Lawrence –

Best of luck
with your
maturity
accountability –
journey

Michael

The Marketing Accountability Imperative

Driving Superior Returns on Marketing Investments

Michael E. Dunn

and Chris Halsall

JOSSEY-BASS
A Wiley Imprint
www.josseybass.com

Published by Jossey-Bass
A Wiley Imprint
989 Market Street, San Francisco, CA 94103-1741—www.josseybass.com

Jossey-Bass books and products are available through most bookstores. To contact Jossey-Bass directly call our Customer Care Department within the U.S. at 800-956-7739, outside the U.S. at 317-572-3986, or fax 317-572-4002.

Jossey-Bass also publishes its books in a variety of electronic formats. Some content that appears in print may not be available in electronic books.

Library of Congress Cataloging-in-Publication data has been applied for.

978-0-7879-9832-5

Printed in the United States of America
FIRST EDITION
HB Printing   10   9   8   7   6   5   4   3   2   1

━⁓━ Contents

To my amazing Ethan, whose feisty spark lights up my world,

and to all of my wonderful family, colleagues, and friends,

without whom I would be rudderless

—⌇— Acknowledgments

This book draws on the experiences that we have had over the past fifteen years, side by side with our many clients tackling tough issues around how to get better returns from their marketing investments. Sometimes the focus was on diagnosing performance problems, sometimes on building investment cases, sometimes on cost-cutting; but in every case, we worked with committed, dedicated professionals who were trying to figure out how to drive more value and better results for their companies. Although the confidential nature of most of those relationships prevents us from listing these individuals and client companies by name, we want to express our appreciation for every one of those learning opportunities. These people challenged our assumptions, pushed our thinking, and never let us settle for "just good enough." They are definitely the coarchitects of this story.

Within Prophet, our principal collaborator over the life of this effort, with all of its many unexpected twists and turns, was Cindy Levine. Her insightful and pragmatic direction helped us shape and improve the overall storyline. Her specific feedback on each chapter as it developed helped us to stay focused on the needs of the reader and ensure that the implications were clear and actionable. Finally, her willingness to play an all-around utility role in terms of case research, chapter outline development, project planning, and resource management saved our bacon on more than one occasion over the life of the writing. Cindy—you rock!

The content of this book also benefited directly from the efforts of a number of individuals who have been spearheading the development of Prophet's marketing effectiveness practice. Andy Pierce, the de facto leader of that practice, provided a clear anchor point for us with his early and passionate advocacy for a "test and learn" approach to marketing accountability. Chiaki Nishino and Jay Milliken, also seasoned colleagues at Prophet, were excellent thought partners around much of the content, and provided very hands-on leadership in developing the detailed arguments throughout Part Two of the book. Jeff Hennige, another hands-on practitioner, also provided useful feedback and direction, especially for Part Three. David Aaker, Jill Steele, Aneysha Pearce, and Joerg Niessing also provided valuable contributions that helped to shape this story.

We also received critical operational and logistical support from another group of Propheteers, without whom it would have been impossible to complete the book. Megan Bigelow had the thankless task of keeping the wolves from our "day" jobs at bay, so that we could find enough significant blocks of time in a month to actually get the writing done. She also kept the authors well-fed and well-supplied with her many lunch and Starbucks runs. Dianna Martin also helped lighten the load with her many humorous door and Facebook postings. Finally, Vincent Chou, Tobias Ammann, Michelle Lev and Knox Bricken helped with the crafting of figures and exhibits, and doing case research that fed its way into the meat of the story.

We would also like to thank the rest of the senior leadership team at Prophet for supporting this effort and for picking up some extra work to create the space for Michael, in particular, to move this project forward. These team members include Kevin O'Donnell, Mike Leiser, Simon Marlow, Scott Davis, Andrea Ivey Harris, Alix Hahn, and Laura Moran. That appreciation should also get extended to the rest of Prophet's board of directors as well, including Niels Nielsen, Mark Leiter, and Kenichi Kobayashi. No matter how much you try to insulate the impact of an effort like this from the rest of your "day" job, it definitely takes the help and willingness of a lot of players to make sure all of the trains keep running on time.

Finally, we would like to acknowledge the patient support of our team at Jossey-Bass, especially our editor Kathe Sweeney. This project definitely ended up following the road less traveled, but it was not always clear it was going to have as positive an outcome as that promised in the Robert Frost poem. Thanks for sticking with this and helping us to get it across the goal line.

San Francisco, California
February 2009

—⁓— Introduction

Google? "Do not call" lists? Digital video recorders? Podcasts? XM radio? Direct response TV? Micro-targeting? "National" cable TV buys? Yelp? Bus wraps? Spam blockers? YouTube? Affiliate marketing? Spot Runner? Declining newspaper readership? Guerilla marketing? On-demand? Satellite TV? LCD billboards? Mobile couponing? Immersive "theatre" retailing? Paid product placement?

If you had put a few top-tier marketers from the early 1990s into a time capsule, put them into a deep sleep for the past fifteen years, and then dropped them into a global CMO role circa 2009, what a bewildering world they would find themselves in. We have to believe that most would eventually have their *Planet of the Apes* moment, walking along the beach and seeing the top of the Statue of Liberty anchored in the sand, but it nonetheless might take them significantly longer than it took Charlton Heston to realize that this wonderful, dynamic, and at times outrageously complex monster was indirectly of their making.

Innovation, it would appear, is alive and well in the marketing and communications space. The continued collision of the technology, entertainment, and media worlds has resulted in a rapidly evolving landscape, with more players finding more ways to package entertainment, information, and content across increasingly fragmented delivery systems to an ever-voracious global audience. People are spending more time with media and entertainment, broadly defined, than at any time in the planet's history—and with the rapid emergence of a growing middle class across China, India, Latin America, and the Middle East, this trend seems, if anything, to be accelerating. Ballyhoo!

Whether this trend bodes well for our species is a debate we will leave to the sociologists, historians, and philosophers. What is clear is that if you are a marketer trying to get your proposition or your promise into the hearts and minds of your prospective customers, the potential tools at your disposal have expanded a hundredfold. It must seem as enticing and perhaps overwhelming as it would be to walk into the venerable Harrod's Food Hall in London if you had spent your life shopping at a local farmer's fruit and vegetable stand!

One very important side effect of this explosion of media and entertainment alternatives, however, is an increasing fragmentation of audiences, at least in the traditional sense. Forty years ago in the United States, if you placed a well-designed TV ad in prime time on the three national TV networks for a month or a quarter, you could be pretty confident that 70 to 80 percent of the adults in the country would have had repeated exposures to your messages. We dare you to try to find a cost-effective way to reach that broad an audience in 2009! The fragmentation of audiences makes it harder for a marketer to cost-effectively communicate with a mass-market target, especially without including a much more diverse set of communication vehicles and tactics.

The sunnier side of the fragmentation story, however, is that there are many more ways to communicate with narrower, more granular audiences, especially if you have a deep understanding of the very specific type of individuals you are looking for. If you have a hot new sports drink or an interesting new approach to product liability insurance, you are no longer forced to use communication vehicles reaching an audience of whom 98 percent have no interest in your message and are of no interest to you. By contrast, if you can target narrowly and reach effectively, you can spend and invest narrowly as well. The challenges here have more to do with allowing companies to quickly and efficiently access enough of these narrow audiences at sufficient scale to meet their business objectives. On this point, the media owners and media planning intermediaries are still struggling to provide the tools and transparency that enable this to happen quickly and consistently.

Some of the newer social media technologies are finally allowing people to congregate—irrespective of geography—around shared interests and passions, creating new communities of interest that may live in the virtual world and occasionally move into the physical world too. MoveOn.org is an excellent example of this phenomenon in the political advocacy space, as is TripAdvisor in the travel world. Some of these trends may eventually lead to a reaggregation of some of these audiences, as a countervailing force to the fragmentation trend. But we are still in the very, very early days of marketers actually figuring out how to reasonably access and participate in these communities in a way that still allows the marketers to pursue their commercial objectives; it will remain an interesting area to watch.

The third element in this story has to do with cost. At least on the surface, you would think that there should be a pretty straightforward cost story. If someone is selling you a TV ad that reaches 60 percent fewer people than it may have reached thirty years ago, its aggregate price and perhaps even its price per person should be going down. However, in most traditional media vehicles in the United States—with the exception, perhaps, of newspapers—the cost to purchase advertising has been steadily increasing over the past two decades. So the price of the old stuff keeps going up, while its effectiveness at delivering audiences continues to deteriorate. Many advertisers using traditional media are actually paying more for fewer eyeballs on an ongoing basis. How can this be?

To get at this, you have to think about the demand side of the equation. Could enough new demand for traditional TV or magazine ads have come to the table over the last few decades that it was powerful enough to drive up pricing even in the face of the declining audience reach of the inventory and additional supply? The answer is a categorical yes. Think about it. In 1975, three main sectors drove most of the demand for and investment in advertising across all media vehicles—automotive, manufacturing, and consumer products. By 2005, whole new industries—like pharmaceuticals, financial services, telecommunications, retail, entertainment, and computing—had incorporated some type of material role for advertising and marketing communications investment into their go-to-market models and competitive strategies. With more and more companies starting to leverage classical marketing techniques as powerful growth-enabling tools, this created conditions in which more and more players, with different business models and different cost pressures, were chasing the same inventory, creating the perfect conditions for the paradox of rising prices in the face of declining productivity. Voila—stagflation came to the marketing world way before we had a credit crunch, a U.S. housing crisis, and $150-a-barrel crude oil!

The fourth and final twist to this story of external environmental factors concerns transparency and measurability. With the advent of cheaper and cheaper data processing and computing power, the performance and effectiveness of certain kinds of traditional marketing vehicles—like direct marketing or consumer trade promotions—became easier to capture and understand. From the marketer's perspective, two "classes" of spend started to emerge, one of which had significantly better optics from a transparency, measurability, and financial return perspective than the other. The rapid emergence of some of the internet-enabled vehicles—like paid search (think Google), e-mail, and display advertising, all of which are highly measurable and transparent—only exacerbated these class differences, making the transparency shortcomings in the second class of spend increasingly less tolerable. Of course, just because the financial return of a certain kind of marketing investment was less directly measurable using the existing processes didn't necessarily mean that it was less effective, but that argument became increasingly harder to defend to a metrics-anchored CFO or CEO—to the ultimate chagrin of some companies (as we shall discuss later).

So let's see—media choice proliferation, audience fragmentation and potential re-aggregation, marketing stagflation, and the great measurability divide; so why, you might ask, are we writing a book about marketing accountability now? If you are looking at this situation from a distance, as are many interested but not very engaged observers in the C-suite or on the board of directors, the challenges around how to confidently and transparently invest in marketing communications and promotions to drive profitable growth can clearly seem like a Gordian knot. There are too many moving pieces, not always that understandable, with too much technical complexity associated with each component. If you are sitting up close, somewhere in the marketing function or the agency world, it probably feels more like the ancient Egyptian riddle of the sphinx: there was an immediate penalty of death for every unwitting traveler who failed to solve it. Given that the average tenure of a CMO in the U.S. Fortune 500 is less than the life of an average goldfish—the sphinx definitely appears to still be pressing its advantage.

To be clear, notwithstanding our deep belief in the value of marketing and our warm personal relationships with many CMOs, the sphinx is still on the righteous side of this argument. Even in the United States, where the marketing community has pushed hardest and quickest against this issue, the state of marketing ROI understanding is, for the most part, appalling. Even when we boil the concept of accountability down to its most straightforward definition, looking for some directional linkage between in-period investments and in-period returns, we find that most companies are not hitting the mark. Many organizations are investing millions of dollars of resources in marketing without a shred of defensible, quantifiable evidence as to what financial benefit it is providing the business. In some companies, marketing is the fastest-growing investment line throughout the entire business model, yet it does not have even the most basic "return on investment" mindset surrounding it. Overall, marketers need to make the practice of marketing more evidence-based, without shutting down the contributions that intuitive, instinctual marketing judgment can bring to the party. And an obvious place to start is around the marketing communications and promotions programs.

The good news is that the huge IT-focused and infrastructure-building investments of the last two decades—in areas like customer information management, sales force automation, enterprise resource planning, and decision support—have lowered the overall cost of data capture and have allowed companies to build an attractive set of information assets, ingredients critical to the marketing accountability equation. Other technology-driven advances in marketing science have allowed a sophisticated set of analytic tools to be more easily accessed and deployed with a frequency that is more appropriate to a monthly operating rhythm of business than to the more episodic rhythms of academia. Finally, media-anchored innovations in marketing vehicles allow for much more active, short-cycle time experimentation, with clearer lines of sight into the direct and indirect outcomes the tactics are driving. All three of these forces, when you think of their aggregate effect, make this an excellent time to rethink our approach to marketing analytics and measurement.

Of course, measurement is really just that: measurement, or keeping score. What is even more powerful is the vastly improved decision making that a more comprehensive and real-time measurement system enables. As we will go on to discuss at length in the book, value-creating marketing investment occurs when great analytics underpins compelling marketing strategy development, which inspires world-class creativity and bullet-proof execution. It is so easy to write, yet so hard to do. Highly accountable marketing investment happens when all of these capabilities are working synergistically together to drive compelling returns. The book will discuss common points of failure in each of these capabilities, as well as time-proven approaches to overcoming potential shortcomings within each. The book will also help you understand how to build a comprehensive measurement and decision-making process that will allow you to make continuous improvements to your efforts in real time and deploy marketing communications investment in a nimble and assertive way to engage and win in the market. Our hope is that ultimately you will be able to dramatically improve your marketing performance over the short and long term, while helping to make your marketing teams and investment more accountable.

So who is this book for? CFOs and financial analysts who are supposed to bring some rigor to understanding this cost line and investment category; divisional presidents and CEOs who are trying to engage their marketing leadership in a productive dialogue about how to improve their marketing performance; VPs of product development; board members who are trying to understand and get comfortable with increasingly aggressive executive requests for more marketing investment; marketers of all stripes who are looking for better ways to both measure their performance and improve the overall accountability of their strategies and tactics; and most important, CMOs who want to be seen as integral drivers of the business and need a comprehensive road map for how to get there.

Given the diversity of potential audiences, each with a different baseline understanding of marketing theory and marketing practice, we have tried to strike the right balance in relation to the specific topics that we are covering and how deeply we delve into each topic. For nonmarketers, we may run the risk of occasionally using too much marketing lingo and not always providing careful explanations before we start a conversation about some relatively well-used marketing construct (like positioning) that may not be that well understood outside of the marketing area. For seasoned marketers, we may run the risk of occasionally spending too much time explaining concepts or practices that you have had in your toolkit for twenty-five years. And for the self-described "non-quant-jocks," we may run the risk of occasionally drifting too deeply into technical modeling or analytic realms, where we may not always see the forest for the leaves.

We beg your forgiveness in advance if you end up having any of these experiences. We think that an insight-led, marketing-driven approach is an exciting addition to any company's competitive toolkit, but we understand it will get deployed in the most effective way only if all of the key business leaders—from the board and the CEO to other skeptical C-suite leadership like a CFO or COO—feel confident in their own understanding of how these kinds of investments can create value and how, over time, the company can put itself on the path to highly accountable marketing performance. So we want this book to be a vehicle that can bring everyone along. To do that, we need to provide a common language and a shared understanding that increases everyone's fluency around critical topics that influence a marketing accountability agenda. We may not always be striking the right balance in serving these multiple constituencies, but we hope that, knowing that our hearts are in the right place, you will be more forgiving. Of course, if you end up having one of those experiences in which our level of discussion misses the mark relative to your knowledge and expectation, just look up from the page, take a deep breath, and then move on to the next section in the chapter. You can pick up the storyline there and, we hope, be none the worse for wear.

We offer only one final caveat. As authors, we made a conscious decision not to address the issue of marketing accountability in its broadest sense. The easiest way to explain this may be the shorthand that we have developed with some of our clients to talk about this—the difference between "Big M" marketing and "little m" marketing. "Big M" marketing addresses all of the classic issues that legendary academic Phil Kotler raised in his early books: the Four P's—product, place, price, and promotions. As most seasoned business people understand, a strategic marketing approach incorporates the interplay of decisions taken in relation to the Four P's as a whole when evaluating the overall strength and viability of a strategy. "Big M" marketing resources can be invested to strengthen our performance along the product P or the price P or the place P just as easily as they can be invested in the promotions P. A comprehensive approach to marketing accountability should incorporate a measurement and prioritization mechanism within each of the four P's and across them, not just within the promotional P. This book does not do that.

On the positive side, many of the core value levers that are discussed in relation to the promotions P can be applied to the other "Big M" marketing investment areas, as can the measurement techniques and test-and-learn orientation that is addressed in the back third of the book. But it felt cleaner and more manageable for us to stay focused on the promotional side of the Four P's equation for this effort, so that is what we've done.

Enough with the preamble. Let's get busy figuring out how to drive more value out of our existing marketing investments and take some profitable market share away from our less "accountable" competitors. ¡Arriba!

Michael E. Dunn
Chris Halsall
San Francisco, California
February 2009

PART ONE

Untying the Gordian Knot of Marketing Investment Excellence

CHAPTER ONE

The Marketing Accountability Imperative

Understanding the Marketing Accountability Gap and Beginning the Journey to Close It

T opics covered in Chapter One:

- The marketing accountability gap and its impact
- The root causes of the marketing accountability gap
- The road to more accountable marketing spending

Pressure makes diamonds.
—General George S. Patton

THE MARKETING ACCOUNTABILITY GAP AND ITS IMPACT

Flip a coin. Whether you guessed heads or tails, statistically your odds of guessing right are better than the odds that a major marketing program will be successful. A recent Deutsche Bank study of advertising in the consumer packaged goods industry concluded that only 45 percent of CPG advertising achieved a positive ROI. Another study across a broader cross-section of industries puts the television advertising success rate even lower, at 37 percent. Studies of promotional spending peg its success rate much lower than advertising, with somewhere between 16 percent and 35 percent achieving positive returns. And these are activities that marketers perceive as being *more* effective than the average marketing program. When we recently surveyed senior marketers about the perceived effectiveness of various marketing activities, 53 percent of them considered television advertising to be an effective activity for long-term brand building, versus an average across activities of just 32 percent. In terms of driving short-term sales, 52 percent considered promotions to be an effective activity, compared to an average of 31 percent across other activities.

Why do perceptions of effectiveness matter? Because the vast majority of companies cannot actually calculate the ROI of their marketing spending programs to uncover the hard truth about their performance. Our survey suggests that as few as 19 percent of companies can consistently and accurately determine what they are getting—*if anything*—from untold millions in marketing spending. So how confident would you be in investing in something that has a lower likelihood of success than random chance and an even lower likelihood that these returns will *ever* be calculated to determine your success or failure? For a surprising number of otherwise successful companies, of all sizes and across all industries and life stages, this is business as usual.

And these are not trivial investments either. It is estimated that over $322 billion a year is spent on advertising in the United States alone. To put this in perspective, the United States has 4.6 percent of the world's population and 28 percent of the world's economic output, but accounts for fully 48 percent of global advertising spending. According to Morgan Stanley, promotional spending accounts for another $106 billion a year, bringing the total in 2005 to $428 billion. What if you add to this figure the cost of sponsorships, loyalty programs, sales collateral, public relations, as well as production costs and agency fees, to try and get a sense of the total annual U.S. marketing spending? Given available benchmarks, it is not unreasonable to believe that this figure could as much as double, but to be conservative let's say that the total figure is only 30 percent greater. This suggests a total annual U.S. marketing spending—not including the cost of marketing staff, market research, or product development—of around $550 billion, or roughly $1,800 for each man, woman, and child in the United States.

Not only are U.S. companies spending an extraordinarily large amount of money on marketing, but these investments are growing at a breathtaking rate. The last several years have seen the double whammy of rapidly increasing spending on traditional marketing vehicles, at the same time that these vehicles are being supplanted by a wealth of new—*entirely incremental*—touch points, led by the Internet. Essentially, the media world is fragmenting, and marketers are keeping a foot on each iceberg as the pieces drift apart.

Since the turn of the twenty-first century, spending on traditional forms of advertising has increased by 44 percent more than the rate of inflation. The Super Bowl offers a good illustration of this phenomenon—of *paying more but getting less*—with traditional media. While the Super Bowl audience declined from 94 million viewers in 1996 to 91 million viewers in 2006, over this time period the cost of a thirty-second spot increased from $1.1 million to $2.6 million. Even after adjusting for inflation, this represents a doubling in the cost to reach each viewer.

With customers abandoning traditional media in favor of the Internet, marketers now must expand their presence to less familiar touch points. Forrester estimates that people now spend on average about 23 percent of their "media time" online, compared with 39 percent of it spent watching television, and this gap is closing daily. To keep pace, marketing spending online has gone from nothing to $16 billion a year in less than a decade and is expected to grow by more than 25 percent per year for the next several years. Our recent survey of marketing leaders found that they are being forced outside of their comfort zone by the shift to new media. Although 53 percent of senior marketers suggest that new media will play an extremely important role in their spending mix going forward, just as many (54 percent) acknowledge that they are unfamiliar with how best to use these new tools to meet their business goals.

In this new, higher-stakes game of marketing spending that we now find ourselves in, how well have marketers risen to the challenge? The results are mixed at best. Marketers have done a very good job of acknowledging that they have a problem, which is the classic first step of any self-help program. Our recent survey of senior marketers found a clear consensus around the critical need to focus on marketing accountability and improve marketing spending effectiveness. Three-quarters (77 percent) of marketers in our survey suggest that improving marketing accountability is one of the top three priorities of either their marketing group or their company overall.

Although there is consensus around the need for greater marketing accountability, only a relatively small proportion of companies have found the solution. Since 2004, the Association of National Advertisers (ANA) has conducted its own senior marketer survey on marketing accountability. In 2005 they found that just 16 percent of companies were confident in their ability to predict the impact of a 10-percent cut in their marketing spending and to get senior management to buy in to their forecast. By 2006 this percentage had almost doubled, with 28 percent of companies "capable and confident" in their marketing accountability. Our senior marketer survey tends to bear out the ANA's earlier results—finding just 16 percent of marketing leaders confident in their understanding of their company's marketing ROI. In an environment of finger pointing, the truth may be not that the problem is going away, but that it is becoming more difficult to perpetually acknowledge that you still have the same problem.

Whichever data point you believe about the percentage of companies who now consider their marketing to be accountable, the fact remains that the majority of marketers are still struggling to link the cause and effect of marketing spending and quantify its real returns. Sixty percent of the marketers in our survey said that they lacked the right approaches and analytic tools to drive ROI and accountability (see Figure 1.1). The lack of necessary data, and the complexity of

Figure 1.1.   Barriers to Pursuing Marketing Accountability and ROI

Note: Survey conducted by Prophet among companies with revenues between $1 billion and $10 billion.

Source: Prophet Annual State of Marketing Study, 2007.

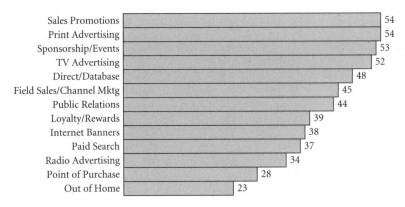

Figure 1.2. **Percentage of Companies Measuring Activity Effectiveness**
Source: Prophet Annual State of Marketing Study, 2007.

their company's spending mix (that is, too many programs, with too frequent changes) tied for second place as the next greatest barrier to more accountable marketing.

Confronted with these challenges, it appears that many companies have reached a stalemate in their attempts to improve their marketing accountability. Perhaps our most telling finding is the relatively small proportion of spending that gets measured at all for its effectiveness.

Figure 1.2 shows that no spending activity is consistently measured for effectiveness by more than 54 percent of companies. In fact, of the 12 most measured activities, the average is evaluated by only 42 percent of companies. Inexplicably, some of the most eminently measurable activities, such as loyalty and CRM programs and internet banners, are among the least measured. Even direct response—*in which the link between cause and effect can be "hardwired" into each campaign*—is consistently measured by less than half of companies.

With seemingly out-of-control marketing spending, dubious program returns, and slow progress by marketers to fix the problems, we can now see how small fissures have widened into seemingly unbridgeable gaps.

THE GAP IN EXPECTATIONS

At its core, the marketing accountability gap is really all about expectations: the expectation that marketing programs will perform as promised and grow the business, and the expectation that these investments will be rigorously measured and managed in accordance with an understanding of their real returns. Clearly CMOs must be disappointed with their progress in linking marketing cause and effect. This is apparent when you compare the 67 percent of CMOs who say that calculating marketing ROI is important with the 60 percent who are dissatisfied with their ability to measure these returns. In turn, CMOs are feeling the heat for not moving the dial on marketing accountability faster. When the ANA asked CMOs whether "pressure on marketing has increased in the last three years," 99 percent of the respondents said yes, with a further 28 percent saying that marketing accountability is among their CEO's top three overall priorities.

Many CEOs have been quite vocal on the topic of the marketing accountability gap—most notably Procter & Gamble's A. G. Lafley and his predecessor Ed Artz, who could indeed be considered the fathers of the marketing accountability movement. Artz is famous for delivering his "Fire the middlemen" speech to an audience of advertising executives in which he decried the lack of marketing measurement, implying that there is more rigor put into evaluating a small-scale facilities investment than there is an advertising programs costing tens of millions. By this point, we are surely preaching to the choir on both the existence of the marketing accountability gap and the critical importance of improving accountability and marketing spending returns. Let's now dig deeper and identify the root causes of this gap, so that we can gain a better understanding of what it will take to close it.

THE ROOT CAUSES OF THE MARKETING ACCOUNTABILITY GAP

Responsibility for the marketing accountability gap does not rest solely on the shoulders of the CMO and the marketing function. There is plenty of blame—for lack of a better word—to go around the executive floors of most corporations. Moreover, many of the largest factors are not anyone's fault at all. Some of the key triggering events that brought the marketing accountability gap to the forefront of executive attention were environmental shocks that no one company caused and few could fully anticipate. It is necessary to understand the root causes of the marketing accountability gap not to apportion blame but to provide context for finding the solution. Each of the factors that had a role in creating the marketing accountability gap can be assigned to one of the following three categories (see Figure 1.3):

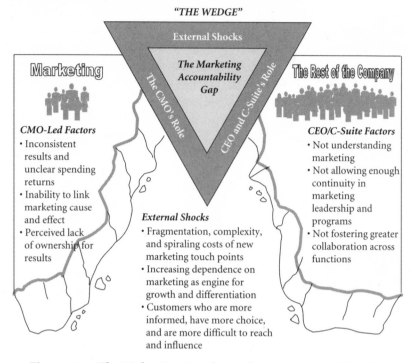

Figure 1.3. The Wedge Creating the Marketing Accountability Gap

- *External Shocks:* The more complex and dynamic new marketing environment
- *CEO/C-Suite Factors:* Greater expectations without greater understanding
- *CMO-Led Factors:* The need to shift the pendulum from "art" to "science"

External Shocks: The More Complex and Dynamic New Marketing Environment

Marketing used to be a lot more straightforward. You developed the best product or service you could, got it distributed, developed a thirty-second television spot and some sales collateral, threw in a promotion or two, and waited for the share to tick up. OK, maybe it was never *that* easy. But it certainly wasn't as complex and frustrating as it has become in the last few years. It takes many more bewildering marketing touch points to track customers down, and when you do find them there are a great many more competitors screaming for their attention. Moreover, even if you can briefly grab your customers' attention, they are less trusting of your intentions, far more difficult to influence, and less likely to become deeply loyal. In this strange new marketing environment, it is has become a Herculean task just to deliver the basics, let alone worry about how accountable your efforts are.

If it is any consolation, many of the factors that are making marketing accountability such a daunting challenge are beyond the marketer's direct control. The Internet and the interactive communications revolution that it triggered are at the core of the marketing transformation that we are living through. New media and technology have reshaped the lifestyle habits of your customers and given them access to comparative information and choice that was never available before. At the same time, technology and innovation have transformed business models to dramatically reduce engineering, manufacturing, and distribution barriers and shift the focus of competition more and more toward marketing. Marketing has become *the* core business of business at the same time that old marketing delivery models are breaking down.

Although technology may have created the trigger for the problematic customer transformation we are experiencing, marketers have to recognize that they are the ones who fired the gun. Negative customer attitudes and behaviors that are manifesting themselves today have been latent for some time. By and large, marketers have harassed and bribed their customer base and treated them as captives; now they are reaping what they have sown. For the purpose of this discussion we will treat these customer behaviors and business model changes as external forces that are beyond the immediate control of any one company, but soon we will get to the culpability of the CMO and CEO.

We have identified several external forces that have contributed to the creation and widening of the marketing accountability gap. In addition to the erosion of traditional marketing vehicles and the complexity of the new marketing landscape that is supplanting them (which we have already touched on), here is a brief overview of some of these other external forces.

More industries entering the marketing spending "big league": Many business model, regulatory, and other changes are drawing new industries into the big leagues of marketing spending. Figure 1.4 shows the dramatic shift in industry advertising spending patterns that has occurred. The effect of this is twofold. First, it creates more demand,

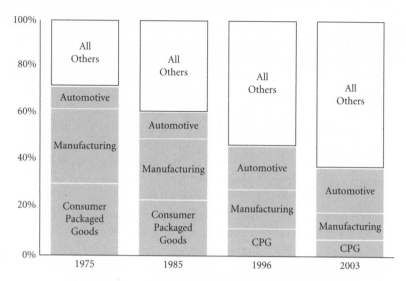

Figure 1.4.   Measured Media Spending by Industry

which is causing general media inflation for all marketers. Second, it makes marketing accountability a top-of-mind issue in these industries as the pace of spending growth far outstrips the speed at which capabilities can be built.

The transparency of information available to customers: Prior to the advent of the Internet, marketers controlled the flow of information. Now customers have ready access to near-complete information on product features and pricing from a variety of sites outside of the marketer's control, including forums for unvarnished peer-peer exchange such as Epinions.com and its B2B equivalents. This information has dramatically shifted power from marketers to customers, as B2B customers broaden the reach of RFPs and B2C customers get comparative pricing quotes in real time. Consider the increase in negotiating power that car buyers have when they can purchase a detailed breakdown of manufacturer and dealer costs and margins for any car model online.

One impact of information transparency on marketing accountability is in changing the basis of marketing spending strategies and activities, from long-term equity building and differentiation to a near-term focus on promotions and churn. This change is occurring in many categories, as transparency contributes to a vicious cycle that is accelerating the spiral toward commoditization—the ability to price-shop creates more "price shoppers," which attracts more low-priced entrants, which erodes perceived category benefits, and in turn creates more "price shoppers."

The shift to word-of-mouth (WOM) marketing: An additional impact of information transparency is the need for marketers to shift from more straightforward "telling and selling" interactions with customers to little-understood "influence" strategies that offer an even more obscure path to ROI. Customers have always claimed word-of-mouth among their top influences. In the past marketers played down the importance of WOM because it was beyond their perceived ability to control, and customers lacked efficient tools of mass exchange. The Internet and mobile technology have changed all this and put customers in much greater control of (1) creating their own entertainment forums and content—increasingly abandoning passive marketing mediums, and (2) the brand dialogue—from being *told by marketers* to *telling others* what they think about the brands that are targeting them.

Although in the past a bad customer service experience may have been shared with only a small circle of friends, now anything with entertainment value has the potential to go viral overnight. A series of dumbfounding telephone exchanges with a bank's customer service team was posted to a blog, and in less than two weeks they were viewed over a million times. The expression "Don't get mad, get even" takes on a whole new meaning when there are thirty-five million blogs alone out there to help spread the word.

With marketers no longer in complete control of medium and message, they are forced to sink or swim in the new WOM world. Some marketers are adroitly adapting to the new influence model. During the 2007 holiday season, P&G's Charmin generated incredible viral buzz by placing free public toilets in New York's Time Square. This was a savvy move, as it hit the trifecta of (1) fulfilling a desperate unmet need, (2) reaching the epicenter of global media—five major networks broadcast from there—as well as the crossroads of tourists from all fifty states, and most important, (3) being clearly on brand strategy. Customers posted hundreds of videos and positive endorsements that crisscrossed the web, giving the brand a reach well beyond what it could afford with traditional advertising. Moreover, the tactics gave the brand's equity a bump that can rarely be purchased at any price.

Most marketers, however, are struggling to get their bearings in this brave new world. PR, the logical home for WOM activities, has traditionally been in the dark ages of marketing accountability—relying on press impressions as a proxy for ROI and only recently adding simple metrics for gauging differences in impression quality. Moreover, PR experts are accustomed to influencing professional media sources, not distributed networks of newly minted individual content producers.

When YouTubers discovered the fun that ensues when Mentos are added to Diet Coke, Mentos marketers became willing accomplices and acted quickly to commercialize the phenomenon—driving a 27-percent increase in sales. In contrast, Coke's official PR efforts to distance their brand from these experiments were met with widespread derision among their target customers. WOM marketing quickly strips away all artifice and demands a much higher level of congruence between marketing messages and the actions that support them. When a single marketing spending misstep has the potential to destroy years of brand equity, marketers may long for a return to the days when all they had to worry about was ROI.

Customers increasingly inoculating themselves against marketing: The fact that marketers have harassed customers to the breaking point is something we will discuss in a moment. The point is that in addition to retreating to their own little worlds, customers now have more tools at their disposal with which to fight back. We are all familiar with the impact that digital video recorders (DVRs) are having, by allowing customers to zap past an estimated over $600 million in advertising a year. If marketers do not do more to create a dialogue that customers want to participate in, we will see more use of approaches such as the following to thwart their attempts.

Techniques for Avoiding the Marketing Barrage

- Being added to the "do not call" list
- Using call blockers and call display
- Installing internet pop-up blockers
- Opting out of e-mail lists
- Having antispamming laws enacted
- Lobbying for disclosure on blogs

New competitive intensity is increasing pressure on marketing to perform: there are forces at work that are shrinking the potential marketing spending prize at the same time that marketing spending is growing dramatically. Many industries are entering a period of slower organic growth, in which the basis of competition is shifting to a costly battle to steal share. We can see this trend in retail white space—where could you place another Walmart, Gap, or McDonald's in North America if you had to?—as well as financial services, wireless, travel, office services, and many others. Even categories that have been in long-term gradual declines, such as many packaged goods categories, are reaching absurd new levels of competition and proliferation, to eke out incrementally more of what is left. When you launch "Vanilla Expressions" flavored toothpaste as your twenty-eighth SKU, where do you have left to go from there?

Shorter life cycles: Increased competitive intensity is now also coupled with shorter and shorter product and value proposition lifecycles. Technology-driven products are experiencing dramatically pronounced declines in the time from launch to obsolescence. As a wireless CMO said, "In the past, it took people three years to replace their handsets; now that is down to one year." Even traditional categories and whole business models are feeling the effect of shorter lifecycles. Blockbuster, which dominated video entertainment for almost two decades with few changes in its go-to-market approach, is now being forced to change its entire business model due to video-on-demand threats that emerged in just a couple of years.

The CEO and C-Suite: Greater Expectations Without Greater Understanding

Today's perceptions about the marketing accountability gap are deeply rooted in old organizational tensions. Marketing has always been a group that stands apart from the rest of the company. No other function is so crucial to business performance and yet so little understood by the rest of the executive suite. Other complex business functions, such as R&D or IT, are characterized by learned skills that smart executives could theoretically master if they put their minds to it. But this is not the case with marketing. Marketing is an invitation-only club because it balances learned skills and hard-to-define intrinsic skills. Although the sales function may also rely on intrinsics, these skills are more easily understood and therefore are not a source of tension.

This intangible nature of marketing, characterized by marketers as "magic" and by nonmarketers as "voodoo," is at the crux of the marketing accountability gap. Because marketing relies on art as well as science, the CEO and CFO cannot confidently collaborate with marketing leaders to help steward the needed improvements. This places them in the uncomfortable position of being able to identify the issues around marketing accountability without being able to proffer a solution. Without collaboration as an option, the CEO and CFO must rely on either nagging the CMO to force changes or taking arbitrary actions to effect change, such as cutting marketing budgets or changing out the marketing leaders.

These differing skills and mindsets are further exacerbated by different timescales. Although the CEO should be a company's most strategic position, the CEO and CFO are compelled to focus most of their attention on the three-month increments between quarterly earning announcements. This often does not jibe with the CMO's long-term investments in brand building—particularly if these programs do not offer proven returns during periods of earning shortfalls.

Although the CMO and the marketing organization may bear the lion's share of responsibility for creating the marketing accountability gap (we will discuss this shortly), ultimately it takes two to tango. All the executives—including the CEO—have had a role in creating the problem and must now play their parts in the solution. Some of these contributing factors are described here.

Allowing value propositions to converge: When did all the cars start looking alike—with an "Oldsmo-Buick" indistinguishable from any other "Camry-ola"? Probably about the same time that all the other functional features started converging and ceasing to be a real source of product differentiation. Sticking with our auto example, we can see that year after year the band between best and worst performance in the same car class has become smaller and smaller on functional features, such as the time to get from 0 to 60, horsepower output, fuel economy, warranty coverage, and defect rate. The same is true across B2B and B2C categories, as new business models give every company equal access to the best innovation, engineering, and manufacturing. The remote on a $500 DVD player may have more buttons, but can you really tell the difference in picture quality from a $50 player?

Without real functional differentiation, companies must place much greater emphasis on brands and marketing spending to fill the void. This is an issue of CEO and C-suite accountability, because non-marketers must recognize that (1) they could have done more to help make their propositions competitive, by investing more in R&D and physical plant and collaborating with marketing to create new sources of customer value (such as financing, partnering, and service); and (2) this reduced differentiation has increased the expectations they are placing on marketing performance, whereas marketing's actual performance may or may not have changed at all.

Short tenure of the CMO: If you knew that you had just twenty-three months to live, how would you spend your time? You probably wouldn't focus on anything long-term that didn't offer immediate gratification. Why then would a CMO be expected to behave any differently, when surveys consistently show their "lifespan" to be just two marketing budget cycles or less? Marketing accountability is a long-term proposition, and it requires a marketing leader with both the vision and the mandate to begin a multiyear journey. Constantly churning through CMOs does not increase their incentive to perform; it simply places an unhealthy emphasis on managing the "optics" of their performance.

Accountability without authority: Not only do CMOs have a short lifespan, but they also are on a very short leash. A senior marketer survey conducted by the Marketing Leadership Council found that the majority of CMOs did not control many of the elements that determine in-market success, including pricing, sales force activities, and customer service (see Table 1.1). Demand forecasting was strangely outside of the CMO's scope, given that officers need to be more accountable for market outcomes. There are also interesting differences between B2B and B2C scope, with B2B marketing leaders having more control over upstream activities (planning and development) and B2C leaders more control over downstream activities (sales force and customer service).

	Business to Consumer	Business to Business
Product Development	67%	51%
Planning	50%	68%
Pricing	46%	46%
Demand Forecasting	42%	22%
Public Relations	38%	41%
Sales Force	25%	11%
Customer Service	21%	19%

Table 1.1.   Accountability Without Control.

Not allowing marketing programs to run their course: Clawing back funding from marketing programs that are already in the field, whether to fund profit shortfalls or other needs, is a classic problem created by the CEO and CFO. Although some changes cannot be avoided, it is hard to justify the frequency with which imposed changes are made. CMOs rightly consider this one of the top barriers to improving marketing accountability (cited by 45 percent of senior marketers), as this renders marketing programs essentially immeasurable. Moreover, it perpetuates a negative cycle of declining marketing accountability—wherein abrupt program changes cloud their returns and make them more likely to be cut again in the future—while simultaneously freeing the CMO of the burden of performance, which in turn increases the likelihood that questionable programs will be fielded. And so it goes.

The CMO's Role: The Need to Shift the Pendulum from Art to Science

It's not easy being a CMO these days. Only 40 percent of CMOs often feel that their groups are "well regarded and respected" within their companies, and fewer than 7 percent believe that they are influential. This derision is not imagined either, with one CEO recently describing CMOs as "more akin to a recalcitrant child than an adult." Other choice adjectives that turned up in a McKinsey CEO survey include "not commercial," "undisciplined," "inconsistent," "self-important," and of course, "not accountable." All of this feedback is coming at a time when the CEO is placing more and more pressure on the CMO to drive growth or step aside. With the ever-looming threat that the axe could fall at any moment, it's not unreasonable to believe that the Four P's that characterize the CMO's role have become *preoccupation, paralysis, paranoia,* and *pension.* It's little wonder that most senior marketers (70 percent) would rather sidestep the role of CMO altogether and leave marketing entirely to assume a business leadership role.

Figure 1.5 demonstrates how the CMO can become caught up in the vicious downward spiral of the marketing accountability gap. These dynamics are illustrative of the countless examples that have played out in the business press in the last two years. Of course CMOs are not oblivious to these dynamics, but knowing that they exist does not prevent marketing leaders from continuing to fall victim to them.

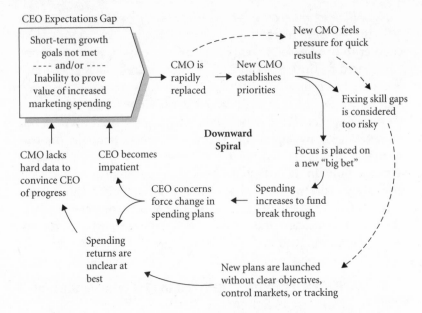

Figure 1.5. The Vicious Spiral of the Marketing Accountability Gap

To break this negative cycle once and for all, CMOs must recognize, acknowledge, and change the several specific mindsets and behaviors that have helped create to the marketing accountability gap.

Hiding behind the art of marketing to avoid its science: The assertion that marketing is an art and a science can no longer be accepted as a defense for weak in-market results or a lack of accountability. Marketing is indeed an art and a science, but the presence of this intangible art can no longer be used as an excuse for the lack of scientific rigor. The pendulum has swung, and marketers must now scramble to catch up to the long-avoided science of marketing and restore balance to marketing's essential equation.

The marketer's ability to generate and leverage compelling, quantifiable customer insights—*the cornerstone of marketing*—has fallen into disarray. Marketing accountability suffers when millions of dollars are invested in undifferentiated brands and messages, and when companies wait for outside vendors to solve their measurement gaps for them. The CMO is accountable for allowing customer insights to wither and erode marketing accountability by (1) accepting persistent data gaps year after year; (2) refusing to complement traditional survey-based research with real-world, observationally driven insights; (3) marginalizing the research function; and (4) accepting a lack of brand differentiation for older brands and mature categories.

The quantitative analytic rigor with which program results are analyzed and evaluated is the other weak link in marketing science. Marketing mix models have been around since the 1980s, and the test-and-learn experimental approach dates back to Archimedes, yet somehow most marketers have not yet discovered the power of these scientific approaches to improve the effectiveness of their spending. The most heavily analyzed category of spending is print advertising, yet only 46 percent of marketers are conducting this analysis. The level of structured experiments is highest with outbound campaigns, but a mere 28 percent of marketers are doing this.

Marketing mindsets must undergo a permanent change to viewing science as *the* critical enabler of the marketing art—by providing clearer direction to create truly breakthrough strategies and programs and by arming marketers with the ability to prove their impact and defend their value. This may not be an easy transition for many marketing leaders who were not required to develop these skills themselves.

Highly visible marketing blunders: Pets.com ushered in not only a new age of marketing spending inflation, but also a new golden age of perceived marketing spending blunders and "What were they thinking?" moments. As we write this, Turner Broadcasting is being fined $2 million for contributing to a terrorist scare in Boston, where devices used for a guerilla marketing campaign were mistaken for bombs. Other recent head-scratchers include marketers trying to bribe a town to rename itself after a beverage and paying pregnant women to advertise on their bellies. Whether some of these approaches actually work or not, they are contributing to the perception that marketers are becoming so desperate to break through that they are just throwing everything at the wall to see what sticks.

Not responding to fundamental shifts fast enough: Most companies currently have a fairly significant gap between where they are spending their marketing dollars and where their customers are spending their time. For example, although only 6 percent of all advertising spending is currently allocated to online marketing vehicles, as mentioned before, people are spending an average of about 48 percent of their "free time" online. By the time many marketers catch up to their customers' new media habits, these habits will have shifted once again, to 3G handsets or some new device not yet imagined.

Perpetuating outdated budgeting approaches: Budgeting is where the rubber meets the road with marketing accountability. Without disciplined use of more sophisticated budgeting approaches, it will be difficult for companies to gain the rigorous understanding of the return on their marketing spending that is needed to improve performance. When we compared research done in 1987 with our 2007 survey of senior marketers to understand how budgeting approaches have evolved, we could see some improvements in sophistication, but little progress in overall budgeting discipline (see Table 1.2). Today, 61 percent of marketers claim that they use an understanding of return on investment to set budgets (this question was not asked in 1987), but this must be balanced by the fact that only 19 percent of companies are confident in their MROI capabilities. There has also been an uptick in the use of experimentation, but in twenty years this has increased only from 20 percent to 26 percent of companies.

Most alarming is the percentage of companies still relying to some degree on less productive budgeting methods, with 77 percent still pegging budgets to last year's spending and 25 percent focusing on what competitors are spending. One acid test of your company's marketing accountability is to ask your top five marketers to describe your company's marketing budgeting approach and see how many different answers you get.

Marketing spending groupthink: Marketing failures do not contribute to the perception of accountability, and neither do the timidity and groupthink that more commonly characterize marketing today. This risk aversion is apparent in the "me too" messaging that pervades

Marketing Budgeting Approaches Employed	1987	2007
Objective and task (1987) / Understanding how customers respond to different types of marketing (2007)	50%	50%
Not asked in 1987 / Understanding of return on investment (2007)	NA	61%
What we can afford (1987) / Last year's budget +/- (2007)	50%	77%
Percentage of sales	25%	49%
Experiments / Testing	20%	26%
Match the competition (1987) / Levels of competitors (2007)	8%	25%

Table 1.2.   Comparison of Marketing Budgeting Approaches, 1987 to 2007.

advertising and in the pile-on of marketers that occurs whenever a cultural phenomenon begins to take shape. For example, the Teutuls of the TV series *American Chopper* may be great spokespeople, but can each of their disparate endorsement partners—Hewlett-Packard, GoDaddy.com, *The Wall Street Journal*, AOL, and so on—extract the same value from this relationship? Groupthink is also evident in the lockstep approach to spend allocation that is often seen among category competitors. Table 1.3 shows the advertising spending mix for two very different auto manufacturers. Although you would assume these companies' distinct customer targets would require different mix strategies, their spend allocation on each medium does not differ by more than half a percent. How can any marketers expect better-than-category-average returns if they are not willing to step away from category norms and do what is needed for their unique brand?

The disconnect between marketers' beliefs and actions: Our 2007 senior marketer survey showed that B2B companies believe that public relations is the most effective activity for long-term brand building and the third most effective at driving short-term sales (after field sales activities and outbound marketing). No form of advertising came close to PR in its perceived long- or short-term effectiveness. Despite this, B2B marketers spend only about 1 percent of their budget on public relations and over 20 percent on advertising. The effectiveness of PR is also rated higher than advertising among B2C marketers and their contradictory spending relationships are even more pronounced. We see this inverse relationship across several other large categories of spend. When you take this together with some of the other points we have discussed, marketers' behaviors seem somewhat puzzling—*they do not believe that the marketing*

Advertising $ Allocation	Mass Market Auto Brand	Luxury Auto Brand
Television	67.2%	66.6%
Print	30.3%	30.8%
Radio	1.4%	1.6%
Outdoor	1.1%	1.0%

Table 1.3.   Comparison of Spend Allocation Across Marketing Vehicles.

activities that they are spending the most on are the most effective, yet they are unwilling or unable to take the steps necessary to quantify this performance.

Thinking more touch is better: Marketers are harassing customers to the breaking point with an estimated three thousand messages each day. Yankelovich research suggests that 65 percent of customers feel "constantly bombarded" by marketing messages, which 59 percent feel have very little relevance to them. Marketers have responded to the increasing difficulty of finding customers and holding their attention by amping up the volume of touch across every conceivable traditional and new touch point. The result of this "more is better" approach is twofold: (1) marketers are wasting huge sums on egregious levels of frequency, and (2) marketers are losing focus on the quality of the touch and are thus losing customers.

Making sure customers see an advertisement or any type of marketing message dozens and dozens of times in a single purchase cycle does not increase its effectiveness, it just wastes money. Numerous studies have concluded that advertising recall plateaus after three to five exposures and ROI is maximized at closer to three exposures. Despite this, we are observing amazingly high levels of frequency today, traceable to media fragmentation and marketers' growing desperation. Worse still, because widespread use of more sophisticated media planning approaches has not caught up with new media complexity, heavy media consumers are sopping up many times their fair share of exposures.

DoubleClick documented this phenomenon by disaggregating the reach and frequency of a recent online advertisement. Although the ad's average viewer frequency of four times ostensibly hits the frequency "sweet spot" of three to five times, when this was broken down by customer it was determined that 54 percent of customers did not see the ad enough (averaging fewer than three times), whereas 36 percent saw it too often. Indeed, 13 percent of customers saw it more than eleven times—representing over 40 percent of all impressions, a great deal of waste, and likely some very annoyed customers.

It's easy to fall into the trap of thinking that this customer frustration is with the marketing efforts of everyone *else*, and that you are engaged in a relevant, value-added dialogue with *your* customers. We examined the issue of quality versus quantity of touch, when we studied the sales force effectiveness of a large B2B manufacturer with an account base of over one hundred thousand customers. The company's sales force made in-person sales calls to the top six deciles of their customers, with the rest buying direct or through other channels. Through our analysis we identified a number of customers across deciles who fell outside of the company's sales territories and were not called on. Customers in deciles 1 to 3 who had sales force contact grew in sales faster than those who did not. However, the reverse was true among deciles 4 to 6, where a customer was more likely to grow in value *if not called on.* Customers can sense when they are not your priority, so if you can't bring your "A" game with each and every touch, it may be better not to bother.

With customers able to tune out the quantity of messages that reach them, the quality of touch is more important than ever before. Moreover, accountability will require marketers to increase their skills in the science of reach and frequency—*across all marketing spending activities*—to drive, rather than outsource, these critical decisions.

Being an undemanding partner: Only in the last few years has there been a movement from marketers to insist that their agency partners have more "skin in the game" and should be compensated—at least in part—based on in-market performance. There is still a long way to go, but one must ask why this move was so long in coming in the first place. As this is being written, Neilsen has just changed their TV ratings scheme to include students away at college, addressing one more measurement gap that has contributed to less accountable marketing spending decisions. Although many more measurement fixes are needed to make spending more accountable and effective, you rarely hear a hue and cry from marketers to demand better service from their providers. To get more accountable and effective contributions from your partners, you have to ask for them.

There are several other CMO-led factors that have contributed to the marketing accountability gap (see Figure 1.6), and probably many more that we have not captured, but at this point you have probably heard enough about the problems and are eager to begin discussing the solutions.

- Emphasizing "art" over "science"
- Spectacular increases in spending
- The lack of well-quantified returns
- Highly visible marketing blunders
- Thinking more touch is better
- Marketing spending groupthink
- Being an undemanding partner
- Disconnected beliefs and actions

- Not agreeing on the definition of success
- Overly simplistic budgeting approaches
- Not managing the full accountability equation
- The "marketing" of marketing results
- Spending to overcome weak propositions
- Stretching brands to their breaking points
- Eroding customer trust

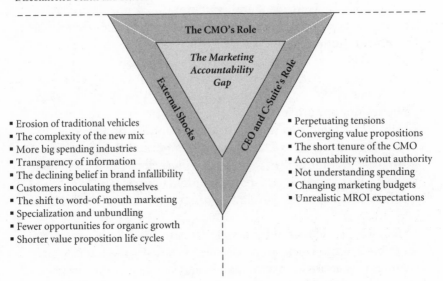

- Erosion of traditional vehicles
- The complexity of the new mix
- More big spending industries
- Transparency of information
- The declining belief in brand infallibility
- Customers inoculating themselves
- The shift to word-of-mouth marketing
- Specialization and unbundling
- Fewer opportunities for organic growth
- Shorter value proposition life cycles

- Perpetuating tensions
- Converging value propositions
- The short tenure of the CMO
- Accountability without authority
- Not understanding spending
- Changing marketing budgets
- Unrealistic MROI expectations

Figure 1.6.   Summary of Factors Contributing to the Marketing
Accountability Gap

THE ROAD TO MORE ACCOUNTABLE MARKETING

It is easy to lay blame—and indeed, it may appear that we have done more than our fair share of that in the first few pages of this book— but we are by no means dismissive of the critical role of marketing and the value of marketing investments. We are passionate believers in the power of strong brands and effective marketing programs to deliver truly breakthrough business performance. Moreover, we are empathetic to the challenges facing marketers today, because we have been in the trenches with CMOs when they have been forced to debate marketing spending cause and effect—and its fundamental value—with their companies' CEOs, CFOs, and business unit leaders. We have seen how perceptions about the marketing accountability gap can destroy trust and subvert marketing's well-meaning efforts to drive business performance.

In the last few years much has been said—perhaps too much—about the nature of this marketing accountability gap and the problems it has created. There is been a wealth of discussion about the problem but precious little said about the solution. We will take no more of your time discussing the problem of marketing accountability and will instead dedicate the rest of this book to providing you with a practical solution.

Defining Marketing Accountability

The first step toward a solution is to agree on a definition of *marketing accountability* so that we have a shared view of what success would look like and an understanding of the challenges we face in getting there. We begin by calibrating your expectations around what we mean by *marketing*. Our definition of marketing, as it pertains to marketing accountability, is both narrower *and* broader than classic definitions.

It is *narrower*, because our focus is on the communications interface between marketers and customers, not on the holistic product or service propositions that marketers are bringing to that interface. We are concerned about where the money is going for traditional and nontraditional marketing communications activities and what companies are getting back from that investment. You may have heard the expression "It's not what you have, it's what you do with it." Marketing accountability is breaking down around this issue of what marketers are doing with the ever-growing millions in marketing spending that is entrusted to them.

The company's proposition—which includes the brand, the product or service itself, and its pricing, features, benefits, and distribution channels—is of course critical to business success. The proposition is, however, a very large topic unto itself. Optimizing the proposition gets at broader, albeit complementary, strategic marketing issues. Although we believe that many of the principles of accountable marketing communications investment are equally relevant for these "Big M" marketing issues around product, pricing, and distribution, we will not attempt to solve these proposition issues here.

We have addressed how our definition of marketing is narrower; now let's discuss how it is simultaneously *broader*. Customers build perceptions based on the totality of all of their direct and indirect interactions or experiences with the company and its products. Marketing, as the primary steward of these accumulated customer perceptions, understands the importance of consistently delivering the brand promise across this "total" customer experience. Any activities that have a material influence on customer perceptions or behaviors—*whether by design or not*—are essentially marketing-related. Any activity that meets this criteria—*wherever it resides in the company, in whatever budget*—should be subject to the discipline of marketing accountability.

When we adopt a broader view of marketing spending that accounts for all company-controlled spending that could influence the customer experience, the spending pool naturally becomes quite large. Figure 1.7 illustrates how this spending grows for a discount brokerage firm. Although the official marketing group controls a sizeable budget of $55 million for advertising, promotions and loyalty activities, when you consider the other spending that significantly influences the customer experience, the total spending balloons to over $180 million.

The first thing you observe is that there are many activities that would be considered "traditional" marketing in many companies

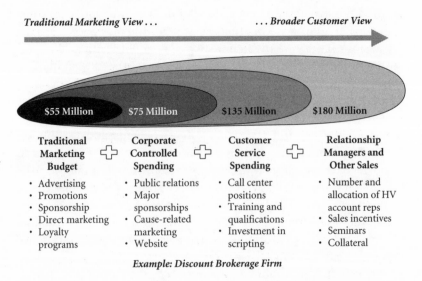

Example: Discount Brokerage Firm

Figure 1.7.   Broader View of Marketing Spending

that are instead being managed out of corporate communications, the office of the CEO, or other nonmarketing budgets. It is highly likely that such spending is being applied without a detailed understanding of current marketing strategy priorities. Beyond this spend, the vast majority of customer-facing spend is controlled by customer service and sales. Even if these organizations align to a common overall marketing strategy and have various points of integration, how truly integrated do you imagine their customer investment is? How integrated is it in your business, and what would a similar set of concentric circles look like for your company?

We are not academically arguing for expanding the scope of marketing to the point where it subsumes everything a company does, but rather for taking a more expansive view of all the customer activities and investments that work together to influence customer perceptions and behaviors. In the end, achieving true "marketing" accountability demands that all customer touch point activities and investments be understood, managed, and optimized as a single integrated system—*regardless of whether the activity is driven by marketing, sales, customer service, or finance*—because it is the whole system that should work together to drive short-term customer behavior and long-term customer and brand equity. This book will discuss how to improve the accountability and returns of a broader suite of spending activities—how far you choose to take this in your own company is up to you.

Now that we have calibrated around the scope of marketing we are addressing, we can define what we mean by *marketing accountability*. If Webster's (or Wikipedia) ever sees fit to tackle this definition, it might look something like this:

Marketing accountability *noun* : The practice of simultaneously optimizing company growth and the return on customer facing spending, through disciplined planning, rigorous tracking and evaluation, and continuous performance improvement. The result of being an effective steward of marketing investments, able to link marketing spending cause and effect, diagnose the root cause of spending performance issues, and make timely fact-based decisions to improve spending returns.

This definition leads off with the real "prize" of marketing accountability and the reason why any of this matters: the promise of improved financial performance—specifically, the goal of simultaneously optimizing *both* company growth and marketing spending returns. This duality is an important point often missed in the discussion of marketing accountability. Programs that optimize their own ROI at the expense of overall growth are not accountable. Similarly, programs that maximize company growth but do so with significant waste or inefficiency are not accountable.

To truly achieve marketing accountability success requires changes to both behaviors and mindsets. Behaviorally, marketing accountability combines the capabilities and processes needed to improve budgeting and planning discipline, perform quantitative tracking and ensure evaluation rigor, and continuously improve spending performance and returns. A marketing accountability mind-set implies responsible, fact-based decision making, which emphasizes discipline and learning over ego and blame.

There are innumerable permutations to how you might define *marketing accountability*, but definitional semantics matter less than what you get from your improvement efforts. The approach to improving marketing accountability that we describe throughout this book offers the following ten important benefits, and you should accept nothing less from any program that you design for your company:

1. Accelerated in-market earnings growth

2. Stronger ROI from each marketing spending program

3. CEO and top-management alignment with marketing accountability as a critical priority and support for the improvement plans that are in place

4. Ever-increasing rigor in quantifying program returns, diagnosing the root causes of performance, and making fact-based, objective decisions

5. Systematic budgeting, planning, and execution processes that are simultaneously faster and more disciplined

6. Elimination of persistent marketing spending, brand, and customer segment data gaps that are a barrier to understanding and decision making

7. Greater cross-functional collaboration, with less organizational tension and finger pointing

8. An ongoing program of in-market experimentation, adaptation, and improvement

9. A long-term road map for improving marketing accountability and performance, which includes investments to build capabilities and improve processes

10. A culture of accountability and performance that is reinforced by formal measurement systems and informal messaging from the top down and from peer to peer

The Value of Improving Marketing Accountability

Over the past decade we have had an opportunity to work with countless companies in their efforts to improve the effectiveness of their marketing spending and the accountability of their marketing function. This work—across industries and geographies, and with companies of widely varying scale, life stage, sophistication, and brand health—has revealed some universal truths about the value of pursuing greater marketing accountability.

First and foremost, it *is* possible to significantly improve your marketing accountability and the business performance of your marketing spending in a short period of time. In the first few months alone, companies can typically identify marketing spending waste equal to 15 to 25 percent of their marketing budgets, which can be redeployed to invest in new growth opportunities. In terms of the extent to which the effectiveness of marketing programs can be improved, the sky truly is the limit. We have observed as much as triple-digit improvements in the rate of return for already effective advertising, promotion, event marketing, and other programs. Over time, these improvements to marketing spending effectiveness have led to much higher rates of revenue growth and in some instances have helped reverse the declines of major brands (see Figure 1.8).

Beyond just getting more from your marketing spending in the near term, we believe that marketing accountability should be pursued in a way that creates an even more valuable ongoing performance "annuity." Creating this annuity will require companies to develop a test-and-learn capability, invest in closing critical skill gaps, improve the speed and efficiency of core MA processes, and foster a

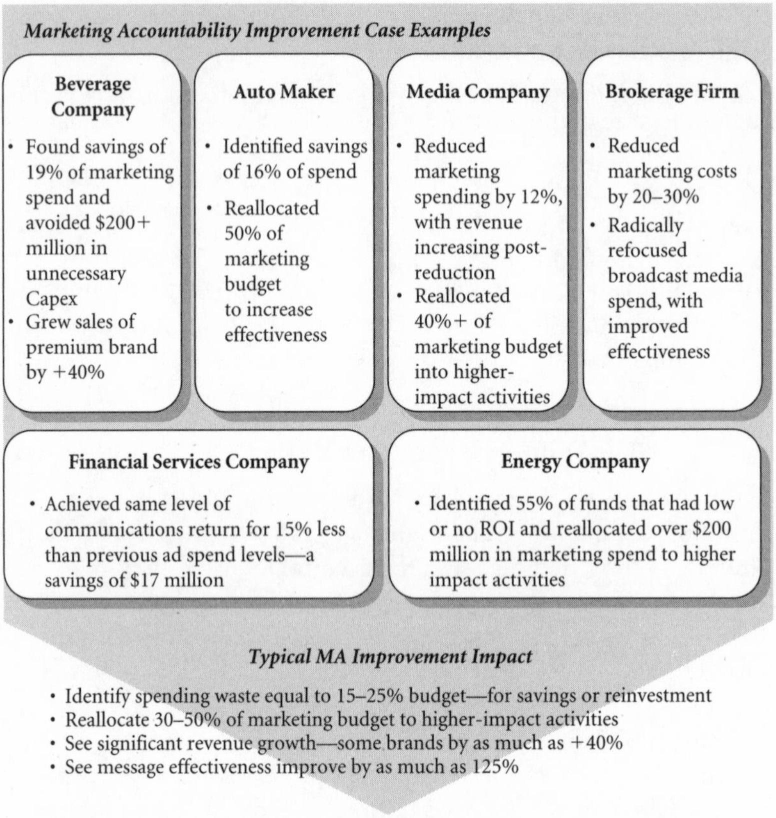

Marketing Accountability Improvement Case Examples

Beverage Company

- Found savings of 19% of marketing spend and avoided $200+ million in unnecessary Capex
- Grew sales of premium brand by +40%

Auto Maker

- Identified savings of 16% of spend
- Reallocated 50% of marketing budget to increase effectiveness

Media Company

- Reduced marketing spending by 12%, with revenue increasing post-reduction
- Reallocated 40%+ of marketing budget into higher-impact activities

Brokerage Firm

- Reduced marketing costs by 20–30%
- Radically refocused broadcast media spend, with improved effectiveness

Financial Services Company

- Achieved same level of communications return for 15% less than previous ad spend levels—a savings of $17 million

Energy Company

- Identified 55% of funds that had low or no ROI and reallocated over $200 million in marketing spend to higher impact activities

Typical MA Improvement Impact

- Identify spending waste equal to 15–25% budget—for savings or reinvestment
- Reallocate 30–50% of marketing budget to higher-impact activities
- See significant revenue growth—some brands by as much as +40%
- See message effectiveness improve by as much as 125%

Figure 1.8.   The Power of Marketing Accountability Improvement

truly performance-based culture within the marketing organization. When companies take marketing accountability to this next level, the financial benefits of increased efficiency, effectiveness, and growth are clear.

What is perhaps less tangible, but no less important, is the fundamental shift in perceptions that takes place across these organizations around the role and importance of marketing. Companies that can maintain a long-term focus on marketing accountability improvement develop a much better understanding of the challenge of marketing and a greater collective trust in marketing's intent and abilities. The marketing accountability gap that may have once divided the company is replaced with a more productive focus on working together to fix *business performance gaps*.

There are several pioneering B2C and B2B companies—including HP, Pitney Bowes, Kraft, and Citigroup—that have gained significant traction in their overall marketing accountability journeys and are beginning to reap the value from their own marketing accountability "annuities." Many more companies have solved important pieces of the marketing accountability puzzle that we can learn from. Throughout this book we draw upon the lessons provided by these companies, as well as many more masked examples, drawn from clients we have served on this critical topic for the past fifteen years.

Our Approach to Improving Marketing Accountability

The good news is that there is a clear path forward, which relies more on business fundamentals and discipline than on some little-understood "black box." The less good—but not unexpected—news is that there are no quick fixes to creating an accountable marketing organization. Although a marketing accountability initiative will offer plenty of early wins, the real improvement prize may take two or three years to come to full fruition. Much like in the story of the tortoise and the hare, the company that is able to maintain a long-term commitment to marketing accountability improvement will reap far greater rewards than the most sophisticated and data-rich company that loses its focus after making initial gains.

In our experience, one common characteristic of companies that lose their way on the marketing accountability journey is that they tend to eschew the basics and instead seek a more rapid "silver bullet" solution. We are all for improving the sophistication of MA decision making, but we will spend the majority of this book discussing basic proven MA analytic approaches and processes. Although most companies are already using bits and pieces of what we will discuss in this book, we are certain that few companies are using the full suite of these tools and approaches to their full potential. Fewer still are doing so in an integrated way, consistently, year after year.

Our approach to marketing accountability is to establish a foundation of fundamental MA skills and practices and then layer progressively more sophisticated approaches on top of this foundation, to continually improve your marketing accountability and in-market results.

It may not be fair that the CMO and the marketing department have taken the brunt of the blame for what is going on in today's marketing environment and for perceptions about the marketing accountability gap. Fair or not, the situation is what it is, and it requires a solution. And more likely than not, it will be up to the CMO or equivalent marketing leader to find that solution. For marketing leaders, this book provides an effective road map for the journey to marketing accountability.

We also wanted to make sure that this book was relevant to the line marketers who live with marketing spending activities on a daily basis and who will be on the front line of marketing accountability improvement. For these readers we have attempted to dive a little deeper in some key areas, to arm them with practical step-by-step approaches and key success factors. As we attempt to add value for both marketing leaders and practitioners, we run the risk of getting too far into the minutiae for some and not far enough for others. We think that the benefits of getting this content in front of marketers of all levels—*who will need to work together to improve marketing accountability*—are worth the trade-offs.

Moreover, this book is not just for marketers. Although primary responsibility may fall to marketing, this does not absolve the CEO, CFO, VP of sales, business unit heads, or other senior business leaders of their responsibility to better understand the issues. This book will help nonmarketing executives recognize what marketing accountability success will look like and understand the type of long-term, cross-company commitment needed to make lasting improvements and foster a more collaborative and productive partnership with the CMO and the marketing function.

CHAPTER TWO

Recalibrating Basic Beliefs About Marketing Spending

When Marketing Can Create Accretive Value and When It Is the Wrong Tool for the Wrong Problem

T opics covered in Chapter Two:

• What is the value creation potential of marketing spending?
• What are the limitations of marketing spending?
• Is ROI the best measure of marketing spending performance?

> *These days man knows the price of everything, but the value of nothing.*
>
> *—Oscar Wilde*
>
> *To note an artist's limitations is but to define his talent.*
>
> *—Willa Cather*

In Chapter One we framed the issue of the marketing account-ability gap and the internal and external factors that have contributed to creating and perpetuating this gap. To respond to these challenges, we put forward a definition for what true marketing accountability can and should be in every company. In this chapter, we address three questions about the role and usage of marketing spending and the basic beliefs that form the basis for our answers. We refer to these as *basic* beliefs because they involve fundamental issues about your company's orientation to marketing spending that will have a material impact on how it pursues marketing accountability. Without calibrating around these beliefs where necessary, it is possible to charter very different MA improvement programs with, in turn, very different outcomes.

You or your organization may have additional and potentially diverging beliefs about marketing investment—whether they are explicitly stated and formalized or simply implicit in how marketing spending decisions are made in your company. As you read this chapter, consider your own organization's beliefs about marketing spending or investment and whether any of these could in fact be limiting your progress toward greater marketing accountability and therefore must be challenged.

In this chapter, and indeed throughout the entire book, we will sometimes discuss concepts that are not "new news" to experienced marketers. We do this because we want this book to be just as relevant to the CFO and CEO, and any other senior executives who have a stake in marketing investment and accountability, as it is to the CMO and senior marketing leaders. Throughout this book, when you encounter concepts with which you are in fervent agreement, or that you consider to be old news, please think about how much easier it might make your life if your nonmarketing peers also shared these views; then skip ahead to the next section. We'll rejoin you there.

WHAT IS THE VALUE CREATION POTENTIAL OF MARKETING SPENDING?

Basic Belief:

Marketing spending *can* create significant value by generating short-term revenue and building long-term brand and business value.

With all of the generalized concern about marketing accountability, it is easy to see how many are losing faith in the ability of marketing spending to drive business performance. The CMO's nonmarketing peers may feel vindicated for all the years spent doubting why companies are spending millions of dollars on advertising, promotions, sponsorships, and countless other marketing touch points. But marketing spending is no more or less effective than it ever was; it is just much more challenging than it once was to yield attractive returns. There are certainly many clear and compelling recent examples of companies that have leveraged marketing spending to drive both short-term sales *and* long-term brand equity. Moreover, the value of this long-term brand building is not just warm and fuzzy good feelings, but tangible and significant bottom-line dollars. These examples, however, have understandably been overshadowed in the business press by the many recent spectacular failures of marketing investment.

As we stated in the first chapter, we are not agnostic about the overall potential of marketing spending to create significant value. We do remain objective, however, about its potential and current performance in each particular situation. This is an important distinction and the reason why we believe that you must first inform your beliefs about whether marketing spending *can* work for a business like yours, *before* evaluating whether it *does* work for your particular business.

The way in which a company views the role of marketing spending and its perceived value will significantly shape its marketing accountability improvement efforts. Companies that grudgingly participate in marketing spending activities only because their competitors do, that cannot conceive of how any real value could come from these activities, are likely to create an MA program that validates their beliefs and cuts spending levels. Although your marketing spending may be ineffective today, that does not necessarily mean that it cannot be improved to become a significant driver of new value. Without uncoupling your company's beliefs about whether marketing spending *can* add value from whether it *does*, your marketing accountability efforts run the real risk of throwing the baby out with the bathwater.

The majority of this book's readers may not have an initial bias against marketing spending. Indeed, for many it will be necessary to examine the other side of the coin and discuss the limitations of marketing spending, which we will do in the discussion of our next principle. But even if you yourself are confident in what marketing spending can accomplish when used effectively, many of your colleagues may not be. Whether it is your colleagues who have significant doubts about what marketing spending can do, or you yourself have such doubts, we should take a moment and calibrate around its potential, so that your MA improvement efforts don't become a "go/no go" plebiscite on investment.

We have stated our belief that marketing spending can be a significant driver of both short-term (within the current budget period) and long-term (beyond the current budget period) value. The ability of marketing spending to drive short-term revenue—whether through promotional offers, call-to-action advertising, or the like—should be readily apparent. Although it may work better in some sectors (such as packaged goods, for which there is a low-involvement purchase decision) than in others, or from company to company within a sector, we are not aware of a groundswell of concern about the fundamental capacity of marketing spending to drive short-term impact. Surely there are not too many senior executives—*even among nonmarketers*—who would doubt that marketing spending programs *can* drive near-term sales. The real open questions about marketing spending as a driver of short-term value—*What returns are you getting? Which activities work best? How can you improve your effectiveness?*—will all be addressed at length in the chapters to come.

It is the power of marketing spending to deliver longer-term goals—*at a positive rate of return*—that is most frequently called into question. And inseparable from this question are questions about the value of investing in brands and indeed the real value of brands overall. A lot of big thorny issues, to be sure, but it's best to get them all out on the table and address them, if there is any confusion that could be standing in the way of an objective assessment of your marketing spending.

Marketing Spending as a Driver of Long-Term Brand Value

Figure 2.1 provides a framework for examining the value created by marketing spending and in particular its role in creating long-term value. As the arrows in the graphic suggest, investments made in the long-term health and equity of your brand feed short-term revenue-generation activities. Essentially, all value creation is realized at a point in time, or a series of points in time, but much of this value is possible only because of long-term equity-building investments. For example, short-term spending on a promotion will generate much lower sales and ROI on the promotion if the company has not invested over the long term in building the equity of the brand and fostering meaningful product differentiation. As we suggest, this intrinsically ties long-term

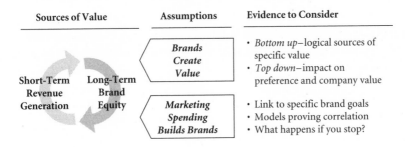

Figure 2.1.   The Role of Marketing Spending in Long-Term
Value Creation

marketing investments to brand building. It would be pointless to discuss how long-term marketing investments build brands if you do not first believe that brands create significant long-term value. It's a fair question, which we will tackle from a few different angles to prove the point. First, we will look at the logic of long-term brand value from the bottom up, by considering all the sources of value made possible by strong brand equity. Next, we will examine the top-down evidence for long-term brand value, by considering different modeling approaches that explain the brand's impact on corporate value and as a driver of customer preference.

Sources of Long-Term Brand Value

As we suggested with our first principle of marketing accountability, the ultimate goal of marketing spending—indeed the *only* goal—is to make money. Although we are strong advocates of the power of brands, this belief is pragmatic rather than sentimental. Brands are a means to an end, and that end is increased profitability. Those new to branding may take as an article of faith the need to make long-term investments in building intangible brand value (see sidebar). But the sources of long-term brand value are in fact highly tangible and quantifiable. Consider these ten sources of brand value and whether they could potentially justify long-term marketing investment:

1. *The ability to grow faster than the market*—by stealing share from competitors or by earning the trust needed to expand usage occasions

2. *The ability to price at a premium*—particularly when your goods or services are functionally undifferentiated

3. *Lower customer acquisition and retention costs*—which means you don't have to bribe new customers to join you or existing customers to stay with you

4. *The ability to leverage your equity into new margin pools*—customer permission to extend your brand into contiguous categories and beyond

5. *The freedom to reject less attractive customers*—or at least price them according to their real value (net of the cost to serve them)

6. *Greater influence over intermediaries*—who must offer you their customers and collaborate with your strategies to be successful

7. *The ability to win the war for talent*—attracting a stronger cadre of staff, who will in turn create superior value for the company

8. *The resilience to survive catastrophes*—Tylenol is the classic example of a brand strong enough to rebound after an unexpected PR disaster

9. *Higher share prices*—investors are willing to pay more to acquire your stock and are more likely to hold on to it despite temporary dips in earnings

10. *The ability to command a higher transaction multiple*—creating either more value for shareholders or greater freedom to spurn unattractive suitors

---

Intangible Equity **Versus** *Intangible Value*

Crisco Oil has developed a powerful emotive bond with its loyal customers, who consider it a trusted partner in helping them express their love for their family through their cooking. This deep equity goes beyond what is tangibly in the bottle, because the oil in the bottle is a commodity that is essentially no different from the oil found in the bottle of any good generic. Amazingly, most consumers know this, or at least suspect this to be true, yet this does not lessen Crisco oil's brand equity. Although this equity could be described as somewhat intangible, the value that it creates is not—consumers pay 50 percent more for Crisco oil than they do for the same oil packaged with a generic label. Was P&G wise to use marketing spending to maintain and extend the equity of the Crisco Oil brand? Absolutely. Is the payoff from this investment "intangible"? No way, as evidenced by the "handsome bonus" P&G shareholders received when the brand was sold to J. M. Smucker in 2002.

From the Top Down: Modeling Brand Value

The overall value created by a brand can be assessed using many different modeling techniques. Because you can question the methodology of any given brand valuation models, we will examine several different approaches to understand the role that brands play in creating long-term value.

MODELING TOTAL BRAND VALUE GROWTH AT UBS You may be familiar with a few different approaches to quantifying the overall value of a brand through modeling. *BusinessWeek* runs an annual cover story that ranks brands by the value they create, drawing on Interbrand's "outside-in" modeling of brand value. Many other companies have similar methodologies for explaining how much of company's valuation or cash flows can be attributed to the strength of their brands. Let's look at Swiss Financial services giant UBS as an example of a company that was able to grow this brand valuation significantly through its brand-building efforts and in turn show that this brand value is indeed real value for UBS's shareholders.

UBS realized a few years ago that their brand's strength was inferior to their business strength (operations, offers, and so on); as a result, they were not getting their fair share of new customers, and existing customers were not granting them adequate permission to deepen their relationship with them. Coming out of a series of mergers and acquisitions at the start of the decade, UBS was perceived by customers and analysts as being somewhat of a hodgepodge of businesses, with varying levels of awareness from market to market and with limited integration and synergy. To create a stronger brand that would better leverage its business strength, UBS announced at the end of 2002 that it would consolidate all of its various holdings under a single master brand strategy and embark on a long-term effort to align its operations and the perception of customers to the promise of this brand. Within the first two years of launching its brand-building push, UBS saw its brand value increase from just $2 billion in 2003 to almost $8 billion by 2005. If there is any doubt that this brand value is indeed real value, you can see from Figure 2.2 that during this period the value of UBS's shares appreciated by more than 70 percent—double the industry average and triple the Financial Times Stock Exchange (FTSE) 100 Index's performance.

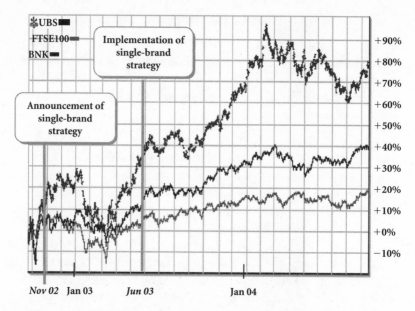

Figure 2.2.   Growing Long-Term Brand and Business Value at UBS

MODELING BRAND AS A DRIVER OF PREFERENCE IN HEALTH INSURANCE
Many senior executives find it difficult to fully trust the output
of "*über*" models of total brand value, because it is difficult to test
the logic of their assumptions. This is why it is helpful to also look
at other, more granular approaches to valuing the role of brands. For
example, Figure 2.3 shows the output of a preference model in the
health insurance industry. A preference model examines the relative
importance of many different factors in explaining why a company is
chosen by customers. Comparing this output across competitors can
help a company assess its strengths to be exploited and weaknesses
to be overcome. Figure 2.3 shows the drivers of preference across all
companies in the health insurance category. We can see that several
factors play a role in driving customer choice, but brand is consistently the number-one or number-two factor across stakeholders—
including employers and intermediaries, who many might assume
would discount the importance of brand.

In the two examples just discussed, we consciously chose industries
that are not traditionally known for being hugely dependent on their
brands (financial services and health insurance). Even in these industries, though, there is a clear relationship between brand strength and

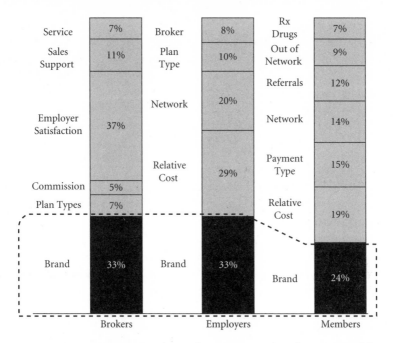

Figure 2.3. Importance of Brand as a Driver of Preference (Health Insurance Example)

business success. CoreBrand, which measures and tracks the brand value contribution across over a thousand brands, suggests that on average brand accounts for 8.5 percent of the market capitalization of these companies. Some packaged goods companies derive a significantly higher proportion of their market cap from their brands— for example, 16.9 percent for Procter & Gamble and 20.5 percent for Coca-Cola.

Having discussed the benefits of building long-term brand equity, let's consider the role of marketing spending in making that happen.

Using Marketing Spending to Build Brands and Long-Term Value

The CoreBrand study just quoted suggested that of the average 8.5 percent of market cap that is attributable to brands, fully 50 percent can be traced to marketing spending—with about 30 percent traced to advertising and the remainder to other marketing activities. As further evidence of the link between marketing spending and long-term brand equity and corporate value, we will consider how marketing spending is used to drive specific dimensions of long-term brand equity and then consider an example of what happens to your business when you stop investing in your brand.

Marketing Spending and Awareness

Building customer awareness is one way that marketing spending can be used to deliver a single tangible brand goal that creates value over a longer-time-horizon investment. Although customers can be made aware of a brand very quickly through marketing spending activities, they will create value for the brand only at some later point—once you have built up their consideration for your offer and when they are in the market to buy. In many big-ticket or high-involvement categories, this conversion from awareness to value realization may take two or more budget periods to occur. Awareness should also be considered a long-term goal because it never goes away. Even if you reach your structural ceiling of efficient awareness, you will not be able to stay at this level without some continued marketing spending activity, because of the constant cycling in and out of new cohorts of customers to the market. Do you think many twenty-somethings making purchases for their first home would be aware of the once-ubiquitous household brands Zenith, Waring, or Electrolux?

Awareness is also a good place to start in our examination of the role of marketing spending in driving long-term value, because this link should not be contentious. Logically, a potential customer who is not aware of you is not likely to buy from you. Assuming a constant marginal conversion rate from those who are aware to those who become your customers, every point of awareness you gain will create value for your company. Now all we have to do to close the loop is to show that marketing spending activities can drive awareness. Figure 2.4 shows the very clear and strong correlation between Aflac's brand awareness investments and their awareness gains over a three-year period. Over this period, Aflac increased its awareness advertising spending by 68 percent and grew its awareness by over 100 percent (46 points). Similarly, E*TRADE increased its awareness spending from 1998 to 2000 by 180 percent and grew its awareness by 170 percent (or 57 points).

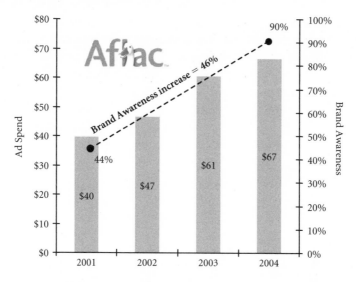

Figure 2.4.   **Relationship Between Advertising Spending and Brand Awareness**

So there you have it. Building awareness creates long-term value, and marketing spending can effectively build awareness—ipso facto, marketing spending can create long-term value.

What Happens When You Stop Investing in Your Brand?

Perhaps the plainest evidence of the link between marketing spending and long-term value is an understanding of what happens when you significantly change your marketing investment level of your brand, through a simple empirical examination of changes in marketing spending and changes in market share.

The best time to capture data on a large number of companies reducing their marketing spending levels is during a recession, when many companies cut their marketing budgets to make up for falling revenues. Two years after the '74–'75 recession in the UK, companies that maintained or increased marketing spending during the recession had revenues 27 percent higher than those of companies that temporarily cut their spending. Moreover, this advantage was still in place when the same companies were examined five years after the recession. The long-term differences in value creation between those who maintained investment and those who cut spending was even greater after the 1981–1982 recession.

You can conduct another simple empirical assessment yourself by looking at data available on www.adage.com. We examined spending changes versus share changes for ten product categories over a two-year period. We found that almost 70 percent of the eighty brands experienced an expected outcome (that is, spend up and share up, or spend down and share down) rather than an unexpected outcome (that is, spend up and share down, or spend down and share up). If there was no correlation between marketing investment and year-over-year value for so many brands, we would expect this number to hover somewhat randomly around 50 percent. Indeed, in some categories the proportion of expected outcomes was as high as 86 percent (for mobile phones) and even 100 percent (for credit cards).

Can marketing spending create value? It can—*in some form, and to some extent*—in virtually every company we have encountered that sees fit to have a marketing organization. In the space of a few pages we don't expect to convert all doubters about the power and potential of marketing investment as a driver of both short-term revenue and long-term brand equity and business value. But by recalibrating your company's beliefs on whether marketing spending *can* create value or, at the very least, by approaching this question with an open mind, you can ensure a more objective assessment of the real question of marketing accountability—*does your marketing spending work for you?* And if it does not, why not, and what can be done about it?

WHAT ARE THE LIMITATIONS OF MARKETING SPENDING?

Basic Belief:

All the marketing spending in the world won't overcome a weak value proposition, unclear path to value, or poor execution.

Objectivity about the potential of marketing spending must, of course, work both ways. This is why we must now discuss the limitations of marketing spending and why it should not be considered a panacea for all marketing ills. We will discuss two core limitations of marketing spending that can stand in the way of realizing the potential that we discussed in the last section:

- *Marketing spending won't overcome a weak proposition.* Fundamental issues with your value proposition cannot be effectively addressed by just adding more marketing spending to the problem.
- *Marketing spending requires a clear path to value, with crisp strategy and solid execution.* There may be critical structural obstacles that limit the potential of marketing spending to help you reach your marketing goals, which get exacerbated by poorly conceived executions.

Marketing Spending Won't Overcome a Weak Proposition

In Chapter One we drew a clear distinction between a company's "proposition" and the decisions and investments required to deliver this proposition to customers—with our definition of marketing accountability focused on the latter delivery choices. Having said this, we cannot escape the critical role of the proposition in driving marketing spending returns and ultimately a company's in-market success or failure. This book won't guide you on how to improve your proposition, but it will reinforce what, it is hoped, you already know: a weak proposition leads to weak marketing spending performance. Moreover, many companies may realize a greater ROI by investing their next marginal dollar on proposition improvements than from a similar investment in marketing delivery touch points that attempt to work around proposition shortcomings. For the most part, you can't use marketing spending activities to spend your way out of a proposition problem. There will be situations in which marketing spending can be used as a temporary workaround to a proposition gap, but these instances are few and prohibitively expensive. More often than not, it will be cheaper and quicker to close the proposition gap than to try to patch over the problem with marketing spending.

PROPOSITIONS RULE In the preceding section we discussed the significant value that marketing spending can create. When competitors are pretty evenly matched with their basic value propositions (features, pricing, service, quality, and so on), then marketing spending, to build brand differentiation and drive revenue, forms the real basis of competition and value creation. It is when these propositions are not equal—*when customers can clearly recognize an inferior offer and act accordingly*—that we must recognize the overwhelming importance of the proposition and the limitations of marketing spending.

Figure 2.5 shows a model we constructed of the differential value created by three retail gasoline brands. It's a straightforward regression model that includes detailed data for all the thousands of sites in the market. The data is shown as an index to all the other brands in the market, so you can compare across these three brands and between each brand and the market. The model compares expected site volume, based on proposition elements, to actual site volume, with the residual attributed to the impact of brand and marketing spending. You can clearly isolate the relative importance of each proposition element in explaining site volume, because there is such rich data available for every site (see sidebar).

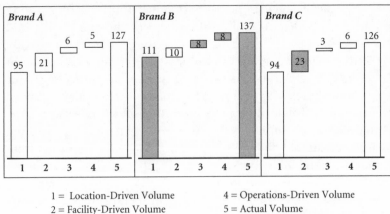

1 = Location-Driven Volume   4 = Operations-Driven Volume
2 = Facility-Driven Volume   5 = Actual Volume
3 = Brand-Driven Volume (linear)   ■ = Best Practice Performance

Figure 2.5.   Drivers of Business Strength: Retail Gasoline Example

Note: Gasoline Modeling Factors

Location: Type of location (highway, neighborhood, business district, etc.), hourly traffic volume, number and proximity of other stations, and so on

Facilities: Site size, size and type of signage, quality of access and egress, number and type of filling positions, number of parking spaces, lighting quality, back-court (store) facilities, mid-court (carwash, oil change) facilities, and so on.

Operations: Ownership (for example, dealer versus owner-operator), hours of operation, labor ratio, site cleanliness, and so on.

So now that we know what the model is, what does it tell us about the relative importance of value propositions and brands? First, brands, and the marketing spending needed to build them, do matter. Each of these brands creates more brand value than the market as a whole, but one brand (Brand B) creates almost three times the value of one of the others (Brand C). Brands, however, represent a fraction of the value created by these companies' proposition elements (that is, site volume attributed to brand ranges from 3 to 6 percent). In contrast, site location alone accounts for an average of 77 percent of the volume on these sites. Brand B can overcome a significant deficit in the quality of its site facilities only because of its outstanding locations, which include the largest share of high-volume highway sites.

If Brand B could close its facilities gap, its advantage over the average market site would grow from 37 percent to 50 percent. But if you have hundreds or thousands of sites to improve, how would you fund this change, and how quickly could you make this change? Brand B's brand value is higher in part because they recognized their facility weakness and are spending more aggressively than competitors on marketing while their site upgrade program (a five-year plan) is under way.

There is no such stopgap measure with marketing spending, however, for Brand A and C's location gap. It is not reasonable to believe that they can triple the value that they extract from brand and marketing spending, and the underlying proposition problem with their locations may never be fixed because their lower cash flow makes them less competitive for new real estate as it becomes available. Thus the gap in their proposition can only continue to widen.

This model correlated elements of the proposition to customer behavior. In the previous section we saw a model that did the same thing, but with customer preference—*showing that proposition accounted for about 80 percent of preference in health care insurance.* No matter which way you analyze it, or which category you look at, propositions matter a great deal.

WHY COMPANIES ATTEMPT TO SPEND THEIR WAYOUT OF PROPOSITION GAPS Some proposition gaps, or gaps in the customer experience, can be addressed with marketing spending activities and others cannot. If customers are not familiar with a brand's points of differentiation, marketing spending can make them familiar. If customers are familiar with the brand's benefits, but these do not resonate with them, marketing spending could potentially be used to convince them otherwise, but it would likely be expensive, with an uncertain outcome. For customers who have experienced the brand and were fundamentally dissatisfied, there is not much that marketing spending can do at all to fix this. Figure 2.6 suggests the role that marketing spending may or may not play in addressing significant gaps in the customer experience for companies in different industries.

So why would a marketing group attempt to use marketing spending to address a problem that it is ill-suited to solve? We saw in the first chapter how little control the CMO has over many fundamental elements of the proposition—features and benefits, pricing, and service. Even if the CMO recognizes that it would be best to address the proposition gap head-on, the only tool that many CMOs have at their disposal is marketing spending—advertising, promotions, sponsorships, direct mail, and so on.

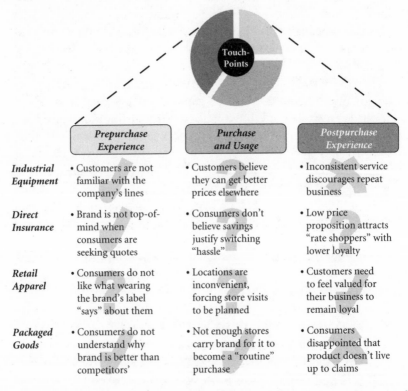

	Prepurchase Experience	Purchase and Usage	Postpurchase Experience
Industrial Equipment	• Customers are not familiar with the company's lines	• Customers believe they can get better prices elsewhere	• Inconsistent service discourages repeat business
Direct Insurance	• Brand is not top-of-mind when consumers are seeking quotes	• Consumers don't believe savings justify switching "hassle"	• Low price proposition attracts "rate shoppers" with lower loyalty
Retail Apparel	• Consumers do not like what wearing the brand's label "says" about them	• Locations are inconvenient, forcing store visits to be planned	• Customers need to feel valued for their business to remain loyal
Packaged Goods	• Consumers do not understand why brand is better than competitors'	• Not enough stores carry brand for it to become a "routine" purchase	• Consumers disappointed that product doesn't live up to claims

Figure 2.6.   Role of Marketing Spending in Addressing Customer Proposition Gaps

Where the CMO has responsibility for marketing results without authority to change elements of the proposition, the CMO is forced to work with what is at his or her disposal, and the owners of the proposition (such as product groups and business units) can shift the blame to marketing when the spending doesn't solve the problem.

Sometimes this lack of control over the customer experience extends beyond the entire company. Companies that depend on intermediaries (brokers, agents, distributors, retailers) or franchisees to deliver much of their overall branded experience to their customers have even greater control issues. These companies may feel compelled to use marketing spending, even when it is clearly inefficient, because they lack other options to address proposition or experience gaps (see sidebar).

Working Around Intermediaries

For years after a big automaker acquired a certain niche auto brand, there was a disconnect between the brand image the acquirer was trying to build with its aspirational advertising for the brand and what potential customers experienced when they went into the acquired brand's dealerships for a test drive: the dealerships were run down and service levels were low. But the new owner's hands were largely tied by agreements already in place with these dealers. This problem resolved itself in time, as the legacy dealers saw the benefits of improving or were bought out. For a period of several years, however, the automaker had to spend more than its competitors on marketing—to essentially stuff more customers into the funnel—knowing that they would lose more than their fair share of prospects once they reached the dealership.

Even when the CMO or company has complete control over all aspects of the value proposition and customer experience, there may be a tendency to rely on marketing spending rather than confront a proposition gap that is particularly difficult to address. This is particularly true when it is likely that it will take months or years to close the gap. As we saw in Chapter One, the short average tenure of the CMO does not give that officer a real incentive to tackle issues that will likely take a year or more to resolve.

A more optimistic CMO will recognize the need to address the weaknesses in the value proposition and realize that with the insights and customer information at their disposal they can guide their cross-functional peers. We saw this firsthand at Prophet when the CMO at Carlson Hotels, Yvonne LaPenotierre, recognized that the beds were key to guest satisfaction and a quality brand experience. She willingly turned over millions of dollars from her marketing budget to fund the operational needs of upgrading the beds in every guest room. We do recognize that this type of collaborative, cross-silo behavior is not common—but we are doing our part in promoting this for stronger business results.

THE IMPACT OF USING MARKETING SPENDING WHEN YOU SHOULDN'T
Perhaps the most egregious example of selling the sizzle over the steak was the questionable marketing spending that characterized the dot-com bubble. In this period billions of dollars were wasted on advertising, promotions, and sponsorship deals, based on the mistaken belief that there was a first-mover advantage to building ubiquitous awareness, which would in turn overcome a flawed or incomplete value proposition. It is very telling that the companies that survived this period and went on to dominate their online categories—Amazon, Google, and eBay—all placed a much greater focus than their peers did on developing their propositions than on big-ticket marketing spending plans.

Although few would argue with the logic of marrying accountable spending to an attractive proposition, many companies are still attempting to simply spend their way out of a weak proposition. For example, you can observe several retail banks and wireless providers that have higher customer churn rates than their peers but choose to react to this problem by increasing their acquisition spending instead of addressing the root proposition causes of their problems (such as the number of ATMs, network coverage areas, or poor customer service training). The belief appears to be that forcing a greater number of potential customers through the marketing funnel can overcome the company's particular weaknesses in customer conversion. But this is a very expensive stop-gap measure for fundamental problems that will not go away on their own.

Gaps in the proposition that trace to poor customer service are a particularly interesting challenge, because customer service can be considered both a part of the proposition and an element of our broader definition of marketing spending (that is, a touch point with a critical influence on customer behavior). With this broader view of marketing spending, traditional marketing dollars can easily be real-located to add variable capacity to call centers, to improve scripting and service levels, and the like. This is why it is particularly troubling when a company with significant customer service gaps instead chooses to address this issue by increasing their spending on traditional marketing activities such as advertising and promotion.

Value proposition gaps are relative. If everyone in your category is perceived to have horrendous customer service or poor product quality, then in essence no one does. But the dynamics change once the first competitor begins to differentiate itself on these factors; everyone in the category must adapt to the basis of competition or be left behind. Let's consider the actions of two brands that scored very poorly in an MSN-Zogby poll of 2007, which asked customers which brands they believed offered the worst customer service.

Earning the title of worst customer service in America was Sprint Nextel. Sprint earned the honor by having 40 percent of its customers rate their service as poor. This compares with 22 percent for their telecom rival Verizon (which also performed poorly). This makes Sprint essentially twice as bad at customer service as their competitor. Now *that's* a value proposition gap. In response to the survey, a Sprint spokesperson pointed to a new website, www.buzzaboutwireless. com, which includes a customer service–focused message board. A visit to the site gives the impression that Sprint created it so customers would be able to work out their problems among themselves. The vast majority of Sprint responses to customer message posts go something like this: "Your issue has been passed along to our customer care center" (although there were occasionally typos, so you got the impression that this response was not computer-generated).

When your customer service has been voted the worst in America—by a large margin—you would think there would be a lot of activity to fix it, as well as messaging to let customers know it is being fixed. But if you search the company's press releases, customer service is referred to in only fourteen, whereas there have been two hundred press releases referring to the company's "sponsorships" (NFL, Nas-car, Bon Jovi, and so on). In addition to its vast spending on these sponsorships, Sprint is also one of the largest advertisers in America, spending $1.2 billion in 2006. Although there were few announcements by Sprint about new customer service initiatives, the company did say that it planned to increase 2007 advertising spending by $200 million and replace its advertising agency as well. Cold comfort, perhaps, to the Sprint customer who said on an online blog that he has become so used to Sprint's overcharge mistakes that he "plans for a 30 minute call each month to wait on hold and have it fixed."

So how well does marketing spending address Sprint's overwhelming value proposition gap with customer service? If you allocate their advertising expense alone (ignoring the cost of their sponsorships, promotions, and any other marketing) to each net new customer Sprint acquires, it costs Sprint about $500 per customer. This compares to an advertising expenditure of about $270 per net new customer for Verizon. If you are someone interested in coincidences, the size of the customer service gap between Sprint and Verizon corresponds exactly to Sprint's relative advertising inefficiency compared with Verizon. For our part, we don't believe in coincidences.

Compare Sprint's behavior with another "winner" in the survey, Comcast, which tied for second worst in customer service, with 30 percent of respondents rating their service as poor. After an even poorer showing in 2008 (42 percent of respondents rated their service as poor), Comcast has revamped their customer service using online outreach to dissatisfied customers. Comcast has dedicated resources of the human kind to monitor what is said about the company online and responding directly via Twitter and e-mail. In addition to responding more directly to consumers, the company is also getting a good deal of online buzz and PR in support of their efforts. We'll have to see where they land in 2009!

DRAWING THE LINE BETWEEN PROPOSITION AND SPENDING It is not always easy to draw a clear line between problems that can be solved only with proposition fixes and those that can be addressed effectively with marketing spending. Consider, for example, the multitude of companies that are attempting to extract a price premium for their product or service. For these companies, is it better to *tell* customers and prospects about a premium image through brand-building marketing communications investments, or to invest in the R&D, design, or service levels needed to truly *be* a premium offer? Of course, the best companies do both.

Apple's iPod, for example, commands a clear premium over other category competitors with similar functionality—as measured by the simple metric of dollars per gigabyte of memory. Although iPod's branded communications masterfully extend their proposition's strengths—allowing the iPod to maintain a hip, leading-edge image, despite its growing ubiquity—this is not simply a triumph of brand-building investments over their customers' common sense. With all of the attention generated by iPod's strong branded communications, it is easy to overlook the fact that the iPod is also a *superior product* on several key drivers of category choice, including

- *Ease of use*: The simplicity and ease of use of the iPod's wheel interface has been imitated but rarely duplicated by other devices.
- *Design aesthetics*: The simple, clean aesthetics of the iPod's over-all design contribute to both its premium perceptions and its adoption by the mainstream of less technically savvy consumers.
- *Proprietary library*: Apple's iTunes software, with its extensive song library, gives it a significant advantage over other devices, which lack a customized plug-and-play interface.

We recognize that few companies occupy the rarefied air of Apple's iPod, where exceptional brand intersects with strong value proposition. The vast majority of companies will be confronted with some minor proposition gaps that they must decide to work through or work around. Although there are precedents for using brand communications to work around minor proposition deficiencies—by elevating the importance of other category benefits—it may in fact be much easier and less expensive to fix the underlying proposition problem than to convince customers that something else should matter more to them.

We will now introduce a simple framework for helping to assess the trade-offs between proposition fixes and marketing spending fixes; we will return to this framework later in the book. The "Antes and Drivers" grid in Figure 2.7 provides a means of assessing the strengths and weaknesses of your proposition and brand relative to your category competitors. The vertical axis of this grid suggests the relative importance that customers give to features and benefits in the category. The horizontal axis suggests the extent to which brands are differentiated from one another on these benefits. Attributes that appear in the upper right quadrant are considered to be *drivers* of a brand's proposition and equity that can be exploited for growth. Attributes in the upper-middle quadrant are essentially *antes*—things that are important but won't really drive a differentiated choice among

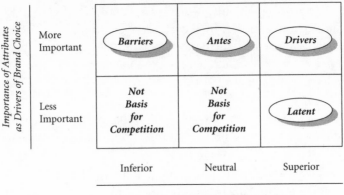

Figure 2.7.   "Antes and Drivers" Brand Assessment Framework

brands, because all brands perform equally well against them. Think of the importance of a clean bathroom in a restaurant; this matters to customers, but they expect that all restaurants will perform adequately on this dimension, so it is an ante or a "ticket to the game." The same attribute in retail gasoline might be a driver of choice for some brands, because customers in that category have highly variable expectations of brand performance. Attributes in the upper-left quadrant are considered *barriers* that could be holding a brand back if they are not overcome, because competitors are strongly associated with these characteristics. Finally, attributes in the lower-right quadrant have the potential to become drivers, if the brand can somehow elevate their importance with customers in the category.

In Figure 2.8 we have layered onto this framework the potential marketing actions that can be taken in each cell of the grid. Some of these solutions require proposition fixes ("eliminate") and others are purely the domain of marketing spending ("emphasize"). You can use this framework and these potential marketing actions to assess the tradeoffs between a proposition fix and a spending fix. For example, if the brand lacks any drivers, it can invest in improving their proposition to build them or in marketing spending to elevate its potential drivers.

Harley-Davidson offers an example of a brand that has shifted the basis of choice for enough customers to create and occupy a successful niche, where image and affinity matter more than certain aspects

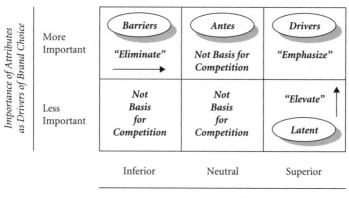

Figure 2.8. Marketing Actions Suggested by "Antes and Drivers"

of pure technical performance and value. Despite Harley-Davidson's success, it is inadvisable to bet your company's future on creating such powerful brand equity that you too can shift the drivers of choice and overcome your brand's proposition weaknesses.

Marketing Spending Requires a Clear Path to Value, with Concise Strategy and Solid Execution

Beyond the shortcomings of your product or service value proposition, there will be many other marketing issues and opportunities, ranging from difficult to impossible to solve with traditional marketing spending activities. For example, in some categories, brands with a 90-percent awareness level can go no higher by using marketing spending, because the remaining unaware individuals are not media-reachable consumers. Essentially, these brands have reached a structural ceiling that limits the further impact of marketing spending. As another example, before customers were able to take their telephone numbers with them from one wireless carrier to the next, there were structural limits on the amount of customer switching that could be accomplished through marketing spending activities. When obstacles in the path to value are less obvious, they may be uncovered by asking a series of "what would you have to believe?" questions. Asking these questions will help you determine whether marketing spending is going to help you reach your goal.

For example, it is reported that Microsoft spent half a billion dollars to launch Vista, its new version of the Windows operating system, when they already had a more than 92-percent share of the category. The vast majority of OS purchases are bundled with new hardware purchases, and after the initial hardware purchase most OS software users are characterized by high degrees of inertia. If you are nearing the structural ceiling of potential market share in a highly inert market in which you have a dominant position, what could be the theory behind this spending strategy? Let's examine "what you would have to believe" about the different paths this $500 million in marketing spending could take to create new value—and what obstacles may stand in the way.

PROTECTING FRANCHISE FROM SHARE EROSION BY COMPETITORS
Perhaps the scale of Vista's launch marketing is a defensive move to protect Windows' dominant share in the face of emerging threats from Linux and others. The problem is that any really dominant player has more to lose than to gain from increasing the intensity of competition. This plays out in two ways. First, the dominant player has much more to lose from the acceleration of marketing spending. For example, we have seen dominant brewers with an over-70-percent share match the price discounting of rivals with a less-than-10-percent share and pay a dramatically disproportionate penalty. It rarely makes sense in an oligopoly to disrupt rational behavior and accelerate spending levels, and it almost never makes sense to do so with a quasi-monopoly.

The second risk of Microsoft's prominent spending is that it could backfire against them, and an attempt to defend or gain share could actually precipitate share loss. Again, it is helpful to ask yourself some "what would you have to believe?" questions:

- Between a dominant and a niche brand, which is more likely to have a higher proportion of "inertial" rather than "emotively loyal" customers?
- What would happen to any dominant brand if a low-involvement purchase decision became a high-involvement one?
- Could aggressive spending that draws attention to a category create a multiplier effect on the spending and messaging of much smaller players—essentially creating a platform for their response?

CHANGING CATEGORY PURCHASE DYNAMICS Perhaps Microsoft was attempting to change underlying OS category purchase dynamics to its advantage—say, by decoupling the OS upgrade cycle from new hardware purchase decisions to make it shorter and increase frequency. A strategy that focuses on disrupting existing purchase dynamics is always highly risky, especially for the incumbent. In this example, the first risk is the assumption that Windows would be the net beneficiary from making OS software a more considered and separate purchase, which is clearly not an obvious outcome. The second risk is that the decoupled OS upgrade cycle is actually longer than the hardware upgrade cycle, so it ends up slowing down demand patterns in the category as opposed to speeding them up.

INCREASE INCREASING CATEGORY DEMAND It could be that the strategy is to grow Microsoft's volume by growing total category demand for operating software. When you have a dominant market share, this can be an effective strategy. In recent years De Beers has promoted new diamond-giving occasions, hoping that they would become as *de rigueur* as the diamond engagement ring. Similarly, if Microsoft could encourage a second or third PC in every home, they would benefit greatly no matter what version of Windows ran on each PC. Unfortunately, it's hard to see a similar category growth benefit in the features Microsoft is promoting with Vista.

BUILDING THE CORPORATE BRAND In general, we are proponents of using product marketing spending to efficiently build meaningful differentiation for the corporate or parent brand. Electronics manufacturers like Samsung and LG do this well with handset marketing, and later we will discuss how Anheuser-Busch did this in the 1980s with its Bud Light marketing spending. Perhaps Vista will become such a silver bullet for Microsoft. But this assumes that affiliating corporate and product brands will create value rather than destroy it. Said a different way, the equity that Microsoft (the corporate brand) acquires through its affiliation with Vista should benefit the other Microsoft-branded businesses—think game platforms like Xbox or portable media players like Zune. Is it possible that Microsoft's ubiquity may work against it in some of the new high-growth categories the company has entered—game platforms (Xbox), portable media players (Zune)—in which individuality and edge hold sway?

Moreover, even if there was a positive affiliation between the product brand and the corporate brand, the economics of this strategy seem questionable. Let's make up a fictitious analogy to walk through the "what would you have to believe?" assumptions around these economics. Let's say our fictitious product is the *Gotcha* media player. We'll keep things consistent and always use 20 percent as our key assumption. Although our made-up example in Table 2.1 did not pay out, you can see how running simple "what if" scenarios can help you understand the structural potential of marketing spending to create value.

Lest you think us overly critical of Microsoft's strategic rationale for the $500 million Vista launch campaign, consider our primary goal: simply to illustrate the thought process around understanding the marketing spending path to value. As the Vista example illustrates, sometimes the path to value for certain marketing investments is less than obvious. But just as challenging for proponents of marketing

Economic Factor	Illustrative "What If" Assumptions	Impact on "Gotcha"
Investment allocation	20 percent of $500M intended to benefit category	$100M in spend
Category growth	100M unit category growing by 20 percent per year	20M units in play
Current market share	20 percent share of 100M unit category	4M unit fair share
Halo perception benefit	Incremental 20 percent of purchase intenders consider	+3.2M units in play
Halo behavior benefit	20 percent of new consideration converts	640K incremental units
Incremental margin	20 percent of average price of $250 per unit ($50)	$32M incremental margin
Residual benefit	Ongoing impact 2x of year one (NPV basis)	$64M total value created
ROI of halo strategy	Loss of $34M in marketing investment	ROI of −34 percent

Table 2.1. The Structural Potential for Marketing to Create Value: "Gotcha."

accountability is the great variability in results that companies introduce with their strategy and execution choices. Marketing spending no doubt *can* drive exceptional performance results, but it would not be wise for most companies to take best-practice performance expectations to the bank. Lack of data or incorrect assumptions can drive faulty marketing spending strategies, and lack of skill or discipline can lead to poor execution. Either factor can turn an otherwise attractive marketing program into a waste of money. And worse than simply wasting money, poorly designed and delivered marketing programs can actually destroy value and leave you with fewer customers than you would have had if you had done no marketing at all.

Consider the findings from the Deutsche Bank report on the return on investment of different packaged goods television advertisements. Although on average the thirty-six commercials examined delivered $1.63 for every dollar invested, there was tremendous variation around this mean. The best advertisement yielded $6.82 for each dollar invested; the worst, a negative $0.64 for every dollar spent. Even within brands from year to year, the same brand could swing from a positive to a negative result. Whether a brand achieved a highly positive or highly negative ROI was by no means random, however. None of the ads for one large company had a negative ROI, but one-third of the ads for a similar company were. Clearly, some companies enjoy an "executional premium" above average marketing spending performance, while others are handicapped by an "executional discount."

We are all aware of the variability of marketing spending performance; we don't need to say more about it here. The rest of this book will discuss how to diagnose the value you are extracting from your marketing spending—*whether premium or discount*—and show you how you can improve it.

IS ROI THE BEST MEASURE OF MARKETING SPENDING PERFORMANCE?

Basic Belief:

Narrowly focusing on marketing ROI can destroy value—real marketing accountability is about improving returns, not simply measuring them.

In Chapter One we saw the critical priority that companies have given to quantifying marketing ROI and how a large portion of these companies are struggling with how to make it happen. CMOs have compared the quest for marketing ROI to seeking the Holy Grail or achieving nirvana. Given these heady comparisons, we should understand how marketers are defining success in this quest. Table 2.2 suggests the various definitions that marketers are using to describe marketing ROI. As you can see, they were allowed to pick more than one option, and many must have gone with several. Even assuming different business models and different roles for marketing, clearly all these definitions can't be right.

Rarely do good things come out of such a combination of desperation and confusion. Without a clear understanding of what marketing ROI is and is not, what it will and will not give you, and how it should and should not be used, for many companies it is very likely that their quest for marketing ROI will end badly. To ensure that marketing ROI is developed properly and used effectively in your company, we should calibrate what you and your company believe about marketing ROI. To this end, please complete the quiz in Figure 2.9.

66 %	Incremental sales revenue generated by marketing activities
57 %	Changes in brand awareness
55 %	Total sales revenue generated by marketing activities
55 %	Changes in purchase intentions
51 %	Changes in attitudes toward the brand
49 %	Changes in market share
40 %	Number of leads generated
34 %	Ratio of advertising costs to sales revenue
34 %	Cost per lead generated
30 %	Reach and frequency achieved
25 %	Gross ratings points delivered
23 %	Cost per sale generated
21 %	Post-buy analysis comparing media plans to actual media delivery
19 %	Changes in the financial value of brand equity
17 %	Increases in customer lifetime value
6 %	Other / none of the above

Table 2.2. Definitions of Marketing ROI Used by Marketers.
Source: ANA / Forrester (2004).

1. **Marketing ROI and marketing accountability are the same thing.**

   a. True   ☐

   b. False   ☐

2. **Which marketing activity is better?**

   a. An activity with a precise ROI   ☐

   b. An activity with only directional   ☐
   data on returns

3. **Which of the following marketing ROI is best?**

   a. Every $1 spent returns $3.41   ☐

   b. Every $1 spent returns $2.17   ☐

   c. Every $1 spent returns $1.78   ☐

   d. Every $1 spent returns $1.36   ☐

Figure 2.9. Marketing ROI Quiz, Part One

Pencils down. Pretty straightforward, right? The answer to the first question is of course "False," but we gave that away in the basic belief presented earlier, and we will say more about it in a moment. Unfortunately, questions 2 and 3 cannot be answered with the limited information provided. What if we reworded the options in questions 2 and 3—the same options, mind you, just more context (see Figure 2.10)?

Now these questions can be answered, and the answers are quite obvious. For question 2, the answer is clearly *b*—we should always choose a program that is directionally positive over one that is precisely negative. Remember that *directional* does not mean *inaccurate*. You may be confident with the ranges that bound your returns, but

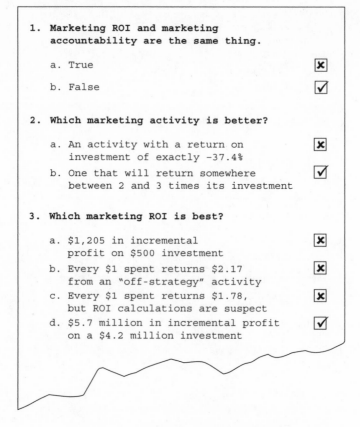

1. Marketing ROI and marketing
   accountability are the same thing.

   a. True   ☒

   b. False   ☑

2. Which marketing activity is better?

   a. An activity with a return on   ☒
      investment of exactly -37.4%

   b. One that will return somewhere   ☑
      between 2 and 3 times its investment

3. Which marketing ROI is best?

   a. $1,205 in incremental   ☒
      profit on $500 investment

   b. Every $1 spent returns $2.17   ☒
      from an "off-strategy" activity

   c. Every $1 spent returns $1.78,   ☒
      but ROI calculations are suspect

   d. $5.7 million in incremental profit   ☑
      on a $4.2 million investment

Figure 2.10. Marketing ROI Quiz, Part Two

not able to pin down the precise rate of return. In question 3, we can discount all of the other options to determine that *d* is correct:

  a. Just not worth the bother: An attractive "rate" of return, as implied by the absolute profit numbers, is not that meaningful a metric by itself—unless your marketing department has unlimited executional capacity to chase down hundreds of small programs. Before category management became more sophisticated, grocers lost a lot of money by focusing on profit margin (that is, percentage profit per unit) over realized profit (that is, margin times price, times facings, times turns.

  b. ROI does not drive the bus: A narrow focus on maximizing ROI may lead you to activities that are not consistent with your strategy that can erode brand equity and destroy long-term value.

Strategy drives tactics that can be measured by ROI—ROI does not drive tactics absent of strategy.

c. *Precise and wrong is precisely wrong*: Richly quantified ROI can be calculated based on a house of cards of nested assumptions, driving outputs with spurious accuracy, which are sometimes just plain wrong. When you can no longer validate every assumption, that's when you've lost control of your ROI calculations.

If these false options looked like easy pitfalls to avoid, keep in mind that they are all real examples of misunderstanding or misusing ROI that otherwise-sophisticated Fortune 500 companies are falling prey to today.

Putting Marketing ROI in Context

It's hard to imagine that a simple little formula such as this one could cause such anguish:

The Marketing ROI Formula

Incremental Returns – Total Cost of the Marketing Activity =
Marketing ROI

But beneath the simplicity of the marketing ROI formula is a tangle of complex issues—*How to get at the number? What trade-offs must be made to get there? How do you know if you're right? What does the number really mean? How does it change how marketing spending decisions are made?*

We would like to challenge some of the narrow, limiting beliefs about marketing ROI—not to rebuke its importance as a goal, but to put it in the appropriate context of a broader marketing accountability improvement program. Marketing ROI is not an interchangeable synonym for true marketing accountability. The ultimate goal of marketing accountability is not to improve the rigor of ROI measurement, but rather to make more money faster, through better, more effective and efficient marketing investments—*that both ring the cash register and build the brand.* To do this, a much better understanding of marketing spending returns is a necessary but, by itself, insufficient step forward. Marketing accountability is concerned not only with the *what* of ROI but also the *why* needed to diagnose performance issues, improve returns, and accelerate growth.

True marketing accountability is also about the discipline to make the right choices for your brand and business. When something is as desired and elusive as marketing ROI seems to have become for many marketers, there is a real danger that the wrong trade-offs will be made to achieve it and that it will be used in ways that destroy value once it is available to you. Throughout this book, we attempt to demystify marketing ROI and the tools that purport to help you determine it, as well as to offer our perspective on how to leverage ROI to create value rather than destroy it. We begin this dialogue by introducing the following topics:

- Using marketing metrics in an accountable way
- Pursuing marketing ROI in an accountable way

Using Marketing Metrics in an Accountable Way

The following examples illustrate how misusing marketing ROI information can actually *destroy value*. They are offered as cautionary tales showing why you cannot be complacent—once the complexity of calculating marketing ROI is behind you, the *real* complexity actually begins. We end the section with a brief discussion of what it looks like to use marketing ROI in a more accountable way.

DON'T EMPHASIZE ROI PRECISION OVER PROFITABILITY The first companies that were able to calculate ROI with some degree of rigor were consumer packaged goods companies in the 1990s. The key technological enabler that made this possible was the widespread availability of retail scanner data, which made it possible for the first time to know where, when, and at what price a CPG brand was being purchased by consumers. Mix models were constructed that combined this new performance data with data about the CPG company's marketing inputs (advertising GRP levels, price features, in-store displays, ads in the retailers' flyers, and so on). These early mix models were able to discern the impact of price promotions very easily, because the results were readable instantly (that is, during the five- to seven-day life of the discount), and because they created significant variation for the model to detect; namely:

- Price features were either "on" or "off" in a binary way.
- Features were dispersed throughout the marketing calendar, based on when trade support could be secured.

• Feature promotions were chain-specific, generating highly readable variation between where the promotion was available and where it was not.

In contrast, more strategic marketing spending activities, which created longer-term benefits, were much more difficult for the ROI modeling approaches of the time to evaluate. Seeing a brand-building television advertisement today might have a cumulative effect on reinforcing or changing the customers' perceptions, but this may not translate into new value-creating behaviors for months to come. Moreover, each customer would experience this lag effect over a different period of time—unlike with a price promotion, which doesn't allow customers to act outside of the offer period. To the early ROI models, any sales improvement resulting from these lagged behaviors would appear to be just general "noise" impacting the entire mix. In addition, more strategic marketing spending activities, like advertising (particularly at this point in the early 1990s), were more likely to be deployed in a highly consistent way throughout the year and from year to year. Media levels rose and fell with the tides of category seasonality in what was described as a *continuity strategy*. Although this may have been exactly the right thing to do, in terms of building your brand and business, it was the worst thing to do if you wanted the results to be read by an early ROI model, because there was no variation to read.

With this data as the input, the modelers went about assessing marketing ROI and arrived at the following conclusions:

• Short-term tactical activities—*particularly temporary price promotions*—have a strong ROI with a clearly discernible response curve (that is, you can conduct very specific optimization of discount levels and supporting flyer and display activities).

• Long-term strategic activities—*particularly brand equity advertising*—do not correlate to sales results. Worse than not having a strong ROI, they could not generate any detectably significant impact at all.

Many of the more sophisticated marketers could balance this new ROI input with their own experience and what they saw from market tests, advertising pretests, and split-cable tests at the time—which was that *brand-building advertising does indeed have an important positive impact on long-term value.* Despite this, CPG firms largely acted on the new ROI data, shifting their focus and spending toward these more richly analyzable short-term in-store activities (CPG's share of overall ad spending fell to its lowest point during this period). This shift away from brand-building activities had a serious effect on CPG and retailer profitability. Not only did the equity of specific brands erode, but so too did overall beliefs about the importance of all brands (allowing the further propagation of generic and private label alternatives). Customers were trained to purchase many products only at their frequent "deal" price—loading up during sales— which significantly eroded margins. All of this resulted from a misuse of "ROI" and the technology that supported it, by focusing on the most easily quantifiable activities with the quickest apparent returns, rather than triangulating across data sources to determine the real value created.

CPG companies have since returned to the notion of brand building with a longer-term view of marketing investment and ROI. The CPG share of advertising spending has returned to its former levels, and companies like Kraft and P&G have publicly recommitted to building up their brands. In 2007, Kraft announced that they would forgo profit growth for the next two years, so they could reinvest in marketing—increasing their spending as a percentage of sales from less than 7 percent at the time of the announcement to 9 percent in 2009 (an increase of as much as $750 million over the next 2 years).

Packaged goods companies, widely believed to be among the most disciplined all-around marketers, have learned the hard way how to model ROI and work with the output over a period of many years. All marketers pursuing ROI should take these lessons to heart.

ONLY AN INTEGRATED VIEW OF MARKETING ROI IS MEANINGFUL Activity- and campaign-centric ROI optimization can win the battle but lose the war by maximizing the returns of one activity at the expense of another. Consider the multiple outbound offers that a company might target at the same customer. Accepting one offer cannibalizes another, shifting ROI between the two in what is ultimately an internal zero-sum game. Pursuing these activity- and campaign-centric ROI efforts rather than customer-centric ROI often destroys real value, as there are rarely two offers that provide exactly the same margin potential.

EASY ROI CAN LEAD TO LAZY MARKETING You may have heard the axiom that if you put a hundred monkeys in a room with a hundred typewriters, eventually they will reproduce one of Shakespeare's plays by unwittingly banging away at the keys in the right sequence. Although fun to imagine, it's not really a best-practice model for marketing. Unfortunately, many CRM efforts look eerily similar to this when they marry a too-narrow focus on ROI with a blind experimentation approach—essentially throwing all the possible campaign permutations at the wall to see what sticks. Here, ready access to precise ROI can become an excuse for avoiding the up-front work needed to find new customer insight and define more differentiated offers from the outset.

USING MARKETING ROI IN AN ACCOUNTABLE WAY Now that we recognize what improper use of marketing ROI can look like, we should consider what good proper use will look like. To begin, we should calibrate our expectations about what the actual ROI "number" should be in an accountable company. The most accountable marketing organizations will deliver solid, respectable levels of marketing ROI—at a rate that provides more attractive risk-adjusted returns than the company's other competing investments, but well below the level of junk bonds. Going beyond this, to suggest a specific numeric benchmark for ROI would be irresponsible, because there are too many factors to list that would make this number meaningless to your company's unique situation. Indeed, for some companies less is more. For example, a highly accountable company with consistently strong marketing performance may actually experience declines in their marginal rates of marketing return, because they are pursuing more and more subtle optimization opportunities. Other behavioral, rather than numeric, benchmarks for strong ROI performance include:

- *Investing in the right opportunities*: Going after the portfolio of initiatives that will best support corporate and marketing strategy—many of which will offer a lower marketing ROI in the near term in exchange for a strong NPV

- *Investing at the right levels*: Investing in programs where dollar returns, rather than percentage returns, are maximized

(underinvesting may spike ROI but will leave money on the table)

- *Experimenting*: Testing new marketing activities, messaging, and go-to-market approaches that may have lower or even negative returns in the testing phase, but hold the promise of exceptional long-term returns

The sidebar sheds some light on the limits of marketing ROI.

Understanding Minimum ROI Threshold

For these companies, marketing ROI will fall above the *weighted average cost of capital* (WACC); otherwise, it would probably make sense to retire debt or increase ownership. Marketing ROI would probably also come in above many other competing uses of investment, such as operations improvements or geographic expansion. Given that many of these activities would have a lower risk profile than a new marketing investment, marketing spending returns would naturally be expected to deliver an additional premium to account for that risk.

Understanding the Upper Bounds of ROI

The upper bounds on marketing ROI will be subject to even more variation, as emerging high-growth companies will have more attractive marketing opportunities to exploit. Accountable mature companies in mature industries, which are growing at or slightly above the rate of inflation, should not expect to consistently deliver risk-adjusted rates of return on large marketing programs, which are wildly above these overall growth levels.

Pursuing a Marketing ROI Agenda in an Accountable Way

Although there is no question that marketers have to raise their game in measuring spending returns—*quickly and significantly*—they must be careful, even in their haste, to do it properly. There are many business press and vendor claims raising expectations about what is now possible with ROI measurement. It is easy to see why the companies that are the furthest behind with measuring returns might want to leap-frog ahead by implementing a whiz-bang new system. This is, however, a very dangerous approach, because the companies that have the most to gain from understanding ROI also have the most to lose if this understanding is not built on a foundation of basic marketing accountability capabilities. These companies would benefit greatly from simple but fundamental improvements to their marketing spending targeting, measurement, and analytics, but instead they get bogged down in the quest for CFO-quality ROI.

Getting the CMO, CEO, and CFO on the same page. The CEO and CFO have to meet the CMO somewhere in the middle with their expectations about marketing ROI. They must (1) recognize that marketing ROI is more difficult to quantify than many other types of investments (due to the number and complexity of variables and general market "noise"); (2) realize that the real goal of marketing is to achieve better "returns," not just more rigorous measurement; and (3) adjust their expectations about the burden of proof, while structural changes are actively being made to increase the rigor of ROI estimates.

Without a more balanced, collaborative view from the CMO's peers, there is a danger that the wrong behaviors could be encouraged. For example, if the CMO were to retrench the company's marketing mix to only a handful of the most measurable activities, it is likely that he or she could calculate a very robust ROI, but it is just as likely that the company would underperform its competitors who are employing a more complex, albeit less measurable, mix of activities. There is also a danger that the CMO will plunge the organization headlong into a complex systems-based solution for leapfrogging ahead of your current ROI capabilities. Such an approach risks draining resources and significantly delaying your attempts to get to more accountable marketing approaches. An all-or-nothing approach to marketing ROI will likely leave you with nothing; instead, we encourage the CMO, CEO, and CFO to compromise and agree on a schedule for measurement improvements with clear milestones.

"Owning" the ROI Solution

There are many complex issues that you will need to struggle with as you build the algorithms and models that will help you calculate ROI. Given the complexity, there may be a temptation to outsource ROI modeling efforts to outside "experts." We encourage you to drive and "own" this process, understanding the pros and cons of making specific choices around all key decision points, while building your knowledge and capabilities. Only in this way can senior leaders be sure that the organization has the fundamental skills to pursue these efforts pragmatically and extract rich insight from them as they are completed.

To illustrate, let's take as simple an assumption as one around the time frame for a marketing program's impact. When your model calculates "the" ROI for a marketing activity, logically you are asserting one of two things: (1) you have stopped counting returns, or (2) you have estimated all the future returns that might accrue from the activity being evaluated. Either of these might be absolutely the right thing to do, but you should be aware that you are taking a stand on this when you declare a program's ROI, and you should be able to defend why the path you have chosen is correct. Saying that your model has stopped counting returns is a bold choice. Even something as short-lived and straightforward as price promotion can play out in many different ways in the weeks and months after the discount is removed (see the following example).

Temporary Price Reduction Example
Typical Marketing Outcomes

- Forward loading of intermediaries who didn't pass along the discount
- Incremental consumption among your current users
- Stocking-up by current customers—removing them from the market for months
- Temporarily shifted market share
- Some share permanently shifted, due to successful trial of your product

Unintended Marketing Outcomes

- Further erosion of your brand's "quality" equity past the tipping point
- Delisting by intermediaries who were not allocated enough supply
- Inspired retaliation by competitors—ultimately igniting a price war
- Feeding of the "gray market"—leading to off-shore market, or retaliatory dumping
- Catalyzing of "off-label" use as an inappropriate substitute—leading to a PR disaster

---

Saying that your model has estimated all the future returns from an activity, whether positive or negative, and has captured them accurately in your ROI number is bolder still. Deutsche Bank claims that it is common practice to estimate long-term advertising ROI by simply doubling the short-term ROI. This type of general assumption, which has a major impact throughout the model, is noted only in a footnote—shocking!

Why would companies invest the time and energy in pursuing ROI assessments, which purport to be rigorous and balance short-term and long-term objectives, when they're going to make such an important assumption in such a ham-fisted way? You should recognize that any ROI model you commission must make hundreds of similar assumptions and that it is up to you to own what your model's view of the market says about you as a marketer.

Remember That ROI "Ain't Nothin' But a Number"

The number that many ROI initiatives narrowly focus on can be both elusive and unsatisfying. Elusive, because most companies lack the simplicity of marketing mix and the richness of performance data needed for immediate, rigorous ROI quantification (once identified, these gaps can be quickly closed). Unsatisfying, because the companies that achieve "the ROI number" find that that number by itself is not instructive for how to improve returns (see sidebar). It is *improving returns*—or more accurately, *increasing company value*—that is the focus of marketing accountability, and the focus of the remaining chapters of this book.

The Limitations of a Number Without Context

The limitations of answering the "what" of an ROI number, without addressing the "why" needed to understand it, can be illustrated with this analogy from *The Hitchhiker's Guide to the Galaxy*. The fable goes that the inhabitants of a far-off planet became restless once all the necessities of their lives were met. In response, they spent generations building a great super-computer with the sole purpose of answering the question "What is the meaning of life?" Once the computer was built, it took many more generations to ponder the question. Finally, after more than a hundred years had passed, the computer's calculations were complete, and it summoned the planet's elders to receive its answer. "The answer to the question…what is the meaning of life?…is…42." With that, the computer shut itself down, never to be heard from again.

Well-quantified marketing ROI is an important milestone on the path to greater marketing accountability. But rather than viewing ROI as the end point of your accountability journey, you should consider it a new beginning. Once you have a stable platform for calculating accurate marketing spending returns, the real work to improve them can begin.

We have covered a lot of ground with these three questions about your company's orientation toward marketing spending. By acknowledging, challenging, and, where necessary, recalibrating our basic beliefs around these questions about marketing spending, we can turn our attention to a productive dialogue on five new questions, which center on the marketing accountability improvement opportunity:

1. How well do our marketing investments align with our most valuable marketing opportunities and goals?

2. Which marketing investments are working and which are not— and for those that aren't, what is the root cause of underperformance and how can these issues be resolved?

3. What is the best suite of marketing spending tools and tactics for our company, given our goals, past performance, target customers, industry context, competitive intensity, available resources, business life stage, and brand health?

4. How can we optimize the effectiveness and efficiency of our marketing investments to do more with less marketing spending and maximize our company's growth?

5. How can we capture the opportunities that we have identified and sustain long-term marketing accountability impact?

The Core Principles of Marketing Accountability

Describing the Critical Competencies and Value Levers That Enable Accountable Marketing Investment

T opics covered in Chapter Three:

- How marketing spending works to create value
- The four core competency domains of marketing accountability
- The six critical value levers for improving marketing performance
- The advantaged few: how companies segment in terms of MA prowess

> *Franklin Roosevelt was a great leader. He saw how to use the levers of power to affect change.*
> *—Pete du Pont*

> *The rung of a ladder was never meant to rest upon, but only to hold a man's foot long enough to enable him to put the other somewhat higher.*
> *—Thomas Huxley*

Without further ado, let's dive into the core principles of marketing accountability.

First off, we need to ground this conversation in some initial truths by restating, and then underlining for emphasis, how marketing spending works to create value for companies. These truths sometimes get lost or forgotten in the face of what seems like a staggering amount of change and complexity. Said simply, marketing's job is to make money for the company by inducing an economically advantageous behavioral response from customers, with only a few clear angles into the behavior change game. We refer to this as the *path to value*. Every material investment idea should involve a crisp and clear path to value. Then, to consistently guarantee great marketing performance, we need strength in four competency domains: strategy, creativity, execution, and analytics. We will describe the core types of contributions that are needed from each domain and how leading companies focus on the interdependencies and linkages across the domains—not just capability development within each silo—to get the most from their investments. Finally, we have identified six critical dimensions to accountable marketing investments. We have labeled these dimensions *value levers*, for when the lever is applied properly, a tremendous amount of value can be unlocked; conversely, when the lever is incorrectly applied, a tremendous amount of value can be lost. Strong performance in any one of the value levers depends heavily on the underlying competency domains.

These three concepts—clear paths to value, competency domains, and value levers—are the core principles of marketing accountability. We'll explore each in much greater depth, then close the chapter with a detailed look at the landscape of existing companies and how they segment in regard to their current proficiency at driving a marketing accountability agenda.

HOW MARKETING SPENDING WORKS TO CREATE VALUE

Chapter One discussed the many environmental and internal factors that are making marketing spending decisions increasingly complex. Making these decisions is challenging enough even if you exclude these factors. We believe that marketing spending decisions are bogging down in unnecessary complexity, even though the mechanics of how marketing spending works to create value remain very simple.

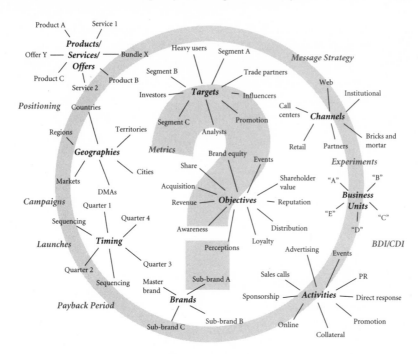

Figure 3.1.   The Complex Universe of Marketing Spending Strategy Decisions

Figure 3.1 highlights myriad strategic decision gates that marketers must pass through as they develop a marketing spending program, with each gate presenting its own unique trade-offs.

Making the wrong choice at any of these gates can doom a marketing spending program to failure. For example, investing in the wrong customer segment, targeting the wrong behavior change, or allocating too much to a given channel all run the risk of compromising returns and placing the brand at a competitive disadvantage. Moreover, even if the strategic foundation is solid, putting creative in the field that fails to capture the imagination of the target audience or is put in the wrong communication vehicles at the wrong investment levels will similarly undermine the effectiveness of your marketing. The stakes are high; the number of opportunities to be considered, trade-offs to be assessed, and potential courses of action must seem overwhelming. It is easy to see how marketers can get bogged down in the complex choices that surround marketing investment decisions.

We can greatly simplify the morass of strategic issues surrounding your marketing investments by grounding your strategic decisions in three simple, inviolate truths, which are often overlooked as marketing becomes more and more complex:

1. The only reason to invest in marketing is to make money.
2. The only way marketing activities make money is by inspiring the right kind of behavioral response.
3. The only way to change behaviors is to change perceptions, change access, or change incentives.

Let's discuss each of these in turn.

#1: Making Money

Simply put, "cash is king." The only reason to put any marketing program in the field—to spend anything at all on advertising, promotion, sponsorship, sales, customer service, or any other marketing activity—is to make money. Blindingly obvious, perhaps, but we still see many marketing investment decisions that don't establish a clear path to ultimate cash value. Marketing spending objectives tend to get muddiest when we are considering the trade-offs between investments that apparently have different return horizons: some more anchored in the short term, others more anchored in the medium to long term. This trade-off is frequently expressed as the choice to drive "revenue" or "sales response" in the short term, or build strategic "brand equity," which may not pay out as immediately in the current period but should build intangible asset value that the company can take advantage of over time. Ultimately every marketing spending activity has to convert to revenue—or more precisely, margin—to be worthwhile. Indeed, long-term equity-building activities must drive higher margin returns to justify the time value of the investment and the greater inherent risk associated with their less direct mechanism of action. The example in Table 3.1 illustrates the return premium that a typical long-term program would need to yield to be more attractive than a typical short-term program. In this example, an investment in long-term equity advertising would need to generate 83-percent higher returns, just to reach parity with the in-period promotion illustrated.

Example of Required Rates of Return on Short-Term Versus Long-Term Spending	In-Period Promotion	Equity Advertising	Rationale
Company's investment hurdle rate	12 percent	12 percent	Cost of capital
Average time to revenue conversion	Immediate	36 months	Time from activity to sale
Risk (percent of programs with +ROI)	85 percent	65 percent	Tracing to time and complexity
Required return on $1 invested	$1.18	$2.16	Adjusting for risk and NPV
Return premium required for long-term programs	-	+83 percent	Given greater risk and time frame

Table 3.1.   Example of Required Rates of Return Depending on Time Horizon Differences.

The implication of this illustration is not that marketers should avoid long-term investments in building deeper equity, or entering new markets or segments, or changing limiting brand perceptions. Quite the contrary; long-term marketing investments are critical to the growth and health of every customer-facing business. Without these investments, brands wither, prices commoditize, and strategic options evaporate. The real implication of the higher returns demanded from long-term programs is that we need much greater precision in understanding how these investments ultimately convert to cash value. The debate about focusing spending on "tangibles" versus "intangibles" is moot—all spending must be evaluated based on the tangible value it creates. The only questions concern how and when this cash conversion takes place, and the optimal portfolio of these investments. Remember, "cash is king"—this always helps bring clarity to the strategic priorities for marketing investment.

#2: Inspiring the Right Behavioral Response

If making money is the only reason to engage in any marketing activity, the question becomes, how does marketing make money for a company? Once again, the simplest answer is also the most meaningful. The only way marketing makes money is by inspiring the right behavioral response—*period*. Taken by themselves, strong brand

Customer Behaviors	Intermediary Behaviors	Investor and Analyst Behaviors
Trial or become a customer	Agree to carry or represent	Purchase the stock
Pay relatively more	Agree to favorable terms	Pay more for the stock
Increase share of wallet	Increase relative focus	Hold shares longer
Remain a customer longer		Recommend the stock
Recommend the company		Assign a higher valuation or multiple

Table 3.2.   Value-Creating Behaviors Driven by Marketing Spending.

perceptions, a great corporate reputation for this or that, exceptional trade relationships, and so on are all very nice to have, but they are essentially meaningless unless they inspire incremental value-creating behaviors, such as those described in Table 3.2.

These choices can be simplified even further by asserting that it is really only "customer behaviors" that create sustainable long-term cash value. Efficient markets cannot be fooled into perpetually overvaluing stock in companies that lack customer fundamentals, and intermediaries are ultimately driven by the pull that customers create for a company's products or services. This leaves us with just five customer behaviors—five marketing spending value-creation goals to concern ourselves with. Every dollar spent on marketing must at some point inspire the right response in one of these five customer behaviors, to create new value for the company.

#3: Changing Behaviors by Changing Perceptions, Access, or Incentives

It would make marketers' lives much easier if marketing spending directly changed customer behaviors. Unfortunately, there is always at least a two-step process separating marketing spending activities and changes in customer behavior. If we believe in the concept of free will, the decisions to *try, buy more, stay,* and so on remain firmly in the control of the customers themselves. Marketers have of course tried to cut the customer out of this decision-making process. One notorious example is "negative option billing," which was attempted by certain cable companies, whereby new channels and services were directly added to customers' statements unless they proactively opted out. Needless to say, that experiment was short-lived.

Thus marketers are forced to use more roundabout approaches to change customer behaviors in value-creating ways. We believe there are essentially three strategic angles into material customer behavior change—(1) target changing customers' fundamental perceptions or beliefs about a product or service, (2) reduce friction points that impede customers' actual or perceived access to a product or service, or (3) offer temporary time-based incentives to increase the relative attractiveness of a product or service's value proposition. Table 3.3 explains how each approach works and provides some illustrative examples of the kinds of programs that align with each approach. By offering up this simple framework, you can encourage or require your team to be crystal clear about how they intend to drive the necessary customer behavior change to deliver against projected business requirements.

Figure 3.2 shows how these three approaches can be deployed via a variety of marketing spending activities along the customer touch point wheel. This is of course an illustrative example. Most activities serve dual purposes, although they often would benefit from being more focused. For example, there is little doubt that the annoying advertising for "Head On" pain reliever—ubiquitous on syndicated game shows—could do little more than build awareness when its copy consists of "Head On, apply directly to forehead" repeated three times in fifteen seconds. Maintaining, improving, or changing customer perceptions is of course the primary goal of most marketing activities. We will say more about the multiple objectives nested in perception building later in the book. It is a helpful exercise to try and align all of your marketing spending activities to their primary purpose; it exposes a great deal of overlapping or otherwise "mushy" objectives and helps reveal whether your spending aligns to your stated objectives.

We have now established the preeminence of the almighty dollar as the ultimate goal of all-marketing spending. This helps us cut through the clutter of all the competing investments to focus on only those that have a clear path to cash value—*whether short-term or long-term.* We have aligned these investments with five value-creating customer behaviors that are the basis for all marketing spending objectives.

Change Perceptions	Improve Access	Offer Incentives
Positively influences customer's fundamental beliefs about the relevance and attractiveness of a company's brand, products, or services relative to competitive alternatives. This can be achieved in several ways; for example: • Promoting a point of positive differentiation (a benefit or reason to believe) • Mitigating a perceived weakness • Drawing attention to competitors' vulnerabilities • Changing the basis of category choice (for example, elevating a less important benefit)	Creates new points of access to transact with the company, without necessarily changing the customers' underlying beliefs about the company's brand or the attractiveness of its offers. For example, a consumer may prefer a particular brand of beer but he won't cross the street to purchase it if the bar he is in doesn't carry it. Awareness advertising is essentially focusing on "access" by informing new customers of the company's participation in the category.	Temporarily increases the relative attractiveness of a company's proposition, without changing the customers' underlying beliefs about the brand or proposition—when the incentives cease, the customers usually revert to their preexisting behavior. Although transient in nature, incentives can create value in several ways; for example: • *Transactional*: incremental margin greater than spend— particularly when category consumption is not fixed (for example, potato chips) • *Acquisition:* as a means to overcome customer inertia to drive trial or switching, especially if a winning "usage" experience might promote longer-term behavior change
Examples: • Advertising to inform and influence consideration • Sponsorships that borrow affinity equity, building deeper bonds with brands • Sales presentations and collateral to influence choice or rejection process	Examples: • Adding distributors, brokers, retailers, and the like • Advertising to drive awareness (that is, accessing the customer's mind-space) • Increasing visibility at POS (such as signage at broker's, share of shelf)	Examples: • Promotional price discounts or volume incentives • Short-term changes to offer features or functions • Contests, sweepstakes Rewards-based loyalty programs

Table 3.3.   Three Distinct Approaches for Catalyzing Customer Behavior Change.

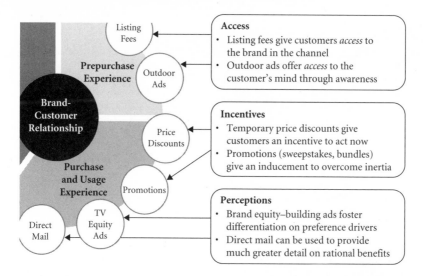

Figure 3.2.   How Touch Points Drive Customer Behavior Change

Finally, we understand the three angles we can take to influence those value-creating behaviors, which in turn are the basis for all marketing plans. This simplified approach is designed to cut through the clutter of marketing spending strategy decisions and get to the heart of where value is created. We will say more about these strategic inputs and outputs in the chapters that follow.

THE FOUR CORE COMPETENCIES OF MARKETING ACCOUNTABILITY

As we will see throughout the discussion in the last two parts of the book, four kinds of competency "contributions" are consistently needed to guarantee powerful marketing performance: great strategy, great creativity, great analytics, and great execution. As seen in Figure 3.3, we refer to each of these as a *core competency domain*, which when effectively developed and appropriately connected into the other competency domains leads to consistently powerful business results and highly accountable marketing investment decisions. So if your company figures out a way to build all of these pieces and fit them together into a coherent system, with tight processes, clear governance, a great data infrastructure, and flexible technology

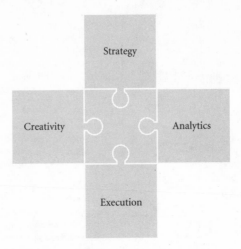

Figure 3.3.   The Four Competency Domains: Essential Pieces
in the Marketing Accountability Puzzle

support, you will have gone a long way toward cracking the marketing accountability code. We will spend a lot more time on the enabling elements around process, data, and technology in the last third of the book, so we will not go into depth on those points here. For now, let's explore each of these core competency domains in a little more depth, using Figure 3.4 as a reference point for the core responsibilities and contribution areas of each.

Earlier in this chapter we spent some time talking about aspects of the strategy competency. Strategic skills ensure that any proposed investment has a well-understood and well-supported path to value. Discipline in this area forces your marketers to be clear about how they intend to make money from specific programs—with which specific customers or prospects, with which anticipated behavioral response (inducing trial, increasing frequency, and so on), and with which angle to try to induce the desired behavior change (perceptions, access, or incentives). In addition to helping the company get clearer on its strategic marketing priorities, this competency also needs to help drive planning around strategic brand equity development, as well as detailed benefit prioritization and value proposition development efforts. So it must help build fact-driven arguments for why certain positioning territories or customer benefit anchor points (such as hassle-free shopping or low prices or attentive service)

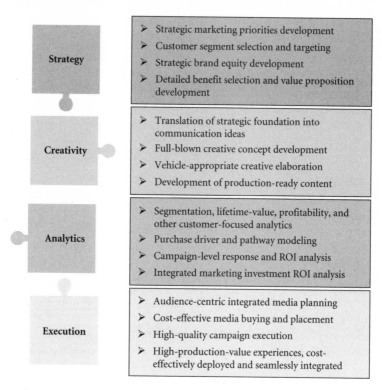

Strategy
- ➤ Strategic marketing priorities development
- ➤ Customer segment selection and targeting
- ➤ Strategic brand equity development
- ➤ Detailed benefit selection and value proposition development

Creativity
- ➤ Translation of strategic foundation into communication ideas
- ➤ Full-blown creative concept development
- ➤ Vehicle-appropriate creative elaboration
- ➤ Development of production-ready content

Analytics
- ➤ Segmentation, lifetime-value, profitability, and other customer-focused analytics
- ➤ Purchase driver and pathway modeling
- ➤ Campaign-level response and ROI analysis
- ➤ Integrated marketing investment ROI analysis

Execution
- ➤ Audience-centric integrated media planning
- ➤ Cost-effective media buying and placement
- ➤ High-quality campaign execution
- ➤ High-production-value experiences, cost-effectively deployed and seamlessly integrated

Figure 3.4.   Core Responsibilities and Contribution Areas for Each Competency Domain

are the best ways to build brand equity and direct any investments. Marketing strategy relies most heavily on the output of the analytics domain, and individuals who are focusing on strategy need to be highly capable in understanding, interpreting, and applying analytic output to inform strategic decision making. There are also more intuitive skills that play a role here, as well as the ability to apply more analogy-driven and qualitative insights into the overall strategic framework, but left-brain skills are more dominant.

Creativity, as a discipline, needs to work within the strategic framework and be used to develop communication vehicles and content that have an ability to connect, to be seen as relevant, and at a minimum to resonate or at best to inspire the intended target. This translation of the strategic positioning into communication ideas that will resonate with the target customer is where the magic of this domain comes into play. To find its inspiration, this domain relies not just on analytically driven customer understanding, but also on other methods of customer insight development. A deep understanding of and empathy for the target customer is considered critical in driving successful outcomes here. Often, marketers also heavily rely on creatively focused outside agency partners to infuse this domain with life, energy, and vitality. Once the core ideas have been established, this domain is also responsible for full-blown creative concept development, vehicle-appropriate creative elaboration (translating the idea for various marketing vehicles, like outdoor or radio or direct mail or on-line), and the development of production-ready content in all of the chosen media.

The analytics domain has gotten most of the recent "ink" in the rapidly escalating debate around marketing accountability. This is probably so in part because it represents that biggest and most consistent deficit area for the majority of companies around the globe. Also, because one critical role for the analytics domain is to provide the essential fuel for marketing accountability via high-caliber metric development and measurement calculations about the effectiveness of marketing programs, it is an intuitive place to focus. The analytics domain tends to have two distinct subdisciplines: one that is more anchored around primary customer research, and another that is more focused on operational data, financial analysis, and more advanced quantitative modeling. The analytics domain is supposed to supply a rich fact-base of quantitatively driven insights that help the company make critical decisions, most specifically in the strategy and execution realms.

The execution domain is responsible for getting all of that great thinking and creative output into the market in a way that delivers high production values, is cost-effective and efficient, and, most important, is on strategy. The types of marketing tactics deployed by any given organization will drive the range of execution skills required, as well as the depth needed in any given area. If your company is very reliant on direct marketing via letters or catalogs, for example, then the required execution-related skill sets would include excelling in execution areas like microsegmentation, list management, cohort-size determination for any given mailing, active campaign management, print, paper and postage cost management, and working with third-party fulfillment houses. However, if your company promotes premium-branded alcohol primarily through on-premise event marketing (at bars and nightclubs) and via trade promotions, what you need from an execution competency will be completely different. In general, though, this competency is expected to generate audience-centric integrated marketing plans, enable cost-effective media buying and placement, guarantee high-quality campaign execution, and deliver high-production-value experiences for target customers and prospects across every marketing communications touch point. On the front end, the creativity and execution domains are highly interdependent; on the back end, the tighter interdependencies are between this domain and the analytics arena.

Each of these competency domains is important as a stand-alone idea, with each having critical responsibilities and making critical contributions in its own right. A root-cause diagnosis of many ineffective marketing programs points to a single point of failure—either poor thinking, ineffective decision making, or subpar deliverables from one of the four domains. However, as we have already pointed out, what matters just as much is the interdependency of these competency areas. Poorly managed interface points between the competency areas lead to disjointed marketing program development, ultimately leading to poorly performing programs. The outputs of one domain need to be used as inputs to drive, or at least inform, the decision making and execution in another domain. For that to happen, the people within the respective domains need to know how to value, internalize, and then apply the outputs from the other domains in their own processes, without being overly crushed or stymied by them.

Cross-competency team constructs are a helpful technique that can be used to achieve this effect, but clearly it is not easy to deliver excellence across all of these disciplines nor to effectively integrate and harmonize the diverse perspectives that spring from each. Many people who excel in analytics or marketing strategy are hard-wired very differently from people who excel in execution or creativity. Not only does the leadership need to commit to developing some fluency in each of these disparate areas, but it also needs to commit to developing processes and culture wherein the value from each kind of contribution is respected and people know how to apply and integrate the insights from across these disciplines into the specific area that they are driving. An alternative may be to follow the consumer goods model, with generalist "brand" managers taking responsibility for cross-competency fluency and interface management. Although typical brand managers may not be experts in any one of the domains,

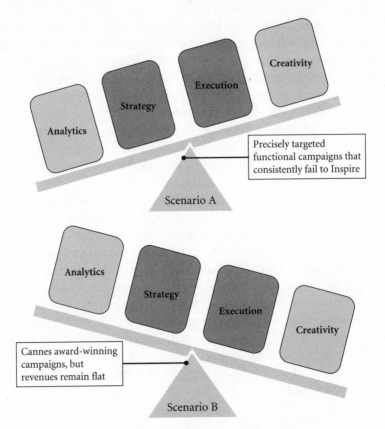

Figure 3.5.   Keeping the Competencies in Balance

they are clearly expected to be able to work with the thinking, approaches, and outputs of all of the domains, dialogue across the competency domains, and bring it all together. But if a company does not have this kind of organizational heritage, just creating these generalist roles out of nothing is rarely a recipe for success.

When the competencies are out of balance, it can also be seen immediately in terms of the marketing performance. As depicted in Figure 3.5, Scenario A is something that you might typically find in a customer analytics–anchored, direct marketing–oriented company. The analytics and strategy competencies are overwhelmingly strong, but creativity tends to be weak—and execution elements outside of direct marketing tend to be very weak. Often the company ends up with marketing programs that do a reasonable job at driving short-term revenue performance and that are very functional in nature but not very effective at inspiring the target customers, capturing their imaginations, or building deep, committed engagement. Alternatively, Scenario B reflects another common situation in which the creativity competency tends to dominate all of the other areas. In this scenario, you can end up with some award-winning campaigns that have edge or energy or warmth or humor, but fail to ring the cash register or move product. Neither is a healthy place to be from a marketing accountability perspective.

Figuring out the right "relative" balance across the competencies and how much of any given competency you are going to build internally rather than source through external partners is critical for any organization. When a relatively well-balanced competency model is underpinned by a strong measurement system and a culture of mutual understanding, empathy, and respect, companies tend to get consistently great decision making in the marketing arena and consistently great in-market results that reflect an appropriate weighting of short-term and long-term considerations and priorities. We will continue to come back to these topics as we move through the rest of the book, but we wanted to introduce the high-level concepts here.

THE SIX CRITICAL VALUE LEVERS FOR IMPROVING MARKETING PERFORMANCE

With an understanding of these foundational competency areas, we can now turn the discussion to the main course—what can a company do in its search for more accountable marketing performance? Based on our extensive work in this arena with countless large and small organizations, we have identified six dimensions critical to accountable marketing performance that is both efficient and effective. When the decision making is flawed or the execution is poor along any one of these dimensions, it can fatally undermine the effectiveness of a company's entire marketing investment. We describe each one of these dimensions as a *value lever*—for when the lever is applied properly, a tremendous amount of value can be unlocked, and conversely, when the lever is incorrectly applied, a tremendous amount of value can be lost.

Figure 3.6 presents all six of the value levers in a single view. The *strategy* lever (#1) and the *content (messaging/creative)* lever (#2) reflect work and contributions that should get made early in the

1 Strategy

2 Content

3 Marketing Vehicles

4 Investment Levels

5 In-Market Execution

6 Fixed Cost Management

Figure 3.6.   The Six Value Levers That Drive Accountable
Marketing Investment

lifecycle of any given marketing investment program. The *marketing vehicles* lever (#3) and the *investment levels* lever (#4) may get adjusted on an ongoing basis during the life of any given marketing investment program. The *in-market execution* lever (#5) and *fixed cost management* lever (#6) center on decisions and activities that are ongoing during the life of any given marketing investment program. Although there is some logic to the sequencing of the value lever discussion, with the strategy and planning topics coming before the execution and monitoring topics, there is no implicit rank order to the levers. Any given company's marketing investment portfolio could be underperforming because of small missteps across all of the value levers or an acute misstep in a single lever. Moreover, there may be just as much upside in addressing issues with the content lever as there is in addressing issues with in-market execution. We'll now step through a detailed discussion of each of the value levers.

Value Lever #1: Strategy

Getting it right with the first value lever, the *strategy* lever, is of utmost importance, as it sets up a series of choices that inform most of the subsequent activities across all of the other value levers. In essence, the strategy lever embodies a series of decisions about strategic marketing choices:

1. Which set or sets of customers present the best business opportunity for your company

2. What kinds of behavioral responses from that target group are the most achievable

3. What unique set of benefits, attributes, and ideas—if communicated and delivered by your company—has the highest probability of eliciting the desired behavioral response

4. Any specific deficits or roadblocks that your brand or company has that will stymie your efforts

Erroneous assertions around any one of these issues can fatally undermine the effectiveness of all of your downstream marketing investments. You want to have a high degree of confidence that your company's answers to these specific questions are right, or at least are the best possible answers given what you know to be true about the category and customer behavior at the time that you make the decisions.

But how can you arrive at that level of confidence? Some organizations rely on an approach that uses the business instincts of an entrepreneur—a passionate believer in an idea who understands the potential target customer so deeply that he or she intuitively understands where the best growth opportunities are and what value proposition will resonate most clearly with them. The business landscape is filled with success stories built around this kind of recipe.

For most organizations, though, it is essential to have a disciplined and transparent approach for answering these questions, because it allows all relevant participants to understand the set of facts, data, beliefs, and assumptions that each of these decisions is based on. "How do we know?" becomes the most common refrain in this kind of process. This allows everyone to stress test the thinking, question the fact base, and look for the hidden underbelly of any decision, in a way that ultimately improves the final answer.

Of course, either approach may get you to the right set of strategy answers—it is just harder to create the right conditions for the first approach if it does not exist already. For organizations that need to follow a more disciplined process, there are a set of well-understood analytic techniques involving customer segmentation and targeting, customer driver analysis, pathway modeling, brand equity modeling, and purchase funnel analysis, which can be used to help your company begin to triangulate on the right answers. When these analytic approaches are used as a foundational input into the decision, without shutting out equally valid qualitatively driven insights and intuitive thinking, a company typically ends up with a strategic value proposition that is worth its weight in gold. A lengthier discussion of this value lever continues in Chapter Four.

Value Lever #2: Content

The next value lever, which we have labeled *content*, anchors on the translation of the strategic foundation into compelling and engaging messaging ideas appropriate for the medium. Although using the word *messaging* might focus the reader on the narrower idea of words or copy, for these purposes we are referring to the whole creative package of taglines, copy, visuals, color, sound, and iconography that are usually part of a broader communication or content platform. Messaging in this sense focuses on the distinctive areas of the strategic value proposition that are most important to communicate to the strategic target audience, finding a verbal and visual language that is uniquely suited to bring these ideas to life in a way that is particularly relevant for that target. The best content platforms originate from a magical combination of strategic insight and creative expression and find a way to connect in authentic yet emotionally compelling ways. When Staples laddered its "hassle-free shopping experience" strategic insight into the "that was easy" campaign, with its big, red, playful "easy" button, and when MasterCard translated its "enabling my purchases for life" insight into the "Priceless" campaign, both companies delivered outstanding performance in relation to this value lever.

Clearly, most companies rely heavily on external agency partners to help bring forth ideas and drive decisions around this value lever. Figuring out how to build the best collaborative partnerships with your chosen creative partners to inspire both sides to do great work remains the ongoing challenge. Of course, you want the best creative talent in an agency working on your business, whereas the agency wants to move its best talent to the most interesting or at least the largest clients for the agency. Agencies tend to get restless—bored a little too easily, perhaps—and may leap to places that are creatively interesting but too loosely connected to the strategy to be effective. Companies may start to shut down ideas prematurely or be unwilling to consider seemingly risky ideas if they reflect too big a break from the past. Companies also have a tendency to put all of the blame for failures in this area on the agency and to have a knee-jerk reaction of opening up an agency search every time they hit a speed bump in messaging platform development.

It is important to remember that great content ideas can come from anywhere. Sometimes they are sourced through collaborative brainstorming, other times by getting similarly briefed teams to pursue independent and somewhat competitive paths. Sometimes they are the work of a single contributor finding some quiet time on a walk or in the shower; other times they result from the contributions of many players in an open-source process driven on the Internet. Irrespective of how the potential messaging platforms get sourced, smart companies make certain to validate their messaging ideas with a robust set of testing before deploying their choices across a full-scale creative campaign. Moreover, the latest academic research also suggests that testing multiple communication ideas is the right way to go. A much lengthier discussion of this value lever continues in Chapter Four.

Value Lever #3: Marketing Vehicles

Once you have gotten the right strategy, supported by strong communication ideas, you are only halfway there. You then need to make a series of decisions about which kinds of marketing vehicles are the most compelling and effective in delivering against the strategy and messaging objectives with expected financial return parameters that will meet your business requirements. We use the term *marketing vehicles* to refer to the wide variety of marketing program types that you could invest in: (1) mass media vehicles like TV, magazine, newspaper, radio, outdoor advertising, PR, internet display advertising and other emerging on-line vehicles; (2) addressable-media vehicles like direct mail, catalog, e-mail, paid search, or mobile advertising; (3) experiential vehicles like trade shows, events, sponsorships, some types of guerilla and "pop-up" marketing; (4) point-of-purchase vehicles like in-store display, in-store couponing, in-store sampling, weekly inserts, and other forms of trade promotions; and (5) the infamous *other* category, including loyalty or rewards programs, affinity marketing, viral marketing, and product placement. This list is not meant to be exhaustive, as ceaselessly innovative entrepreneurs and marketers are always going to piggyback on emerging technology and social and media trends to find new platforms to communicate and engage, but it gives you a sense of the range of activities that we are talking about, as well as some high-level groupings.

Vehicle choices, when made effectively, should enable your multisensory messages to reach and connect with your strategic target audience in a timely, relevant, cost-effective and, increasingly, multiplatform way. To do this effectively, first you must understand where your target customers spend time interacting with media or media-enabled experiences and how open they are to receiving messages in that setting that achieve the specific strategic marketing objectives of the campaign (induce trial, change perceptions, encourage repeat purchase, and so on). As we have seen, consumers and B2B customers are voracious users of media across channels, with the emergence of broadband and compelling Web 2.0 experiences and content just adding momentum to this trend. But even as overall media consumption continues to rise, consumers have more effective tools to shut out your messages if they so choose. So you need to understand both dynamics as you weigh your vehicle decisions.

Additionally, you need to understand the intrinsic characteristics of each of the vehicle alternatives that you are considering. For example, what kinds of marketing objectives are best served by specific vehicles? Is vehicle #1 more appropriate for awareness building and general perceptual shifts and vehicle #2 more appropriate for offering incentives and generating trial? Understanding the optimal strategic applications of each vehicle, as well as the core challenges that any given vehicle poses, is essential for understanding relative trade-offs. Finally, you will need to understand the underlying economics of each vehicle—what drives its cost equation and what drives the type of anticipated revenue response that you might achieve.

Making the wrong choices here can torpedo your entire effort to pursue more accountable marketing, no matter how "correct" your strategic thinking and messaging ideas tend to be. If you mismatch the vehicles with the marketing objective or audience or you fail to have adequate coverage across the required mix of vehicles, all of the hard work up until then will be for naught. Conversely, if you pick the right mix of vehicles from a reach and engagement standpoint but don't understand the underlying economics and potential revenue response dynamics, the implications are just as unpleasant. A much more detailed discussion of this value lever is presented in Chapter Five.

Value Lever #4: Investment Levels

The next important value lever, *investment levels*, operates in two ways:

1. Are we investing appropriately in marketing activities relative to the overall income statement?
2. Are we investing appropriately in any given marketing vehicle, relative to its intrinsic return characteristics and relative to the other investment alternatives that are available to the company?

With this value lever we are trying to diagnose whether the overall marketing investment amount is too high or too low, relative to the intrinsic financial return characteristics of the proposed marketing activities in relation to our strategic marketing objectives. We are also trying to determine whether the amount that we are investing in any particular vehicle, program, or activity is too high, too low, or just right relative to its intrinsic return characteristics and the intrinsic return characteristics of alternative investment options.

Typically, most companies have well-socialized boundaries around how much they are prepared to invest in marketing activities; say, between 2 and 4 percent of revenues or between 22 and 25 percent of revenues, depending on the business model. Traditionally, companies have built an operating model around a certain investment level and, if successful, have carried that forward from year to year with a rolling budget process. This may have been supported by standard share-of-voice analyses done by external media agencies that help to benchmark the investment levels relative to competitive spend. But in rare cases there is a strong empirical foundation to back those boundaries up. We feel that an iterative approach that combines robust point-in-time activity analysis and historical modeling with experimentation is the best way to build that empirical foundation and to understand how much amplitude significant increases or decreases in your overall investment levels might provide to the business.

This is made complicated by a number of factors. First off, marketing program returns are not static. Changes in brand maturity levels, overall category development, and competitive intensity can all materially impact program-level returns, all other things remaining constant. Rapidly evolving media habits of the target audience and changing cost dynamics of any particular vehicle can also materially change a vehicle's return characteristics. Second, marketing program returns are not always linear. Said a different way, if a $5 million investment in program Y gets me X, does a $10 million investment get me 2X? If the return characteristics of any given program are linear, you could answer that question in the affirmative. But many kinds of marketing programs have rapidly decreasing returns to scale above certain kinds of investment levels. Others may even have increasing returns to scale within certain investment boundaries, as captured in the hypothetical S-shaped return curves (S-curves). These curvilinear scale effects are often difficult to estimate, but they definitely tend to imply that there is an "efficient" frontier of investment at the marketing program level that must be well understood. The third issue that complicates this is the existence of portfolio or interaction effects across marketing programs. With certain combinations of programs, you may get materially positive interaction effects, whereby $1 + 1 = 4$; in other situations you may get the opposite.

For these reasons, and a host of others, figuring out how much additional value we can drive by making changes to this particular value lever is a challenging task, but one that ultimately holds a ton of upside. A more detailed discussion of this value lever is presented in Chapter Five, along with the discussion on marketing vehicles. In addition, much of the discussion in Part Three of the book—especially in the analytic approaches section of Chapter Seven, the state of play and diagnostic findings section in Chapter Eight, and the whole dynamic experimentation section of Chapter Nine—help to illuminate how we can tackle the investment level question in much greater depth.

Value Lever #5: In-Market Execution

Even if your company's performance with the first four value levers is top-notch, your overall marketing investment performance can still be adversely impacted by poor decision making and activation around the fifth value lever, which we have labeled *in-market execution*. The nature of your company's particular mix of marketing activities will determine your level of in-market execution risk as well as the upside opportunity that you may realize by improving performance with this value lever. Regardless, great marketing content still needs a great delivery mechanism, one that is consistent with the strategic intent of the overall program and that delivers the same high-quality, high-production-value experience each and every time you deploy it. Diligence with this value lever ensures that your marketing content and your delivery mechanisms are working together as harmoniously as possible.

There are myriad tactical decisions that need to get made to enable, say, a $20 million campaign with a certain bundle of marketing vehicles to get into market in a way that creates maximum impact and with an eye toward cost-effectiveness. On the planning level, you need to make choices about reach and frequency, geographic coverage, and scheduling, in light of insights around seasonality, purchase frequency, and key decision points in the purchase cycle. You need to make these choices across all types of programs, including direct mail, internet search, and point-of-purchase, even though we may be using the "reach and frequency" language of mass communications. On the buying level, in an ever-fragmenting media landscape you need to make hard placement choices that hit the financial parameters set out in the marketing plan on cost-per-point or cost-per-thousand or cost-to-acquire basis while overlaying the qualitative aspects of media reputation, specific audience demographics, and other editorial-related cross-effects. You need to do this in the most fluid media environment ever, with rapidly evolving audience profiles and unreliable tracking figures, while at the same time you audit the "buy" or the "drop" to ensure that it got in market at the intended time and in its intended slot. If your marketing programs are more experiential in nature, you still have the same overall issues about picking the range of venues and ensuring high-production-value experiences every time an "experience" is in market; you just have the added complexity of delivering consistency with an intrinsically more variable format!

The cross-channel visibility that the converging media landscape creates puts even more pressure on this value lever. A lack of symmetry across the channels in terms of the strategic messaging target, creative strategy translation, tactical offer elements, or in-market timing can create huge problems for brands and companies over time. The customer's or prospective customer's experience must be consistent and seamless. If your various programs are not working together synergistically to create that effect because of poor in-market planning and coordination, the instantaneous viral communications platform called the Internet will enable your critics to amplify these mistakes and call you to task for it in a highly embarrassing manner. This value lever is covered more extensively in Chapter Six.

Value Lever #6: Fixed Cost Management

To fully realize the benefits of a marketing accountability program, a company needs to focus on improving cost efficiency as well as improving effectiveness. Driving efficiency through better fixed cost management is a reliable way to do this, whether this is oriented toward explicit cost cutting or cost containment. By *fixed cost management* we mean focusing explicitly on all of the costs that go into producing the various marketing programs that your company may employ, like external agency costs (advertising agencies, event marketing agencies, design agencies, and so on), other production costs, and costs for critical supplies like postage, paper, give-away trinkets, displays, and the like. We think of these as fixed costs because they are the costs required to produce an internet display ad or a TV ad irrespective of whether you decide to show it a hundred times or a thousand times or a hundred thousand times. The nature of your fixed cost base depends on the mix of marketing programs that you employ. But given that some have estimated fixed costs amounting to anywhere from 20 percent to 60 percent of the overall marketing budget in some companies, this is not a trivial matter. If important gains are made around fixed cost management, some of these savings can get redeployed into actual media or other targeted response programs, which could then serve to improve overall effectiveness if properly targeted and executed.

Applying more of a hard-nosed purchasing or procurement manager mind-set to this value lever is a critical step in terms of trying to unlock value here. For marketing, which is an area of the organization that tends to be very relationship-driven and people-centered, this is not always as straightforward as it sounds. An easy way to get started is to understand whether the ratio of "working" to "nonworking" spend on the fixed costs of production, fees, rights deals, paper, postage, packaging, and other production assets seems to make sense. If this ratio seems out of whack, the next step is to ascertain whether you can selectively apply some strategic sourcing principles to pay a little less for what you buy, to redefine some of the core programs to allow you to execute them more cost-effectively, or to reengineer overall processes to reduce costs without compromising quality.

The big risk here, of course, is that, driven by a relentless desire to reduce costs, we end up seriously eroding the quality of our supplier base and our production assets. That would be throwing the baby out with the bathwater. A more detailed discussion of this value lever is presented in Chapter Six.

THE ADVANTAGED FEW: HOW COMPANIES SEGMENT IN TERMS OF MA PROWESS

Over the next few chapters, we will explore each of these value levers in much greater depth, providing you with a good understanding of how to diagnose performance weaknesses within each of them as well as how to design more winning formulas. Some of the levers lean heavily on a single competency area; others require strong contributions across the strategic, creative, analytic, and execution realms to deliver material changes in performance. All of this will become clearer as we walk through the next three chapters. But before we head there, we thought it would be helpful for you to take a closer look at how the existing marketplace is segmented in terms of current MA proficiency. Even though some of these concepts around competency domains and value levers appear pretty straightforward, you may be surprised to see how few organizations feel that they have a good handle on the current state of their marketing investment returns.

Within our study of global companies (which admittedly had an oversampling of U.S.-based respondents), the findings are somewhat startling. Based on a combination of attitudinal, behavioral, and firmographic variables, six discrete segments emerge, only two of which feel confident that they can adequately measure short-term or long-term returns on at least 50 percent of their marketing budget. So even the two segments with the strongest self-assessed proficiency in marketing accountability still have somewhere between 30 and 45 percent of their marketing investment budget deployed against unmeasured programs and vehicles! Within those two segments, only one segment, "The Experts," has a robust system of metrics in place—metrics that account for both income statement and balance sheet effects of marketing investments and also incorporate the interaction effects across programs. Even most companies that live in The Experts segment are cautious about describing their proficiency in marketing measurement—signaling that much of the current system is

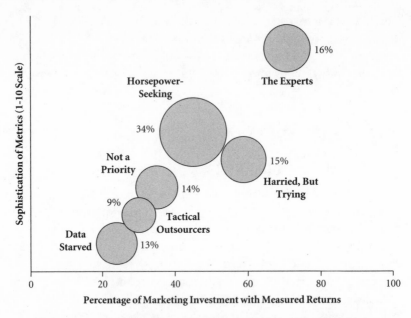

Figure 3.7.   A Current-State Snapshot of Self-Assessed Marketing
Accountability Proficiency

still a work in process and acknowledging that many growing investment areas still have not been fully incorporated into the measurement systems and models.

In Figure 3.7, we depict all six segments in relation to the percentage of their current total marketing investment with measured returns and to the overall sophistication of metrics. Companies that score higher on the sophistication scale have a diverse set of metrics that assess income statement (sales and profit) and balance sheet (equity) impacts, incorporate stand-alone as well as interaction effects in their return estimates, and have multiple longitudinal measurement observations. Interestingly, each segment has fairly even distributions when it comes to company size, ranging from companies with more than $50 billion in sales to companies with less than $500 million. Moreover, even though there is some spikiness, there are companies from all of the major sectors in each segment. Even in the vaunted consumer products industry, with its data-rich environment and early-adopter status around many of the leading-edge analytic and measurement techniques, only 30 percent of those sampled qualified for inclusion in The Experts segment.

The three least-well-positioned segments—"Data-Starved," "Tactical Outsourcer," and "Not a Priority"—represent almost 35 percent of respondents; on average, they understand the returns on less than 30 percent of their existing spending. The largest segment, "Horsepower-Seeking," also represents almost 35 percent of the market, and understands the returns on only about 45 percent of the total current marketing investment. The remaining segment, "Harried But Trying," represents about 15 percent of the market and understands returns on about 60 percent of the overall spend. Not an overwhelmingly bullish assessment of the current state of marketing accountability, but all the more reason for a good book like this one!

Companies in the three least proficient segments share some things in common, but also differ sharply from each other along other dimensions. They all deploy very narrow sets of tactical effectiveness metrics, have fairly evenly distributed marketing mixes, and invest, on average, less than $100 million a year in marketing programs. Companies in the Data Starved segment, however, cite data quality and availability issues as their primary roadblock to more accountable marketing. Of all the segments, this is the only one that has a firmographic skew, with an overrepresentation of small to medium-sized companies. Consistent with this, these companies are significantly more likely to cite more effective pricing and global expansion as critical to short-term growth goals, and the least likely to cite a need for more investment in marketing to drive near-term growth. The only vehicle that at least 50 percent of them measure effectively is sales promotion, and interestingly, they are the segment least likely to outsource marketing mix planning to an agency.

Companies in the Tactical Outsourcer segment, conversely, are almost two times more likely than average to leave the optimization of marketing investment mix questions to an outside agency. This segment uses the prior year's budget as the primary input to marketing planning and is particularly ill-equipped to measure the effectiveness of mass media vehicles and emerging internet vehicles. Finally, companies in the Not a Priority segment have the most diverse set of roadblocks to more effective marketing measurement— data issues, capability issues, analytical issues, and process effectiveness issues. Interestingly, less than 10 percent of the respondents say marketing accountability is in the CEO's top three priorities list, and more than half say marketing effectiveness is not even a priority for the marketing group! Perhaps this is why they struggle to make systematic progress against a marketing accountability agenda. If you find yourself in any of these three segments, we encourage you to spend a fair amount of time in the next three chapters to understand the power of more accountable marketing and then focus heavily on Chapter Eight.

Companies in the Horsepower-Seeking segment, the largest segment by far, assert that the biggest barrier to better marketing accountability is a lack of effective analytic and modeling horsepower. This shortcoming is exacerbated by shortfalls in data availability, quantitative customer insight development, and process effectiveness, particularly in relation to marketing planning and execution. Interestingly, this segment has the most evenly distributed marketing mix of any of the segments, with mass communication vehicles accounting for 30 percent of total spend, direct response and experiential marketing vehicles accounting for 25 percent each, and the rest of the investment in sales promotions. Moreover, they find all of the vehicles equally challenging from a measurement perspective, with no single vehicle being effectively measured more than 50 percent of the time. A large majority of financial services firms and retailers live in this segment, as do significant portions of the high technology, telecommunications, automotive, and industrial sectors. Of all of the segments, it's notable that the Horsepower-Seeking members are most likely to state that better marketing accountability is at the top of the CMO agenda, but least likely to state that it is one of the CEO's top three priorities. This may be why these companies have not been able to secure the resources necessary to effectively tackle these gaps. If you identify with this segment, we encourage you to spend some extra time in Chapters Five, Seven, and Nine.

Companies in the Harried But Trying segment believe that their largest barrier to better marketing accountability is that they have too many programs in field at any one time and that they change their programs too quickly. It's interesting to note that on a relative basis this segment's marketing mix is overweighted toward direct-response vehicles, like direct mail, e-mail, and paid search, and toward more experiential vehicles like events, sponsorship, field marketing, and PR. These kinds of vehicles make up almost 65 percent of their total investment mix, almost double the weighting of companies in The Experts segment. Their proficiency around direct marketing returns is the highest of any segment, but they have failed to keep the same level of prowess with the migration of investment to the Internet, and they still lag significantly in effective measurement of the experiential vehicles. High technology, telecommunications, and media and entertainment companies are overrepresented in this segment, along with some players from the retail, health care, and industrial sectors. Understanding marketing effectiveness is high on the agenda for both the CEO and the CMO inside these companies, but they feel caught in a little bit of a doom loop in terms of the pressures to drive the business versus the discipline to measure the effectiveness of their marketing investments. If you self-identify with this segment, focus a little extra time on Chapter Seven and then key in on the dynamic experimentation section of Chapter Nine.

What can else can we tell you about The Experts? Although your first instinct may be that this segment is populated exclusively with consumer goods companies, we actually find companies from a wide range of industries, including sectors as diverse as health care, financial services, media, entertainment, technology, and telecommunications. We also find a pretty wide distribution in terms of company size, from middle market companies through the Global 50. From a marketing mix perspective, companies in this segment spend dramatically more on TV advertising and dramatically less on experiential marketing vehicles like sponsorships and events, and somewhat less on direct-response vehicles. This segment has the second heaviest weighting for internet marketing vehicles and sees this proportion growing over time. We do not know whether this mix is more business model–driven or reflective of the segment's understanding of the relative effectiveness of these various vehicles. Companies in this segment are three times as likely to have robust effectiveness measures for point-of-purchase marketing and twice as likely to have robust effectiveness measures for TV, radio, and print advertising. The only area in which this segment struggles from a measurement perspective is with newer internet marketing vehicles and some of the experiential marketing vehicles like sponsorships and events.

None of this may seem too surprising, given how the segments were derived. TV is the most expensive vehicle by far, so—especially in a fragmenting media market—continuing to invest a lot in that vehicle probably requires a lot of substantiation. What is perhaps more revealing is The Experts' more sophisticated approach to marketing planning and in-market execution. Companies in this segment are dramatically more likely to use an understanding of relative returns on investment to determine next year's investment—and it is notable that these companies are much more likely to incorporate anticipated competitive spending levels as a vital input into the planning process. Much more than their agencies, companies in this segment feel accountability and ownership for driving strategic mix decisions. Further, much more of their planned marketing investment is long-term-oriented, even though they cite cost cutting, operational efficiencies, and new product launches as the three initiatives most critical to meeting short-term growth targets. The Experts are also significantly more likely to look at a combination of metrics to assess the effectiveness of marketing investments, including the impact on revenue growth, profit growth, market share growth, and long-term brand value. Even if your company self-identifies with this segment, we still encourage you to spend extra time with the dynamic experimentation section of Chapter Nine and all of Chapter Ten.

Irrespective of which segment your company may slot into, it is clear that everyone has a lot to learn in the pursuit of more accountable marketing, even The Experts. With so many parts of the broader marketing ecosystem in flux right now, you may have a unique opportunity to reset the playing field inside your company and get everyone pointed in the right direction. First, we need to take a deeper look into the six value levers in Part Two. After you have built a better understanding of how the value levers work, we can then, in the third and final part of the book, get into the detailed planning for how to turn your company's performance around and start building some positive momentum via highly accountable marketing investment decisions.

Driving Material Performance Improvements Across the Six Value Levers of Marketing Accountability

CHAPTER FOUR

Strategy and Content

Enabling Purposeful Strategic Decision Making and Creating Engaging, Compelling Content

T opics covered in Chapter Four:

- The new prerequisite: a clear line of sight between marketing strategy and business performance
- A quantitative approach to purposeful, strategic decision making
- The art and science of strategic positioning
- Unlocking the secrets to compelling content
- Managing an effective and efficient content development engine

> *Strategy is about making choices, trade-offs; it's about deliberately choosing to be different.*
> —*Michael Porter*

> *It takes great skill to tell a compelling story in under 60 seconds.*
> —*Michael Apted, British film director*

The *strategy* lever and the *content* lever are the two fundamental anchoring points for all accountable marketing investment. The decisions that get made here set up all the rest of the marketing

investment equation. Get it *wrong* here, and even pristine performance across the other four value levers will not salvage the anticipated
returns on your marketing investment. Get it *right* here, and even
disastrous performance across the other four value levers may not sink
your returns. Strong performance on both of these levers typically
requires a well-balanced contribution across the four competency
domains of strategy, creativity, execution, and analytics, which is not
always easy to come by.

When we talk about the strategy lever in this context, we are
focusing on the questions of marketing communications strategy
and strategic positioning. Obviously these decisions get made in the
context of the broader "Big M" marketing strategy development and
in light of the company's overall business strategy. But when we talk
strategy, we are talking more narrowly, focusing in on decisions that
need to be made about the frame of reference definition, customer
targeting, key benefits to highlight, and the critical reasons to believe
our marketing promise. This strategic thinking needs to be rooted in
a clear line of sight to how the company intends to make money in any
given year, particularly on the revenue and gross margin lines.

When a company is struggling with the strategy lever, typically
one of two different patterns is at work. The first pattern—which we
playfully refer to as either "strategy lite" or more sarcastically as the
"Where are my ads?" phenomenon—is characterized by a brisk rush
through the strategy discussions as an unwelcome diversion that is
tolerated only as long as it does not slow down the creative process.
No one has much patience for stress testing any of the assumptions
underlying most of the strategy decisions, to the extent that any of the
critical strategy choices have been made explicitly at all. The second
pattern—which we describe as "analysis paralysis" or more impa-
tiently as the "a penny for an insight" phenomenon—is characterized
by an overabundance of market research or other behavioral data
from which it is impossible to glean any actionable insights. The players are more than happy fielding yet another custom market research
study, but no one can serve up compelling evidence-based arguments
for how we should anchor our strategic choices. Neither pattern is
particularly helpful, but both can be remedied with some discipline
and effort.

When we speak of the content lever, we are focused on the
processes, talent, and decisions that enable development of the full
range of marketing vehicle–related creative content. Depending on

the type of vehicles in the mix, the discrete content components can range from copy to graphics to imagery to sound to video to long-form written content to full-fledged live productions, and on and on. Sometimes marketers refer to this as the *messaging* lever, but in the world of rapidly proliferating media, we just want to be sure you understand that we are talking about the full content package, not just the copy or the written or spoken word. Often a content platform may get described using a higher-order theme or tagline (such as MasterCard's "Priceless" idea or Apple's "Think different" campaign), which is often a helpful organizing principle.

When a company is struggling with the content lever, typically one of three patterns is in play. Within the first pattern, a stream of potentially engaging content ideas gets served up, with a consistent disregard for the strategic foundation of the marketing program. We jokingly refer to this as the "out in left field" syndrome, because all of the key sides of this debate sincerely believe that the rest of the players are out in left field, as they do not see either the obvious connection or the blatant disconnect between what is being proposed creatively and what has been decided strategically. There is typically more going on here than the usual friction between the creatives and the suits, but it is not always clear how to fix it.

The second pattern is characterized by content ideas and output that are consistently flat. The content is neither interesting nor emotionally resonant. It lacks imagination and energy. And despite being technically sound and on strategy, it lacks a compelling insight communicated in an engaging way, so it is deemed not particularly relevant by the audience. Sometimes this has to do with the tenure of the agency relationships or the quality of creative talent. Other times is has to do with the risk-taking appetite and direction setting of the client. What is clear is that you have a stream of marketing investments that are flat and overlooked.

The third pattern, which we affectionately refer to as the "Tower of Babel" effect, involves a lack of consistency and direction setting throughout the whole content development process. There are no clear decision rights, multiple disconnected content efforts run concurrently, senior management randomly redirects content efforts at the last minute, vehicle-specific content experts are not consistently leveraged—you get the picture, and it ain't pretty. Content breakdowns are often the hardest to fix, because so much of this has to do with effective management of a creative process. Nonetheless, some companies have been developing great marketing content for the last fifty years, through many different economic cycles and management regimes, so there are some well-understood mechanisms to drive more consistent performance here.

So let's dive right in. In the first section of this chapter, we will address the importance of requiring a clear line of sight between intended marketing outcomes and business performance. Too often this rigor is not applied and a company has nothing to vet its strategy alternatives against to see how well any given alternative stands up to deliver the goods from a revenue or margin standpoint. We will introduce a robust toolkit that can be deployed to bring more quantitative rigor to the strategy conversations, and then show how art and science can come together to drive powerful strategic positioning choices. Then we will uncover the secrets to engaging and powerful content, and close with a discussion of how to drive an effective and efficient content development process.

THE NEW PREREQUISITE: A CLEAR LINE OF SIGHT BETWEEN MARKETING STRATEGY AND BUSINESS PERFORMANCE

In the twenty-first century, senior executives of the most successful companies in their sectors—such as PepsiCo, American Express, and McDonald's—expect marketing to own part of the responsibility for achieving a company's overall business and financial goals. They demand to understand how marketing and marketing activities will help increase revenues, in this period and in future periods. Executives no longer tolerate generic, directional linkages between marketing activities and revenue growth; they expect marketing to be able to make explicit linkages between its activities and the anticipated sales response at a granular and behavioral level, as discussed in Chapter Three. In the process, they are making a new, more strategic marketer a business reality.

This has not always been the case. Indeed, in many companies across the globe today, it is still not the case. More commonly, the planning processes that the marketers follow and the planning processes that the operators follow occur in parallel and quite separate universes. The marketers plan for campaigns, tactics, and initiatives, and if those plans have any metrics associated with them at all, those metrics focus on how these activities will drive changes in awareness or favorability or other kinds of customer perceptions—or what we refer to in Chapter Seven as marketing outcomes. The operators plan for revenue and margin targets, perhaps at the geographic, channel, or product-line level. In this world, when a CEO wants to understand how potential changes in the marketing plan change the risks inherent in the operating plan, the answers tend to be vague and unhelpful. Without explicit linkages between these two kinds of planning processes, that is the best that the teams can serve up.

Detailed Revenue and Margin Planning Is Key

At the more forward-looking companies, executives began to ask the question: How do we ensure that the achievement of our marketing objectives will favorably impact the achievement of our operating plans and our business objectives? These executives want clear linkages between the financial goals of the operating plan and the anticipated sources of underlying sales volume that would deliver the aggregate number. Requiring the marketers and the operators to come together to do detailed revenue planning—in which the revenue line gets disaggregated by and attributed to various customer or consumer types, different distribution channels, different geographies and product lines—enables the necessary transparency around the intended sources of all of that revenue.

Figure 4.1 provides a masked example of how one company, an owner of destination resorts, tackles this issue. The revenue plan for this property, one of many in the company's portfolio, for the upcoming year is $175 million. But this company has a reasonably deep set of customer-level data that allows it to slice and dice this number in relation to a number of key customer characteristics and dimensions of customer behavior. In Chart A, we can see that 23 percent of the revenues are expected to be driven by customers living less than nineteen miles from the property, with less than 3 percent coming from customers living more than seven hundred miles away. Chart B depicts that customers in the Tier 3 segment are expected to contribute over 42 percent of the revenue plan. Chart C shows that newly acquired customers (less than a year) are expected to contribute only about 13 percent of the revenue target. Chart D shows how important visit frequency is in driving next year's numbers, as customers with an annual frequency of eight visits or more are expected to contribute almost 46 percent of the total

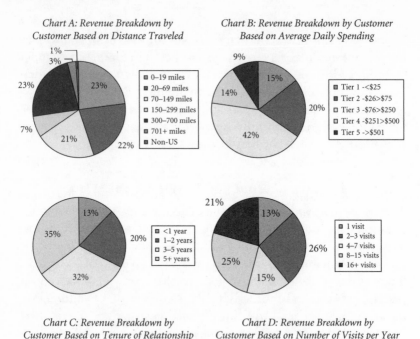

Chart A: Revenue Breakdown by Customer Based on Distance Traveled

Chart B: Revenue Breakdown by Customer Based on Average Daily Spending

Chart C: Revenue Breakdown by Customer Based on Tenure of Relationship

Chart D: Revenue Breakdown by Customer Based on Number of Visits per Year

Figure 4.1.   Detailed Revenue Planning

revenues. What you cannot see from that chart is that those customers represent fewer than 6 percent of the total guests the property expects in the plan.

As you can see, this kind of a detailed customer-, channel-, or product-based build on the overall revenue and margin plan allows you to build very explicit linkages between marketing actions and financial outcomes. The resort owner's marketing team can now tailor its marketing strategies to support the assumptions that have been baked into the operating plan. For example, new customer acquisition represents a very small portion of the overall plan, so they want to make sure the majority of the investment is focused on driving repeat visitation and providing compelling reasons to increase frequency. In a similar vein, there are two clusters of trading areas for this resort: a very local market (less than seventy miles away) and the area within a one-and-a-half-hour flight (three hundred to seven hundred miles). So the marketing strategy and vehicle choices should take this into account.

All of the proposed marketing programs can still target specific types of marketing outcomes or the building of specific brand equities that matter to target customers. But now you can insist on understanding how these marketing outcomes enable the specific types of customer behavior outcomes we are banking on in our revenue plan. In this case, we would look for outcomes such as improving consideration and preference while targeting purchase funnel blockages for repeat visitation. Moreover, you can immediately see which elements of the marketing plan have no connection to any of the critical detailed revenue plan components. In the same way, you can see where there are detailed revenue plan components unsupported by the marketing strategy—raising doubt as to whether those components are truly achievable.

Not every company has the assortment of readily accessible data assets to allow the kind of slicing and dicing available in this last example. But there are ways to use custom market research to build stop-gap data bridges that will get this kind of conversation going at your company. As one executive told us, "Having clear revenue objectives is great, but it only helps to answer the 'what,' not the 'how.' Having clear marketing objectives is also great, since it helps build confidence in the 'how.' Having a repeatable process that requires clear linkages between the 'what' and the 'how' is every CEO's dream." We could not agree more. We have found that competitive success increasingly depends on this more sophisticated approach to marketing's revenue and margin responsibility.

Operating Within the Constraints of the Broader Marketing Strategy Context

The other critical ingredient for establishing a clear line of sight between the strategy lever and business performance is having a clear understanding of the broader marketing strategy context within which your marketing communications investment is operating. As we discussed in Chapter Two, the effectiveness of your spend will partially be a function of the strength of your proposition, broadly defined. Put at its most basic, a $50 million investment in marketing for Apple's wayward PDA entrant Newtown in the 1990s had dramatically different optics than a similar sized investment for the iPod in 2005. You need to have an unvarnished but balanced understanding of your current state of play across the key aspects

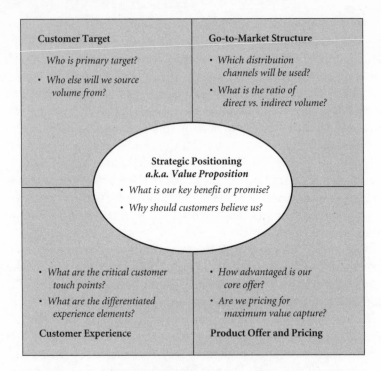

Customer Target

Who is primary target?

• Who else will we source
  volume from?

Go-to-Market Structure

• Which distribution
  channels will be used?

• What is the ratio of
  direct vs. indirect volume?

**Strategic Positioning
a.k.a. Value Proposition**

• What is our key benefit or promise?

• Why should customers believe us?

• What are the critical customer
  touch points?

• What are the differentiated
  experience elements?

Customer Experience

• How advantaged is our
  core offer?

• Are we pricing for
  maximum value capture?

Product Offer and Pricing

Figure 4.2.   Marketing Strategy Development Framework

of your proposition to anchor the strategic positioning in a place of optimal value.

Holistic marketing strategy development encompasses four main domains—customer targeting, go-to-market structure, product offer and pricing, and the overall customer experience. All of these come together in an integrated way to form the basis of our broader proposition, shown in Figure 4.2. Strategic positioning, at the center of our framework, is intended to crystallize our broader proposition into a key benefit or promise that is compelling, supported by a set of reasons to believe that help to carry the story. In an ideal world, an executive would start with a blank sheet of paper in each domain and design a holistic, synergistic approach across the whole proposition that makes articulating a strategic positioning as easy as dropping the cherry on top of an already irresistible hot fudge sundae. If things were only that easy . . .

The goal for the long term is to clearly get all of these proposition elements working together synergistically, but the reality is that some of these things take significantly longer to change than others. Making material changes in a company's go-to-market structure or product offer or customer experience is often a multiyear endeavor at best. An empowered CMO needs to keep his or her eye on all of these balls and help the CEO ensure that the right investments are being made across the proposition over a diversified payoff horizon. More often than not, in any given planning cycle, a company's reality in terms of its customer experience, product offer and pricing, and go-to-market structure is relatively fixed; it is the job of the strategic positioning to optimize around it. You may need to anchor on a strategic positioning that emphasizes specific things in order to compensate for some material deficiencies in the customer experience or product offer, or vice versa.

Thus your questioning about the strengths and weaknesses across each element of the broader proposition needs to be direct and pointed. What is fixed for any given point in time? What can be changed? Is the company committed to resourcing the efforts to fundamentally alter its customer experience or its product offer or its pricing or its go-to-market structure, and within what time frame will these changes hit the market? Just as important, how much risk is associated with any of these initiatives to change the broader proposition?

Understanding the underlying strengths and weaknesses of the broader proposition in its current state, as well as understanding the likelihood and impact of any anticipated changes, becomes the critical contextual building block for the strategic positioning work to follow. You will still have tough questions to wrestle with—like, should you point the strategic positioning toward anticipated changes or the existing reality? If you are going to stretch the positioning to cover some anticipated changes, how far can you stretch before you lose credibility? The next section showcases an approach and some techniques that can help you confidently answer these kinds of questions.

A QUANTITATIVE APPROACH TO PURPOSEFUL, STRATEGIC DECISION MAKING

In essence, the strategy lever embodies a series of decisions about strategic positioning—which for any specific short-term time horizon must be made in light of the existing product portfolio, pricing environment, channel structure, and competitive context at play for your company or division, as we outlined in the previous section.

In particular, your decision making should involve purposeful choices in the following areas:

- Which set or sets of customers does your company have the best business opportunity with?

- What kinds of behavioral responses from that target customer group or groups are the most achievable (consider and purchase us; buy more often, buy bigger ticket items, renew their business; consolidate their spending with us)?

- What unique set of benefits, attributes, and ideas, if communicated and delivered by your company, has the highest probability of eliciting the desired behavioral response?

- Are there any specific deficits or roadblocks to your brand or company that will stymie your efforts, especially in light of existing market conditions and the current competitive context? Conversely, are there distinctive brand strengths that should be focused on and leveraged?

Erroneous assertions about any one of these issues can fatally undermine the effectiveness of all of your downstream marketing investments. You want to have a high degree of confidence that your company's answers to these specific questions are right, or at least are the best possible answers, given what you know to be true about the category, customer behavior, and the strength of your brand and proposition when you are making the decisions.

But how can you arrive at that level of confidence? Some organizations rely on the business instincts of an entrepreneur—a passionate believer in an idea who understands the potential target customer so deeply that he or she intuitively understands where the best growth opportunities are and what value proposition will resonate most clearly with them. The business landscape is filled with success stories built on this kind of recipe, whether it is Steve Job's Apple, Howard Schultz's Starbucks, or Chuck Williams's Williams-Sonoma. The problem, of course, is that there are many other companies in the global economy who are not blessed with these intuitive, entrepreneurial marketing-connected leaders, yet are making overarching, broad-based strategic decisions based on only qualitative data or the gut feel of the decision maker. This is usually a recipe for disaster, and it may be one of the root causes of the pervasive disappointment of most CEOs in their marketing performance.

For most organizations though, it is essential to have a disciplined and transparent approach for answering these questions, because it allows all relevant participants to understand the set of facts, data, beliefs, and assumptions—the body of evidence, as it were—that each of these decisions is based on. "How do we know?" becomes the most common refrain in this kind of process. This allows everyone to stress test the thinking, question the fact base, and look for the underbelly of any decision, in a way that ultimately improves the final answers.

Of course, either approach may get you to the right set of strategy answers—it is just harder to create the right conditions for the first approach if it does not exist within the business already. And it is too easy to fall into the trap of believing that the conditions for the first approach exist when they in fact do not. For those reasons, we strongly advocate a more quantitative, transparent process for organizations that are not blessed with a visionary, instinctive marketer at the helm. There are a set of well-understood analytic techniques involving customer insight development and segmentation; brand equity modeling; purchase funnel analytics; and driver, pathway, and choice modeling—all of which can be used to help your company begin to triangulate on the right answers (as shown in Figure 4.3). Each of these strategic building blocks will be explained in further depth throughout the rest of this section. When these analytic approaches are used as a foundational input into the strategy decision, without shutting out equally valid qualitatively driven insights and intuitive thinking, a company typically ends up with a strategic value proposition worth pursuing.

Finally, any reader who considers him- or herself a seasoned marketing professional may see in the following section some high-level concepts, like customer segmentation or brand equity modeling, that have been in use for years and years. You may be thinking that these are constructs you have been working with since your first marketing course at your MBA program, so what else could there possibly be to learn? That may be the case, but we believe that the continued advances in marketing sciences have enabled a set of new and vastly improved applications of these constructs to enable better decision making. We highlight some of these new approaches in each of

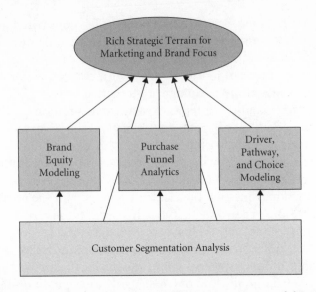

Figure 4.3.   Framing a Quantitative Approach to Purposeful Strategic
Decision Making

the sections that follow, and we encourage even the most seasoned
marketing professionals to give this section a perusal.

Framing the Market Insightfully by Defining the Right Customer Segments

Every good business person understands intuitively that not all
potential customers respond to the same proposition in the same
way. Some may need to see lower price points, others may need
more features, and still others may not be motivated to change their
existing behavior regardless of what gets put into a proposition, at
any price point. Thus an important step in the marketing strategy
process is using techniques to frame the potential customer landscape
of a market in an insightful way. Are there distinct clusters or groups of
potential customers that appear to have similar distinguishing
attitudes and beliefs about the category, similar purchasing behavior,
or similar channel preferences? If so, how financially attractive are
those potential customer groups and how entrenched are their existing brand preferences within the category? We refer to this overall
process as *customer segmentation analysis*.

Approach:	Demographics, Firmographics	Behavior	Channel	Occasion	Attitudes and Needs
Key Question:	Who are our customers?	What are they doing?	Where and how are they doing it?	In what context are they doing it?	Why are they doing it?
Dimensions to Explore:	• Lifestyle and life stage • Geography • Ethnicity • Family structure • Industry type (B2B)	• Product usage • Brand awareness, usage, and loyalty • Price paid, share of wallet, and purchase frequency	• Purchase and shopping behaviors • Variety of distribution alternatives considered • Levels of usage across channel types	• Various situations, contexts for purchase • Various situations, contexts for usage	Category needs, desires, and beliefs

Tactical ⎯⎯⎯⎯⎯⎯⎯⎯⎯⎯⎯⎯⎯⎯⎯⎯⟶ *Strategic*

Figure 4.4. Different Approaches to Segmenting a Market or Category

Iconic consumer product companies, like Procter & Gamble and Unilever, have developed legendary methodologies to provide ongoing substantive understanding of the consumer needs that affect choice of goods or services, as well as consumer satisfaction with current offerings and, more important, the resulting list of unmet needs and priorities. But these techniques are now being used increasingly by other companies in other industries—no matter who the customer. The framework shown in Figure 4.4 depicts the variety of customer characteristics that a company can use to do customer segmentation analysis, the range of which can yield insights from the tactical to the strategic. By focusing on the key questions—(1) who the potential customers are, (2) what they are doing, (3) where and how they are doing it, (4) what context they are doing it in, and (5) why they are doing it—companies hope to develop unexpected insights into what motivates different kinds of customers to think and act the way that they do. Ultimately you often find that different kinds of customers have different needs and expectations from a category or a brand, but not necessarily in an infinite variety. Rather, you uncover a handful of manageable *segments* that can be clearly identified, analyzed, and assessed through this kind of process.

Companies can use a variety of approaches to uncover this understanding about customer motivations and behavior. Many of the iconic consumer goods companies like P&G have pioneered innovative ethnographic research techniques to develop rich and powerful insights about individual consumers, which they then attempt to validate and refine through quantitative research techniques. Other companies, like Harrah's Entertainment, have built extensive repositories of behavioral data about customers, focusing on how individual customers actually spend their money during each visit to a casino, how much they gamble, how likely they are to use other on-site amenities, which marketing offers they respond to and which they ignore, and so on, and based on these have then build out actionable insights.

As you can see, the data can come from lots of different places— new primary market research, existing customer information management systems, order tracking systems, marketing campaign management systems, operational systems that track service interactions, information from third-party data sources like Dun & Bradstreet, and so on. Ideally you can design an analytic approach that can accommodate most of the material customer-level information you have access to as a business. And insightful qualitative techniques can be used to unearth new insights. Finally, quantitative analysis and modeling approaches are critical here, because ultimately the segmentation solution needs to be rigorous and defensible. Advanced mathematics can be used to derive powerful segmentation solutions that deliver high within-segment homogeneity of needs, motivations, and behaviors, with high across-segment heterogeneity of needs, motivations, and behaviors (see Figure 4.5). Once you have a solid understanding of the needs, motivations, and behaviors of these different customer segments, you can then also do detailed analysis of their size, their current and future potential value, their preferred brands and purchase channels, how easy it is to identify and serve them, and how costly it is to acquire and retain them.

Customer segmentation analysis is relevant irrespective of your industry or category. Here is one example that was developed for a B2B component supplier, which had a large contract with a dominant customer but was hoping to diversify its customer base. As Figure 4.6 depicts, the company discovered that its potential customer targets naturally fell into four different segments: price-driven, consistent basics, value-added partners, and status seekers. As you can see, each of these segments had diverse attitudes toward the category and suppliers in the category, which cascaded into a different set of needs for and requirements of potential suppliers. By looking at the market in

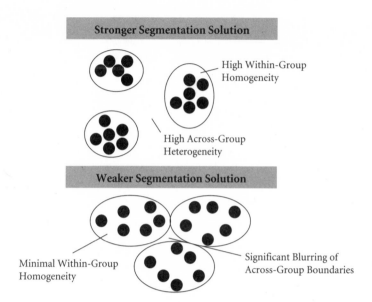

**Figure 4.5.   Powerful Segmentation Solutions
from Advanced Mathematics**

this way, this company was able to see that different kinds of customers valued different things. It was then also better set up to have the debate about whether it should relocate some of its manufacturing to lower-cost geographies to go after opportunity with the price-driven segment, or whether it was best positioned to go after more business with the value-added partners segment, as many of the requirements for this segment were very similar to the requirements from its current dominant customer.

Obviously we could write a whole book on how to use and deploy customer segmentation analysis; this technique has been around for a while and has been well covered in the business and marketing literature. Our main point is that it is a foundational analysis for quantitative marketing strategy development and that the best applications of it develop multidimensional views of the distinguishing attitudes, needs, behaviors, and firmographics of the various customers in the marketplace. When it is used well, it helps companies focus by helping them understand which customers or potential customers matter most and by encouraging them to assess whether existing resources are being deployed in a matter consistent with that. It also provides companies with a clear understanding of what is needed to

Customer Type:	Price- Driven	Consistent Basics	Value- Added Partners	Status Seekers
Dominant Factors:	• Views product as commodity	• Values time-tested, trouble-free functionality	• Desires innovative stuff	• Stakes reputation on brand imagery
	• Perceives no value in brands	• Has modest support requirements	• Values partnership and brand	• Wants premium products and services
	• Shops on price	• Seeks quality, consistency, and reliability	• Wants flexible financing alternatives	• Desires exclusive access
Key Needs:	• Lowest cost per unit	• Time-tested performance	• More exacting technical performance	• Brands with strong differentiation
	• Multiple suppliers	• Guaranteed, consistent supply	• Value-adding innovation stream	
	• Minimal threshold performance	• Freedom from thought or worry	• Personal attention	
Size:	40%	35%	20%	5%
Share of Spend:	25%	20%	40%	15%

Figure 4.6. Findings from a Segmentation Analysis for a B2B Component Supplier

win with each potential segment and how feasible it is to win that segment, relative to a brand's existing equity, a company's purchase funnel blockages, and other detailed purchase driver modeling, which will be covered in the subsequent sections.

Unearthing Critical Strategic Priorities—Approach #1: Brand Equity Modeling

Brand equity modeling is a quantitative technique that provides a comprehensive snapshot of a brand's current equity across a core set of dimensions. David Aaker has written extensively about the importance of brand equity development for the last twenty-five years. Prophet has recently updated its brand equity model to reflect our

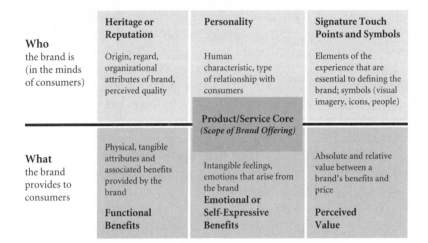

Figure 4.7. Prophet's Brand Equity Model

rich array of strategic brand work over the past decade. As depicted in Figure 4.7, Prophet's brand equity model explores a brand's equity along two fundamental dimensions—*who* the brand is in the minds of its stakeholders and *what* the brand provides to its stakeholders in the form of functional and emotional benefits and in perceived value. There are other brand equity models that may be equally valid for any specific situation. What is most important is that the brand equity modeling exercise provides the empirical foundation of a brand's current assets and liabilities, which can then be used in marketing strategy development. In the case in which a company is working with a customer segmentation analysis, the brand equity modeling is most effective when it is done by customer segment.

Through this process, you are trying to understand the dominant perceptions about your company, your products and services, and your overall reputation—the good, the bad, and the ugly. Certain kinds of beliefs or perceptions (or equity) may be very superficial; others may be deeply felt or held. Some perceptions may be present across all of the core customer segments; others may be concentrated within a single customer segment or a narrow audience. Some of the equity may reflect a fair and unbiased view of in-market company performance, whereas other equity may have no factual basis whatsoever. But all of it becomes part of the canvas for your marketing strategy development and informs what kind of strategic terrain is actually credible for your company to try to own. If all of your brand equity is anchored in perceptions of no frills, reasonable quality levels, and cost-effective products, a strategic positioning anchored in performance or luxury would not be seen as consistent with your existing equity and would have a high probability of being rejected by the market. It would be a waste of money and time to put a lot of investment behind marketing programs amplifying this strategic positioning idea, falling far short of your accountable marketing aspirations.

The other critical component that effective brand equity modeling is designed to help you understand is how differentiated any hypothetical strategic positioning terrain may be in relation to your competitive set. This matters for a couple of very important reasons. First, typically it takes a lot of energy and investment to dislodge a key equity element that is clearly owned by a competitor—much more energy and investment than it would take to build a new equity element that no one in the market already owns. Second, companies that go after the same strategic positioning as the competition and thus put similar messaging in the market run the risk of having their messages get lost in a sea of similar, like-sounding communications and having to spend that much more to get their messages to land and stick. As the barrage of messages continues to increase, you need some strategic angle that helps make your messages memorable. So looking for strategic terrain where your company can be credibly differentiated is usually a smarter starting point—as long as it addresses material purchase funnel blockages and is relevant, as you will see in the next two sections.

We tend to find that the most useful synthesis for strategy development lies in some quantitative framing technique that maps your firm's brand equity against the equity of the competition. As shown in Figure 4.8, Prophet has developed a framing tool with quantitative underpinnings that has six equity quadrants, mapped in relation to the credibility and relative differentiation scores of all major competitive brands. Equity elements for which your brand is highly credible and are distinctly owned by your brand relative to the competition fall into the strategic drivers quadrant; equity elements where all of the brands are credible but no one is distinctive fall into the table stakes quadrant; and so on. If you use this technique, or some other visualization technique like battleground charts or competitive mapping, the end game is to understand the range of viable options for your marketing strategy and how to sidestep strategic value propositions that may be a no-win battle for your company or that

	Distinctive to Competitive Brands	No Distinctiveness	Distinctive to Your Brands
High	*Competitive Neutralizers* Brand elements distinctive to a competitive brand but also strongly associated with your brand	*Table Stakes* Category requirements or antes delivered by more than one brand	*Strategic Drivers* Brand elements distinctively owned by your brand
Low	*Competitive Drivers* Brand elements distinctively owned by a competitive brand	*Opportunities* Brand elements that are "white space" opportunities for both your brand and competitors	*Potential Drivers* Brand elements that may potentially be owned by your brand

Credibility (vertical axis, High to Low)

Differentiation (horizontal axis)

Figure 4.8. Prophet Framework for Analyzing Brand Performance Data in a Competitive Context

have the potential to trigger an ever-escalating arms race to own the same idea—which no one will have the resources to win.

Unearthing Critical Strategic Priorities—Approach #2: Purchase Funnel Blockages

If the brand equity modeling helps us understand the strategic questions about credibility and differentiation, the next two analytic approaches help us understand the issue of relevance. What kinds of features, functions, and benefits matter the most to different kinds of customer segments and, when present, ultimately drive different kinds of customer behavior? The first of these techniques uses the construct of a classic purchase funnel and attempts to uncover high-potential areas to anchor your marketing strategy.

To understand a classic purchase funnel, you have to put yourself in the mind-set of a prospective purchaser in a category. Once a potential customer is thinking about a prospective purchase in a given category, we say that the customer has entered the purchase funnel. If your brand or product hopes to be the one that ultimately gets selected, your brand will need to successfully move through all of the key stages of the decision process. To begin with, a potential customer needs to be aware that your brand exists, either from personal experience and memory or through some aided technique like finding it on a Google search. Although top-of-mind awareness is good, having a potential customer believe that he or she is highly familiar with your brand is even better. This says that the customer understands its strengths and perhaps its weaknesses. But just because a customer is familiar with your brand does not mean that the customer would actively consider it as one of the viable alternatives for an upcoming purchase. So moving from familiarity to consideration is the next big step in the purchase funnel, which typically involves the purchase decision itself and then, depending on the category, potentially different kinds of repeat purchase behavior that may lead to preference, loyalty, and advocacy. The number of steps in the purchase funnel will vary depending on the product category, the purchase cycle, and the nature of the purchase decision (impulse or considered), but this should give you a feeling for the general construct.

Purchase funnel analytics can help you in two important ways when it comes to marketing strategy development. The first is just to understand the absolute performance of your brand or product or company in relation to the overall purchase funnel for key customer segments, as well as your purchase funnel performance in relation to your key competitors. Put another way, they demonstrate the company's opportunities for improvement within the funnel when a brand is underperforming relative to competitors. Figure 4.9 presents the purchase funnel performance for three companies in the U.S. financial services sector. Competitor B is the eight-hundred-pound gorilla in this category, with an incredibly broad funnel and strong conversion at each step of the funnel through purchase. The hypothetical "Your Company" has the weakest funnel of the three companies. It does a very ineffective job of converting its awareness into familiarity. In spite of this, it holds its own, converting the familiarity that it does have into consideration, purchase, and loyalty. Competitor A may have the trickiest challenge to tackle, because it faces challenges converting reasonably high familiarity into consideration and purchase, likely due to a lack of relevance. As every improvement in a conversion rate at a higher level of the funnel has the potential to improve the flow through to purchase, you can quickly understand the economic opportunity associated with fixing critical funnel bottlenecks.

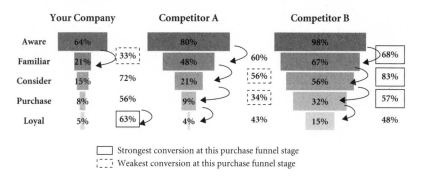

Figure 4.9.   Representative Purchase Funnel Performance for Three
Different Companies

Second, purchase funnel analytics can help you understand which
components are the critical drivers of conversion at each step of the
funnel—information you can then use for strategy development. By
analyzing the purchase funnel behavior of each segment to determine
the perceptual roadblocks or bottlenecks that routinely delay a particular customer from moving to the next stage of the funnel, you may
better understand how you might resolve key bottlenecks to maximize the business impact of your marketing investment. Figure 4.10
shows this kind of application in action, in a disguised example for
a consumer technology product targeted at college students. From
the purchase funnel analysis, we can see that our company clearly
underperforms its main competitor in converting reasonably strong
consideration into familiarity. In diagnosing the key drivers of conversion from consideration to preference—its critical bottleneck—
the most important factors included having the products in plain
sight, with competitive prices, while ensuring that the sales associates
understand the product and know where to find it.

Armed with this knowledge, the company could dig into the
opportunity and explore how to tackle this issue strategically. It found
that college students often did not purchase the product because
it was not in plain view, but rather stored with other products the
company made that were unrelated to data storage. Moreover, few
college bookstore employees understood the product's capabilities. So
the company picked a strategic value proposition anchored in availability and ease of use. It also activated a set of field marketing programs targeted at the sales associates of its channel partners, giving

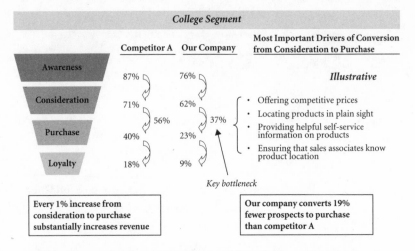

Figure 4.10.   Understanding Key Bottlenecks for Your Brand and
Targeting Marketing Strategy at Critical Conversion Drivers

away free data sticks to the trainees, and then positioned the new product in displays near cash registers. This increased the number of customers who bought the new version by 27 percent and sales by $35 million. In the most telling example, the product development group determined that the target segment was more interested in increasing the storage capacity of the data stick, rather than in adding any other cosmetic touches.

When the company analyzes the segment opportunity in this way, the marketing team gains a deeper understanding of the different levels of customer engagement that are possible, given the variables that affect the customers' ability to purchase that product or service. Companies can use this technique to better focus their investments in relieving the purchase funnel of key bottlenecks, thereby ensuring that its strategic positioning is targeted at a highly relevant pain point— whose correction is guaranteed to start ringing the cash register.

Unearthing Critical Strategic Priorities— Approach #3: Purchase Driver Analysis and Pathway Modeling

The use of purchase funnel analytics is just one tool in the toolkit to help you understand which strategic opportunity areas may exist for your company or your brands. A complementary approach is the use of quantitative research techniques to better understand what combinations of factors—be they product features, brand personality elements, service elements, or emotional benefits—are the most salient in driving specific behavioral outcomes at the individual customer level. These behavioral outcomes might include things like propensity to purchase, willingness to recommend, willingness to consolidate purchases, or propensity to purchase at a premium price. This kind of approach is often referred to as *driver modeling*, in which you attempt to understand the specific interplay of factors most likely to account for certain behavioral outcomes. Improving your company's actual and perceived performance against these critical drivers then becomes the focus of your marketing strategy.

There are some straightforward ways—and some more complex ways—to quantitatively model the universe of relevant drivers for your company. As with all of these analyses, this is most robust if done by customer segment, in combination with a segmentation analysis. The most straightforward way is to simply ask potential customers what matters most to them, using a survey technique. A more advanced approach uses mathematical techniques to correlate the importance of certain factors in explaining actual underlying behaviors. Table 4.1 presents a masked example of this kind of driver analysis in the roofing industry. The ratings market participants assigned to certain product, service, or reputational attributes were correlated with their actual purchase behavior over the previous twelve months. As you can see, customer perception of the company as having "deep expertise in roofing installation and repair" was correlated twice as strongly with purchase as was a perception that the company "uses sustainably harvested materials and supplies." In terms of discrete individual ideas, you can start to determine where to build relevance hierarchies and unearth the most fruitful strategic positioning platforms.

Pathway modeling is an interesting methodology used to perform sophisticated driver modeling. It is designed to help marketers and senior management better choose among several variables or levers it can pull in developing the tactics necessary to achieve strategic goals. It is important to remember that it is not simply a question of learning which variables drive business outcome, but also how they relate to each other and which are more important. Pathway modeling provides insight into the customer-brand relationship through an understanding

Ranking	Attributes	Attribute Type	Correlation Index
1	Has deep expertise in roofing installation and repair	Functional benefit	216
2	Offers convenient ways to get estimates	Touchpoint	174
3	Makes me feel like I have made a smart choice	Emotional benefit	163
6	Has fair and transparent pricing	Functional benefit	143
12	Has a strong reputation for honesty and ethics	Reputation	126
13	Makes me feel like I made a smart choice	Emotional benefit	116
19	Known for very good on-time and on-budget project execution	Reputation	110
20	Uses sustainably harvested materials and supplies	Functional benefit	110

Table 4.1.   Basic Driver Modeling Example Using Correlation Indices.

of how various brand dimensions (capabilities, functionalities, perceptions) are connected in the minds of customers as they move up the customer pathway toward a desired outcome. Put another way, pathway modeling demonstrates graphically how functional attributes and higher-order brand associations work together to drive customer behavior—and how they're connected in the minds of customers.

Figure 4.11 illustrates a simplified pathway model for an upscale retailer of modern, contemporary home furnishings, for a specific customer segment identified in a segmentation analysis. The arrows in the figure show significant pathways or relationships among the product, service, and reputational attributes. This particular pathway model is designed to show which combinations of these attributes are the strongest in driving a welcome feeling and a corresponding likelihood to recommend the company to a friend. As you can see, being perceived as having the widest selection of furniture is only the starting point for building relevance, but the truly powerful duo of providing a relaxed setting for decision making and providing a place where I, as a customer, can meet the designer helps reinforce a critical feeling of showing others that I shop at only the best places, which in turn is a powerful driver of recommendation.

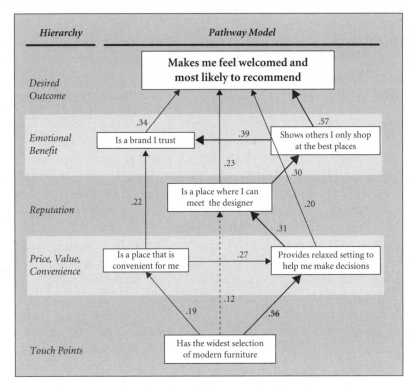

Figure 4.11. Pathway Modeling Example: Differing Relevance of Competing Positioning Ideas

Using tools such as brand equity modeling, purchase funnel analytics, and pathway modeling can give the company a deeper understanding of the interrelated factors that drive customer behavior and beneficial economic and business outcomes. This understanding in turn helps senior management diagnose factors critical to influencing the customers in the targeted segment in order to achieve the desired behavioral outcome (repeat purchase, purchase at higher price points, switch brands, and so on) stipulated by the marketing plan. It also helps provide a quantitative basis for making trade-off decisions in the marketing strategy development process, because the expected impact of alternative positioning platforms can be modeled financially.

By integrating these kinds of approaches into the strategy development process, not only do you get more rigorous and vetted strategic decision making, but through this evidence-based approach you also create more transparency for everyone. It also moves this most critical of value levers out of the domain of personal opinions and long-held biases, instead creating the conditions for more people to actively participate in the strategy debate by discussing how to interpret this shared body of evidence and how to determine the most important implications for the business and its approach to marketing.

Successful companies have begun to realize that connecting marketing with business strategy will filter and prioritize marketing objectives, helping to leverage these scarce resources more effectively so that they help the company achieve its most important goals. At one software company, for example, the chief marketer developed an entirely quantitative approach to determining how to prove that his strategies opened up new markets in the small to medium-sized business segment, and how to then track the continued progress in opening up new segments within that broader sector. Within one year of the inauguration of the new marketing program, the senior marketer could point to increases in sales to the high-growth segment—increases that came at the expense of the company's major competitor. Just as important, stock analysts began to praise the company for its ability to develop deep relationships with these companies that are the engines of the economy. As a reward for his success, the marketer was given a seat on the global strategic management committee and put in charge of the entire global marketing budget for the first time in the company's history.

THE ART AND SCIENCE
OF STRATEGIC POSITIONING

Although we spent a lot of time on quantitative techniques in the previous section, we firmly believe that the truly powerful strategic positioning concepts emerge through the application of both art and science, as depicted in Figure 4.12. On the science side of the equation, in addition to the quantitative market research and comprehensive analytic approaches just outlined, other ingredients essential to a comprehensive strategy development process are framework-enabled structured thinking, a deep operational understanding, and business case modeling. On the art side of the equation, brainstorming and creative problem-solving techniques are critical in helping to unlock customer insights and to articulate compelling positioning concepts,

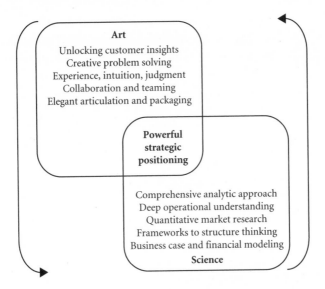

Figure 4.12. A Finely Tuned Balance of Art and Science Leads to Great Strategic Positioning Outcomes

then package those concepts in an equally powerful way. Further, tremendous value can be added to the discussion and debate by including the input of seasoned individuals with years of experience, strong intuition, and sound judgment. Companies that can harness these complementary forces of art and science in a positive and synergistic manner can develop truly distinctive strategic positioning concepts that enable creation of long-term shareholder value.

Consider the story of Staples, which became the first office supply superstore in 1986 and rode the wave of that innovation for almost fifteen years. At the start of this decade, Staples was competitor-whipped directly by Office Depot and Office Max and indirectly by Walmart, Best Buy, and even Costco. Office Depot, a primary competitor, had just launched a new positioning that centered boldly on knowledge and expertise in office products, with a tagline promising "What you need. What you need to know." Was this going to be a winning formula for their competitor, and if so, how should Staples respond?

Fast forward to 2004, when Staples publicly changed the game—and came out on top again in its sector. Who could forget the Staples commercial that burst on the U.S. market—in which an administrative assistant, burdened by a seemingly impossible task, suddenly pushed a red button emblazoned with the word *easy*. The "easy" button was born, and with it, Staples clearly signaled that it intended to own the concept of a "no-hassle" shopping experience within its category. The key to the Staples strategy—and its eventual success—was the company's commitment to a disciplined strategy development process that built on the best its teams had to offer in both art and science.

The basic principle behind "easy"—making the shopping experience hassle-free—was conceived and proofed in the strategic laboratory based on analytic research, creative problem solving, and operational improvement initiatives before it became part of the creative ad process. In 2002, a joint strategy and marketing team wanted to anchor Staples' renewed growth efforts in a better understanding of its most profitable customers. Customer research helped identify a number of different segments, each with its own set of needs, attitudes, and behaviors.

Four segments were the most intriguing in terms of their commercial appeal, but each appeared to have very different expectations from the category, at least on the surface. One was more relationship driven and would pay a slight premium for reliability. Another viewed the category as a necessary evil and placed a premium on highly efficient interactions that did not waste their time. A third was very demanding, expecting a broad assortment with 100-percent availability, plus fast and easy service. The fourth segment was downright enthusiastic about office products, derived a lot of enjoyment from the category, and wanted high product variety and knowledgeable sales associates. Despite Staples' having high awareness, there was significant room to drive penetration in key categories across each of these profitable target segments. But could the company come up with a strategic positioning platform that would be relevant for all of them?

Within these important segments two key drivers emerged: one focused more on efficiency and personal attention, another focused more on category involvement and assortment. Initially, alternative positioning platforms were developed that anchored on each of these ideas discretely. However, as the company continued to push the team to think creatively about the segments and their needs, a seed of a new idea emerged. The first segment wanted a hassle-free and consistent buying experience, and the second segment wanted to maximize its efficiency in terms of effort and time. For the third segment, ease of doing business was more important than the lowest price, and the fourth segment wanted to access a wide assortment in a hassle-free manner. So the idea of a hassle-free buying experience emerged as a "golden thread"—an alternate positioning hypothesis that might stretch across the four segments and be meaningfully differentiated from Office Depot.

As the team started to elaborate on and visualize these alternative positioning hypotheses, they also went back to the science side of the equation to unlock a deeper understanding of what constituted a hassle-free shopping experience for these segments. They unearthed key triggers like finding what you need in stock, fast checkout, courteous service, and an easy reordering process, and assessed whether the company was willing to make the operational investments needed to deliver against these triggers. In this way, the team could assess whether the company had the appetite to invest in the idea of "easy," so that it would not merely become some empty marketing slogan, but rather would indicate a fundamental shift in corporate priorities.

Even after the internal team anchored on a hassle-free shopping experience as the strategic positioning recommendation, they did one more final thing right. They convinced the senior executive team to start investing in the operational improvements and internal culture change before going public with a new advertising campaign. In the words of a senior executive, "We created a culture throughout Staples so that everything begins and ends with the customers and we make it easy for them to buy." Additionally, the creative team was able to turn the strategic positioning idea into compelling content, including the "that was easy" tagline, the "easy" button, and a variety of compelling and humorous advertising dramatizing the need for a hassle-free solution in our lives.

At the end of 2007, the result of the marriage of strategy and marketing was clear: Staples had become the largest office supply superstore in the world, with total global sales of $19.4 billion, increasing its internet sales to a record $5.6 million. In a slow market, Staples was one of the few companies that continued to pay a cash dividend to shareholders—and the company repurchased $750 million in shares.

The Basics of Strategic Positioning

As you can see through the Staples example, a good, solid strategic positioning recommendation has a number of critical components.

To start with, it includes a clear delineation of the target audience, clarifying in as granular a way as possible who to focus on. It helps us understand to whom the marketing needs to be relevant, and it is usually composed of at least one discrete customer segment—and perhaps multiple segments. The second contextual component is a clear delineation of the frame of reference, which is designed to clarify the primary purchase or usage occasion being targeted and establishes the competitive set against which we are trying to differentiate. The next component is the key benefit: identifying the critical need and want of the target audience that will be uniquely valued and distinctive if we are to provide it. In the Staples example, the key benefit was a hassle-free shopping experience. The fourth component, labeled *reasons to believe*, identifies the key proof points that validate our ability to deliver the key benefit, as well as establishing additional things that the company needs to do to credibly deliver on that benefit. Compelling reasons to believe have to be squarely rooted in the company's proposition and operational platform, taking this debate out of the realm of marketing communications and into the heart of the business. Finally, as an optional element, a strategic positioning might include a recommendation of key elements of the brand's personality to focus on as part of the strategy.

So every good strategic positioning recommendation needs to include, at a minimum, thoughts on the target audience, frame of reference, the key benefit, and proof points. But how do you develop confidence in your eventual strategic positioning recommendation? In addition to investing in the solid quantitative foundation that was described in the previous section of the chapter, you are encouraged to follow a process that leverages a blend of art and science disciplines to arrive at and build alignment on an optimal answer. Figure 4.13 depicts the six stages in this process of the strategy development process, each of which will be discussed in more detail in the following pages.

Target Segment Identification and Prioritization

Target segment identification is the first place to start in the development of strategic positioning alternatives, as much of the rest of the thinking should get done in the context of the prioritized segments. Ultimately this set of prioritized customer segments, in aggregate, will form your target audience. As we discussed in the

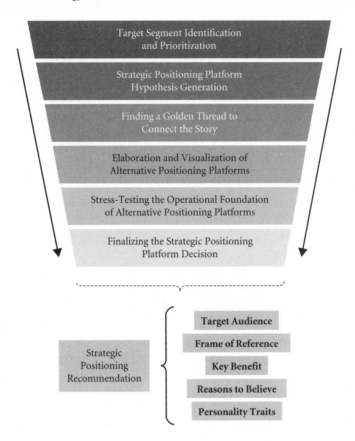

Figure 4.13.   Strategic Positioning Decision-Making Steps

segmentation section earlier in the chapter, we believe that a rich multidimensional segmentation analysis lies at the heart of most good marketing strategy development. But the task of prioritizing specific segments, which by its very nature means that you are giving others a lower priority, presents a difficult bridge for many companies to cross. Unless you are in a dominant market share position covering a significant portion of the market or have a business model that allows you to invest to create a disproportionate share of voice within the category, you are likely to fatally undermine the effectiveness of your marketing investments by failing to prioritize—and thus tailor and optimize—your appeal to a priority segment or a subset of high-priority segments.

The problem is, many executives internalize this kind of discussion and mistakenly assume that a prioritization process implies walking away from profitable sales or volume opportunities from the deprioritized segments. But this is not the case at all. Often it is helpful to differentiate among strategic targets, for which we are optimizing our strategic positioning, and those volumetric or consumptive targets from which we expect to source demand and volume, even though we are not prioritizing their needs in the strategic positioning decision. The prioritization process that we are advocating here is about aligning with the strategic target segments.

There are a number of analyses that you can do to help understand and evaluate overall segment attractiveness. Typically you will want to understand the overall commercial attractiveness of each segment, by understanding its average annual spending in the category; repeat purchase, retention, and switching behavior; cost-to-serve metrics; and profitability potential. All other things being equal, segments with higher commercial value are more intriguing than those with lower values. Then you will want to understand the level of brand performance alignment between the segment's satisfaction and purchase drivers and your company's existing brand equity. In a similar way, you want to understand the level of affinity of each segment with competitive brands, and the extent to which we can deliver against their loyalty and satisfaction drivers. In this situation, you want to understand which segments you already are in a strong position with, and to understand whether you should be building on that strength or looking for white space opportunities with segments that none of the competitors truly own.

Strategic Positioning Platform Hypothesis Generation

Once you plant your initial stake in the ground for prioritized customer segments, the main focus during the next stage of the process is to explore interesting directions for the positioning, in light of the prioritized customer segments. The latter stages of the process are more geared toward weeding out ideas that do not make sense, but for now this should not be your overriding motivation. Rather, you should have more of an ideation and brainstorming mind-set, infused with creativity and a willingness to explore. Your starting points should be insights gleaned about the needs of the target segments (Figure 4.6). Obviously, ideas that are seen as distinctive drivers of purchase and loyalty should rise to the top of the list, as you might discover through driver analysis (Table 4.1) or pathway modeling (Figure 4.11). To the extent that your brand is somewhat or highly associated with these ideas, per the brand performance framework (Figure 4.8), this is helpful. But do not rule out ideas that may reflect distinctive or sought-after benefits that no one in the category is truly delivering on yet, because they may also represent rich strategic positioning terrain for your company.

Each distinctive idea can become a strategic positioning "platform"; then you can develop discrete positioning concepts, a little more evocative in nature, that hang off of each platform. Figure 4.14 depicts a cloaked example of this kind of thinking in action for a company that develops residential housing and communities. One of the core drivers that emerged through the customer research was the idea of competent reliability, especially given the relatively nascent nature of the residential home-building market in this company's base territory. In addition, a number of other interesting customer-centric drivers

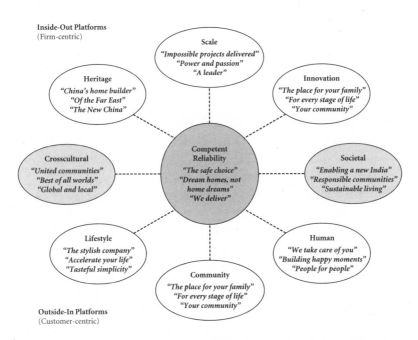

Figure 4.14. Strategic Positioning Platform Hypothesis Generation for a Residential Real Estate Developer

were uncovered during the exploration, concerning ideas about community, a premium lifestyle, a human touch, and a commitment to societal development. Similarly, a number of other firm-centric elements were unearthed during the brand equity analysis, concerning capabilities associated with innovation, operating scale, the firm's heritage, and its cross-cultural sensitivities. With each of these ideas serving as the inspiration for an alternative positioning platform, evocative positioning concepts can be developed around each one. In this case, three concepts—"the stylish company," "accelerate your life," and "tasteful simplicity"—branch out of the lifestyle platform.

Usually this is the start of an iterative creative development cycle, in which some platforms fade in priority, some rise in priority, and new concepts are developed that draw inspiration from multiple platforms or ideas. Visual mapping techniques can also help the group identify the strengths and appeal of the varying concepts. For example, the competing concepts could be mapped on a two-by-two grid, comparing their tangibility to their emotionality or comparing their appeal to segment A versus segment B. The concepts could also be mapped along these dimensions in relation to the spaces occupied by key competitors. The main objective here is to complete this phase with a rich set of options that are well understood and have been strategically vetted.

Finding a Golden Thread to Connect the Story

The previous stage was designed to be expansive; this stage is more about narrowing down the field so you can put your remaining energy and investment into exploring the most viable options. Often some of the analytic techniques highlighted in the previous quantitative approach section can be highly useful here, particularly pathway modeling and purchase funnel analysis. Evaluating the different concepts in relation to a deep understanding of the underlying drivers of purchase and choice is the ultimate currency. When you are doing those analyses by target segment, however, you often find concepts that score fairly strongly for a specific target segment but are not so clearly relevant for other segments. Rather than let such a finding become a roadblock, we encourage you to turn it into an opportunity. This is when you should begin your hunt for the ever-elusive but infinitely desirable "golden thread" introduced earlier in the Staples story.

What is a golden thread, you may ask? A golden thread is usually a simple, single unifying idea that can be woven through your whole marketing story to give it coherence and make it understandable. Its presence at the heart of your strategy makes the whole marketing proposition work, even if it does not address some of the specific parts required for any given target customer segment. Usually it reflects or captures a benefit that is relevant across all of the target segments, yet is flexible enough to be translated and activated for each different audience in a way uniquely relevant to them. Ideas that can serve as a golden thread therefore make the best strategic positioning alternatives.

Let's go back to the Staples story for a moment. The initial driver analysis pointed to ideas of efficiency, personal attention, and assortment breadth as the critical enablers for each segment. The main competitor was building on the idea of authority and expertise, pointing to a supposed desire for a highly knowledgeable, expert-enabled service experience. But when each segment was revisited in relation to the idea of a hassle-free, easy shopping experience, interesting and attractive connections could be found. For one segment, a hassle-free shopping experience might have much more to do with one-click on-line reordering. For another segment, it might mean having courteous store associates who could help them navigate through the deep line of basic products. But the idea of hassle-free could be translated in a way that was highly relevant and compelling for each of these stakeholders and could serve as a unifying idea for the Staples marketing strategy and subsequent communication investment. Ideally you can find two or three concepts of comparable golden thread quality among your concepts and narrow them down from there.

Elaboration and Visualization of Alternative Positioning Platforms

Once you have a couple of attractive, viable strategic positioning alternatives, it can be highly instructive to elaborate on each idea verbally by building stories around the idea, as well as to round out each idea visually by developing unique color palettes, iconic imagery, visual symbols, and photographic style. These early-stage attempts to bring an idea to life creatively can illuminate in an alternative the inherent power or unfortunate shortcomings that do not jump out immediately during the hypothesis generation phase. By deploying these techniques, you can both sharpen your thinking about a given alternative and make the possibilities of each alternative come to life in a manner that is often more accessible for all of the stakeholders in the process, not just the marketing strategists.

Elaboration techniques are designed to sharpen and enrich each person's understanding of the intended underlying meaning of each of the core words at the heart of a strategic positioning hypothesis. For example, if the ideas of authority or fairness are critical to one of your platforms, does everyone on the team have a shared understanding of what you mean? You can use different elaboration techniques to tease out a sense of shared understanding. For example, as seen in Figure 4.15, the development of ideation spectrum can help ensure that everyone has the same definition of the word *authority*: Are you anchoring it more in concepts of personal authority that might fit naturally within peer-based or mentoring relationships or in concepts of professional authority, such as those that might be associated with a religious or institutional context? In a similar manner, you can develop a mood board with different visuals to elaborate on your

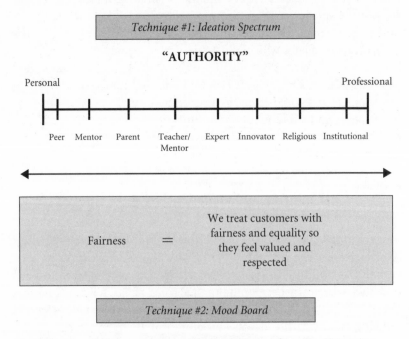

Figure 4.15.   Sample Elaboration Techniques: Ideation Spectrums
and Mood Boards

intended meaning of the word *fairness*; for example, is it the fairness of a judge or courtroom setting or the trustworthy support of your closest group of friends? Techniques like these will allow for an open debate and eventual alignment.

Visualization techniques are designed to create a preliminary visual language for competing hypotheses, both to clarify how the intended meaning should come to life visually and to better understand whether each of the concepts has equally strong potential to get interpreted and enriched via a complementary visual system. Although you do not want to overinvest in design, photographic, film, or architectural resources at this stage of the strategy development process, you should always create the time and space for some amount of visual discovery. You will immediately see how different ideas get interpreted creatively, which will help you anticipate potential land mines and start to lay the groundwork for eventual content development of the winning idea. Moreover, this starts to give key executives and nonmarketing stakeholders a better sense of the complete feel and overall package implicit in any strategy choice, which typically makes it easier for them to evaluate and compare competing alternatives.

Stress Testing the Operational Foundation of Alternative Positioning Platforms

As we saw in the Staples example, the final critical analysis that must occur before a strategic positioning platform is finalized involves stress testing how feasible it is for the company's existing operating model and processes to support the implied promise of the strategic positioning under consideration. For example, if one of the elements of a hassle-free buying experience is having a strong in-stock position, but Staples currently has frequent stock outages across most of its core assortment and inaccurate or delayed delivery information, it would be highly risky to select a strategic positioning anchored on the hassle-free idea. Similarly, if hassle-free promises that service interactions with the store associates are respectful and helpful, but the current customer satisfaction data states that customers experience most interactions as uninspiring and unproductive, then, in NASA-speak, "Houston, we have a problem."

The knee-jerk reaction to these kinds of findings should not be to immediately kill what appears to be an otherwise attractive positioning hypothesis. In fact, the most interesting strategic positioning alternatives will usually require some amount of operational stretch for a company. It is meant, however, to force you to become crystal clear about how different positioning ideas will affect expectations for the overall product offer and holistic customer experience and then to succinctly identify the relevant strengths or gaps in your current operating model. Then you can have the tough conversations with the senior team to assess the company's appetite for investing to close some of the most critical gaps and the probability that these efforts will be seen as successful by customers. The single action most likely to undermine the effectiveness of your company's marketing investments is anchoring on a strategic positioning concept that the company cannot or will not operationally support. It is the kiss of death for any campaign.

Finalizing Your Strategic Positioning Decision

As you have stepped through each stage of the strategic positioning process, the relative appeal and attractiveness of each of the competing concepts should become increasingly clear. The final few stages—elaboration, visualization, and operational feasibility—are designed to tease out the potential of each of the concepts, as well as to give each more substance, more depth, and more stature. As their creative and operational potential are explored, the team should also circle back to the customer and competitive fact base to refine and fine-tune their understanding of the upside and risks associated with each alternative.

Ultimately each of the remaining viable alternatives should be evaluated against these five criteria:

• Its ability to provide differentiation

• The extent of its customer relevance

• How credible your company or brand is in making this promise

• The ease of implementation

• Its ability to stand the test of time

All criteria are shown in Figure 4.16. In situations in which you have heavily leveraged the science-led parts of the problem-solving process, you will have a quantitative and perhaps even a financial basis for

DIFFERENTIATION	CUSTOMER RELEVANCE	CREDIBILITY
How unique is each positioning relative to competitors' promises?	• What perceived benefit does the positioning offer customers or prospects? • How important is that benefit?	• How credible is it for the brand to consistently deliver on the idea? • How well does the positioning idea map to the current brand equity?

EASE OF IMPLEMENTATION	SUSTAINABILITY
How feasible is building and delivering the positioning with existing resources and limitations (technical, human, financial)?	• Will this positioning stand the test of time? • How easy will it be for a competitor to copy this or knock it off?

Figure 4.16.   Important Criteria for Finalizing Your Strategy Choices

rating each concept against each criterion, as opposed to just a qualitative, judgment-based assessment. For example, through purchase funnel analysis and pathway modeling, you will have modeled the incremental revenue upside potential associated with achieving any of the competing positioning platforms. Or you might have done detailed business cases to understand the implementation costs associated with each alternative, or used brand equity modeling to quantitatively understand the differentiation potential of each remaining alternative.

With all of that said, let us not downplay the role of experience, intuition, and judgment in finalizing our strategy decision. Sometimes strong entrepreneurs or marketers have an instinctive feel for the potential of a positioning idea even when its attractiveness is not that apparent to the rest of us. However, in situations in which the science is pointing to an answer in one direction and judgment is pointing to an answer in the other direction, the burden of proof is disproportionately higher on the team to try to make sense of the recommended solution. If the direction is not making sense to you, do not be afraid to throw a flag on the field and stop play. Push the team to try to creatively rethink the analysis to find some support for the recommendation in the underlying fact base. Because there is one thing that we know for certain: a series of marketing investments based on a flawed strategic premise are guaranteed to deliver disappointing returns.

UNLOCKING THE SECRETS TO COMPELLING CONTENT

Once the company has developed its strategic positioning, it faces an incredibly important next step: content development. This lever anchors on the translation of a strategic positioning platform into compelling communication ideas, promotional programs, and other forms of consumer and customer engagement. Many marketers have historically thought of this phase as messaging or message development. But because the word *messaging* might focus a reader on the narrower idea of *words* or *copy*—whereas we are referring to the whole creative package of taglines, copy, visuals, color, sound, iconography, and experiential elements that are usually part of a broader communication or content platform—we have opted to label this the *content lever*.

When Staples laddered its "hassle-free shopping experience" strategic insight into the "that was easy" campaign, with its big, red, playful "easy" button, or when MasterCard translated its "enabling my purchases for life" strategic positioning platform into the "Priceless" campaign, both companies delivered outstanding performance in relation to this value lever. The most visible part of the "Priceless" and "that was easy" campaigns may be the TV advertising, but the full range of content that it encompassed is much broader—from promotional experiences to in-store point-of-sale merchandising to the approaches to key sponsorships and events. The best content uses strategic insight to drive creative expression. It is not a chicken or egg question. Rather, it emphasizes the importance of the strategic positioning as the springboard for creative expression. Without a strategic anchor, content development can veer off in myriad directions, and content gets developed that is not grounded in customer insight or competitive strategy.

Creativity is the mother's milk of this value lever. Without access to world-class creative minds and creative talent, most content development efforts fall flat. For most global corporations, with operating cultures built on structure, controls, and risk mitigation, being so reliant on a creativity-fueled engine presents challenges. They must embrace and nurture all of the wonderful and unsettling parts of the creative process—its nonlinear, highly iterative nature; the fact that you're nowhere and then suddenly you're somewhere; the need to withhold premature judgments. At the same time, marketers need a light-touch approach to channel that creativity in a way that is relevant and applied, without sucking all of the energy and life out of the participants. It is a tough act to balance. But some companies and marketers do it, decade after decade. In the rest of this section we focus on how creativity and inspiration get channeled into great content ideas. In the closing section of the chapter, we focus on how to effectively and efficiently manage the content development process.

Why Great Strategy Does Not Always Lead to Great Content

Running a great strategy process and landing on a logical, sound, and bullet-proof strategic positioning does not guarantee that you will end up with a compelling content platform. It is not preordained that great strategy will lead to great content. In their attempts to breathe life and energy into the strategy through creative expression, the teams can travel down an infinite number of paths, only some of which have the potential to become truly compelling and durable content platforms.

The recent experience of the Ford Motor Company with its relaunch of the Taurus model showcases a very common problem—literal and unimaginative interpretations of the strategic positioning, which led to bland content ideas. To be fair, when Ford revived the Taurus brand, it set out to do everything by the marketing book: the new design tested well with consumers, both Taurus stalwarts and new customers; the engine was judged fuel efficient by national standard-setting groups; *Consumer Reports* announced that the car was a real buy. With these good reviews as its foundation, and with a target market of families, Ford developed a content strategy that emphasized the vehicle's world-class adherence to safety standards, trying to go directly against Toyota's Camry and the Volvo family. The company developed the tag line "Taurus, the safest full-sized car in America." Unfortunately, the content platform did not resonate, and Ford watched as Taurus sales went straight into the decreasing column. Even consumers who were Taurus enthusiasts from the late 1980s, who would ordinarily have considered buying the new reformulated model, judged the ad campaign as "boring"—when they even remembered seeing it at all. This is in sharp contrast to Ford's relaunch of the Focus vehicle, which featured drivers of other cars "blind" driving the Focus and ultimately deciding to switch—and to BMW's ability to bring its strategy to life with engaging content across a broad content platform.

Sometimes the issues that undermine the strategy-to-content translation are more subtle but just as lethal. Consider the story of UBS. Formed by the merger of Swiss Capital and Union Bank of Switzerland, UBS wanted to build an integrated, one-firm model across wealth management, investment banking, and asset management. The company decided that investing behind a single global brand was the right way to enable this. In 2002, the executive board gave the go-ahead for marketing to move forward with a new brand management strategy, with a strategic positioning that emphasized the key benefit of passionately enabling client success. The positioning was supported by three key reasons for clients to believe in the company: (1) its proactive advice and guidance; (2) its active listening, leading to a deep understanding of needs and goals; and (3) its position as a global financial powerhouse.

With that strategic frame, the marketing leadership worked with its preferred agency partners to develop some initial content platforms. As the creative teams wrapped their heads around the issue, the most interesting initial concepts leaned heavily on the first proof point—proactive advice and guidance. The two leading concepts, "Be Sure," and "You Are the Decisions You Make," anchored on headline copy and voiceover emphasizing advice—for example, "The right advice can turn doubt into confidence"; "With the right advice, a guess can become a choice"; and "Good advice—sometimes it can hurt a little." They developed print ads and storyboard TV ads, which were tested in June 2003. And the pressure was on to make a decision. The company had already gone into the market with a "name change" campaign that announced the launch of the new single brand and, by implication, the retirement of the PaineWebber and Warburg brands. Name change advertising was developed at the same time, then launched. The executive board expected the new content to launch in the fall of 2003, after six months of the "one firm, one UBS" name change messaging.

But interestingly, when the two content concepts were put into prototype print and TV executions and tested for brand and industry identification, as well as specific message recall, the results were not encouraging. Although the concepts proved directionally okay, the overall message was not clear, and the key themes (about being passionate about client service) and attendant associations were not coming through on any level. Rather than push one of these "on strategy" content concepts into the market and invest millions of dollars behind it, the marketing leadership had the courage to ask the executive board for additional time to develop content platforms with greater potential to resonate with the target audience. Even though those conversations advocating a delay were probably met with some fear and trepidation by the marketers and the agency, as they were not without material professional risks, it was clearly the right call.

Ultimately, out of this setback a new concept emerged. "You and Us" anchored on a different reason to believe—active listening reason and understanding—rather than on proactive guidance. It also had other attractive dimensions, in terms of its simplicity, the natural way it reinforced the UBS name itself, and its ability to scale up to corporate clients and down to wealthy individuals. When the scores came back from pre-testing this time around, the "You and Us" concept, with its sample executions, had "home run" written all over it. Launched in February 2004, this concept spawned five years of powerful and accountable marketing content, helping UBS break through the clutter and catapult into the top tier of financial services brands. In this case, patience and discipline around the content development process yielded dramatic financial rewards.[1] But it should also illuminate how easy it is to drop the baton between the strategy and content levers, even with a cadre of world-class, well-intentioned strategic and creative resources working hard on your behalf. The UBS case also shows how incredibly difficult it can be to discern the difference between content decisions that with hindsight will look either wildly courageous or astoundingly short-sighted. Mediocrity and brilliance may be separated by only the thinness of a razor's edge.

What Makes for a Great Content Platform

When it works best, a content platform focuses on a big idea, usually a simple truth, packaged in a fresh and engaging way. The best content platforms originate from a magical combination of strategic insight and creative expression, and they find a way to connect in authentic yet emotionally compelling ways. In addition to the big idea, well-grounded content platforms also create a complete verbal and visual system uniquely suited to bringing the key benefit within the strategic positioning to life, in a way that is particularly relevant and engaging for the primary target audiences.

Of course, all of this is much easier said than done. As we noted earlier in this chapter, the content lever is plagued by a couple of standard illnesses—the "out in left field" syndrome, the "flat and boring" phenomenon and the "Tower of Babel" effect. All of these maladies can be traced back to how fundamental tensions that run through any content development process get resolved. The tensions emanate from the often competing priorities that are fighting for mind share during the content development process. As seen in Figure 4.17, we think of this as a multipolar battle, in which the forces for *engaging*

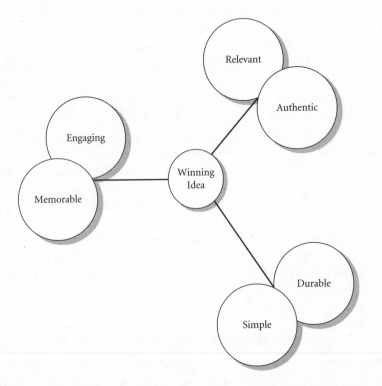

Figure 4.17.   Competing Priorities in the Content Development Process

and *memorable* go up against the forces for the *relevant* and *authentic*, both of which battle with the forces for *simple* and *durable*. When any one of these poles overwhelms the others, the result is lopsided, ineffective, and highly unaccountable content. When each of these poles is treated with thought and consideration and is given adequate airtime in the overall content solution, you get a winning idea and great content.

You may wonder why this is so. The answer should become self-explanatory as we think about each of the poles. Relevance and authenticity are great starting points for content, because focusing on those priorities helps to ensure that we are speaking to the target about something of meaning in a way that is credible and believable. But if too much weight is put on authenticity and relevance in the absence of other considerations, the content that gets developed runs the risk of being more of the same—standard industry fare that fails to grab anyone's attention.

In this media-saturated world, with consumers being bombarded with message after message, creating engaging, memorable content is also an important priority. The choices for diversion are so bountiful that you have about five seconds to pique a listener's curiosity or they will move on to the next thing. If you cannot get the target to even perk up and pay attention to your content, you will have lost the match before you even get a chance to put your team on the field. Similarly, if no one can remember the content within thirty minutes of seeing or hearing it, that is a problem. But, as is often the case, if too much weight is put on these priorities in the absence of the other considerations, you get content that fails to drive your business performance.

Finally, given the exploding complexity of our world, many people are drowning in too much information with too little time to process it. Thus it is also an important priority to establish a content platform that is both simple and durable. By pushing the creative team to keep an eye on simplicity, you increase the probability that the core message is understandable and digestible. By pushing the creative team to test for durability, you require them to think about how well any given content platform will stand the test of time. It can take six to eight quarters for an idea to get firmly planted in the consciousness of your target. If your content ideas do not have the potential for durability, you could be setting yourself up for a self-fulfilling cycle of questionable effectiveness, triggering frequent content shifts, which in turn undermine effectiveness.

But as you think about these six priorities for content—relevance and authenticity, engagement and memorability, and simplicity and durability—it is easy to see how some of these priorities put conflicting pressures on content development. When you couple this with the natural hard-wiring of many creative thinkers to be enamored of things that feel new and fresh, it is easy to see why so many well-intentioned content efforts veer off course. General Motors' recent experience in the U.S. advertising market brings these issues into stark relief.

At the beginning of 2007, General Motors executives were intent on investing in a new strategic positioning: General Motors vehicles are tops in quality. The company had done the legwork, understood that lagging quality perceptions were a key purchase funnel blockage for the brand, and were determined to put their marketing muscle behind a content platform that would bring this idea to life for their target audience. But they had two competing content strategies to bring the strategic positioning to life. One, which showcased customers who traded in their Japanese cars for GM cars—because GM cars had higher quality standards—seemed to score high on relevance, simplicity, and possibly authenticity. The other, a vignette about a factory robot who takes quality issues to heart, seemed to score high on engagement, memorability, and possibly relevance. Just one day before the 2008 Super Bowl weekend, for example, GM executives said they were considering running the testimonial ads, but chose to run the robot ads instead.[2] During the Super Bowl, General Motors debuted the commercial—and a firestorm of response ensued.

In the ad, viewers see a robot being thrown off an assembly line because he dropped a bolt and didn't live up to GM's standards. The robot goes into a psychiatric tailspin and commits suicide by throwing himself off of a bridge. Then the robot wakes up to see that it was all a bad dream.

The creative types at Deutsch, a unit of Interpublic, the same agency that had brainstormed the consumer testimony ads, had come up with the "edgy" ad concept with the hopes of getting across the message in a new, more modern and different way. At first the spot was so praised by ad execs that no less an authority than *The Wall Street Journal* announced that General Motors had won the battle of the automotive titans. The robot ad got high marks from advertising executives for using a different approach . . . Many said the ad was "epic."[3]

But the first few days after the airing saw a 180-degree reversal in prevailing opinions about the spot, from positive to decidedly negative. The American Society for Suicide Prevention protested first by letter, and then by interview, asserting that the ad could encourage people to solve their problems by suicide. "We wouldn't see this ad around cancer or heart disease," said Robert Gebbia, executive director. "Why is it OK to make fun of mental illness or depression?"[4] General Motors first responded by suggesting this was an isolated response and announced plans to run the ad during the Academy Awards later in February. As the public protest grew, however, the company first announced plans to edit the ad, then announced it would pull the ad altogether. Finally, in March, GM fired Interpublic from its multibillion-dollar account.

No one knows for sure whether the testimonial-driven content strategy that GM had considered would have broken through the clutter and connected with the target audience in an engaging and memorable way. GM did not share publicly any results that they may have run during a pre-testing phase to ascertain the appeal of that content strategy. But it is clear that the content platform that GM went with, although engaging and memorable, resulted in people talking about the wrong thing—mental illness and suicide, instead of the dramatically improved quality position of GM's cars and trucks. But it is easy to see the allure of content platforms in which priorities about engagement and relevance dominate—they have surface-level sex appeal, they are more interesting, and they are ideas that the creative teams get excited about. However, it can be a siren song.

It is the senior marketer's job is to ensure that all of the content development priorities have an equal voice in the debate. Do not be afraid to blow up a process and ask the teams to go back to the drawing board if the emerging "favorite son" is seriously deficient along one or more dimensions. We acknowledge that coming up with a winning content platform that effectively addresses all six priorities can be hard, frustrating work. Teams will question your judgment and complain that you are asking for the impossible. But stick to your guns and remind them that nothing undermines an accountable approach to marketing investment more than investing in ineffective content. Money gets wasted to produce the content and to buy the time that delivered the wrong message, and time is lost with ineffective marketing not helping to drive the business. Moreover, you can explore some approaches that will increase your probability of developing content that falls squarely in this sweet spot, as you will see in the following section.

Using Observation and Empathy to Source Your Zone of Authenticity

The most reliable springboard for winning content ideas and break-through creativity is deep customer or consumer understanding. This deep understanding, at its most powerful, acknowledges the consumer's emotional, situational, and cultural context, just as much as it addresses the consumer's rational motivations. When it works best, it balances sincere empathy with well-intentioned inquisitiveness. It is nuanced enough to understand how the small details stitch together into a coherent story. When you are operating from this place of deep consumer understanding, it is as if you have the ability to be completely in and of that consumer's world, accessing its fears, hopes, desires, symbols, and language as if you were an insider. Ultimately, with this confidence of the insider, you unlock a zone of authenticity from which new content ideas can emanate. You unearth a simple truth, an overlooked belief, an unstated assumption that becomes the catalyst for the killer insight around which magical content is formed.

In many ways, finding a zone of authenticity is a critical prerequisite for world-class content development. But if you do not have it instinctively, how do you get it? Some people can source a zone of authenticity instinctively, perhaps because they actually are the target consumer or have unusually keen intuition. But for the rest of us, it takes work. In this case, unlike with the strategy lever, qualitative techniques tend to be much more effective than quantitative techniques. Ethnography, in all of its various forms, can be particularly powerful. Deep immersive dialogue, contextual observation, journaling, video diaries, shop-alongs—all have the power to pull you further and further into the real world of the target. Some companies, like P&G, are bringing the consumer into the business in a more semiperma-nent way, by creating standing communities of interest among teens (Tremor) and moms (Vocalpoint) to create ongoing engagement, interactions, and debate. The social media tools are also creating mechanisms to listen in on and observe the peer-to-peer interactions of a wide range of consumers, via next-generation message boards (think Twitter), fan/hater sites (think Dell Hell), peer reviews (think

Yelp), and blogs (think Digerati), to name but a few. Irrespective of how you unearth it, establishing that zone of authenticity is a critical success factor for content development.

Embracing Nontraditional Sources of Creativity and Inspiration

We do not want to imply that there is a "one solution fits all" method of creative development. What is important to remember is that great content ideas can come from anywhere. Sometimes they are sourced via collaborative brainstorming, other times by getting similarly briefed teams to pursue independent and somewhat competitive paths. Sometimes they are the work of a single contributor finding some quiet time on a walk or in a bath; other times they result from the contributions of many players in an open-source process driven by the Internet. In fact, there are a variety of ways to create real inspiration. It is important to seek different ideas from different sources and to not be wed to traditional approaches. Ideas come from people, but not always from the people that you expect. And once an idea has taken flight and gotten recognition, it is very difficult to determine its source.

Recently, many good ideas have come by asking the target audience to create or cocreate the content themselves! In the 2007 Super Bowl ad derby, for example, when GM struck out with the suicidal robot, Doritos scored a home run with an ad concept created, developed, and produced by a twenty-one-year-old customer. Doritos was so happy with the results that it aired other commercials created by customers in February and March of that year. In addition, American Express's fifteen-second clip competition, L'Oreal's You Make the Commercial, Firefox's Flicks, MasterCard's Write a Priceless Ad, JetBlue's Travel Stories, and McDonald's Global Casting campaigns emanated directly customer- and consumer-generated content. These kinds of initiatives only scratch the surface of this broader crowdsourcing phenomenon.

Other companies are looking outside of their industries for ideas about their creative push. But rather than tapping into the wisdom of crowds, they have a curator's orientation and are looking to assemble a distinctive collection of creative minds sourced from a community of world-class talent to infuse new life and energy into a company's creative engine. Over the past decade, for example, American Express's

CMO has opened a running dialogue with an eclectic set of individuals like Robert De Niro, Jerry Seinfeld, Annie Leibovitz, and Ellen DeGeneres, all of whom have creativity at the core of their identities, to serve as role models and disruptive thought partners in the search for engaging content ideas. Other companies, like BMW, have asked world-class directors to develop content vignettes to bring the brand to life, through the acclaimed BMW Films series. Whether through crowd-sourcing, a curator's approach, or some other mechanism, the CMO, as manager of the process, must identify how to continually enliven and energize a company's creative engine.

The Accretive Effect of Durable Ideas

The final hidden secret in the content equation is the concept of durability. Given all of the noise and clutter in the market, plus how little time most people spend thinking about most categories and potential purchases, it often takes sustained investment over long periods of time to influence and change people's perceptions in an enduring and sustainable manner. So the idea of content durability is incredibly important to accountability, as it has been shown that effective content platforms with longevity gain in efficiency and effectiveness over time, while helping to build measurable and significant brand equity value. The effect can be nonlinear and highly accretive. GE's "Imagination at Work," BP's "Beyond Petroleum," Staples' "That Was Easy," Accenture's "High Performance. Delivered" and MasterCard's "Priceless" are all iconic examples of durable content platforms. Now, every idea eventually fatigues, crossing a threshold beyond which it delivers decreasing marginal returns and can even become a hindrance to the business. But with a belief in durability, rather than just rushing immediately to change the overall concept, you will first be encouraged to actively explore how you can refresh the execution to keep it engaging and relevant. You have a much better chance of effectively activating your strategic positioning if you are investing behind a dominant content idea over a five-to-seven-year cycle, as opposed to switching out your core content ideas every twelve to eighteen months.

So how do you test to see whether an emerging content idea has the potential to be durable? As some of the iconic examples from GE, Accenture, and MasterCard demonstrate, the idea needs to have a core foundation, speaking to some essential truth, and simultaneously be flexible enough to spruce up and refresh in new and engaging ways over its lifecycle. Specific creative executions evolve innovatively, but they contain core elements of continuity. The idea must manage the difficult task of leveraging the momentum of the previous storytelling without repeating the exact same story. Rather, it needs to feel like a familiar, likeable, and relevant narrative that has now been extended or advanced in a new, interesting, and perhaps unexpected way. Accenture's use of Tiger Woods as an overriding metaphor for high performance, as well as the episodic unveiling of the key ingredients of high performance ("40 percent playing it straight, 60 percent staying ahead of the curve," or "70 percent flexible, 30 percent unbending") is a well-executed example of this. Durable content ideas are solid gold from an accountability standpoint, so don't settle for anything less from your creative teams.

MANAGING AN EFFECTIVE AND EFFICIENT CONTENT DEVELOPMENT ENGINE

Having spent a fair amount of time discussing what makes for world-class content, let's switch our focus to how to manage an effective and efficient content development engine. As we said at the beginning of the chapter, the third ailment that often plagues the content lever is the "Tower of Babel" effect, which includes a lack of three crucial elements: leadership, timely direction setting, and effective coordination throughout the whole content development process. Under these conditions, agency relationship management is all over the map, with no clear metrics for evaluating quality and efficiency, resulting in either a revolving door across the agency roster or little to no turnover in agency relationships when it is clearly time for a change. Moreover, there is no strategic logic to how the roster of agency relationships has been assembled, in terms of its breadth, its concentration, or its alignment with the content needs of the business. Vehicle-specific content experts are not consistently leveraged; great, successfully implemented content ideas from different parts of the organization are not reused; and the use of a variety of pre-testing and "test and learn" approaches to validate content in advance of significant investments is haphazard at best. Finally, content process governance is usually a train wreck. There are no clear decision rights, multiple disconnected content efforts focused on the same opportunity run concurrently, anyone has the authority to initiate content efforts, and senior management randomly redirects content at the last minute.

We believe that the design and delivery of an efficient and effective content management engine requires these elements:

- A strategic yet flexible approach to agency relationship management
- A leadership process that inspires your creative partners to do amazing work
- An ability to break down silos and leverage the best ideas from across the system
- A healthy balance of generalist versus specialist participation
- A religious commitment to pre-testing and experimentation
- A coherent, transparent approach to content governance

When you can apply these elements over time to your content development investments, you will see efficiency and effectiveness benefits that are extraordinarily valuable. Let's dive in and discuss each of these ideas in turn.

Enabling Your Creative Partners to Deliver Compelling Work

Most companies rely heavily on external agency partners to help bring forth ideas and create content, although occasionally some of the creative and production resources associated with content development reside in-house. The ongoing challenge is figuring out how to build the best collaborative partnerships with your chosen creative partners—be they external or internal—to inspire everyone to create great work and to have the courage to invest behind it.

Of course, the desires and needs on both sides of this equation are not always aligned. As a client, you want the best creative talent in an agency working on your business, whereas the agency wants to move its best talent to its most interesting or at least its largest clients. The talent inside an agency tends to get restless, bored a little too easily perhaps, and may leap to places that are interesting creatively but too loosely connected to the strategy to be effective. Clients, on the other hand, may start to shut down ideas prematurely or be unwilling to consider seemingly risky ideas if they reflect too big a break from the past. Clients also have a tendency to put all of the blame for failures here on the agency and to have a knee-jerk reaction of opening up an agency search every time they hit a speed bump in content development.

To overcome some of these challenges, we believe you need to start by applying strategic logic to the choice of how many creative partners you need and across what range of specialties. To ensure that the goals are achieved and the business metrics realized, best practice dictates that the CMO take charge of the process. Having developed the strategic positioning, the CMO is in the best position to determine which agencies are the best to add, with which capabilities, and which agency the company should develop a relationship with— and what kind of relationship that should be. We will spend more time in Chapter Six on the fixed cost management lever, discussing the forces that may necessitate use of a narrower or a broader roster of agencies. But wherever your company ends up falling on that spectrum—which should be dictated in part by your brand portfolio strategy, the content needs of your brand, and the extent of decentralization in your organization—you should be able to articulate the strategic logic behind the structure of your agency roster. If you have a few preferred overall partners and then a select few supplemental specialist vendors, why is that structure best suited to support your needs? If you let each country and product line chose its own agency partners, why does that structure make sense? Again, we have seen a wide range of structures be highly effective for different companies, providing that there is a clear logic for why a particular structure of agency relationships is best suited for that company's content needs.

Just as important, whether you are working with five or five hundred agency partners, you should have a clear rationale for why you have selected and are sticking with your chosen partners. For example:

- Does a particular agency add a unique set of skills or industry knowledge?
- Is its stable of creative directors deep beyond belief, or is there a particular creative director with a history of doing great work in the category?

- Does it have an account management or planning approach that helps to drive consistently great content from the creative teams?
- Does it have an efficient, effective network with the breadth to manage complex, global rollouts?
- Is it flexible and responsive in a way that allows you to get high-quality yet fast-turn work?
- Does it have a unique set of skills in a particular marketing vehicle—like promotions or digital or direct—that is particularly important to your marketing plan?
- Does it have a price-value position well suited to your overall investment posture?

Being very clear with the agency and with your own team as to why they have the business and the unique kinds of value you are expecting them to add helps everyone understand what success looks like. It also allows you to quickly identify places in the roster where there is no compelling logic to the relationship and no clear source of value, forcing the team to either clarify the source of value or eliminate the relationship.

Many companies have aligned with a more limited roster of preferred partners for their most important content development work, for reasons beyond cost. It takes time and investment to build the right kind of collaborative partnerships with agencies, and a collaborative partnering dynamic is critical to successful content development. To get the most out of the partnership, marketers learn to empower the agency and inspire their marketing partners. As a positive track record is developed, marketers will give the winning creative teams a greater degree of control than they have been getting. As companies begin to use multiple specialist agencies rather than a single agency—despite the fact that larger agencies are marketing themselves as "one-stop" shops—the CMOs must know how to rate agencies properly, given the proliferation of new media and the belief that smaller, less traditional companies understand this space.

In forming a framework to manage the relationship with the various ad agencies, the best CMOs learn to nurture agency knowledge about the company's brand and customer base. Agency partners have developed historical knowledge about what works for a brand—and what doesn't. In many cases, the talent on the agency side may have more history and context for the business and the consumer than fast-trackers who have just been rotated into a three-year placement on the client side. But ad agency partners are not necessarily compensated for their brand knowledge, and as the agency moves its talent off of brands to move up their career paths, this knowledge base can be lost. The best companies do not allow this knowledge to leave their accounts; they respect and nurture the agency knowledge base with the help of agency management, because managing an effective balance of tenure and institutional knowledge with new thinking is the best way to maintain a durable zone of authenticity for your content.

This understanding of history can spare the CMO from making the mistake of attempting to put his or her stamp on a brand by going with a new shop. Instead, the new CMO will succeed if he or she moves forward carefully, setting out to work with the agency to determine what's been working and what hasn't, then moving forward with the agency on a new strategy. Miller did not follow this advice with its advertising of Miller Genuine Draft—and sales of the beer have declined as a result. Since 1991 the MGD brand has used four agencies to develop its campaigns. As of this writing in 2008, it is about to launch its eighth tagline. In that seventeen-year period, research shows that the MGD messaging has anchored on "both juvenile sexual humor and the maturity of the people who drink the beer; cited both its lack of pretense and its inherent sophistication; and touted its cold-filtration brewing as superior while being marketed in tandem with its heat-pasteurized siblings."[5]

Finally, as with any good partnership, there are a few other basic tenets that help enable it to remain healthy, mutually rewarding, and highly productive. It is important to respect and value the distinctive contributions of all of the various players. It is important to be crystal clear about setting expectations and defining what success looks like. It is important not to micromanage the process. It is important to allow the process an adequate gestation period and to not commit to unreasonable or unrealistic time pressures. It is important to give timely, constructive, and consistent feedback throughout the process. And it is important for everyone to understand the key decision points, how those decisions are going to get made, which criteria will be used to evaluate deliverables, and who ultimately owns the final decision. Nothing is more demoralizing to an agency partner than a murky or random governance process.

Religiously Commit to Pre-testing and Rapid Adaptation

Irrespective of where the inspiration gets sourced, smart companies make certain to validate their content with a robust set of testing before deploying it across a full-scale creative campaign. Because of the resources involved, the best marketers know that content creation is an iterative process. Once initial content has been developed, it must be tested and refined. Despite constrained resources, senior managers are putting greater demands on marketers to pressure test the messaging. This causes tension between the drives for accountability and measurability and the challenge inherent in testing a concept so new to the market that most consumers do not have the ability to adequately evaluate it through a traditional research approach. Notwithstanding such constraints, it is becoming increasingly indefensible to put significant investments behind content that has not been tested in some way.

Historically, marketers have tested for robustness, across all media, across most target customer segments, across most geographic markets, and over time. Now, with the pace of change in the market, continual in-market testing and improvement is becoming more important than getting the perfect message out in the marketplace. At a minimum, it is important to have some preliminary prelaunch read as to whether the content is hitting these basic requirements in terms of its understandability:

- Is the message clear?
- Does the consumer understand precisely what is being communicated?
- Is the consumer clear what company or brand the message is for?
- Is the consumer clear about the category of the company?

After these requirements have been met, you can test for more nuanced aspects of the content's effectiveness; for example:

- Did they relate to content and its underlying message?
- Did they see it as relevant?
- Were they moved by it, intellectually or emotionally?

• Did they see it as a memorable?

• Was it entertaining?

• If there is a call to action embedded in the content, was it actually motivating?

In addition to these classic, market research–based approaches to pre-testing, some companies are taking advantage of a rapid experimentation orientation and the emergence of faster, short-production-cycle vehicles like digital and direct mail to do small-scale live market tests of competing content platforms, then rapidly applying the insights gained and deploying the new "winning" content on a much larger scale. When many companies used TV as their dominant vehicle, with its four-to-six-month production schedules and high production costs per execution, this type of in-market experimentation approach took too long and was cost prohibitive. But with the exceedingly short-cycle times associated with some forms of digital content or direct marketing, it is both cost-effective and highly feasible to run informative and scientific in-market content experiments over a three-to-six-week cycle, which is a huge game-changer from a content development and testing standpoint.

Moreover, the latest academic research from places like Wharton suggests that testing multiple content ideas concurrently is the right way to go, given the disproportionate upside associated with great content ideas. The best marketers understand that as long as the cost of evaluating multiple content approaches is less than the potential opportunity of getting the right content in market, there is only an upside to creating multiple content vehicles, getting them out into the field in a limited test environment, and tracking their response rate. The most successful marketing companies understand that they can use some types of media, such as online surveys and direct mail, to test multiple content executions.

Of course, the framework of such tracking is defined depending on the medium. With more open and innovative channels and the proliferation of open dialogue rather than one-way messaging, it is becoming important to test alternative two-way messaging media. The best marketers are not wedded to traditional messaging media only; they experiment with interactive mechanisms that allow the customers or prospects to respond to the messages. They learn to incorporate these interactive mechanisms into a test-and-learn approach—continually not only measuring the effectiveness of the message but also improving the message by incorporating some of the feedback.

Break Down the Silos and Leverage the Network

Another way to reframe this idea of stress testing the effectiveness of your content through rapid, in-market experimentation is by actively encouraging people in your company to look for winning content ideas from the active stable of content assets already deployed within the company, in either a local market or a regional market context or in a related but different brand or product area. Often a myopia develops from the corporate center or from the global brand management structure, signaling that great content ideas flow only one way—from the center out to the market. But in reality, given the mix of global, regional, and local market activities, a winning content idea may already have been developed in India or China or Brazil and run the effectiveness gauntlet through six or twelve or eighteen months of in-market investment. In a sense, the in-market experiment has already been run and its effectiveness has been proven; you just need to stress test its applicability in other market contexts.

To do this, you have to have an active commitment to breaking down the silos within your own company, an issue that David Aaker elegantly tackles in his recent book *Spanning Silos*. P&G has made excellent headway on this issue, initially by changing its mindset and opening itself up philosophically to great content from around its network, around the globe. It has sourced what have become highly successful global content platforms in its health and beauty and home care businesses by reframing its perspective about the value of its wide-ranging set of local market activities and identifying the winning formulas that have already been battle-tested. For large, decentralized organizations with a fair amount of marketing investment, breaking down silos is one of the largest overlooked sources of effective content ideas, enabling them to save time and resources, improve quality, and reduce risk.

The Governance Process

We would be remiss in closing our conversation about content without addressing the issue of governance. The lack of a clear governance process—concerning who gets to initiate new content initiatives, who gets to put new content into the market, who needs to participate in the content development process, who gets to decide what content gets in market, and which criteria content will be evaluated against—is the source of an incredible amount of frustration, inefficiency, waste, and lost opportunity. Pushing yourself and your teams very hard for governance clarity is probably one of the most effective things that you can do very early in your tenure to stimulate step-function improvements in the efficiency of your content development engine.

Governance in terms of content issues is unnecessarily challenging for one very basic reason: unlike in other areas of the operational value chain, content generally—and advertising specifically—is a realm in which everyone inside the company feels capable of having an opinion and even *entitled* to have one. Said another way, when it comes to content, all of us tend to see ourselves as expertly qualified to judge quality and make assessments. In one way, this is understandable; we are all voracious consumers of content in our personal and professional lives, and thereby are making explicit and implicit snap judgments about content effectiveness almost continuously. On the other hand, no one without the proper training and pedigree would feel the same confidence in rendering an opinion on the supply chain optimization strategy or the product technology strategy without some more formal basis and expertise in that area. When it comes to marketing content, however, everyone feels like it is fair game.

Rather than whining about this state of affairs, we simply encourage seasoned marketers to get out in front of it and actively manage it. If the opinions of the CEO, the CEO's spouse, the chairman, the chairman's spouse, and the head of IT all legitimately matter in the final authorization of any given content strategy, figure that out early, then bake them into the process in a way systematic enough that you solicit input early and often. If the powers that be tend to feel backed into a corner if they don't see at least three content options each time you ask them for a decision, then make sure you serve up three. What is most disconcerting to the teams and creates a highly dysfunctional process is when none of these realities are understood until too late in the game. At the same time, as credibility is established and in-market success happens over time, you can start to advocate for a more rational and streamlined governance model, which should ultimately allow you to reduce the amount of rework and wasted content development effort.

CHAPTER FIVE

Marketing Vehicles and Investment Levels

Selecting Which Vehicles to Deploy and How Much Investment Gets Put Behind Each

T opics covered in Chapter Five:

- Reexamining the tried and true: TV, print, direct, point-of-sale, and PR
- The rapid rise of experiential marketing and the Internet
- Choosing the right mix: bet on the proven, but never stop experimenting
- How market, message, and media factors inform investment levels
- Using business case thinking and advanced marketing analytics to triangulate on your best answer

> *The universe is full of magical things, patiently waiting for our wits to grow sharper.*
> —*Eden Philpotts*
>
> *Life is a constant oscillation between the sharp horns of dilemmas.*
> —*H. L. Mencken*

*Whenever I have to choose between two evils, I always like
to try the one that I haven't tried before.*

—Mae West

After a strategic value proposition is set, in conjunction with finding compelling ways to creatively express the strategy in messaging
and communications, the next biggest challenge faced in achieving marketing excellence lies in determining the right mix of
marketing vehicles and the levels of investment necessary to fund
those vehicles. Our research has shown that these two elements—
marketing vehicle mix and investment levels—are inextricably tied
together. Best practice dictates that the CMO should solve the mystery of the mix by linking its composition closely with strategy and
objectives. The first step is to create a vision for your optimal portfolio of marketing vehicles and then compare this optimal portfolio
with the available investment levels to see what you can afford.

But here CMOs face a stark contrast, as hinted at in the opening quotes. There are so many beautiful, even magical, alternatives
out there when it comes to marketing vehicles, but so few objective
criteria, strategic or performance-related, on which to base those
decisions. Choices, choices, choices—these we have in abundance. But
how to choose? And most important, how do you gain the confidence
that you are choosing wisely?

In this age of constrained resources, it is often not easy to make
choices, especially given the plethora of media channels available—
from the explosion of cable alternatives to the reality of internet
advertising to the importance of advertising on search engines to the
alternatives that traditional companies have begun to investigate in
the Web 2.0 era, including blogs, wikis, social networks, podcasts,
on-line games, virtual worlds, viral, mobile, consumer generated,
branded entertainment, video advertising—and more. As we depict
in Figure 5.1, the universe of potential marketing vehicles continues to expand at an exponential rate. The possibilities for marketing within these new channels are exciting—but there is very little
real historical data available on the reality of their impact on a target
market. There is little data that could be used to develop an effective
ROI calculation.

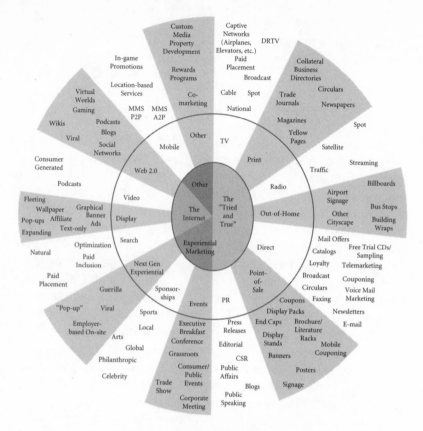

Figure 5.1.   The Ever-Exploding Universe of Marketing Vehicles

No matter what you decide, as a CMO you have to analyze whether these emerging media can create the right forum with which to meet your brand's objectives or, even better, create a two-way forum in which to engage your customers. Communication is part message and part medium—and you have to balance the second to maximize the potential impact of the first. Pick the wrong vehicles for deployment and you will never achieve the right outcomes, regardless of how compelling your strategy and creative you are.

Then once you have sifted through the marketing vehicles, you look at the total marketing budget to determine which level of investment can be made in each vehicle. Can the ideal portfolio of marketing vehicles that you have identified be funded at reasonable and effective levels, given your existing budget? If not, why not? Is the company prepared to invest at an optimal level, to capture all of the profitable growth opportunities that may be available when supported by the right kind of marketing vehicles, or are there other constraints that limit the company's investment posture? The optimal investment level is, of course, a dynamic, not a static target. At a single point in time an optimal investment level may exist, but depending on a number of market, competitive, and proposition-level dynamics, the optimal investment level will vary over time and situation. Ultimately you typically run through an iterative process wherein you explore trade-offs between marketing vehicles and investment levels until you reach an allocation decision that you feel best serves the needs of the business, given the investment constraints.

That's what this chapter is about—helping you to have the insights necessary to begin to evaluate your own situation. As a first step to developing an optimal mix, we have structured the chapter to provide the pros and cons for each class of marketing vehicle. Initially we will look at the "tried and true" vehicle types, like TV, print, and direct mail; then we will move over to the two fastest-growing parts of the marketing vehicle ecosystem: experiential marketing and the Internet. Once you know what each can—and can't—do, you can better judge which are more likely to help you maximize your outcomes, and we will provide some framing devices to help you prioritize your vehicle mix. We will then go back to some fundamental principles of marketing strategy to help you do a "bottom-up" framing of what kind of investment levels might be required to achieve your marketing objectives. Finally, we will demonstrate how you can combine business case thinking with advanced marketing analytics to determine your overall optimal investment levels, as well as how to make the best use of the available budget for any given operating cycle.

REEXAMINING THE TRIED AND TRUE: TV, PRINT, DIRECT, POINT-OF-SALE, AND PR

When we talk about the tried and true marketing vehicles, we are focusing on vehicles that have been a part of the traditional marketing arsenal for at least forty or fifty years. These vehicles—including TV, print, radio, out-of-home, direct marketing, POS, and PR—have been practiced with discipline and flair for most of the modern age of marketing. However, many of the disruptive media innovations are putting pressure on these formats, in terms of audience appeal, relevance, and overall economics, at exactly the same time that companies are pushing harder for the accountability story behind each. So it is an interesting time for proponents of the tried and true approaches. The reexamination is absolutely warranted, but some of the critics may be rushing to write premature obituaries for many of these vehicles. Let's start with a discussion of TV.

When Is Television Worth the Investment?

Television is inherently a mass-media vehicle, although you can make more targeted purchases designed to help you reach a single specific market. As a result, you must determine whether your marketing strategy requires that you focus your investment dollars at the top of the purchase funnel, to reach the largest audience, or near the bottom of the funnel, to reach one particular segment. In the age of global media, you must also determine whether you want to piggyback on a global brand strategy.

Because of the expense of the television investment, you must remember that there are tried and tested rules about its use. In fact, we've found that the objectives can vary depending on the current state of your brand. If your brand is relatively new, with low awareness, then TV is more likely to be effective in raising awareness. If your brand is fairly mature and already has strong top-of-the-funnel metrics, then you can use TV advertising to drive the bottom-of-the-funnel performance—designed to nudge the consumer to buy.

Of course, TV offers the opportunity for your company to make a big splash, especially if you purchase time during a showcase event like the Super Bowl. It can launch a new wave of purchasing, such as the legendary 1984 ad developed by Apple Computer and shown during Super Bowl XVIII—it was credited with the solidification of the Apple market that sustains the company to this day.

In addition to this well-known, and inherently risky, potential, television has been proven to give you the best bang for the buck:

- When you need to reach large numbers of customers in a short period of time
- When your target customers can be fairly broadly defined; say, M18–34 (men between eighteen and thirty-four)
- When you need to convey your message with sight, sound, and motion

• When you can precisely identify the target customer who would be in the market for your product

Take the case of the real-estate company RE/MAX International. When RE/MAX advertises with local cable operators, it typically asks them to air its commercials during home-improvement shows like A&E's *Flip This House* and HGTV's *House Hunters*. RE/MAX's marketing strategy is to attract the viewers of such programs, who might be in the market to buy or sell a house.

Have DVRs Changed TV Opportunities?

Marketers are beginning to question the effectiveness of TV. Three out of four advertisers (78 percent) say traditional TV commercials have become less effective in the past two years, according to a survey by Forrester and the Association of National Advertisers (ANA). Nearly two-thirds (60 percent) of those polled in 2006 say they will reduce TV spending once digital video recorders (DVRs) are in thirty million households, which is expected to happen by 2010.[1]

At the same time, however, some sophisticated marketers are questioning the DVR's impact. Information Research (IRI) conducted a three-year study of DVR use from 2005 to 2008. The findings were as complex as the impact of any new medium. Overall, homes without DVRs had only 5 percent higher purchases of packaged goods than those with DVRs. At the same time, one-fifth of the "pace-setter" brands did lose a significant amount of purchases. In addition, some brands actually saw their sales increase in DVR homes. The study also pointed out "that even modest diversification of media plans away from TV can minimize or eliminate the impact of ad-skipping. Brands that spent 20 percent or more of their media budgets outside TV had no significantly lower volume in TiVo households than non-DVR households."[2]

At the very least, the best marketers will not automatically look at TV, or at least mass market TV, as a first choice. Television remains the most expensive media channel available—and as such, the best marketers are carefully analyzing TV's effectiveness for their particular strategy or value proposition. The TV commercial is, after all, the quintessential "flash in the pan." The message is always going to have a temporary impact, and it may require multiple exposures for your ad to rise above the clutter. It is important to keep in mind the limited time element. Because most ads are only thirty seconds long or less, the company must remember that it is limited in the amount of information it can communicate. It takes a real measure of brilliance to make the call to action more effective.

If the DVR has not completely changed the impact of advertising, however, its ubiquity has helped shine a light on the real measurement challenges that television has always faced: trackability and traceability. Researchers have made significant efforts to measure and track consumers' TV watching habits, but there still is some debate as to its effectiveness. Nielsen Media Research, in particular, provides ratings estimates for TV programs using a variety of methodologies including diaries and set-top meters.

Some companies have begun to meet the challenge of the advent of the DVR. NBC Universal is attempting to measure the effectiveness of television ads that viewers skip through with their digital video recorders. By tracking biometric measurements such as eye movements, heart rate, and sweat, the NBC study found that the ads people concentrated on the most and recalled the most shared several traits. The most successful ads concentrated the action and the brand's logo in the middle of the screen; didn't rely on multiple scene changes, audio, or text to tell the story; and often used familiar characters. People were also more likely to remember an ad in fast-forward mode if they had seen it once before live.

At least one major marketer has already begun to tweak how it crafts ads in the DVR world. In 2007 Visa ran a commercial set in a deli, where patrons were paying for their lunch using Visa check cards. At the end of the commercial the company's "Life Takes Visa" tagline appeared in bright blue on a white screen. Visa decided to focus on the slogan for a few extra seconds so it had a better chance of being seen if the ad was being zapped. (Visa didn't participate in the NBC study.[3]) And most marketers know that if they run their ads during programs that mesh with their products (say, ads for Calphalon cookware during *Top Chef*), as this preliminary research into DVR use confirms, consumers do not fast-forward through their commercials at the same rate.

The Continued Appeal and Potential Downsides of Print, Radio, and Out-of-Home

The traditional media channels of print, radio, and out-of-home (OOH) are considered together because they play similar roles in a company's mix and are affected by similar trends in media usage. Although none of these three media types is cutting-edge, all three can be used effectively for both mass and narrow targeting applications.

First, print, radio, and OOH can help you impact a wide-ranging mass audience and allow for some form of targeting. Second, these media are easily accessible by all types of organizations, so that smaller local businesses can participate. Third, these media types offer some format flexibility, allowing for the individual company to customize its offering with different sizes, lengths, and locations. Finally, the three types are much more cost-effective than television advertising.

The Internet has dealt a real blow to the possibilities provided by these kinds of vehicles, however, because the Net provides an alternative channel for print and radio in terms of time and information. Although it is most pronounced with daily newspaper format, we are seeing a consistent audience migration away from some of these media formats as sources of information or entertainment. Equally troubling, the effectiveness of all three traditional media types is difficult to measure. Many companies continue to focus their marketing measurement for these three media squarely on ad recall research. Others are using dedicated toll-free numbers or micro-site URLs to give them some additional trackability, similar to more direct response media. Many companies have found, however, that even with direct response tools it is difficult to effectively trace and track the complete impact of these traditional forms of media, as not everyone who may have been influenced by the vehicle may respond immediately via the toll-free number or the other ad-specific call-to-action mechanism.

Why Direct Mail Can Still Add to the Bottom Line

The use of direct mail continues to increase because of its value proposition—it is relatively inexpensive and can provide a more effective ROI than most other marketing media. Successful CMOs understand that direct mail is most useful to focus a specific message on a target segment that will create a call to action in the mind of the consumer and hence a purchase. We refer to direct mail in all of its forms—from high-production-quality hundred-page catalogs to simple "10 percent off tomorrow's purchase" postcards—as an addressable vehicle, because you address it to a single individual or household. The good news is that direct mail is one of the most well-developed vehicles in terms of its ability to target a specific type of customer or region. Because it is a mature type of marketing, it has increasingly allowed CMOs to tailor their message to the needs of much narrower audiences in a cost-effective manner, increasing the likelihood of a hit, as the piece is seen as more relevant by that specific individual.

Capital One Corporation has built the foundation of its franchise on a sophisticated use of direct mail, using a precise combination of snail and e-mail to convert its segments into sales, clearly offering each segment a very specific value position designed to make the sale. The success of Capital One's strategy is of particular interest because it has been replicated in countries outside of the original U.S. market.

Direct mail provides opportunities for B2B as well as B2C companies. In fact, the use of e-mail letters to CEOs of client companies has been shown to be especially effective when properly targeted and customized. Both direct e-mail and a personalized handwritten note can be targeted to specific individuals from a mailing list fulfilling specific criteria for a particular company. If a database is tagged with the attributes of particular customer segments, the company can send specific offers and messages to specific customers. In a recent study performed by a professional services firm, for example, targeted CXO communications were effective in over 78 percent of the cases—effectiveness was defined as anything from opening a door to resuscitating an old relationship to starting the close of a sale or to reopening a door that had been closed.

One reason that companies continue to use direct mail is that direct e-mail, personalized notes, and even direct snail mail campaigns are relatively inexpensive media that can prove more effective ROI than many other media. The best marketers realize that direct mail offers the possibility of tailoring many different elements fairly easily—whether it be the format, teaser, greeting, offer, or call to action. A test mailing can help the marketer cost-efficiently determine what is and is not effective. As a result, direct mail can provide the marketer with a quick cycle of test-and-learn—so that the marketer could see real results within a month. In addition, direct mail is a very trackable medium if it includes a specific micro-site for a visit or a phone number to draw hits.

Although an institution such as Capital One can use direct mail effectively to home in on a specific segment, a direct mail campaign can be blocked as a result of the regulatory trend toward protecting customers from unwanted advertising. Increasingly, consumers can stop direct mail campaigns in their tracks through a variety of means. Secure corporate systems can block spam; telephone services block annoying calls; websites help customers keep away unwanted mail.

Customers—both consumers and businesses—have become so overwhelmed with incoming mail (and other "mail" in electronic media) that some studies show that response rates are declining. The average response rates for a direct snail mail or e-mail campaign are less than 1 percent. Our experience shows, however, that if a direct mail campaign is carefully conceived and planned, with the right target and offer and message put into place, a company can achieve the same level of response rates as Capital One—as high as 3 or 4 percent.

For this reason, marketers increasingly are testing to determine the response rate for a particular direct marketing campaign. They make certain that the piece will hit the target. Given the size of the investment, however, another measurement challenge resides with the sophistication of a company's IT systems. As companies expand through merger and acquisition—and pick up a mountain of legacy systems in the process—they need to develop integrative capabilities across the company, to be able to access the data necessary to track the call to action to the source.

How Point-of-Sale Drives Value

Because point-of-sale (POS) promotions (including elements such as coupons and display) are controlled by the sales team, not the marketing team, they are often neglected in the development of a marketing strategy. The objective for POS promotions is to influence the consumer at the point of purchase—the immediate audience for the product. Of course, they are designed to generate impulse sales, but can also subliminally, gradually build the long-term brand image.

According to marketing research, POS promotions can be among the most cost-effective because if placed in the right way—in front of customers—POS nudges the consumer to make a purchase. Sales executives always use POS techniques to target particular segments, but in the last few years we have found that technology has impacted the POS technique. Point-of-sale mechanisms become more pointed when pushed through the mobile phone with mobile POS ads—so the offers can be even more closely targeted to a specific customer's needs. Because they are so focused, POS mechanisms are relatively inexpensive to use. More important, sales executives believe they can more easily achieve a positive ROI with POS than they can with most other media.

P&G is one of the most aggressive companies in its unearthing of powerful and imaginative ways to drive more consideration and trial through innovative POS vehicles. The company has made a material shift toward POS vehicles over the past seven years, because they saw a huge opportunity to partner with their retailers to drive more value for their consumers in the shopping experience itself. Some of their efforts are related more to packaging and display, all of which focuses on how to make the visual merchandising of the product more appealing at the point of sale. Some of it is focused on unique bundling opportunities and co-op promotional investments that tie into some broader merchandising theme of the retail partner. P&G has even reinvented its approach to couponing—taking a dying, aging vehicle significantly up-market, involving higher-production-value booklets packaged around interesting themes and content. P&G understands the importance of fighting the battle as close to the point of purchase as possible, and the organization has retooled to get sharper and smarter in that area.

Although in some ways the right kind of POS display can help reinforce the image of a brand, the wrong kind of POS offer can *lower* the value of the brand, especially if the offers focus exclusively on price reductions or heavy discounting. Using price-based offers at the point of sale is typically a surefire way to get a prospective customer to take a second look or create that sense of a "limited time deal" that certain types of customers find highly motivating. But when it is overdone, you can start to erode the overall economics of the brand. Because of these risks, one company that has traditionally shied away from POS mechanisms is Gold Toe socks. The company does not do on-the-spot promotions, and it limits sales discounts to one or two times a year—and does not allow its brand to be put on sale by the retail distributor.

In the opposite end of the spectrum, however, sits Kraft, which is probably the poster child for the overuse of POS couponing. In the late 1990s and the early part of the 2000s, Kraft shifted too much of its marketing budget to POS couponing, because it drove short-term sales lift. However, after a few years, the company saw that it was actually "training" its customers to wait for the sale and buy the product on discount. Without any other marketing support for the brands to counterbalance this effect, the brands gradually saw their price premiums erode, and they became dramatically more price elastic. This example illustrates the fundamental problem with most traditional discount-based POS vehicles. No matter what the aim of the sales executive, POS is first and foremost focused on pushing a short-term sale, and the easiest way to do that is to cut the price. Depending on how often it is used and the way in which it is used, POS mechanisms have been found to lower the long-term value of the brand and product, if not balanced with other brand-building activities.

In addition to this problem, however, POS mechanisms are often ignored because they are outside the control of the CMO. As a result, the marketing team cannot coordinate the use of POS with the other aspects of the marketing strategy. In the best case, POS might reinforce the brand, but in the worst, it might counter the marketing messages going out to prospects and customers through other media about the product or the brand.

Public Relations: The Energizer Bunny of Traditional Marketing Vehicles

Public relations always comes under scrutiny by companies—but it has survived for decades because companies value the PR shield from time to time. PR is a very global medium, given the ease with which information spreads around the world at a rapid pace. The problem with investments in PR is rather simply stated: because a company has little control over the "take rate" for any given PR investment by the legitimate editorial and media owners, PR is inherently a tool of indirect influence, grounded in an optimistic belief that by repackaging company-specific stories in a reporter- and media-friendly manner or by steering company-specific narrative toward issues that are topical for the media at the moment, great editorial coverage will ultimately materialize for the company. But the problem is that usually the inherent strength or attractiveness of the company's story is a much bigger factor in driving favorable coverage than anything a PR firm ends up doing. And most editors and reporters can smell spin a mile away and are highly cynical about any attempt by a company, via its PR firm, to repackage its stuff into whatever the flavor of the day happens to be. The "iffy" nature of the potential outcomes from a PR investment is always the big elephant in the room. As the old saying goes, "advertising is paid for, publicity is prayed for."

Companies realize that they can maximize the value of public relations when it complements other elements of a marketing campaign and the core story is compelling. The power of public relations, when it works, can be priceless. A seemingly independent source provides a good review of a company, in some way. This source is viewed by the market as objective and hence credible. Research has proven that consumers are more likely to pay attention to news reports than to advertising. Sometimes, depending on the agency, the costs of a public relations campaign can be significantly less than for other forms of media. When you combine this with the added protection PR investments provide if a company stumbles into a string of mishaps that generate bad publicity, you can understand why most companies make room for at least a little bit of PR in their overall marketing mix.

When being compared with other investments, however, PR tends to lose on a relative basis, as the probability for systematic and consistent message exposure is not as great as with other forms of marketing vehicles. This vehicle has a high beta in terms of its performance, and it is not clear that if you doubled or tripled your investment in PR you would gain commensurate increases in the probability of more favorable outcomes. In dealing with a public relations firm, the company has little or no control over messages, their timing, or their placement. Moreover, it is difficult to determine whether the hit buys as much for the company as either the publication or the public relations firms say that it buys. In fact, this limitation provides the most significant barrier to PR effectiveness. Companies, especially new high-growth entities, often believe they need PR, so they jump into a relationship with an established firm armed with obscure objectives. Unless the company figures out exactly what objectives it wants to achieve through a public relations campaign, it is very difficult to measure PR effectiveness.

Just as important, it is difficult to measure impact—even when you've drawn up objectives—and tie that impact to specific activities. The wide variety of tactics and tools used in PR—such as publicity, publications, editorial road shows, events, press releases, reporter/media management—makes tracking the impact very difficult indeed. And because PR campaigns cast a wide net and can exercise little control over the outlets that pick up the story, it is very difficult to effectively track the way these publications assess and use the information provided through your PR resources. Unless you have good knowledge about which medium is optimal, you need to build in some inherent experimentation and risk mitigation.

THE RAPID RISE OF EXPERIENTIAL MARKETING AND THE INTERNET

In addition to all of the innovation and disruption that has been occurring within the tried and true marketing vehicles, the two most powerful emerging forces in the marketing vehicle world over the past decade have been the rapid recasting of "face-to-face" marketing as experiential marketing, and the indomitable rise of the Internet. Each of these forces is powerful in its own right, and they are also reshaping the balance of power and influence across the other viable marketing alternatives. Experiential marketing, when executed well, has that multisensory authenticity that can be powerful and show-stopping. The Internet is changing the rules of the game on many levels, even as it passes through its third or fourth incarnation. These marketing innovations are fascinating and exciting. Let's dive into the experiential marketing world first.

Experiential Marketing via Events and Sponsorships

Sponsorship of events continues to be an attractive strategy for many companies because they can target specific audiences or customer segments. Professional services businesses are adept at sponsoring clients to golf tournaments; many professional services firms have a golf professional on contract to teach during these sessions. The slow-paced nature of the tournaments lends itself to discussion and relationship development. Retail companies have long tried to build their brands through various events, such as NASCAR races. Best Buy began to broaden this strategy in 2008 by marrying the brand-building use of NASCAR with a community awareness initiative about autism. Held at Dover International Speedway, the race was called "Best Buy 400 Benefiting Student Clubs for Autism Speaks."[4] These events have the benefit of allowing the sponsor to emphasize regional and national brand-building. Equally important, you can alter the size of events depending on the type of brand strategy you're emphasizing.

Events are a classic play for longer-term brand building or top-of-the-funnel initiatives (to build market awareness and familiarity with the company). They are rarely used for bottom-of-the-funnel impact to increase consideration of a product or an immediate conversion to sale. Depending on the customer segment, events can be very easily customized and targeted. As we indicated by the preceding examples, they can work for both consumers and business audiences, especially when built around leisure activities outside of the business environment. In some cases, for example, yearly brand-building exercises are proven vehicles for building relationships—and sales—in the B2B environment. Both Oracle and SAP have created legendary event venues, going back twenty years. They are so well known that customers look forward to them, and the software companies use the events to introduce prospects to their capabilities and praise those customers that have succeeded with their investments.

The Challenge for Experiential Marketing Vehicles

In the cost-constrained marketing world, cost-benefit analysis of these events is difficult. In the case of B2B events, because sales cycles are so long, a company's long-term track record of success is used as a justification for ongoing sponsorship. In the case of B2C, companies do look for both a short-term and a long-term boost to sales from events.

Best practice for events dictates that a company chooses the right event for the right target customer segment—in the right region. What works in the Southeast may not in the West. Our experience has shown that there are diminishing returns for some events in some regions. Moreover, the company cannot make the target audience too narrow—or too broad. The idea is to choose both the target customer and the event carefully.

Even when a company can identify the right segment or can leverage its investment with multiple sponsors, the company must make certain that, given the hierarchy of brands, its brand is the most visible. When PricewaterhouseCoopers sponsored a golf event in the late 1990s, following the merger of PW and Coopers and Lybrand, and after a long absence from such sponsorships, the marketing director in charge did not worry about the hierarchy of brand names, because he thought that the PWC brand was golden in the accounting industry. Unfortunately, the brand of golf equipment outshone the evidence of PWC's new name. When clients were asked what they remembered, PWC was never mentioned. Instead, the name of the golf ball, golf club, and golf cart, were top of mind—right after the event! Understandably, the marketing director was fired, the partner in charge of brand development was forcibly retired, and PWC waited two years before sponsoring anything again.

Events are well liked and respected by the market. Even so, companies do not rush into sponsorship, because they understand that the ROI is too complex to measure until you figure out the full "leverage" that could be obtained from the sponsorship, rather than simply the potential for direct sales. The complex elements include whether it helps create marketing cost efficiencies (for example, through additional media and merchandising opportunities or the driving of retail or website traffic, or by providing access to niche market) and whether it helps increase perceived brand equity, leads to additional benefits from the sponsor as a potential customer, blocks competition, or helps recruit or retain employees, depending on the attractiveness of the sponsorships.

The best marketers analyze the pathway of relationships that events can help the company pursue. They must specifically determine whether the sponsorship exposure leads directly to improvement in brand perceptions and then to improved brand outcomes, which in turn could lead to improved business outcomes in the long run.

The New Secrets of On-Line Marketing

There is no doubt in anyone's mind that on-line advertising remains the fastest-growing way for companies to share marketing messages. Group M, the media planning and buying agency owned by WPP Group, forecast that spending on Internet advertising in the UK would surpass spending on TV ads in 2009—making the UK the first of the world's major economies to see TV spending overtaken by the Internet. ZenithOptimedia predicted internet advertising would pass three milestones over the following three years. First, it would overtake radio advertising in 2008; second, it would attain a double-digit share of global advertising in 2009; and third, it would overtake magazine advertising in 2010, with 11.5 percent of total ad spend.

In fact, on-line media stands apart from other media because it allows companies to

• Impact a wide variety of activities across the marketing spectrum
• Drive sales through an alternative sales channel

• Easily reach global locations, allowing marketing executives to leverage web investments for global exposure

The increase in on-line advertising and the use of the on-line channel to drive marketing messages stems from its ease of use, ubiquity, and cost-effectiveness. Unlike the experience marketers have with other channels, they can easily trace the impact of marketing message sent on the Net; the majority of on-line vehicles can be tied to a single customer target. This micro-targeting advantage has taken on more power for marketers as the number of web outlets for on-line advertising continues to proliferate and expand, increasing the opportunities for CMOs to narrowly focus marketing strategies on the specific customer they're trying to reach. Such potential for truly narrow focus has been proven to increase not only the likelihood of a hit but also the ROI for the marketing investment. In addition to the narrow focus, the marketing team receives feedback throughout the campaign cycle and can further tailor, or change completely, the basic messages as they go along. This feedback comes in a variety of ways—but in the main, the internet culture encourages responses from proposed customers or users. These responses can be incorporated in order to increase the likelihood of purchases.

Another reason that on-line advertising generates an excellent ROI is the low production costs involved with on-line campaigns. As the production costs for printed materials and advertising campaigns continue to skyrocket, those for on-line have reached a certain plateau, given the increased competition among vendors. The result is an even greater business value for the marketing investment.

In our work, the challenges we've found in this area actually come more from the newness of the on-line opportunity than from inherent difficulties with the basic concept. In the first place, many traditional marketers think in traditional marketing patterns and do not understand the possibilities that digital and on-line media offer. For example, in a recent study of automotive marketing executives, whose average age was fifty, and who were fired between 2006 and 2007, many complained about the lack of budget, and opined that marketing was used as a scapegoat for a more general state of corporate failure.[5] These are, in fact, the traditional complaints made by marketers.

The survey's more interesting finding was the reason given for one marketing executive's being released; it stood out from the others because it was different. A former SVP of marketing pointed out that he was shown the door because he was supposed to familiarize himself with over thirty different media outlets or marketing channels. He not only had to become an expert in each, but he also had to know enough to negotiate for the right price mix with myriad vendors. In fact, although the SVP managed to land on his feet in a retail company following his ouster from the auto company, he was fired from *that* job within six months—for the same reason.

In our work with companies, we have found that both the lack of internal expertise with on-line campaigns and the unique approach offered by on-line advertising have held back many marketing organizations from realizing the full potential of the media.

Just as important, confirming the auto marketing executive's experience, many marketers simply don't know what questions to ask, or what variables to assess, when analyzing an agency's on-line capabilities. All of the larger public relations agencies have been developing in-house on-line capabilities for the last five years, and they will argue that their successes in certain campaigns illustrate the strength of their capabilities. Until and unless the marketing executive has experience with an on-line campaign—in gauging the substance of consumer feedback, or in learning how to judge the various measures vendors use to judge campaign effectiveness—the marketer risks a poor ROI for on-line.

The Power of Web 2.0

In addition to needing experience, the marketer also must keep up with the pace of change with respect to on-line marketing. We have found that changes come so swiftly and with such regularity that many marketers are overwhelmed. Add to this pace the fact that so many different on-line media vehicle options continue to be developed, and it's no wonder this medium has become exceptionally difficult for most companies to navigate without help from agencies of a kind that differs from their traditional agency relationship. Although on-line advertising has been more significantly developed for B2C industries than it has for B2B companies, the pace of change will affect B2B in the long run. One particular aspect of the Net, the phenomenon known as Web 2.0, is most likely the source of real technological innovation in the twenty-first century, and it will heavily affect the B2B market.

Web 2.0 refers to a transition from a focus on information and e-mail to an emphasis on network and community on the Internet. This transition holds out enormous opportunities for marketers to harness both the information and the potential that these communities of web users create. Credit for the creation of the concept of Web 2.0 goes to Tim O'Reilly, who coined the phrase.[6] According to one of Tim O'Reilly's many definitions:

> Web 2.0 is the network as platform, spanning all connected devices; Web 2.0 applications ... [are] delivering software as a continually updated service that gets better the more people use it, consuming and remixing data from multiple sources, including individual users, while providing their own data and services in a form that allows remixing by others, creating network effects through an "architecture of participation," and deliver rich user experiences.[7]

As was the case with on-line advertising, the impact of Web 2.0 has been felt, in the first wave, by B2C companies. This phenomenon can be traced back to the 1990s, when Amazon.com is credited with having innovated one of the first visible aspects of Web 2.0, in which retail companies encourage their customers to write reviews and comment on books. Increasingly, however, the companies at the forefront of on-line advertising have also become adept at developing the concept of community. Harley-Davidson has taken its natural community and increased the impact exponentially through the effective use of net meetings and community development campaigns. The impact on continuing to increase the value of the HD brand, even in the face of a business downturn, has been significant.

Contrast Harley's effectiveness with the ineffectiveness of professional services firms attempting to tap into the Web 2.0 sensibilities. Although these firms, whose strategies are inherently client-focused, should be among the first to develop a real sense of community with their clients, they have not been able to catch the wave. Their attempts at blogging, for example, fall flat. For the most part, they treat on-line as an adjunct to traditional media placement—without taking it to the next level of interactive or network-related functionality.

Even more important than the inability of the traditional companies in the B2B market to seize control of the Web 2.0 initiative is the fact that in other areas, such as politics, the communities have grown so quickly, and gathered so many adherents, that they have transmogrified into nations. In the political world, for example, what started as the community of Daily Kos, which helped shape the outcome of the 2006 election, has grown into the nation of NetRoots. This phenomenon obviously has potential to catch a market of interested, like-minded "customers."

Networks expand exponentially as each individual participating in the network responds and adds his or her opinion. Communities have grown to the extent that they invade the space of one another. In the presidential campaign of 2008, for example, the two sides of the Democratic contest—those supporting Hillary Clinton and those supporting Barack Obama—each invaded the turf of the other to add their negative comments about the partisans of their opponents. If you think of these comments as potential criticisms, you can immediately see the potential for mining these criticisms to hone the brand of Clinton or Obama.

As the campaign of 2008 revolutionized the use of the Net as a community of donors and partisans, it also galvanized the attention of corporate executives who can recognize an opportunity for influencing the market—in addition to further developing the brand. Amazon.com, for example, has not stopped with the development of a reviewer community among its customers. As Amazon expanded its product base, it also expanded the concept of the Amazon community. The members offer their own suggestions for lists of books in the same topic area. Amazon has taken the data generated by the customer community to offer other ideas for purchases to the customers who are buying a particular book on a certain subject matter.

Taking such concepts created in the B2C space and developing them to create communities of suppliers or business customers in the B2B market has proven more difficult for B2B operations. For one thing, the proprietary nature of their integrated systems makes it more difficult for them to bring clients into their community. For another, they continue to believe that in the long run face-to-face interaction with clients is more effective than virtual contact.

Some companies are using the principles of Web 2.0 to increase their access to new ideas. Best Buy and Procter & Gamble, for example, have leveraged the National Innovation Marketplace, "an on-line registry where researchers and inventors ... post ideas ... Businesses (including large companies) will browse through the ideas," as if it were a job search site. The idea is to tap into the networking and

community-development aspects of like-minded inventors by putting together inventors with small businesses, and ultimately, larger
companies.[8]

What Web 2.0 Means for Marketers and Measurement

In the course of its still very short history, Web 2.0 has created a variety of media such as blogs, wikis, social networks, podcasts, on-line
games, virtual worlds, viral, mobile, consumer generated, branded
entertainment, and video advertising. In the long run, these media
have the potential to create entirely different forums in which a CMO
could tell a brand story or create two-way forums through which her
company could engage with its customers.

The majority of companies are not familiar with these "bleeding-
edge" technologies and do not have the capabilities (internal or external) to take full advantage of them. This lack of familiarity does not
mesh with the experience of most of their customers, however, and
could hold them back. Customers are managing their own participation more than ever, so it is becoming critical for companies to create forums in which the customers can participate and engage with
the brands—whether it be directly, through some type of consumer-
generated media, or indirectly, through branded entertainment that
cuts across multiple media that customers may engage in.

The most important aspect of Web 2.0 is the creation of a more
direct emotional connection with customers by tapping into their
natural inclination to tell other people about their experiences. As
a result of these trends, marketers increasingly understand that, in
the world of Web 2.0, branding is becoming more important than
ever by becoming part of the consumer storytelling. When you no
longer have a full thirty or sixty seconds worth of advertising to tell
your story, brands become their own content creators and channels
to manage this change.

Starbucks Corporation has decided to wet its feet in the Web
2.0 world by launching a new website, www.mystarbucksidea.com.
Starbucks customers will have the opportunity to offer their own
ideas for everything from products to services to any other aspects of
the company's operations. The main goal is to increase the innovation components of its brand equity.[9] Many marketers jumped into
Web 2.0 initiatives because they were attracted by such ideals. As with

the beginning of any new internet phase, however, companies experimenting with Web 2.0 ideas have been wasting money. As a result, "Digital marketing executives say they had a hard time justifying the tens of thousands or sometimes hundreds of thousands of dollars needed to build and maintain a campaign in the virtual world when there are few ways to measure return on investment."[10]

One way traditional marketers can justify expenditures is by finding the right partner with whom to harness the opportunities of community—and the data and information that it generates—to understand just how best to use community to increase the power of their brands. They need to collaborate more with experienced agencies to create the "story" for a particular medium that would most effectively communicate their value proposition to customers. These experts understand that the new media do not work well as stand-alone mechanisms but are meant to be integrated and interconnected with each other and with traditional media. In addition, marketers must also learn to take advantage of their customers' penchant for multitasking and consuming multiple media.

The experts understand what Web 2.0 is all about: consumers and customers are voracious users of media, and there are many more sources of available information now than in the past. They are consuming the mix because they are multitasking. The best marketers have found that no single medium can be completely effective at meeting all the objectives for a marketing campaign. Some media resonate better with specific target segments. Some are better suited to a call to action vs. building brand awareness (top-of-funnel versus bottom-of-funnel). Other media complement one another (interaction effects). Combining some media will get you more than a simple additive effect—the result can be called the "$1 + 1 = 3$" effect.

As the pace of change has hit the variety and potential of on-line advertising, so it has also affected the challenge of on-line measurement. The development of the Web 2.0 capabilities—including blogging, networking, user-developed services and applications, and, most important, the collection and use of myriad data generated throughout the Web—will become an important piece of competitive advantage. The marketers who know not only how to collect data on the users that become part of their community but also how to mine, understand, and use that data effectively will be the ones to help their companies maximize the potential of their network for competitive advantage.

There are many capabilities to be learned. The evolution of Web 2.0 is having a significant impact on how the effectiveness of on-line advertising is measured. Marketers still mastering basic analytics must now deal with Web 2.0. In the earlier internet stage, marketers typically measured a prospect's entrance to and exit from a web page. Web 2.0 analytics focus on user interaction. Where do users click, hover, look, or interact? What data did the user leave behind? What does it tell you about that market segment?

The reality of Web 2.0 is that marketers must track activity and interest across a much broader universe. These "engagement" metrics must span things such as web browsers, web applications such as widgets, RSS readers and destinations including traditional websites, walled social networks, and services like Twitter that extend beyond the realm of any one web location.

That reality has spawned a new generation of measurement metrics, including use rate, interaction rate, click-through rate, conversion rate, distribution rate, and cost per interaction.[11] The biggest stumbling block to maximizing the Web 2.0 opportunities on the Net is the lack of integration between web systems and a company's existing order-tracking systems. The potential for fraud and corruption has pushed many companies to create walls between their systems and the Net. Many companies do not have the capability to seamlessly integrate the Web and their internal systems, an integration that could lead to a good understanding and trackability of leads generated on-line, but a broken link in determining whether those on-line leads have generated any business outcome.

CHOOSING THE RIGHT MIX: BET ON THE PROVEN, BUT NEVER STOP EXPERIMENTING

With so many seemingly compelling alternatives, narrowing in on a specific set of marketing vehicles that are most appropriate for your business situation is never an easy task. Go with too many, and you may overwhelm your execution capabilities, fragment your spend, and invest too much in production and too little in media or other customer-facing spend. Go with too few, and you may be seriously underserving your target customer and hindering your business performance.

Until you start to build better data on the financial effectiveness of the various vehicles, it is always safe to start by letting your strategic

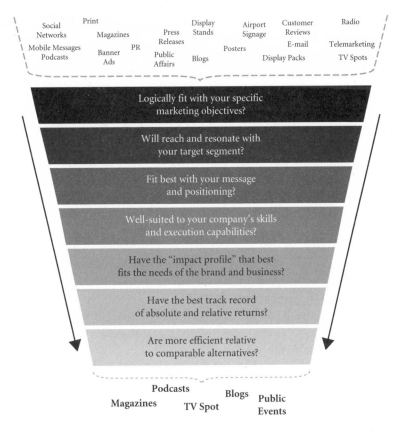

Figure 5.2.   Strategic Filters Used to Narrow the Universe of Viable
Marketing Vehicles

marketing objectives drive the selection process. As you can see from Figure 5.2, which depicts the seven key filters that you should actively use to narrow the universe of viable marketing vehicles, strategic marketing issues dominate the top half of the decision funnel, while execution and effectiveness criteria dominate the lower part of the funnel. Because we will focus on how to marry up the effectiveness criteria with investment-level decision making in the second half of the chapter, we will focus on more of the strategic filters in this section.

Ultimately, marketing vehicle selection is about the intersection of marketing strategy and business strategy—what strategic choices has the business made in terms of how to compete and win, and what role can marketing investment play in supporting those out-comes? How much of what kind of volume needs to be sourced, at what price points, and from which types of current and prospec-tive customers? If you have forced the company to get precise about which customer types or segments will provide this year's volume, you have helped to narrow the playing field of appropriate market-ing vehicles. Do we need to go broad and appeal to mass audiences, or are we going to build deeper relationships with narrow audiences? Are we prioritizing growth from certain kinds of customers, and if so, which ones?

You can see how a similar line of inquiry might play out along other dimensions of your strategic marketing approach. For example, if you have identified your strategic customer target or targets correctly and have unearthed a value proposition that addresses a compelling set of pain points in a differentiated way, you have started to lay an even stronger foundation for vehicle-level decision making. If you have also profiled the purchase funnel blockages for these target segments and understand your company's critical bot-tlenecks in terms of driving more consideration and purchase, you have helped clarify the "problem" around which your vehicle choices should be optimized. If you have augmented these insights with a deep understanding of how your priority segments use and access media in their daily lives, you should have all of the critical elements needed to step through the filtering process. By marrying this stra-tegic marketing thinking with a good understanding of the oppor-tunities and challenges provided by each of the marketing vehicles, you have the makings of a thoughtful process for selecting the right vehicles.

Over the next couple of pages, to help evaluate the appropriateness of the various marketing vehicles discussed earlier in the chapter, we will apply this kind of methodology to specific kinds of strategic and execution challenges, through a series of conceptual maps. Think of these mappings more as starting points for the debate than as any-thing more definitive. We understand that many vehicles have a wide range of potential execution styles, and were we to focus on any one given instance of a particular style of execution, we might end up plotting the vehicle in a totally different place on the map. But as a way to get the filtering discussion started, we offer them up as tan-talizing icebreakers or perhaps playful little hand grenades that shake things up without hurting anybody.

What Behavioral Outcomes Are You Targeting, with What Messaging Strategy?

One important place to anchor, of course, is around the critical behavioral outcomes the business is banking on to drive sales. For example, is the business currently confronted with more of a top-of-the-funnel problem—"people are not familiar with us"—or a bottom-of-the-funnel problem—"people kick the tires but never end up buying"? Or is there a little bit of both? In addition, what kind of messaging strategy is most motivating to the target—one that is more emotive and image-focused, or one that is very call-to-action or offer-oriented?

As seen in Figure 5.3, when we juxtapose these two dimensions, you see a fairly wide spread in vehicle fit. Some vehicles, like direct mail offers or broadcast TV, have the ability to be pretty effective at tackling problems throughout the purchase funnel, but differ sharply in their ability to deliver more emotive messaging versus call-to-action messaging. Other vehicles, however, have a definitive skew toward one end of the funnel, with activities like POS and

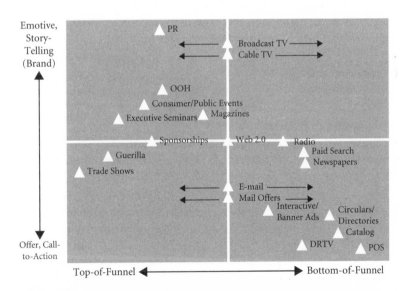

Figure 5.3.   Mapping Marketing Vehicles in Relation to Messaging
Strategies and the Desired Behavioral Outcomes

circulars anchoring at the bottom, and activities like consumer events, PR, and guerilla marketing anchoring at the top. Direct response vehicles are particularly well-suited to develop relationship, or drive toward a near-term purchase, and POS vehicles help convert browsers into purchasers, so this kind of mapping should not be surprising. PR and word-of-mouth vehicles like social networks, paid coverage, and guerilla campaigns are designed to enhance reputation and leverage third-party credibility to build positive buzz, and as such are better suited to top-of-the-funnel needs.

Target Audience Make-up and Level of Permission

Another interesting place to pressure test your vehicle alternatives is around the composition of your target audience and the level of permission they have given to your brand to communicate with them. Does your business plan require you to appeal to a broad, heterogeneous audience with general needs or to a narrow, special-ized audience with targeted needs? This particular decision is often the toughest part of marketing strategy development. Nobody in charge of a P&L wants to believe that we are going to "deselect" cer-tain kinds of customers and potentially walk away from profitable volume. So it is not surprising that this kind of a decision has seri-ous implications for marketing vehicle selection as well. It is even more interesting when you juxtapose this factor against the level of permission the customer has explicitly or tacitly given the company to communicate with them in a certain manner. With customers having an increasing ability to block out unwanted or unneces-sary messages via "do not call" lists, "do not mail" lists, spam filters, TiVo, and what have you, marketers must understand the difference between vehicles that represent the company "interrupting" the cus-tomer and those that represent the company being "invited in" by the customer.

As you can see in Figure 5.4, many of the tried and true market-ing vehicles are more suitable for broad audiences and follow a more interruptive style, with the exception of direct mail. Over time, then, these vehicles run the risk of being increasingly shut out of a cus-tomer's sphere as the customer grabs more control of the messages allowed in. At the other end of the spectrum, many vehicles associated with experiential and internet marketing are geared for more narrow targeting—and have the added halo of customer invitation!

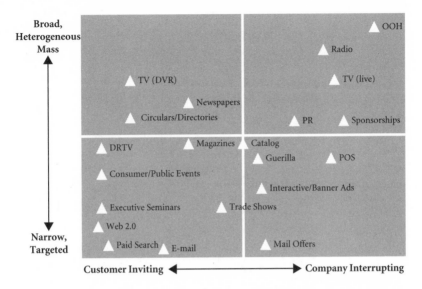

Figure 5.4.   Mapping Marketing Vehicles in Relation to Target Audience Make-up and Levels of Permission

Style of Engagement, Scalability, and Contextual Relevance

The exhibits in Figures 5.5 and 5.6 present two additional conceptual maps that juxtapose various strategic marketing parameters with each other and then map the inherent performance of marketing vehicles in relation to those parameters. Figure 5.5 attempts to look at the communication and messaging needs of the core target audience. During the strategy development stage, we should have identified what kind of value proposition is going to resonate most powerfully with our target: emotional or experiential benefits or more rational or functionally oriented benefits. We also should have identified how much "conversational" participation the target segment expects from the brand. Are they expecting to have a lot of opportunities to engage with the brand in a two-way dialogue and perhaps even co-architect their conversation? Or will a traditional one-way communication mode suffice? Depending on the audience requirements, different marketing vehicles deliver different levels of impact.

Figure 5.6 looks at the scalability question—how easy or difficult it is for you to cost-efficiently double or triple your investment in a given vehicle—in relation to the level of contextual or behavioral

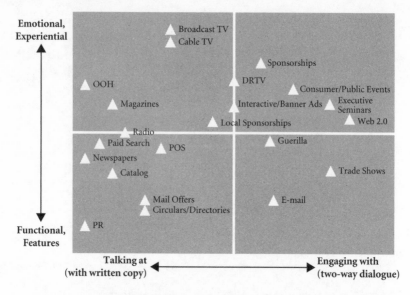

Figure 5.5. Mapping Marketing Vehicles in Relation to Messaging Strategies and Engagement Style of Communication

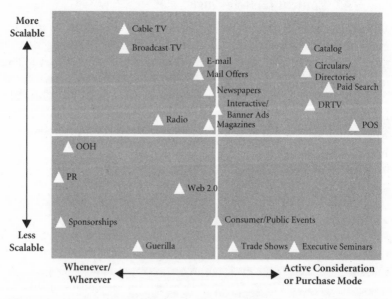

Figure 5.6. Mapping Marketing Vehicles in Relation to Scalability and Contextual Relevance

targeting that each vehicle can deliver. Again, depending on your need for quick scaling of effective marketing vehicles (scaling them either nationally or globally), highly productive good ideas that do not scale easily are unattractive. An activity may not be scalable because it is difficult to access more inventory (like out-of-home) or it has production constraints (like many public events) or it has other operational limitations (like direct mail or e-mail).

As we stated earlier, none of this is meant to be definitive. But you can see how this kind of approach stress tests the logic behind your optimal vehicle choices, forcing you to rigorously assess them against the key criteria that you have identified as critical success factors during your marketing strategy development process. Highly sexy vehicle alternatives that can't deliver against the basic requirements of your marketing strategy should get pushed to the bottom of the list or at least get segregated to the "experimental" side of the spreadsheet. Priority should be placed on proven vehicles with performance characteristics aligned with your marketing needs.

Before we move on to the financial effectiveness screens, the final idea that we would like to close with here is the ongoing need for continuous experimentation of new potential marketing vehicles. Although we are strongly against continued investment in vehicles that clearly do not fit the marketing strategy or deliver proven financial returns, we are also strong believers in the idea that every marketing vehicle portfolio needs to have a process for continuous renewal from within. History has shown that competitors eventually try to erode the effectiveness of winning marketing formulas, and that tactics can lose their effectiveness over time. When you couple this fact with the rapidly changing dynamics in media consumption and consumer experiences, it becomes clear that every company must be vigilantly on the lookout for new marketing vehicles with the potential to become the next big ideas. We will spend a lot more time on this in Chapters Nine and Ten, but we wanted to at least start the conversation here.

HOW MARKET, MESSAGE, AND MEDIA FACTORS INFORM INVESTMENT LEVELS

Having a short list of optimal marketing vehicles is only half the battle, of course. Making smart decisions around the investment levels value lever is the other critical part of the overall marketing accountability equation. Set the investment levels too high and the average returns of your marketing portfolio will suffer. Set the investment levels too low and you may leave profitable growth opportunities to a competitor or, even worse, severely underperform your operating plan. Allocate the investments to a suboptimal mix of marketing vehicles, inappropriately weighted, and you could have the same unfortunate outcomes.

As you think about the investment levels value lever, there are two basic questions that you should keep in mind. The first and most strategic question is whether the overall investment level in marketing vehicles—the total marketing budget—is appropriate, given what you know about your proposition, your competitive environment, the historical financial returns of your marketing programs, and the risk-adjusted returns of other internal investment alternatives—sales force, pricing, distribution, customer service, and the like. Perhaps it is too high? Perhaps it is too low? Most important, on what set of data and analyses are you basing this assessment?

The second question focuses more on the allocation of that budget, specifically asking whether the allocation is optimized in a risk-adjusted manner to help the company hit its overall business objectives. Are you overweighting certain kinds of vehicles because of legacy issues or inertia, while underweighting programs that may have higher potential to drive profitable growth? Are you overweighted toward vehicles with a high theoretical upside, even though they have high performance variability? Have you fragmented your investments across so many activities that none of your activities has enough critical mass to achieve breakout performance? Again (as before), most important, on what sets of data and analyses are you basing your assessments?

Both of these questions—the appropriateness of your overall investment level and the relative allocation of investment dollars across your chosen marketing vehicles—are tough to answer in a rigorous and systematic manner. Moreover, answering these questions requires more emphasis on left-brain, analytical thinking, which does not play to every marketer's strong suit. This may explain why many companies still set overall investment levels and make allocation decisions based on last year's budget, plus or minus a few percentage points. We are not big fans of top-down approaches that do not take into account the relative effectiveness of each of the vehicles in helping to achieve the marketing objectives at hand, regardless of whether these top-down approaches are the carry-forward budgeting technique described earlier, share-of-voice analysis from an agency, a "best guess-timate" from somewhere in the C-suite, or what have you.

We believe that a more robust bottom-up approach, which incorporates a few rounds of iterative planning, analysis, and evaluation, can lead to better answers for the business, more systematic and focused priorities for the marketing team, and fewer risks for everyone. This bottom-up approach should take a few things into account, including

1. An outside-in, marketing-driven view of how much marketing volume is theoretically needed to achieve the respective customer-level behavioral outcomes that the financial plan requires

2. A business case–driven assessment of what the company can afford to invest in marketing communications, based on its profitability targets and current operating model

3. A smart application of your best available current knowledge of the inherent financial effectiveness of each of the marketing vehicles in your business or brand context

We are pragmatists at heart, of course, so if last year's budgeting process incorporated all of these analyses, then we would be happy to use last year's budget as a starting point! Seriously, though, we understand that getting here will take some time if your company falls into the Data-Starved, the Tactical Outsourcers, the Horsepower-Seeking, or the Harried But Trying MA proficiency segments. It may even take some time if you are in The Experts segment. The only thing we can be sure of is that the Not a Priority segment will be spending their energies climbing other mountains, perhaps to the delight of their increasingly MA-savvy competitors. But helping you get there at a pace that makes sense is the overriding purpose of this book, so carry on, carry on.

Behavioral Outcomes, Not Communication Outcomes

As we tackle this issue of investment levels, we believe that the right place to start is with the marketers and their ecosystem of partners. When there are both good dialogue and clear linkages between the business planning and marketing planning processes, marketers are well aware of what the business plan is calling for from a revenue and contribution margin standpoint. Moreover, they also intuitively or instinctively understand the way the proposed marketing vehicles behave and how our current and prospective customers are likely to respond to the various marketing tools in our arsenal. Media planners have a lot to add to this conversation, as do brand managers, creative types, marketing analysts, customer insight specialists, and strategic planners. So based on everything the marketers know and understand about customer behavior, our various marketing vehicles, and our business needs, how much marketing volume or dosing do they believe will be theoretically required to enable us to hit our operating targets without incurring excessive levels of risk of financial underperformance?

This may seem a little bit like giving the fox both the keys and the deed to the henhouse, but bear with us. The benefit of this kind of a bottom-up dosing assessment is that it forces everyone to be more transparent about the forecasted relationships between marketing inputs and business outcomes. In some ways it borrows from the old media planning concepts of reach and frequency, but rather than permitting everyone to stop at intermediate marketing outcomes like awareness or favorability, you would require everyone to drive the analysis down to the specific behavioral outcomes the business needs from individual customers and then to how that aggregates to the overall financial outcomes for the business. This also incorporates the idea of response rates and conversion rates from the direct marketing world. What we are arguing for is a rigorous analysis from the marketers that says "This is how much reach and frequency we will need, sourced by investing at these levels across these optimal marketing vehicles, to achieve this level of initial customer response, which will convert to this level of sales."

The idea is that all of the marketing programs should be driving toward encouraging the necessary behavioral response from the prospective targets—make an order, renew their policy, purchase another item, and so on—even if only indirectly at times. So the question back to the marketers is, how much marketing volume are they going to need to put into the market to ensure that enough of your prospective customer targets have had enough exposures across an adequately motivating mix of marketing vehicles to drive the right behavioral response? You can rephrase the question as, how much dosing or how many exposures to what mix of marketing vehicles is it going to take—not only to change the target audience's perceptions but to actually get enough of them to take the action that it is necessary for them to take so that the company hits its financial targets? The marketing team should see this as their "requirements definition" request, similar to what we would try to collect from our prospective users if we were designing a new product or software system for them. Ultimately we may need to scale back the design for cost or complexity reasons, or we may need to ask them to do some trade-off analysis to figure out their most important priorities, but at least it provides a starting point.

You may think that many marketers would be thrilled to think through the issues this way and provide this input, but you would be surprised how hesitant some are to dive in here. The stereotypical pushback might run something like this: "Our activities can only directly influence people's perceptions, not their behaviors, so we do not know how to plan around behavioral responses." As we stated back in Chapter Two, this ultimately is not an acceptable response. Now, we all understand that it usually takes more than seeing a billboard or a TV commercial to motivate a customer to take the right action. The proposition has to be right, the pricing has to be right, the belief in the service proposition has to be there, the timing has to be right—the list is endless. But ultimately we need to understand— perhaps through research techniques like choice modeling or through direct observation—the role that marketing programs play, however small or large, in contributing to those favorable behavioral outcomes that drive the business, either in the current period or in some future period. Moreover, we need to be able to confidently attribute some proportion of those favorable outcomes to the marketing investment alternatives in a rigorous and believable way.

A Quick Primer on Reach, Frequency, Response Rates, and Conversion Rates

If we can reorient the conversation toward behavioral outcomes as opposed to communication objectives, we believe the ideas of reach and frequency, and response and conversion rates, provide an excellent starting point for this analysis. For those of you less familiar with these terms, here is a quick primer. When media planners talk about "reach," what they mean is the percentage of your target audience or target customer group exposed to your marketing vehicles and messaging. It represents the total number of people exposed to the communication in a defined time frame; for example, targeting a 65-percent reach against a total universe of 10 million 18–35 males indicates that 6.5 million men will be exposed to this communication at least once over the life of the campaign. Reach measures the accumulation over time, so individuals are not double-counted. Frequency, on the other hand, represents the number of occasions on which any given individual will be exposed to the marketing vehicle. Keep in mind that an impression is a single potential exposure of a message to a member of your target audience.

When marketers talk about response rates and conversion rates, they are focusing on the productivity of the marketing vehicles themselves. If the company sends out a million of these promotional e-mails, how many of these pieces are going to generate some kind of a response, triggering either a visit to a store or a website or perhaps an inquiry to a call center? If forty thousand pieces are expected to generate a response, then your response rate is 4 percent. If five thousand pieces are expected to generate a response, then your response rate is 0.5 percent. One reason that Google's paid search offering has proved to be so popular is that marketers pay for the vehicle only each time it actually generates a response.

There is one last step in this cycle for the marketers to close the final loop, and that centers on the idea of conversion rates. Here you focus on how effective the company is in taking all of those responses generated by the marketing activities and converting those responses into actual sales. Do we convert our responses to sales at a 20-percent rate or a 2-percent rate? This is really about the final few stages of the purchase funnel, when the rest of the proposition is expected to take over to help convert marketing response into a sale. Although a company may have some systemic problems with its proposition that lowers its overall conversion rates, most people also look at differences in conversion rates as an indication of the *quality* of the responses that different types of marketing vehicles generate. Vehicles with higher relative conversion rates are perceived to be generating higher-quality responses, meaning those vehicles are more effective at finding and appealing to customers who are naturally attracted to our proposition.

Now, we acknowledge that certain kinds of marketing vehicles—those that are addressable to individual customers (like direct) and those that have great sales response traceability (like POS, most internet vehicles, and mobile)—allow for a more straightforward execution of this kind of analysis. We also understand that some marketing vehicles, by design, may not promote a favorable sales response in this operating period but may do so in some future period. But ultimately more advanced research and modeling techniques can be used to attribute these kinds of productivity characteristics to all of the vehicles in the marketing portfolio. The confidence intervals for some of the less directly traceable vehicles may be wider at times, but at least this starts to give you the basis for an apples-to-apples comparison.

How Different Market, Media, and Messaging Factors Can Dramatically Affect Your Dosing Requirements

We believe that all marketing plans are ultimately about assessing how different combinations of reach (what percentage of what kind of customer audience you are targeting) and frequency (how many times you are going to hit them with a message or an offer) across the various marketing vehicles can be used to trigger a certain level of response that converts to specific levels of sales. Ideally, your company's historical response rate and conversion rate performance, at different reach and frequency combinations across the various vehicles, can help you establish a baseline to inform your dosing requirements analysis. Communications experts also have general rules of thumb to help you understand how many times an individual needs to be exposed to a message before it sinks in. Your own customer research should help you understand how likely you are to get a response from someone in your target audience after your message has sunk in. So this is where you start to do the rigorous, bottom-up planning. Even if you do not have a lot of this kind of productivity data at your fingertips, bringing this kind of discipline to your planning will expose the holes in your understanding and push the team to close its knowledge gaps.

However, it will not be enough to just look at your historical productivity data, especially if you are worried that the historical response and conversion patterns may not hold in your future environment. We know that response rates change over time. Marketing campaigns may fatigue, the competitive proposition may strengthen, or a chosen media vehicle may lose its audience. New pressures in the environment may change how much marketing is actually required to grab people's attention and get them to focus on your proposition or your offer. We think that the Ostrow Model of Effective Frequency[12] provides a good framework for incorporating these forward-looking factors into your overall planning process. Ultimately, you may need to modify your dosing requirements up or down based on a number of characteristics throughout the environment; some market-related, some message-related, and some marketing vehicle–related. Let's start with the market-related factors.

With the market-related factors, the core issues concern characteristics of the brand or product that is being supported, as well as characteristics of the category and the strategic customer target (as shown in Figure 5.7). In situations in which you are working with an established brand, with high share and high loyalty, your dosing requirements to drive a similar response level should be lower—sometimes dramatically lower. However, if you are working with a new brand or one that has low share or low loyalty, you are facing more of an uphill battle, which may require significantly heavier

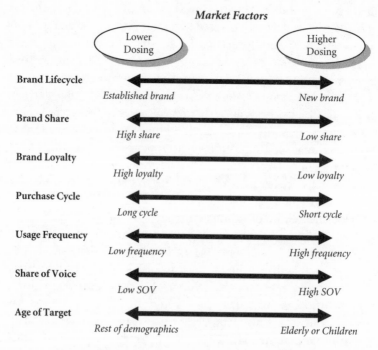

Figure 5.7.   Market Factors Affecting the Extent
of Required Dosing Adjustments

frequency of marketing touches. In a similar vein, categories with long purchase cycles and lower usage frequency may require less dosing to stimulate an adequate level of response, whereas categories with short purchase cycles and high usage frequencies typically require significantly more.

The characteristics of the message also influence how much dosing or frequency may be required to achieve the right level of customer response. The strength, uniqueness, freshness, and relevance of the message all are big drivers in determining how many times consumers need to hear it before it grabs their attention. Although you should be in a never-ending quest to look for compelling ways to improve, strengthen, and simplify your messages over time, this is really about optimizing within the constraints of your existing messaging alternatives in any specific period of time. So if the messaging has high complexity, low uniqueness, or an emotional, image-oriented focus, you will probably need higher than average frequency to achieve the right behavioral response, as depicted in Figure 5.8. In a similar way,

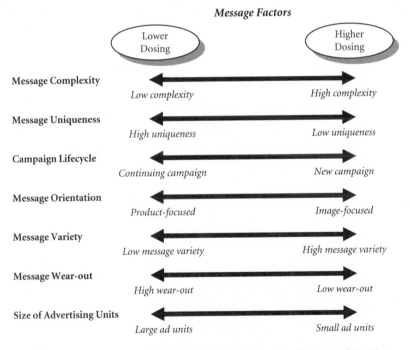

Figure 5.8.   Message Factors Affecting the Extent of Required Dosing Adjustments

a new marketing campaign, or a campaign with high message variety or low anticipated wear-out, will also need higher than average frequency.

Finally, you may need to adjust your required dosing strategy based on characteristics specific to the marketing vehicle and media environment. For example, if you anticipate that your strategic customer target will be operating in a low-clutter environment with a high degree of attentiveness, then you can probably achieve acceptable response levels with fewer overall touches. However, if you are operating with a high variety of marketing vehicles, all with fairly neutral editorial settings, and none of which guarantee a high degree of repeat exposure to the message, then you may need to add additional frequency to your dosing requirements analysis (see Figure 5.9).

Obviously, all of these assertions can be empirically tested with your systematic approach to experimentation over time. But these guidelines are consistent with general understanding of consumer behavior and how consumers respond to different kinds of information, from different sources, provided in different media contexts, so

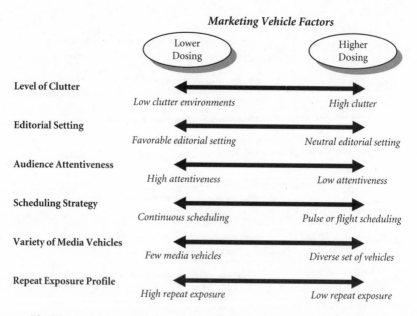

Figure 5.9.   Media Vehicle Factors Affecting the Extent of Required Dosing Adjustments

they provide a good starting point. You can use them to apply some educated upward or downward adjustments to your dosing requirements assessment as you arrive at your final answer.

USING BUSINESS CASE THINKING AND ADVANCED MARKETING ANALYTICS TO TRIANGULATE ON YOUR BEST ANSWER

In the previous section we spent some time adopting the point of view of the marketing experts, allowing them to make the case for how different combinations of market, message, and media factors can work together to make it harder or easier for the marketing investments to get the job done and trigger enough of the right kinds of perceptual and behavioral responses in our target audiences to meet the business plan. In a sense, this kind of thinking helps shape the theoretical volume requirements for our marketing activities. It is like someone saying "Hey, I am an expert in how marketing activities and media affect consumer perceptions and behavior, and given all your particular circumstances, this is how much marketing volume you are going to need to get the job done!" These frameworks are based on solid theories about consumer behavior and media impact, supported by some empirical data and industry observation, and as such, an analysis based on these frameworks should serve as a good starting point. We can think of this as "the ask."

In addition to this, however, we need to incorporate the points of view of the marketing analyst, the financial analyst, and yes, even the CFO, to start to triangulate on the right overall answer for the business. Hmmm, you say; what do we mean by this? We mean two different things, to be exact. The first is that we need to bring a business case mind-set to these investment-level questions, and stress test different scenarios around what the business can theoretically afford to invest in these kinds of marketing activities. The second is that we need to incorporate a robust fact base on the absolute and relative effectiveness of all of these different marketing vehicles for our business and to use this historical performance data to shape our decision making around investment levels and relative allocation. If you work in a company that has little existing knowledge about the relative or absolute returns of your marketing vehicles, note that in the third part of the book we will take you through a detailed primer on how to "up" your marketing ROI fluency, so soldier on. Suffice to say that many companies start with some marketing vehicle–specific, point-in-time financial return analysis, and that best practice companies are using a combination of advanced marketing analytic techniques—including choice modeling, econometric modeling, and portfolio optimization, and a test-and-learn orientation—to continually deepen and solidify that fact base.

Of course, because there is no intrinsic ROI for any vehicle and few published track records that you can use as a template, it is difficult to set an optimal investment level for any of them without some company-specific effectiveness data. Correctly identifying the optimal investment level requires a significant amount of historical spend and performance information. Companies that have tracked marketing investment over a long period of time (P&G, for example) have tested a number of different investment ranges, for marketing vehicles overall as well as for each specific marketing vehicle; this has allowed them to establish a more precise view of the theoretical boundary conditions for their marketing investment portfolio, a concept some refer to as the *efficient frontier* of marketing investment (see Figure 5.10). If your company does this, over time you will gradually be able to quantitatively ascertain where the efficient frontier of marketing investment may be for your brands at any given point in time.

On a conceptual level, the efficient frontier is elegant. It incorporates the idea, supported by the academic literature, that returns on most marketing investments exhibit diminishing returns to scale and that there are natural theoretical and actual limits to the absolute level of sales response that any portfolio of marketing investments can be expected to generate. So you can quickly identify what types of sales response expectations are clearly unrealistic based on your historical marketing performance, as well as what kinds of aggregate investment levels dramatically decrease marginal returns. You will also be able to more effectively identify and optimize relative portfolio allocations, understanding efficient frontier performance benchmarks. The challenge, of course, is that the location, shape, and slope of your company's efficient frontier is going to evolve over time—at times dynamically—based on the strength of your propositions, the actions of competitors, changes in market structure, and your ability to systematically improve your performance on any and all of the other five MA value levers (strategy, creative, vehicles, execution, and fixed cost management). Nonetheless, it remains an elegant way to frame the end game of investment level management, and it can

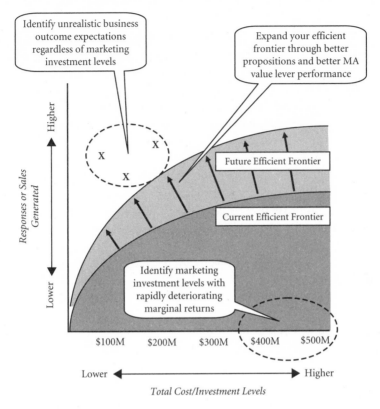

Figure 5.10. Using the Concept of the Efficient Frontier to Drive Your Orientation Toward Marketing Investment Levels

serve as an effective communication tool to help senior executives understand your broader agenda for achieving highly accountable marketing performance.

Now that we understand the end game, let's get back to the basic building blocks.

What Can the Business Currently Afford? Creating a Base Case Affordability Read

First, we need to answer the question of what the business can theoretically afford to invest in marketing communications. In the short term, the sticky nature of most companies' operating models—with a pattern of hard-wired business practices, preexisting sources of volume, and the heavy sunk costs associated with supporting these practices—creates a fair amount of rigidity in the system. Although this may seem like a chicken-and-egg question, because some marketing investments purport to grow the top line and perhaps pay for themselves, the conservative way to approach this analysis does not bank on too much incremental revenue growth or self-funding promises with the incremental investment, especially if it is not supported by rigorous customer-level lift analysis or more robust financial effectiveness data for the proposed vehicle types.

So when confronted with this type of short-term context, the question to ask is, how much can the business afford to invest in marketing vehicles without skating too close to the edge, all other things being equal? If the company has typically invested at a 2-percent-of-revenues level, could it afford 2.5 percent? If the company typically invested at a 25-percent-of-revenues level, could it afford 27 percent or 28 percent, or conversely, does new competitive pressure on product margins require it to reset the bar at a 15-percent or 18-percent level? Typically, if you have a good understanding of the operating P&L and margin targets, coupled with a good understanding of the capital deployment process, you can generally arrive at a reasonable set of upper and lower ranges, or boundary conditions, for preliminary affordability estimates.

A more disruptive way to think about this would be to challenge some of the conventional operating assumptions and belief systems throughout the business, trying to ascertain whether there are some opportunities to profitably redeploy existing non-marketing vehicle investment toward incremental investment in marketing vehicles. For example, if we were to consider stopping use of a specific channel of distribution, for which we pay 17-percent commissions, and attempted to source more of that volume directly, would the business be better off? What kind of incremental investment in the offer and in marketing vehicles would be required to support that transition? What if we were investing a lot in store-level promotions to keep our unit volumes high because our products had high price elasticity? If we explored diverting some of the promotional dollars toward brand-equity building tactics and holding the line on pricing, would the business be better off? If so, what could we afford to invest in marketing vehicles in that scenario? Of course, we referred to this approach as disruptive for a reason. Not only does it explore alternatives that may feel highly risky for the business, especially during the transitional phase, but it will also stir up a firestorm of political resistance from all of the places in the business with a vested interest in protecting the status quo. You may still end up getting the company to consider some truly compelling new ideas that are ultimately in its best interest, but you should have your battle armor on.

A different, and perhaps more pragmatic, way to approach this question of how much the business can afford to invest in marketing vehicles is to anchor it around customer-level economics, via customer-level profitability or customer lifetime value. Although many companies still do not have systems that are easily set up to look at customer-level economics, the intensive CRM-related technology investments of the past decade have laid the foundation for more of this recently. The idea is to use a much more rigorous, financially based view of the value of a customer account or customer relationship to determine how much the company can afford to spend to acquire and then to retain that customer. You need good cost accounting discipline to attribute your costs down to the individual customer level, and then you need to have a good understanding of the cross-sell, up-sell, repeat purchase, and account renewal patterns of your customers or prospective customers to understand the potential revenue stream that could be attributed to a specific kind of customer over time. Ultimately this will allow you to estimate the lifetime value of a current or prospective customer, which can then be used to determine what the company can truly afford to invest in marketing. Wireless carriers and credit card companies are the kinds of companies that have pushed this thinking the furthest and have used it to dramatically reorient their guideposts for what the company can afford to invest in marketing, although it is not without its own set of complications.

Absolute and Relative Returns of Alternative Vehicles

Once you have stepped through the affordability analysis, which helps set the general marketing investment parameters for any planning cycle, you need to assemble and apply the company's working body of knowledge about the absolute and relative returns of the alternative marketing vehicles under consideration. The typical company usually starts with a hodgepodge of effectiveness insights, which we refer to as your company's existing marketing ROI understanding (covered in much greater depth in Chapter Eight). Even if all you have is a dog's breakfast of data points and random analyses about the absolute and relative returns of various marketing vehicles, that still needs to get aggregated to help you form your starting point for this round of decision making.

As we mentioned earlier, we have a robust way of determining the optimal investment level for each specific vehicle and for marketing overall; it is an iterative, analytically driven technique that we call *dynamic optimization,* covered in depth in the latter half of Chapter Nine. It includes a combination of various research and analytic techniques to more rigorously ascertain the absolute and relative effectiveness of various marketing investment alternatives. We use choice modeling to best understand what drives customers to make specific purchase decisions and the impact of potential company investments on that purchase choice. We use point-in-time return modeling and econometric modeling to get at absolute returns and the elasticities, or relative returns, of each vehicle, as well as to better understand the interaction effects or portfolio effects that occur when vehicles are used in combination. Figure 5.11 displays representative elasticity curves for some marketing vehicles in a long purchase cycle, B2B, U.S. market context. We recommend then using different types of simulation and predictive optimization approaches to determine the optimal

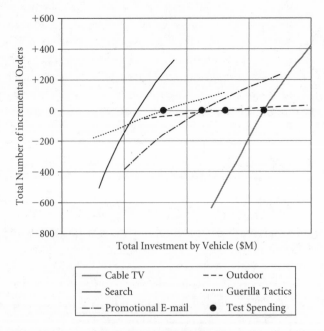

Figure 5.11.   Sample Projected Order Elasticities by Type
of Marketing Vehicle

budget allocation over time. Even though the intrinsic effectiveness of vehicles is evolving over time, with changing media consumption patterns and market factors, dynamic optimization provides a closed-loop process to continually refresh and update our knowledge about relative and absolute returns over time.

For the time being, however, you will start wherever you start. Unless you are in the 16 percent of the market that self-assessed in The Experts segment (see Figure 3.7 for a refresher), you probably have some holes in your understanding. But even given that, the rules are pretty simple. Vehicles with higher absolute return levels and higher elasticities should go to the top of your list. Vehicles with lower absolute return levels and lower elasticities go toward the bottom of your list. You may want to convert these return numbers into some standard, easily comparable metric, like the "ad cost" metric used by direct marketing businesses (marketing vehicle spend/allocated revenues generated) or another form of ROI metric. These now compose your list of vehicles with proven returns, and they should form your starting point for investment level planning. (We will get to the second list, the one with all of the vehicles with unknown returns on it, in a moment.)

As you begin to apply the effectiveness data that you have, it is important to remember two things. First, there can be a high degree of variability in terms of the confidence intervals for any given set of absolute and relative return measures. Some vehicles have ROI assessments with very small confidence intervals, meaning historically these vehicles have very narrow performance bands and behave very predictably. Other vehicles, which may have the exact same nominal absolute returns and elasticities as the previous set, could have very wide confidence intervals around those estimates. So even though at face value both sets of vehicles appear to have the same return profile, the second set actually has very wide performance bands, meaning these vehicles perform very unpredictably. You need to factor this in to build more of a risk-adjusted view of potential returns. Second, you should keep in mind that the majority of companies have historically invested in marketing vehicles within fairly narrow ranges, so the return estimates reflect only those historical spending patterns. If any potential vehicle-specific investments are being considered that fall dramatically outside of those ranges, those absolute and relative return ratios may start to break down.

For our marketing vehicles with proven returns, we also have to start to capture how much incremental investment any given vehicle may be able to take without dramatically eroding its economics. Do any of the proven vehicles have the capacity for profitable, incremental investment? Theoretically that is what the elasticity curves are designed to measure, but there may be execution-based constraints on inventory, list availability, and so on that impede our ability to scale those activities. For example, you may have a series of search marketing or catalog marketing campaigns that have incredibly high returns at say, a $3,000,000 investment level. Could you feasibly double or triple your investment in these vehicles without compromising their return? On the search marketing side, you might have to bid on a wider variety of key words that might be less relevant to your brand or perhaps be willing to pay more for better placement on the key words that you are already purchasing. On the catalog marketing side, you may need to find an additional 750,000 or 1,500,000 names that you could mail to profitably. Are either of these scenarios realistic or feasible? At any given moment, the productivity that you can expect any given vehicle to generate may have hit a theoretical ceiling, and to attempt to put more investment behind is not financially prudent.

Finally, in this analysis you need to make an informed judgment as to what to do with the vehicles and programs—perhaps the vast majority—that fall into the unproven returns column. Obviously our long-term recommendation is to use the dynamic optimization approach to move them out of the unproven column. But in the short term, we recommend classifying them into three categories— those believed to be effective, at least anecdotally; those with highly questionable effectiveness; and those with unknown effectiveness. Although this last component is not data-supported, at least we now have a starting point for building an investment plan.

Iterative bottom-up planning and analysis process. We believe that these three different analyses—(1) the theoretical marketing dosing requirements (in terms of reach and frequency) from the previous discussion, (2) the base case affordability read, and (3) the absolute and relative performance estimates per vehicle—form the foundation for investment-level decision making. We recommend that you use these to guide an iterative bottom-up planning and analysis process to ultimately land on your recommended overall investment level and your allocation by vehicle. Each round of this process has three separate deliverables: (1) a hypothetical investment allocation by marketing vehicle, (2) a supporting cost analysis that stress tests the feasibility

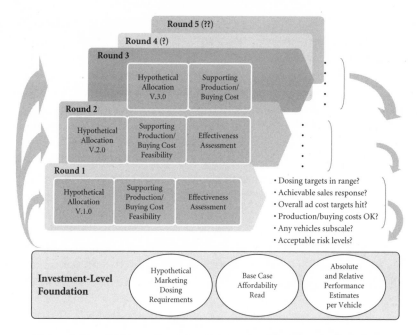

Figure 5.12. Using an Iterative, Bottom-up Planning and Analysis Process to Make Final Investment-Level Decisions

of producing and procuring the recommended allocation within the budget parameters specified, and (3) an effectiveness assessment, which answers six key questions, as highlighted in Figure 5.12.

By comparing and contrasting the findings across the three foundational analyses, you should begin to have a good sense of any potential friction points. The dosing analysis may point you in the direction of certain vehicles at specific investment levels, whereas the affordability and ROI estimates may point you in different directions. We feel it makes sense to build a hypothetical allocation version 1.0 around your proven vehicles first. If you put all of your proven vehicles in up to their theoretical efficient frontier capacity, can you confidently hit your business requirements? If you are still pretty far off, we encourage you to start to pull from your list of vehicles whose financial returns are unproven but that are believed to be effective. Go down to this next set of alternatives and look at how different combinations of them help you close the gap in terms of your business objectives, your dosing objectives, and your marketing efficiency objectives. Eventually you should lock down on v. 1.0 of your hypothetical allocation.

Now you have to do two other important things. First, work with people on the production, planning, and buying side to ensure that the cost estimates you have identified for producing and procuring your hypothetical allocation are achievable. Sometimes production cost estimates are too optimistic, especially for new vehicles. Sometimes seasonal activities, like a U.S. presidential election or a summer Olympics, may be episodically driving up inventory costs. So it never hurts to have someone gut check the cost estimates.

Second, run through a thorough effectiveness assessment of this allocation. In particular, you want to stress test this allocation from a number of different effectiveness and efficiency angles. Is there a large variance between the dosing supplied by this allocation and the hypothetical dosing requirements identified earlier? If so, what is driving that variance? Are your ROI criteria steering you away from providing the investment levels to vehicles that could help achieve the dosing targets? Does the predicted sales response or sales lift anticipated from this allocation seem reasonable? Just as important, does it comfortably allow you to hit the business plan? Does this allocation allow you to manage your overall "ad cost" to acceptable levels? And how much risk is there to those efficiency estimates? At the proposed investment levels, are any of the vehicles in at a subscale? The ratio of fixed costs to working costs may be too high for certain kinds of programs if the allocated budget is too small. Or the amount that you are willing to invest may be too small to deliver to meet the minimum thresholds for impact in a given vehicle. Finally, how do you feel about the overall risk profile of the recommended allocation? Are you trying to tackle too many things, which may overwhelm your execution capabilities? Are you putting too much of your budget into programs that cannot effectively scale?

An open and forthright discussion of these kinds of questions should allow you to complete a fairly robust SWOT analysis of your first hypothetical allocation. Following this kind of process through several rounds of planning and analysis should allow you to finally triangulate on an answer to the investment level issue that is best for you, given your current body of knowledge about the short-term and long-term financial returns from your various marketing investments. As we have said earlier, it is better to be directionally correct than precisely wrong—and it is especially important with this value lever. In the early days, do not overweight precise accountability at the expense of potential effectiveness. Finally, make sure that you are creating enough room in your marketing investment pool to test new programs and vehicles that could prove to be the next big thing for your business. The only way for the business to not be caught flat-footed is to look for ways to continually renew its portfolio of profitable marketing investment opportunities from within.

CHAPTER SIX

In-Market Execution and Fixed Cost Management

Ensuring High-Quality In-Market Execution and Consistently Strong Leverage of Your Fixed Cost Basis

T opics covered in Chapter Six:

- Tactical planning decisions: where the rubber meets the road
- Buying, delivering, and auditing marketing investments for a cross-platform world
- Applying procurement discipline to marketing fixed cost management
- Unearthing higher-risk—but higher-reward—savings opportunities
- Strategic sourcing and agency partners: how far is too far?

> *Execution is the missing link between aspirations and results.*
> *—Larry Bossidy*
> *Obviously the highest kind of efficiency is that which can utilize existing material to the best advantage.*
> *—Jawaharlal Nehru*

TACTICAL PLANNING DECISIONS: WHERE THE RUBBER MEETS THE ROAD

In-market execution provides the fifth marketing accountability value lever. How are you going to connect to your customer in a timely and, increasingly, multimedia platform way? Most of you realize that once you've developed the strategy, brainstormed compelling creative executions, and made thoughtful choices to balance marketing vehicles with investment priorities, you're only halfway to your goal. Only flawless in-market execution ensures that your messaging ideas reach and successfully connect with customers.

Take the case of the marketing of Revlon's Vital Radiance line. Its target was the increasingly strong market for older women; it had the powerful Revlon brand behind it and a substantive budget. Yet poor execution doomed the campaign. According to *The Wall Street Journal*, "The Vital Radiance line failed largely because of marketing missteps. For example, it didn't incorporate the well-known Revlon brand name, hired unrecognizable models as spokeswomen and cost more than consumers cared to spend."[1] The result: the CEO was fired and the company lost millions, laid off 10 percent of its workforce, and scrapped its marketing strategy.

Such high-profile marketing failures, coupled with the increasing difficulty of making the choices among myriad marketing vehicles, whose pros and cons often don't balance out (as shown in Chapter Five) have caused many marketers to hesitate before making decisions—despite the growing array of new opportunities. For example, even as the size of the U.S. internet audience begins to plateau, marketers cling to old favorites like sponsorships. A study by the Yankee Group found that ad dollars have not caught up to internet use. In 2006, advertisers spent less than one-third as much on-line as they did on TV ads.[2]

We would contend, however, that successful marketers do not hesitate but rather develop a cohesive strategy—and then do what it takes to make certain that marketing execution is world-class. They make certain that the customer's experience is consistent and integrated and that marketing messages sent via one medium reinforce the customers' experience with messages learned from other touch points.

In short, successful companies take the strategy and creative execution idea and translate it effectively across all of the implementation opportunities. Winners taken into account the idiosyncrasies of each opportunity in terms of format and medium and in terms of implementation and effective execution. They get the in-market execution basics right. Then they masterfully orchestrate the holistic in-market experience for a customer in light of the totality of their active programs. Although each piece needs flawless execution, the whole composition must make sense to the customer.

The difficulty of decision making and degree of in-market execution risk vary somewhat depending on the type of marketing vehicles in your mix. Tactical planning for most traditional one-way marketing "communications" vehicles—such as advertising, internet marketing, or direct mail—includes three key stages:

- Stage One: The buying process that helps secure actual inventory
- Stage Two: The physical or virtual delivery of the marketing message
- Stage Three: The auditing of the delivered marketing programs, media or otherwise

Tactical planning of more live, experiential marketing vehicles—such as sponsorships, trade shows, business-to-business events, and even most viral or guerilla marketing tactics—includes the same three stages. But your ability to consistently deliver high-production-value experiences every time the program is in market is significantly more complicated. These marketing formats are by their very nature more difficult to control than traditional one-way communications formats, once they get in field. As a result, your level of in-market execution risk and variability is much higher than that encountered in more traditional marketing programs.

Before you concentrate on tactical considerations, of course you will have ironed out the strategy of the overall media plan, including strategic customer target identification and prioritization, the reach required to hit the stated business goals, and the frequency and timing needed to achieve the desired perceptual or behavioral outcomes. You will have made strategic choices in the context of iterative trade-off conversations around marketing vehicles and investment levels, as discussed in Chapter Five.

To finalize your marketing campaign, however, you must make myriad tactical planning decisions. These tactical decisions determine whether your campaign will thrive or flounder. As a result, they are made only after thoughtful analysis and consideration of five key dimensions, as highlighted in Figure 6.1: mapping of the media audience to the strategic target, editorial and contextual synergy, geographic breadth, scheduling and flighting, and depth of buy. You and your planning partners should really understand all aspects of your high-priority strategic customer targets, based on thorough research of off-line and on-line media consumption patterns, as well as real insights into their openness to participate in experiential marketing activities. If you have such an insight-rich, quantitatively based, and relatively recent level of customer understanding, you will be in a strong position to make highly effective tactical planning decisions.

Media Audience Mapping

The first tactical dimension involves a detailed analysis of the audience profiles of media properties or experiential marketing venues you are considering in light of your strategic target customer. Initial research should not only help you understand the media that cater

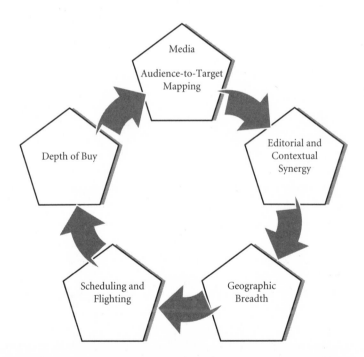

Figure 6.1.   Five Dimensions to Your Tactical Planning Efforts

directly to your strategic targets but also your target's responsiveness to different placements and ad formats. Next, you must align these generic profiles, which are typically based on generic demographic information, with more nuanced—and specific—strategic target segment identification.

Such strategic segment analysis can be challenging, as it adds aspects of attitudinal, behavioral, and contextual data to the insights from demographic data. Even though strategic segment analysis gets trickier as your targeting requirements narrow, such a robust and careful research process will help ensure that tactical planning choices deliver the expected benefits of your media strategy.

The data services offered by larger research houses can help you create the right profiles of audiences across mature media vehicles. With the rapidly evolving nature of media consumption patterns, especially of the under-thirty-five crowd, however, many marketers cannot find robust data that adequately reflects the recent momentum for any given vehicle. Some newer services have popped up to fill in this gap, democratizing the provision of audience metrics across media properties—services like Quantcast's Open Internet Ratings. These services provide a rich and transparent set of metrics for pro-filed on-line properties. They also attempt to estimate the level of engagement and passion for each property's audience, which is an important dimension of audience mapping. Some successful market-ers also supplement these information sources with custom media consumption studies for strategic customer targets. These studies will often provide the best hedge in trying to determine an individual media property audience's precise fit with your target.

Editorial and Contextual Synergy

Optimizing the editorial, contextual, or behavioral synergies from placement strategies is the next tactical planning dimension. Best practice demonstrates that you optimize the probability that your strategic target will be in the right frame of mind to receive and inter-nalize your marketing message if you deliver that message in specific contexts. Using that logic, a marketer promoting a new face cream for women asks, "Would my print advertising be more noticed and effec-tive next to an article on health and beauty tips or next to a celebrity lifestyle feature?" In like manner, the marketer would also determine whether the text ad would be more effective if displayed when people use Google to search for "wrinkles" or "anti-aging," and whether a banner ad is more effective if placed on the Yahoo! home page or the within the Yahoo! Lifestyles section.

Asking these questions and finding data-driven answers is increasingly important. Given the on-line world's traceability and flexibility, some studies show 20-percent to 30-percent lifts in effectiveness from contextual and behavioral targeting. You can apply similar logic to making tactical planning decisions for many types of marketing vehicles; the objective is to increase the probability that your target will receive your marketing message at the point of optimal relevance— for the target!

Geographic Breadth

The breadth of your intended geographic coverage is another avenue for major tactical planning. Whether you chose a national, multiregional, or local strategy depends on existing business strength and the growth opportunity in a specific market. Because media companies in the United States offer significantly lower pricing for national, up-front buys versus geo-targeted inventory in the spot market, mass market brands with national distribution gravitate to the cost efficiency of national campaigns. Because many companies have a high degree of local or regional variance, they do not have enough budget to provide uniform support across their geographic footprint. Other factors, including the widespread adoption of digital cable—which allows for zip-code or even household-level targeting with TV—and the emergence of disruptive players like Google in radio and Spot Runner in TV erode some of the cost advantages of national buys in traditional media. As a result of the aggressive marketing campaigns run by these new entrants, more and more companies are exploring geo-targeted campaigns.

Another important aspect concerns the use of the Brand Development Index/Category Development Index (BDI/CDI). Whether you're considering an overlay to a national media buy or simply want to target your marketing efforts geographically, the indices compare your business concentration (BDI) or the category's concentration (CDI) in various markets against the population. The index is a simple ratio comparing the percentage of business, either for your company or for the category, in a given geography to the percentage population in that geography, multiplied by 100. For example, if Chicago accounts for 2.3 percent of the U.S. population but also counts for 3.0 percent of your company's sales, then the BDI for Chicago is 130: significantly better-than-average performance. A company can buy according to its own business strength, the category strength, or some combination. When making media buys, companies look for concentration with an index of 120 or more for additional/overlay support in strong areas. You might not advertise if very low BDI and CDI indicate either the category or your proposition is potentially irrelevant.

Scheduling and Flighting

The fourth tactical planning dimension deals with scenarios for scheduling and potential flighting. Scheduling refers to the tactical marketing choice of the day, week, or month a marketing vehicle should be active or live in field. Scheduling choices are traditionally based on factors such as

- Whether seasonality makes a difference
- The frequency of the purchase cycle (for example, does the average customer buy the product once every three years—such as a BMW—or once every three hours—such as a Starbucks decaf nonfat latté?)
- The length of the typical sales cycle (that is, how long the customer consciously researches or considers alternatives before actually making a purchase—for example, ninety seconds or ninety days?)

The importance of scheduling is clear: if you manage a brand that does 55 percent of its sales in the month of December, and one priority segment starts considering purchases thirty to forty-five days before the sale, whereas another segment buys on impulse, your marketing vehicles should be in field by late October and stay heavy through December. This scheduling decision is obvious; unfortunately, most are not.

Typically, marketers combine their brand and category-level insights so that they can choose from three basic approaches to scheduling—continuity, flighting, or pulsing. Continuity scheduling spreads the marketing investment evenly across the year, providing a steady and consistent exposure of your brand and its messaging to the target audience. Continuity scheduling is appropriate, for example, if your category is hypercompetitive, your sales are spread evenly throughout the year, and you fear rapid decay rates in recall and consideration when marketing is silent. Be warned, however, that continuity scheduling can be very expensive. It could be necessary to underserve your reach and frequency goals to spread your budget evenly across the year.

In contrast, flighting alternates "live" periods when the marketing vehicles are in the field with "dark" periods when the marketing vehicles are not. Standard rotations may involve six weeks on, six weeks off, or eight weeks on, four weeks off. Flighting works well when your business has strong seasonality skews or when you are less likely to see dramatic decay rates during your dark cycles, perhaps because category decision making is slow. Pulsing combines a lower maintenance level of continuity throughout the year, with "heavy up" periods of flighting. Pulsing and flighting are cost-effective if your target audience and reach and frequency objectives remain the same during live periods. Often, however, many companies adopt flighting or pulsing even though they are also adjusting the reach and frequency objectives to more intense levels. As a result, the hypothetical cost savings never materialize.

Whatever your final decision, it is important that your scheduling decisions reflect your best knowledge about your customer and your competitive context. Putting marketing investments in the market that miss critical windows of opportunity or create huge competitive openings has proven fatal to the careers of many marketers.

The Depth of Buy

The fifth and final dimension of tactical planning involves the depth of buy. Into what depth of the customer or prospect list will you mail? Into how broad a range of magazine titles, TV shows, or radio programs will you advertise? Will you mail only to prospective targets with anticipated response rates that keep your overall marketing costs below 10 percent per revenue dollar generated, or are you willing to mail to lower-yield prospective targets with anticipated response rates that drive overall marketing costs to 35 percent per revenue dollar generated?

Although this is a direct marketing example, you will frame the same types of questions for any type of marketing vehicle. Although the decision may seem pretty straightforward, your overall business model should set the boundaries of marketing spend as a percentage of revenues. In that case, you would include only tactical alternatives that meet the criteria.

Of course, almost no business decision is that straightforward. First, changes in individual customer-level profitability, customer retention rates, and cross-selling success levels can drive significant changes in customer life-cycle value estimates, which can dramatically alter the amount a company can spend to acquire a new customer. Second, the theoretically anticipated ROIs for tactical marketing alternatives are usually not well understood. Hitting the sales goals for a quarter may require more lead flow than the highest-ROI marketing alternatives can deliver. So marketers need to apply their best business judgment to decide how deep the business needs them to go with the buy. The business could hold the line on anticipated cost per lead (or cost per sales or ad) even if it means putting the sales plan at risk. Or it could move into lower-yield tactical planning choices that will put marketing ROI at risk but provide some insurance that you will hit the sales targets.

We developed Figure 6.2 to illustrate how you can best consider this challenge. There are twenty-five different tactical placement choices, each with a potential ad cost, reflected as a percentage of revenues. These ad cost estimates may be based on the actual historical performance of each alternative. Or we could hypothetically derive these estimates, based on the percentage overlap of the specific property's audience with our target audience and the alternative's contextual or behavioral relevance. If we drew a hard line around the 10-percent ad cost, only three of these tactical alternatives would make the cut. If we pushed the ad cost boundary to 20 percent, we could add another nine titles, programs, or customer list sources. But would those twelve tactical alternatives be enough to confidently guarantee the results expected from the sales plan, or does the buy need to go deeper to reduce top-line risks even if it impacts marketing profitability?

Of course, most companies are rarely confident enough to place their tactical alternatives on a grid like this. Over time, you can use this kind of approach as part of a close-looped marketing accountability process to make explicit trade-offs between top-line growth and bottom-line profitability for any given period.

By considering all five tactical planning dimensions—media audience mapping, editorial synergy, geographic synergy, scheduling and

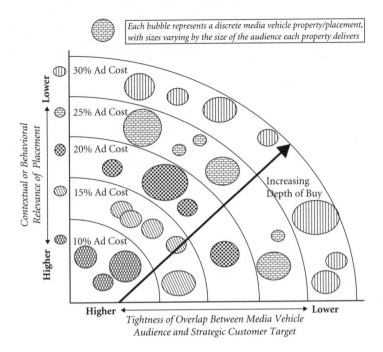

Figure 6.2. Using Audience Mapping and Relevance Screens to Plot Specific Properties and Inform Your Depth of Buy

flighting, and the depth of the buy—you should move closer to optimizing your in-market activities and making your overall execution more efficient. As Figure 6.3 illustrates, companies operate with a tactical marketing mix that falls well below the efficient frontier. As you gradually fine-tune your tactical buying choices, you could choose to migrate horizontally along the x-axis and lower the overall cost necessary to generate the same amount of demand, or you could migrate vertically along the y-axis and generate dramatically more demand for the same basic investment levels.

BUYING, DELIVERING, AND AUDITING YOUR MARKETING INVESTMENTS IN A CROSS-PLATFORM WORLD

Each time CMOs get past the strategic and tactical planning stages, they are still faced with the reality of an increasingly complex and

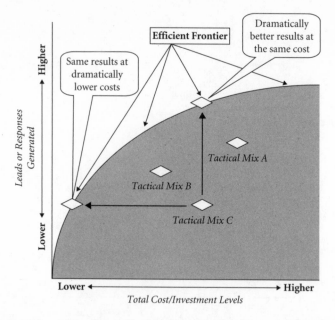

Figure 6.3.   Make Smart Tactical Planning Decisions to Drive Your Programs Out to the Efficient Frontier

expensive process to actually buy the right marketing inventory and ensure that the inventory has been delivered in field as expected, and they also face the added complexity of coordinating all of these activities in a harmonious way so that the view to the consumer is seamless.

Winning companies always step back at this point and analyze the reality of the next stage in the process—how the budgeted money actually gets put to work and how to determine whether the money has bought you what you paid for. Starting with a look at the traditional communications vehicles, we will review how best to buy each vehicle, audit the expected results, and ensure that your in-field execution is flawless—in a marketing world that is increasingly focused on making the most of the opportunities provided by cross-platforms.

Buying Traditional Marketing Communications Vehicles

Up until this point, the marketer is dealing in a theoretical world; now he or she must secure the inventory with an actual buy. Most

companies hire a third-party agency to help with the buying process, although some will cut deals directly with the individual media
or property owners. Some players maintain that more cost-efficient
buying processes can shave as much as 5 to 15 percent from a marketing budget greater than $50 million—typically by combining better
negotiated list rates and better realized pricing. If a buyer can combine such efficiency with small but consistent moves toward slightly
higher-quality inventory, the overall gains can be even greater.

With the explosion of vehicle alternatives and the rapidly changing economic landscape for some traditional media alternatives like
newspaper or broadcast TV, it is more difficult to get desired inventory at the best price. Although new data services help you benchmark your pricing for specific inventory against what others spend,
it is still a challenge to determine whether you are consistently enjoy-
ing the best available pricing. Given this increasing price complexity,
media companies are of course coming up with creative ways to create
win-win situations for advertisers. But they may muddy the overall
economics, either by working with traditional purchasing tactics like
volume discounts, up-front commitments, and cross-property bundling or by using some newer approaches like new-media and cross-
property bundling. Being open to such creative opportunities may help
you bring down the cost per reach, but the buying process will be
more complex, especially as the opportunities could be fast-moving.

Each marketing vehicle brings certain idiosyncrasies to the process
of cost-effective purchase. For broadcast TV in the United States, for
example, marketers have to decide whether to participate in an up-
front buy or purchase through the scatter market, as well as whether to
buy geo-targeted or national inventory. For the Internet, you face massive fragmentation and the resulting challenge in determining how to
deal with niche, subscale audiences. In response, a new set of inventory
aggregators—the internet ad networks like DoubleClick or Google's
Ad Sense—have emerged. The larger networks are consolidating,
while the niche networks continue to proliferate, each with different
strengths. Some have great cost-per-click advertising potential; others,
superior geo-targeting; still others, specialty inventory, the best
rates on pop-ups, or text link inventory. For direct marketing campaigns, list acquisition is a major cost driver, as is the interplay among
the size and complexity of pieces, postage rates, and anticipated
response levels. These insights are only the start; each different marketing vehicle has developed its own unique purchasing characteristics.

As is the case in any B2B marketplace without transparent pricing, marketers have a hard time staying abreast of the latest pricing trends and fast-moving inventory opportunities, especially if they operate a diverse mix of marketing activities across an equally diverse range of geographies. For this reason, the best marketers work with highly informed external buying groups with access to diversified inventory sources and some proprietary information, not only to help make the right choice but also to lower overall costs. Of course, the number and type of buying agencies will depend on your company's individual circumstances.

In our experience, most buying agencies have strengths in dealing with a particular vehicle. Even though many claim to be vehicle-neutral, you will find that most have institutional strengths. Their knowledge of the quality of a certain vehicle's audiences, the diversity of the inventory, and the pricing patterns is particularly deep in specific marketing vehicles but anywhere from somewhat weaker to very weak in other vehicles. For that reason, many companies still work with multiple buying agencies. Regardless of your preferred number of partners, remember that their primary job is helping you procure your planned inventory at the most effective price.

Delivering and Auditing Traditional Marketing Communications Vehicles

Effective execution depends on having your vehicle delivered as planned. This may seem fairly straightforward, but it is often easier said than done. Even for traditional marketing communication vehicles, with their much more controlled delivery environments, in-market execution failure points abound.

Some problems stem from basic operational breakdowns, which are almost never tolerated, such as when your delivery misses the critical timing windows dictated by the planning schedule. For example, if your company's catalog marketing drop was supposed to be in home on November 17, but did not actually get in home until November 25, even though major selling dates were November 23 and 24, the marketer will get the blame. Even worse are incorrectly situated placements. You pay for a full-page ad next to the business section, but it ends up in the lifestyle section! In another unforgivable sin, substandard production qualities hit your collateral, such as poor color reproduction for a print or TV ad or a catalog sent without key product pages. It's even worse when the wrong creative is used or direct mail pieces are mailed to the wrong names on the wrong list! Although greater attention to detail and more operational consistency can avert some delivery failures, such mistakes still happen in a surprising number of ways.

More upsetting, given the amount of a company's marketing budget that may be wasted, are in-market execution failures stemming from an error in judgment or overreach in terms of audience commitments. For example, sometimes a marketer uses a singular creative execution to maintain message consistency even if it does not translate well into some specific vehicles or formats. Take an ad that works well in a magazine format but is too copy-intensive for a billboard or bus stop. Or you may use still photography in an interactive medium that requires video. Another common problem involves inappropriately sourced reach and frequency, whereby a buying group delivers placements that are "off brief" but inserted to help hit the overall exposure or dosing targets the campaign stipulates. It is one thing if the marketer makes a conscious decision to increase the depth of the buy, but another if the marketer believes she is getting X only to have the buying company deliver Y without her knowledge. Even more common failures result when promised audience or viewership does not materialize. Although some mature marketing vehicles like TV bake economic penalties into their structure to alleviate the impact of this circumstance, others do not. Moreover, marketers are not as anxious to get their money back as they are to achieve their marketing goals. Compensation cannot mitigate the business consequences suffered from these kinds of audience shortfalls.

Given the wide range of potential in-market delivery failures, we have found that an auditing process can be an essential way to close the loop and gradually squeeze the failure points out of your execution model. Some companies report positive results from a rudimentary, low-tech, self-managed auditing process; others prefer a more sophisticated, highly automated process that involves objective third-party services. Whatever the technique, the principle is the same: validating that the right piece was delivered, at the right time, with the right production quality per the overall marketing plan, and to the promised audience of the right size. Because the costs of a selected auditing approach must be appropriate for the size of your marketing investment, many companies apply a random, spot-checking methodology instead of something more comprehensive.

Whatever the methodology, its results can help pinpoint oft-repeated failure points and diagnose the root causes of the problems so that you can more systematically upgrade your capabilities and processes and avert operational failures in your future campaigns.

Delivering and Auditing Experiential Marketing Vehicles

As we mentioned earlier, all of the key dimensions of the tactical planning process and many elements of the actual buying process are quite similar across traditional one-way marketing communication vehicles and more live, face-to-face experiential marketing vehicles. Make a decision to host an experience at a larger event where there is poor audience alignment or at the wrong time of year, and your anticipated marketing outcomes will be equally compromised. It may be argued that experiential marketing vehicles have more complex cost structures that include variable line items like labor, equipment rentals, and travel, but even then, most companies can typically manage these cost-based execution risks with relative ease over time.

By far the most profound in-market execution difference for experiential marketing vehicles involves the higher set of expectations that a customer has for a live, face-to-face experience and, given the fact that it is live, the correspondingly higher degree of potential variability in the delivery of that experience each and every time it is in market. After all, most customers expect experiential marketing vehicles to be engaging and energizing. Given the popularity of reality shows, customers want experiential marketing to live up to their fantasies about these shows. They are most excited by the promise of a relevant and personal interaction with a company or its brand. They expect to be immersed in their experience and stimulated multidimensionally—emotionally, psychologically, intellectually, and physically. When an experiential marketing event works well, most leave with a sense of more intimate and personal connections with the brand. Moreover, most believe they can differentiate between a poorly executed and a well-executed experience. With stakes this high, in-market execution must deliver.

When experiential marketers are pushed to identify core opportunity areas for better overall delivery of experiential marketing vehicles, they tend to anchor around a few core themes. As you can see in Figure 6.4, the first theme that emerges has to do with some level of

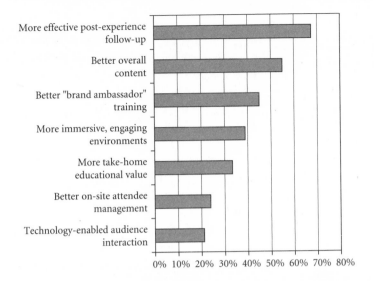

Figure 6.4. Core Opportunity Areas for Better Overall Delivery
of Experiential Marketing Vehicles

personalized interaction with attendees, when they are on-site in the experience itself and as follow-up after they have left the experience. The second theme that emerges involves the quest for ever better content that provides true take-home value. In a B2B context, this may mean more white papers, case studies, or trend reports; in the B2C worlds this may mean product sampling or trial. A third theme centers on the role of the people who are manning the experience for your company—here referred to as the *brand ambassadors*. How well do these individuals know the company story and the connective tissue between your brand and your target customers? Are they authentic, passionate, and knowledgeable? The final theme involves the level of engagement, immersion, and interaction that is baked into the actual experience itself, through either the physical environment, the people, technology-enabled interfaces, or the activities themselves.

Although some of these attributes stem from the experience design, most also become critical success factors during the delivery of the experience. Brand ambassadors play an indispensable role, as does the immersive nature of the overall experience. The diversity of suppliers required for world-class execution, from production companies to caterers to event management firms to logistics providers, creates truly daunting operational management challenges. Directing this array of players to create a consistent experience requires truly experienced drill sergeants, because most companies combine internal and external resources—some with long-standing relationships, others with temporary guns-for-hire. The detail-oriented leaders understand how to keep the platoon in sync while keeping customers enthusiastic and motivated.

Given the potential for disaster, we have seen an auditing mind-set taking root in the experiential marketing world, which tries to better understand the consistency of execution as well as lay a foundation for more robust effectiveness measurement. In the case of experiential marketing, auditing approaches take different forms. Some companies send in random sets of "mystery shoppers" posing as legitimate attendees who evaluate overall experience against critical dimensions. Others use qualitative and quantitative methodologies to measure participant response either during the experience or afterward. They might use mystery shopping, electronic surveillance, or post-experience follow-up both to monitor the quality of the live experience and to drive continuous improvement in design and execution.

The Cross-Platform Effect and Multi-Initiative Synchronization

It is no secret that to achieve marketing success in a world reeling from too many choices and too many media, marketers increasingly must take every vehicle into account when developing the strategy, creating the tactical weapons, deciding on the vehicles, and then measuring their impact. But when multiple marketing vehicles are simultaneously used to increase the impact of a particular message, how does the marketer ensure that all of these messages are working together in concert to deliver an integrated impression to the target customer? Remember, customers are increasingly channel-neutral in terms of where they source their media, but they are also increasingly message purists, taking companies to task if what they are saying in one channel is not consistent with what they are saying in another. If you are delivering the message through on-line marketing, targeted TV spots on MSNBC programs, mobile downloads, interactive blogs, and in-field experiences, can you be sure that this cross-platform communication plan is being executed in a way that is synchronized and consistent?

Even after you get the basics right, recognize shifts in media consumption, and gather together all of the places in which your creative execution will play, the first and most important element must be message integration. No matter what the media, no matter how many touch points, only one message should be disseminated to targets. You must adhere to the basic principles of multi-initiative synchronization, or you will spend money without achieving any of your marketing goals.

The key for some marketing powerhouses, such as Pepsi, has been the *brand manager* in charge of orchestrating the synchronization between the platforms. According to one vice president, "Where we've been successful is where a brand manager has taken a leading role and set up a system for overseeing all aspects of a campaign ... The brand manager has to sit in the middle as sort of a general contractor and conduct business."[3]

The increasing importance of cross-platform marketing has pushed the marketing industry to recognize the need for measuring results—but has not pushed them to know exactly *how* to measure results. In meetings that bring together ad agencies, the talk is all about the need for such measurement, without a clear understanding of what is the most important aspect of this measurement. According to *Ad Age*:

> How is a marketer to know whether the teen watching a scene from "Gossip Girl" online is also watching the full program on the CW or represents an unduplicated viewer who would add to the larger reach of the show and its accompanying ads? Further muddying the waters: Different advertisers want different elements measured, frustrating attempts to create a standardized system ... some ... might measure the success of a campaign with click through rates and cost per clicks, while others think engagement metrics like time spent with video or time spent with widget are more important.

Emerging technologies will allow a marketer to track across media, enabling real-time or close to real-time campaign or media shifts. Factor TG provides a system of continuous marketing measurement that captures the effects of specific marketing tactics as they happen via online consumer surveys. The technology measures brand impact, analyzed with sales data and reported when and how you need it (for planning, execution, optimization, and modeling.) You also can apply insights you receive at the tactical level through continuous measurement and consumer alignment.

With this technology you can collect the insights produced by each campaign that tell you how consumers were influenced, how each creative approach performed, and how each media vehicle delivered. Each campaign is measured discretely and can be rolled into program- and brand-level reporting. The technology provides visibility into performance at all levels across all vehicles in an integrated way. At the tactical level, you can see campaign performance in close to real time, optimizing midcampaign or from cycle to cycle, as well as campaign ROI and consumer segment, creative, and media performance detail.

Such technological innovation can help the marketer determine whether the advertising worked; whether cross-platform efforts increased the impact of the ads or took away from them; the elements of the campaign that generated positive ROI; the synergy effect of cross-media communication; the advertising changes that impacted awareness, opinion, and purchase; and the impact of competitors' advertising. Such a system of continuous marketing measurement captures the effects of specific marketing tactics as they happen via online consumer surveys. Each campaign will produce insight about how consumers were influenced, how each creative approach performed, and how each media vehicle delivered.

APPLYING A PROCUREMENT DISCIPLINE TO MARKETING FIXED COST MANAGEMENT

The sixth and final value lever for driving accountable marketing is anchored in more effective and efficient management of overall fixed costs. The basis of fixed costs is the costs of planning, producing, and managing the various marketing programs that your company may employ, including the following:

1. External agency costs, whether the fees of advertising, research, PR, design, event marketing, or any other type of marketing services agency
2. Costs for critical input materials like postage, paper, give-aways, displays, and all other materials

3. Other associated production costs

4. Costs associated with the internal headcount, processes, and technology systems used to manage the overall marketing investment portfolio

As highlighted in Chapter Three, we consider these costs as fixed because they are required to strategically target, plan, envision, and creatively produce an internet display ad or a TV ad or a trade show exhibit irrespective of whether you will use it ten times, a hundred times, a thousand times, or a hundred thousand times. Your fixed cost base depends on your mix of marketing vehicles, the level of your marketing organization's decentralization versus centralization, and the extent to which you build capabilities with internal resources or through relationships with external suppliers.

Given this definition, we see a high degree of variability in the fixed cost make-up from one company to another. But given that these fixed cost elements can take from 20 percent to almost 60 percent of a company's overall marketing investment, it is important to understand the effectiveness of your company's performance in managing them.

There are many ways to go after performance improvements within this value lever. You can bring to it an explicit cost-cutting orientation, more of a cost-containment sensibility, a right-sizing approach, or something more akin to a strategic sourcing mind-set. But make no mistake, this is a very tricky value lever to master. Use an approach that is overly weighted toward traditional procurement priorities—such as price reductions, low-cost suppliers, or excessively lean internal teams—and you will find endless opportunities to make decisions that will ultimately prove to be penny-wise and pound-foolish.

At the same time, it is just as easy to be coaxed or bullied into believing (1) that the providers of these intangible, talent-based, knowledge-driven contributions across the marketing value chain—whether they are internal or external—need to be protected like sacred cows, and (2) that this is the one remaining cost line on the P&L that cannot benefit from a strategic sourcing mind-set. This point of view, of course, is as wrong-headed as the "penny-wise and pound-foolish" one just described. What you have to do is approach this value lever flexibly and with intelligence; by doing so, you should be able to find many smart and more cost-effective ways to align your fixed cost basis to drive better marketing performance. If important gains are made around fixed cost management, these savings can be redeployed into media, trade promotions, or other targeted response programs, which if properly executed could then serve to improve overall effectiveness.

Understanding the Basics

Depending on your business model and organizational structure, analyzing your marketing-related fixed costs may be fairly straightforward or mind-numbingly complicated. In our experience, global companies with multiple, diverse business divisions and a history of decentralized marketing structures tend to struggle in building a holistic view of fixed costs, but they are not the only companies for whom this is a struggle. A lack of common definitions for internal marketing job classifications, a lack of consistency in the way different marketing spending lines roll up in the general ledger, highly fragmented and decentralized supplier bases, a high degree of variation in the ratio of in-house versus external resources used to perform any given marketing task—all of these factors complicate the development of even a rudimentary view of a company's existing marketing-related fixed costs.

Despite the obvious challenges, however, successful companies learn to pull together an integrated analysis of aggregate fixed cost investment, with the appropriate breakdowns between internal headcount and related expenses, external agency and other marketing service provider fees, marketing supplies costs, other production expenses, and all other marketing-related fixed cost investments, including those around infrastructure, technology, training, and support. In performing this analysis, best practice dictates that you answer the following questions:

- Does the absolute amount of my fixed costs, as well as the ratio of relative investment levels between my fixed costs and my variable program costs, appear to make sense?
- If the absolute amount doesn't make sense, what are the root causes of the apparent inefficiencies around my fixed cost leverage?

You need to answer these questions in aggregate, at the firm level, and then you need to answer them more individually for each type of marketing program in which you are investing.

To be able to understand whether your fixed costs make sense, you must be able to rely on normative benchmarks with which to perform comparative analysis. You can derive these benchmarks through internal company history, ad hoc external data points supplied by recent hires from other companies or any number of potential agency counterparts, or through an external benchmarking process. Our experience with benchmarking large, global companies demonstrates some variability across these numbers, even when you control for industry sector and company revenues. The ratios of fixed costs to variable costs are the most volatile, especially in times of rapid growth or deceleration of marketing program investment.

Exhibit 6.5 provides an example of benchmarked ratios, this time within the financial services sector, based primarily on headcount levels and overall people costs. Note the high levels of variability across the ranges. Despite this, general patterns of absolute fixed cost investment levels tend to emerge, especially when normalized for revenues and go-to-market models, and can give you a solid starting point for your analysis of this value lever. One 2006 study of fixed costs produced ranges of $300,000 to $450,000 in marketing program spend for each internal marketing full-time equivalent (FTE) in B2B companies and ranges of $800,000 to $1.1 million in marketing program spend for each internal marketing FTE in B2C companies.

Determining whether absolute investment levels and ratios make sense at the program level requires a detailed understanding of the drivers of fixed and variable costs for each marketing vehicle, which can vary dramatically. Clearly, the greater your familiarity with a specific kind of marketing vehicle, the more expertise you should have about its fixed cost drivers. In contrast, it will be more difficult for you to understand the fixed cost drivers of emerging marketing vehicles like mobile marketing or on-line video or of vehicles new to your company's marketing mix. In our recent field study, when we asked about the make-up of program costs, most marketers told us they follow unwritten rules of thumb relative to fixed cost investment levels for specific campaigns or programs, although this went from as low as 10 percent of the total investment budget to as high as 30 percent, with the majority of responses in the 15- to 20-percent range. Building a detailed database of the fixed cost

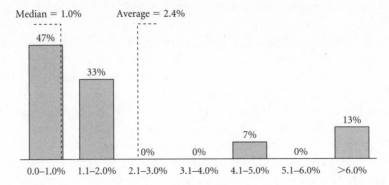

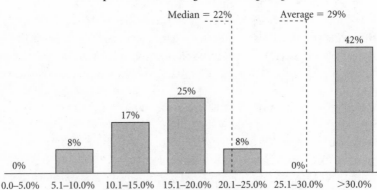

Figure 6.5.   Benchmarking Internal Headcount Investment in Relation
to Total Marketing Investment in the Financial Services Sector

drivers of a cross-section of a company's historical campaigns is
the best way to institutionalize this knowledge. Many of the newer
"marketing resource management" (MRM) software vendors are
seizing this opportunity (for more details, see the next section and
Chapter Ten). You should also have a clear understanding of how
non-program-specific fixed costs—like market research, customer
analytics, or strategy development—are allocated across the different
programs.

Diagnosing the problems with fixed cost leverage can be significantly more challenging, especially at the aggregate level. Sometimes

a company may inherit an internal structure built around different priorities that bloat headcount in specific areas. Frequent strategy shifts, inconsistent agency briefing or project specification methods, poor process management, and a dysfunctional creative approvals approach can drive up fixed costs without creating a proportional amount of deployable, production-ready marketing content. High degrees of fragmentation in the supplier base can also lead to expensive duplication of effort, especially across a global firm.

The rest of this section deals with some of these challenges and opportunities head on. In our experience, most companies have some "low-hanging fruit" cost improvement opportunities, as well as some that are harder to grab but more material over the long term. But before you barrel ahead and take these efficiency gains to the bank, let's explore the kind of organizational challenges and resistance you can expect to face when you start to sniff around in these areas.

Challenges in Applying a Procurement Mind-Set

As we said earlier, going after performance improvements in this value lever is not for the faint of heart. You can quickly run into a wide array of organizational, political, and cultural roadblocks that have historically limited the actualization of any material savings opportunities. First, entrepreneurial and creative cultures throughout the broader marketing organization are likely to resist not only any strong-handed centralized direction but even just some of the basic blocking and tackling of process coordination. Most marketers want autonomy and control, and they strongly believe that they are in the best position to determine what kind of resource, supplier, or investment is needed to drive to a high-quality marketing outcome. In companies with strong local or regional marketing organizations with a history of decentralized decision making, the resistance to any proposed changes to the vendor selection process or purchase decision making will be that much fiercer.

The nature of the marketing process also creates two opposing considerations, both of which are, in their own way, an enemy of cost efficiency. On the one hand, for a company's most material marketing investments—which rely on the magical intersection of great strategy, analytics, and creativity to deliver effective performance—there is a general resistance to either destabilizing the strategy development or creative processes or focusing these important relationship-based vendors around tactical ways to be more cost efficient, especially if the relationship appears to be working. A marketing leader often brings more of a Hollywood director's orientation to his or her star talent—a tendency to create the conditions for optimum performance by removing all unwanted or unhelpful distractions that prevent the talent from focusing, including anything that has to do with the commercial aspects of the relationship. At the same time, because there is so much experimentation and change in the marketing world, many companies can also end up in an environment that is almost exclusively project-based, resulting in a lot of one-off projects that use a wide array of one-time, transactional suppliers and do not provide enough of an opportunity for internal staff to get smarter about how to most effectively and efficiently produce results. So you end up with people bouncing from one inefficiently sourced and executed project to another, without building any institutionalized learning and strategic perspective.

Finally, there are many structural barriers that must be overcome. Usually someone has a vested interest in protecting the legacy internal marketing headcount that exists in an organization and defending the status quo, regardless of whether it is still fit for the purpose in the existing business environment. As we have implied, marketing-related buying decisions get made on many noncost factors, not all of which are always clearly articulated and transparent to process participants, let alone to nonparticipants. Across the overall marketing investment portfolio, typically the buying decision itself is highly fragmented. Most marketing organizations struggle to capture, codify, and then share best practices for fixed cost management, although some organizations are using the corporate marketing center or cross-divisional marketing leadership groups to drive better visibility here. Consistent with the rest of this story, the decision support tools available to facilitate decision making around fixed cost management are very, very limited in most organizations. Most companies do not have timely access to this kind of financial data. It is either poorly tracked, out of date, or completely inaccurate. As one marketing technology vendor frequently reminds anyone who will listen, marketing investments represent $1 trillion of global economic activity that still gets managed via phone conversations, faxes, e-mails, word processing documents, and, if you are lucky, some spreadsheets and GANTT charts.

Looking for the Low-Hanging Fruit

In spite of these challenges, companies can realize significant benefits by merging a strategic marketing sourcing capability with a measured, periodic analysis of the internal resource and infrastructure model. Dramatic and extensive headcount reductions may not be required if you focus on periodic redeployments and fine-tuning. Overall service and quality levels from marketing service suppliers can actually be improved by following some basic strategic sourcing principles. With a proactive stance, marketing can control the process, without letting finance, procurement, or operations jump into the driver's seat. Having marketing remain in control minimizes the chances that the company will make some truly stupid decisions that may save money in the short term but critically hamper marketing effectiveness over the medium term.

The easiest low-hanging fruit to pick is paying less for what you are buying or employing. On the supply side, use a procurement orientation to drive for more clarity about deliverables and terms from contractors, to push for transparency from a cost and margin standpoint, and ultimately to renegotiate prices. You can try to leverage your scale, your market position, and your total spending profile to secure these concessions from potential suppliers. Alternatively, you may find ways to use third-party service providers to access these scale benefits, in the same way that a media buying organization may give you access to better rates than you would get going directly to the media owner.

You can also consolidate your operations or supplier ranks. The highly fragmented and decentralized nature of most marketing value chains allows the achievement of dramatic one-time gains through consolidation. The literature is rife with examples of companies that have gone from 232 market research suppliers to 8, or from 18 in-house outbound telemarketing centers to 2, or from 475 graphic design and packaging suppliers to 6, or from 14 local trade promotions teams to 2 regional teams, all of which may have resulted in cost savings in the 10-percent, 20-percent, or even 30-percent range, while delivering improved quality and service levels. In the case of high fragmentation, focusing on the development of a preferred supplier list that has been certified to meet predefined quality, delivery, and expertise standards, with transparent prenegotiated cost rates, will almost always create value, especially when the price is not overly weighted by decision criteria. Ideally you can align marketing, finance, and procurement around the development of well-understood cost targets for each type of service, as well as a quality index to evaluate supplier performance. Before starting this process, it's best to first do a lot of internal education, teaching people about the pros and cons of supplier selection, cost modeling, sources of value transfer, negotiations, and work planning before bringing an indiscriminate hatchet to the supplier lists. When done well, your company can significantly reduce the supplier base while substantially improving supplier quality, delivery reliability, and lead times.

These basic approaches can be even more powerful if mapped against a more discriminating view of the risk and value-creating potential associated with different kinds of internal capabilities and external suppliers. We have modified a construct found in the supply chain management literature for use here (see Figure 6.6), with a variable tied to complexity, supply risk, and capability-uniqueness on the vertical axis and a variable tied to value, profit impact, and marketing effectiveness potential on the horizontal axis. You can analyze any internal marketing capability or supplier relationship in relation to these two variables and position them on the map. You end up with key capabilities or suppliers plotted in one of four quadrants—a strategic zone, a bottleneck zone, a noncritical zone, and a leverage

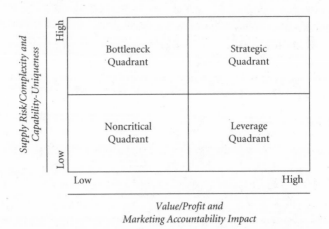

Value/Profit and
Marketing Accountability Impact

Figure 6.6.   Assessing the Importance of the Existing Portfolio
of Supplier Relationships and Internal Capabilities

zone—each of which may merit radically different treatments from a procurement or investment perspective.

Prevailing wisdom would argue for more collaborative partnering and development approaches for suppliers and aggressive in-sourcing of the capabilities that map into the strategic and bottleneck quadrants. By comparison, you would push for a more transactional orientation for suppliers and more outsourcing of the capabilities that map into the noncritical or leverage quadrants. The objective in the noncritical and leverage quadrants is to maximize flexibility and maintain price competitiveness, typically done on the supplier side by spreading the purchase volume around to multiple providers and on the capabilities side by splitting volume between internal groups and outsourced providers. A more aggressive procurement posture may even be established for activities in these quadrants, using tools like on-line auctions, incentive pricing, and episodic new supplier qualification to weed out 25 percent of the suppliers. We have seen companies achieve one-time savings of 15 percent to over 45 percent when deploying these techniques with those kinds of opportunities. But applying those same techniques to activities in the other two quadrants would be tantamount to suicide. Collaborative partnering and proactive development is a better way to coax out efficiency gains in those quadrants. However, pursuing those tactics is a higher-risk, higher-reward strategy, and as such, we will address it in the next section.

The procurement mind-set has taken hold of some marketing organizations, especially those that have based their operations on a solid foundation. For example, DuPont, which has been using the Six Sigma philosophy for some time, decided to take that same commitment to continual quality improvement and apply it to marketing. The Global Sourcing Function took the lead and developed a Six Sigma–oriented methodology based on four criteria: brand building, creative excellence, industry knowledge, and budgetary efficiency. Then the team asked six global agencies to prove that they were experts in all four criteria, using actual data presented to senior DuPont executives. The agencies were then asked to participate in an hour-long on-line auction in which they submitted the best bid for a number of hours by skill and geography. Although DuPont did not choose the agency with the lowest bid, management believed it had been able to persuade the agencies to provide their lowest bids—because of the competition.

UNEARTHING HIGHER-RISK—BUT HIGHER-REWARD—SAVINGS OPPORTUNITIES

Above and beyond achieving some of the basic gains that applying more of procurement mind-set can yield, some companies have more ambitious aspirations when it comes to managing their fixed cost levels. These companies are willing to pursue improvement strategies that have some higher risk associated with them, because the promised rewards hold out even greater promise. Sometimes these rewards come in the form of material efficiency gains with limited risk to overall marketing effectiveness. Occasionally these rewards may pack a double punch, potentially delivering significant efficiency gains while simultaneously delivering material improvements in overall effectiveness. Now doesn't that sound attractive? Through our field work we have identified six different kinds of higher-risk, higher-reward strategies (see Figure 6.7); we will discuss each in turn.

Process-Focused Strategies

The first, called Process Redesign and Overhaul, borrows heavily from the techniques used by business reengineering and Six Sigma.

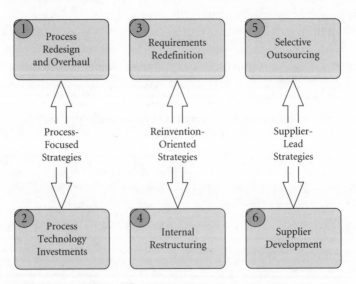

Figure 6.7.   Higher-Risk, Higher-Reward Strategies for Achieving Best-in-Class Fixed Cost Management Performance

Companies implementing this technique use standard process improvement approaches to reinvent core marketing processes to eliminate waste or redundancy, improve the quality of information, streamline decision making, and reduce time to value and the overall cost picture. The best companies find the potential for improvement in myriad marketing subprocesses, such as the creative development process, the analytics and strategy development process, and the marketing operations process. Each generally contains real possibilities for operational improvements.

A typical creative development and production process, for example, is often fraught with inefficiencies and process flaws that escalate costs. Standard challenges include poorly specified creative briefs, premature creative development while the strategy is still in flux, dysfunctional review and approvals processes that lead to excessive revision cycles, inefficient communication and collaboration approaches with outside agencies, an unwillingness to reuse existing marketing assets, and abrupt shifts in a strategic design that is already too far into the production process for any changes. Cummins Engine, a large B2B industrial manufacturer, faced many of these challenges with its marketing collateral development process, which accounted for almost 20 percent of total marketing investment. By applying Six Sigma approaches, the company found the three key process drivers that increased costs and throughput; to address the root causes, Cummins redesigned the processes with supporting technology. The revamped process reduced collateral production cycle time by 61 percent, produced 78 percent fewer revisions, reduced creative development costs by 23 percent, and saved 75 percent in asset management fees.

Smart process redesign can lead to increasing efficiencies in the analytics and strategy development process as well. A large Dutch insurance company, for example, decided to redesign its targeting process for direct mail offers by developing a more robust and predictive model of customer response to different hypothetical offers. The redesigned process allows marketers to efficiently create, optimize, and execute these campaigns without needing technical database specialists or expensive statisticians. After the process overhaul, the new approach enabled the company to reduce direct mailing costs by 35 percent, pare down the volume of direct mail by 40 percent, cut its cycle time for campaign execution by 30 percent, and improve response rates by over 50 percent.

The second higher-risk, higher-reward strategy pairs process improvements with more intensive marketing process technology investments. MRM software solutions attempt to bring more transparency to the marketing planning process and integrate planning more seamlessly with budgeting, spend tracking, and process execution. By enabling marketers to create and manage detailed plans for each marketing campaign on an enterprise platform, with real-time visibility into detailed spending commitments and workflow tools to support better project collaboration and execution, marketers can better monitor their fixed cost investment levels and build institutionalized knowledge about workflow and cost drivers for core marketing programs. Bank of America has used technology to experience gains of 10 to 15 percent in cost efficiency and 15- to 30-percent improvements in cycle times. There is a whole section of Chapter Ten that focuses on how to build faster and more efficient processes as one of the key pillars of sustained marketing accountability, with technology as a key enabler. If this has piqued your interest, look for more details there.

Reinvention-Oriented Strategies

A third, slightly more innovative strategy that some pursue is one we have labeled *requirements redefinition*. We believe it is more innovative than the others we've described because it requires an ability to take a very large step back from the status quo or the standard operating procedure; to try to develop some new insights about what the company is really trying to achieve with a specific marketing strategy, vehicle, or tactic; and then to redefine, at times radically, what that means from a procurement perspective. A company may end up changing the items or services purchased through a better understanding of customer requirements, thereby unearthing opportunities to substitute less expensive alternatives, standardize and simplify materials or production specifications, or perhaps just stop doing something entirely. At a macro level, the shift toward on-demand, high-quality, small-batch collateral or marketing materials printing, or to a 100-percent electronic delivery mechanism, might reflect this kind of thinking in action. A comparable example of this strategy at the individual company level is Samsung's delivering on its aspiration to launch itself as a lifestyle brand at the 2004 Summer Olympics. Samsung carefully thought through which aspects of Olympic

Sponsorship would help them achieve their goals. They chose to sponsor the Olympic Torch Relay (which gave them an emotional connection with consumers) and made sure to provide an experience to Olympic attendees, with an Olympic Rendezvous Spot as a gathering place for athletes, their families, and spectators.

The fourth strategy, typically more politically challenging and definitely more angst-ridden, involves internal restructuring throughout a company's broader marketing organization. Through our work, we have observed three main factors that help explain why any given company's marketing resources are structured the way they are: (1) the degree of centralization, (2) the degree of integration, and (3) the marketing team's orientation (see Figure 6.8). By the *degree of centralization* we mean the extent to which resources in the corporate center drive the marketing activities, versus resources housed in a company's various geographic, business unit, or product/

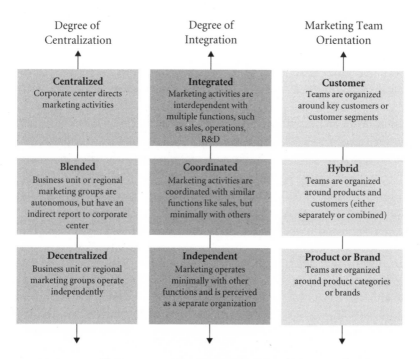

Figure 6.8.   Three Dimensions That Shape Marketing Organization
Structure and Drive Fixed Cost Basis

brand-level organizations. By the *degree of integration* we mean the extent to which marketing acts in an interdependent or autonomous manner in relation to the other customer-facing business functions, such as sales, operations, and R&D. And by the *marketing team's orientation* we mean the extent to which the marketing team is organized around specific customer segments or specific product lines or brands. Specific choices that a company has made along each of these dimensions tends to drive marketing structure, which in turn can have a very significant implication on the nature of a company's marketing fixed cost basis. We have seen companies achieve efficiency gains of anywhere from 5 to 25 percent of their overall fixed cost basis through smart internal restructuring efforts. The question always boils down to whether those efficiency gains can be achieved without a material loss in effectiveness.

Of those three factors, the most material pivot point with regard to the fixed cost basis is the degree of centralization. Whenever a company makes a move toward centralization, whether that is about pulling certain decentralized activities into a corporate center-based shared services model or moving completely into centralized decision making and control over most marketing decisions, significant opportunities usually emerge to restructure the fixed cost basis in a way that cuts overall cost levels—perhaps modestly, perhaps aggressively. Knowing that those savings opportunities are always available to a company making that structural decision, we still must answer a more important question: whether the company has strong business and competitive reasons for making this move. In Figure 6.9, we present a framework for helping to assess whether the underlying business needs are conducive to more centralization or more decentralization. The trend over the last ten years toward fewer, stronger brands for many large companies and, in certain sectors like financial services and technology, to take dominant master-brand approaches—whereby global consistency in messaging and execution are big value creators—has indisputably pushed more companies toward a centralized model and allowed them to achieve significant cost savings and better execution through internal restructuring. However, if the forces in your category require your company to drive more local relevance, be faster to market, and be much more responsive to local competitive forces, you may need to do internal restructuring in a different direction, which is more likely to increase your fixed cost basis, not decrease it.

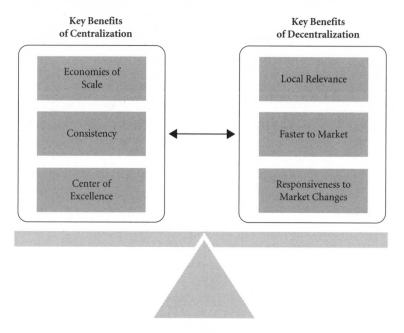

Figure 6.9. Determining the Right Balance between Centralization and Decentralization by Focusing on Desired Outcomes

Supplier-Led Strategies

The fifth strategy that some companies pursue to change their fixed cost profile is to move to selective outsourcing for many elements of the marketing value chain. Although some parts of the traditional marketing value chain have always been handled by external suppliers, like the fielding of market research or the development of TV advertising, companies using this strategy are much more aggressive about evaluating in-house versus external sourcing alternatives across all parts of the marketing value chain. Some opportunities may be driven more by labor cost differentials; other opportunities may be driven more by uneven or peaking needs for certain kinds of services. Sometimes this may be more of a talent play, when in-sourced strategies could never generate a team with the same caliber of talent and expertise that a specialized smaller external firm can achieve. For strategic and bottleneck capability areas, there are more material risks in going down this path, if you are not willing to concurrently think strategically about the sixth and final strategy: supplier development.

Supplier development implies a different orientation to some subset of external vendors, with the emphasis more on partnering and collaboration, as opposed to the adversarial, pricing-obsessed nature of many buyer-supplier relationships. The hope is that through making explicit reciprocal commitments over an extended period of time and more openly sharing relevant information, significant performance improvements will occur, which will create incremental value that can be shared with both the supplier and the buyer. Typically this involves some training of supplier personnel, some co-investing in operations, and usually some hands-on cooperative or joint actions. The benefits usually accrue because of improved communication, better clarification of needs and expectations, proactive elimination of problems and concerns, and consistent operational performance. When companies are willing to share anticipated demand requirements and focus on the total cost of usage over lifetime, not just invoice pricing, and when suppliers are willing to share some of the risks of nonperformance, this can be a powerful approach, but it clearly requires a lot of trust and mutual commitment for it to work well. This kind of an approach makes sense only in the strategic or bottleneck quadrants, but it can be used to drive unexpected benefits on the fixed cost side while simultaneously improving marketing effectiveness.

STRATEGIC SOURCING AND AGENCY PARTNERS: HOW FAR IS TOO FAR?

Irrespective of which of the six higher-risk, higher-reward fixed cost management strategies you experiment with, the guiding principle of fixed cost management should always be to do no harm to your company's ability to produce highly effective marketing programs. Clearly, the way marketing has grown up inside many companies has led to spending patterns, go-to-market models, and cost structures that can seem grossly inefficient, especially to a fresh set of outside eyes. So this is always a surefire and reliable place to source some efficiency wins, and—given the short tenure of many CMOs in their job roles—a common place for newly hired senior marketers to put some quick points on the board.

But how do you know when your efforts to be more efficient with your fixed cost investments start to cut into lean muscle mass, not just unwanted body fat? In the marketing arena, nowhere is this question more hotly debated than around the topic of managing the roster of agencies that serve your company. If a thousand is clearly too many, is one or two too few?

Dell's Attempts at Radical Consolidation and Multidisciplinary Integration with Enfatico

Dell is a recent example of a company taking the idea of radical supplier consolidation combined with targeted supplier development to a new extreme. Toward the end of 2007, Dell announced that it would create a new marketing and communications agency in partnership with the WPP group—initially called Project Da Vinci, later renamed Enfatico (based on the musical notation that means to play each note with emphasis)—which will handle all of the Austin, Texas, computer maker's marketing and communication duties. Although at the time of this writing the detailed plans for the new single agency were still under wraps, the impetus for this is a belief that by working with a single multidisciplinary agency—with skill sets that cut across digital, database marketing, TV and print advertising, PR, and other marketing domains, reinforced by a commitment to disciplined and comprehensive measurement—Dell will ultimately "create a new marketing model to further propel the company's growth." The difference from other recent examples of agency consolidation at companies like Verizon, IBM, and HSBC is that Enfatico is explicitly breaking the traditional above-the-line versus below-the-line split that had historically been preserved under other agency consolidation efforts. The other difference is that Dell wants to drive the same level of measurability and accountability that it has with its direct response marketing programs for every area of its marketing investment. So the idea of measurement and marketing accountability is at the very heart of this agency consolidation strategy.

When you listen carefully to the limited amount that Dell has been willing to say publicly about this initiative, some of the themes are very consistent with arguments that are central to this chapter and the broader book. Once you get past the lead headline about the $4.5 billion, three-year commitment to WPP, the story almost always starts with a comment that Dell had previously been working with over eight hundred different agencies globally, and how inefficient that had to be. The new CMO acknowledges that the first insight was about the need for consolidation, because Dell had many agencies doing the "same exact job and presenting us with different creative ideas, different media ideas, different digital and demand generation ideas. We had to make some sense out of the chaos." Instead of "dating 800 agencies," Dell sees this as creating a deep partnership with one firm. In this way, Dell hopes to keep all of the talented people inside that single agency partner singularly focused on Dell's customers, Dell's competitors, and what Dell needs to do to win, without being distracted with the other commercial or client priorities with which a multiclient agency concerns itself. So at first blush you can see all of the building blocks of a classic strategic supplier development approach at work: extended mutual commitments; deep partnering; the intent to share relevant, highly proprietary information; better clarification of needs and expectations; and so on.

When you dig a little deeper into the story, the cost savings and efficiency component starts to take more of a back seat to the idea of increased effectiveness, not just through better coordination and fewer competing voices at the table, but also by putting a desire for seamless integration across analytics, creative strategy, and cross-platform campaign execution right at the heart of the argument. The parties first picked the code name Project Da Vinci because of the art and science combination that the real Da Vinci's legacy embodies. "Improving shareholder value is the ultimate award for all of us to win. Yes, we don't mind winning industry awards, but our customers and our shareholders are our focus, not what we can win in Cannes. A combination of great analytics and creative is key ... an agency that has both the creative horsepower and ability to measure the impact of their work."[4] The dialed-up importance of analytics, combined with an aggressive push for integrated thinking across execution platforms, is what changes the heat, appeal, and potential power of this argument. Given Dell's aspirations and apparent strategic intent, this move puts them right at the center of the marketing accountability debate on every level.

Fittingly, as the dust started to settle post-announcement, Dell's approach elicited a passionate, animated, and at times heated debate from every corner of the marketing value chain. Some commentators scoffed at the idea that this is anything more than a procurement-led move to cut costs out of Dell's marketing budget. Many were skeptical that this kind of model was actually going to deliver on the "art" side of Da Vinci's legacy. The competition for talent is one factor that keeps many agencies fresh and vibrant, but some questioned the attractiveness of this single-client, multidisciplinary shop to the most sought-after creative types. Just as some question whether this is an attractive value proposition for the highly talented knowledge workers that would need to populate the agency, others also question how attractive the proposition is for Dell. "Through-the-line consolidation is a step too far for most clients right now … Few clients want to put all of their eggs in a single global basket."[5]

Other commentators, however, love the audacity of the move and think it is a natural step for a company with Dell's operating discipline and focus. They see the unrelenting pressure for more accountable marketing investments as the direction in which the world is moving, so they admire Dell's insistence to find an agency that will co-architect and then navigate this journey with them. Finally, with a billion people on-line already and the next five hundred million close on their trail, gaining the right insights, the right analytics, and the right mind-set to build campaigns in days rather than calendar quarters is a big, hairy audacious goal. The looming unanswered question remains—will it work? In Dell's case, we will get to that answer only by waiting and watching. Patience, friends, patience …

Key Forces at Work in the Agency Consolidation Trend

This current consolidation trend has actually developed in response to what was a powerful specialization movement started in the 1990s. At that time, many leading marketers started to move away from the full-service agency model that they had grown up with in the 1970s and 1980s, with its media-commission-driven compensation model, to a dramatically expanded roster of specialized agencies, with distinctive capabilities across various marketing disciplines. These specialized agencies drove the disaggregation of the marketing value chain, and they used output-based or time-and-materials-based fee mechanisms to be compensated for their efforts. As the variety of marketing vehicles continued to proliferate, new ecosystems of specialized suppliers would spring up around each vehicle or medium, like database marketing or CRM or the Internet, creating yet another set of potential players for a marketer to build additional relationships with. Decoupling the payment for the creative development process from the media investment decision allowed many marketers to remove a major conflict of interest from the kind of advice they were receiving from critical marketing suppliers. Working with an array of focused specialists also allowed marketers to feel that they were getting best-in-class, highly tailored thinking for each component of their marketing investment, which probably also led to some powerful, highly accountable programs.

But as we entered the early part of this decade, the problems with this kind of an approach started to become more pronounced, especially as many companies across many sectors started to consolidate their brand portfolios and attempt to operate with fewer, but more powerful global brand platforms. It was clearly much more challenging to communicate integrated, consistent brand messages with a wide array of specialized, and thus highly fragmented marketing partners. Moreover, as consumers and customers started to become more multi-channel in their media consumption, the material risks to brand equity from presenting inconsistent or even contradictory messages across the channels created by different partners continued to grow. Particularly as the companies started to consolidate around fewer brands or even a single global master brand like GE, IBM, or HP, the excessive investment of time that came with managing so many external relationships started to seem more wasteful. At the same time, financially oriented types began to smell an opportunity to drive cost savings through fewer, better managed, and more material supplier relationships.

For all these reasons, over the last five to seven years we saw more and more companies consolidate around a few key agency partners. Many developed a limited roster of preferred full-service partners, occasionally reducing these to one primary full-service agency, usually picking a supplier with a historical strength in whatever the company's dominant marketing vehicle was—perhaps TV advertising for some players, direct or promotional marketing for others. Getting down to a single agency, however, was generally the exception rather than the rule. Many industry insiders argue that getting down to one does not work; they often cite HSBC's or IBM's efforts as the proof. The argument usually is that this decision leaves the company with access to a pool of creative resources with too narrow a focus, and that ultimately their marketing efforts will start to lose energy and creative momentum. Overconsolidating can also tend to shift the power base to the agency and make exiting the relationship exceedingly difficult.

For these reasons, many companies end up with a short-list roster of preferred suppliers in their major marketing investment categories rather than a single agency. Many marketers like the idea of fewer, deeper relationships but also like the idea of keeping the thinking fresh by preserving some diversity in their agency mix. It is also hard to ignore the intangible benefit that comes from agencies knowing that there are others in the mix. A little heat and the sense of competition helps keep everyone focused on bringing their A game to every assignment. When it's done well, companies ensure that the various suppliers on their short list have different kinds of strengths—creatively, geographically, or strategically. They also ensure that each preferred partner has a well-defined and specific role in the overall value equation—sometimes splitting the responsibilities by brand, geography, or type of communication (say, brand versus demand generation). This allows all of the players to understand how and where they are expected to add value. It also helps the company be clear with itself about the unique and targeted contribution that each preferred supplier provides, so everyone understands why any given agency made the cut and is still on the list.

Of course, all of this has been further complicated over the last few years by the proliferation of the number of disciplines in which a company and its agencies need to be fluent. Depending on your industry, you may be experiencing pronounced shifts in the importance of digital or design or PR or promotions in your overall marketing value equation. As the marketing mix continues to shift, without any given media type dominating, it has made the whole supplier consolidation movement more complicated. In the old days, if TV advertising dominated, it might have made more sense to let the TV agency or agencies take the lead role. But in this more fragmented situation, with equal importance across a diverse set of vehicles, what should the configuration look like? Should you have a preferred short list of suppliers in each discipline? If so, who coordinates across them? Or should you push your key short-list agency partners to build multidisciplinary skills, internally or through a third-party ecosystem, and then demand that they manage across them? These trends clearly have added a new twist to the agency consolidation trend and again are pushing the dialogue into uncharted waters.

Figuring Out the Right Answer for You

To be clear, there is still a huge range of configurations being deployed by companies globally. A recent survey of global marketers on this topic of marketing suppliers and agency consolidation elicited a wide range of responses. On one end of the spectrum, when asked how many agencies they were currently working with, a good portion of respondents replied with answers like "hundreds," "thousands," "approximately 3,200 globally" and "so many it is hard to quantify." On the other end of the spectrum, a good portion of respondents gave answers that were south of 25, and some were even in the low single digits.

If your company is truly focused on driving more effective fixed cost management efforts and better marketing outcomes, you need to reach a point of healthy balance that ultimately will result in fewer overall suppliers without compromising your ability to achieve high-quality outcomes. So companies are experimenting with different responses. Some are looking at complete "through the line" consolidation, either with a single agency or a few preferred suppliers, a la Dell with its Enfatico initiative. Others are picking a lead agency for the business and then requiring that lead agency to manage all of the specialist agency contributors and the overall budget. In this way, the lead agency is really responsible for delivering an integrated, internally consistent marketing campaign, and the company does not get penalized if the mix switches midstream. Others are managing a tight, well-qualified short list of preferred suppliers, while developing well-thought-out business rules that enable people to go outside the roster occasionally when the exception conditions specified in the business rules are met. These companies put most of the coordination and interagency management responsibilities on internal resources, but have a higher degree of confidence that they will be getting the right usage, cost, and quality outcomes from their preferred supplier network.

We encourage you to start by asking yourself a series of questions:

- Is there anything fundamentally broken with your existing agency support model? Are you running into problems of consistency, quality, coordination, cost, or prioritization? Is finance demanding more transparency, standardization, or oversight?

- How many full-service marketing communications agencies do you need? What is the value you are getting from each of the ones that you currently work with today? How full-service are they these days—and what is the quality of their work across the spectrum?

- Are there key media elements that are particularly strong in driving your brand's results? Do you have the best providers for that discipline? Conversely, are there others that are less important, so they can follow along with the lead agency for the key discipline?

- Do your different lines of business have dramatically different go-to-market marketing models? How quickly are you experimenting with and innovating around different kinds of marketing vehicles and disciplines?

- How long will your internal brand stewards stay in place such that they can be the guardian of the brand and manage multiple agency partners—or does that history actually need to live with an agency manager? If the agency provides more of a source of continuity, how much of a direct relationship or control do they need to have over how many key vehicles to develop the necessary integrated effect?

When you combine a thoughtful approach to these strategic questions with a disciplined review of the existing agency supplier base, you can usually start to arrive at the right answer for your company. Ideally, a disciplined review of the existing agency supplier base will allow you to ensure that you are getting market-competitive pricing, optimizing agency usage across scope and utilization, and developing tools and policies to monitor usage, cost, and quality outcomes more consistently over time. Figure 6.10 provides an example of how one company evaluated the overall value it was receiving from fifteen of its agencies in relation to the annualized fees it was spending with each. The company used average cost rates per billable hour to place each agency on the cost scale and then used a combination of campaign-level ROIs and survey responses that assessed the agency's performance in a number of critical quality dimensions to place each agency on the quality scale. As you can see, there was a dramatic difference in these dimensions across the agencies. One cluster of agencies was placed in the high-value quadrant,

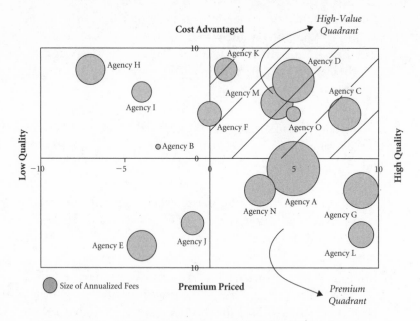

Figure 6.10.   Understanding the Cost and Quality Performance of Various Agency Partners

in which they were cost-advantaged and were driving high-quality outcomes; another cluster was placed in the premium quadrant as more premium-priced but yet were still driving high-quality outcomes. Other agencies wound up in the unattractive quadrants, delivering low-quality outcomes, irrespective of their cost position. If you start to create more transparent data and some analytical foundation to monitor the quality versus cost equation for your agencies over time in a manner similar to that of the company in Figure 6.10, you can manage the low-performing agencies out of the roster and focus on continuous improvements for your high-value agency suppliers over time.

Keep in mind that if you try to consolidate too far, you may lose the ability to bring creative excellence to the problems at hand. Even worse, if you consolidate around the wrong type of agency with the wrong type of core capability, you run the risk of irrelevance. With the increasingly fragmented world of marketing, media, and experience touch points, it is hard to believe that any one firm can bring the best of all of this together—Dell's efforts with Enfatico notwithstanding. Given the importance of the strategy and messaging value levers in the overall accountability equation, you cannot underestimate the risk of getting this wrong. But if you consolidate too little, you run the risk of delivering inconsistent messages, fragmented experiences, and small campaigns that never have the scale to become truly iconic signatures for the brand. And your cost structure could remain bloated, serving only to leave the marketing area with a big target on its back the next time the business hits a soft spot and needs to do some radical cost restructuring.

We have now completed the detailed discussion of each of the six value levers of marketing accountability. Chapter Four dealt with the strategy and messaging/creative levers, Chapter Five dealt with the marketing vehicles and investment level levers, and this chapter addressed the in-market execution and fixed cost management levers. With this comprehensive understanding of the various sources of value that can be explored to drive greater accountability from your existing marketing investments, now, in the third and final part of the book, we turn to a detailed discussion of how to activate a comprehensive marketing accountability program inside your organization.

PART THREE

Putting Core Principles of Marketing Accountability to Work Inside Your Organization

Laying the Tactical Groundwork for Long-Term Marketing Improvement

Planning for Your Journey Through the Three Horizons of Marketing Accountability

T opics covered in Chapter Seven:

• The three horizons of marketing accountability
• Understanding typical landmines in early ROI efforts
• A quick primer of available analytic tools and approaches
• Familiarizing yourself with internal and external MA enablers
• Practical tips for getting started

A journey of a thousand miles begins with a single step
—Lao Tzu

In this third and final part of the book, we focus on how to practically apply the principles and concepts of marketing accountability— including the six value levers—by discussing how to build a long-term marketing accountability program in your company. In this chapter we will introduce you to the three horizons of marketing accountability improvement and offer some practical advice for getting started. The remaining three chapters of the book correspond to these three horizons of marketing accountability and will go into each of those areas in much greater depth.

As you articulate the ambition for and set the ground rules of your overall marketing accountability initiative, you will immediately come face to face with a set of fairly thorny issues concerning ROI measurement, key analytic approaches, and the broader ecosystem of marketing accountability enablers that can either facilitate or, if left unaddressed, materially undermine any improvement efforts. So we will provide a quick tour through each of these areas—ROI landmines, analytic approaches, and MA enablers—that will leave you better prepared to navigate tricky discussions with the broader organization on this topic.

As you will see, the granular long-term road map gets built out as part of Horizon One—the diagnostic phase. But without a good practical understanding of some of these issues and how to address them, you may get tripped up before you even have a chance to get a pony into the race. By the conclusion of this chapter, you should be well prepared to make the case for why the organization should begin this journey toward greater marketing accountability and better in-market performance. You should also be able to make cogent arguments as to why the approach described in this book is best positioned to get the organization there.

THE THREE HORIZONS OF MARKETING ACCOUNTABILITY

There are three sequential horizons of improvement that a company must pass through on its long-term journey toward greater marketing accountability (see Figure 7.1). These horizons are more significant than simply the phases in a typical corporate initiative, as each marketing accountability horizon represents a significant accomplishment in and of itself, and only as you near the end of one horizon will the next come into view.

Horizon One centers on identifying marketing accountability opportunities and building the initial long-term plans to pursue

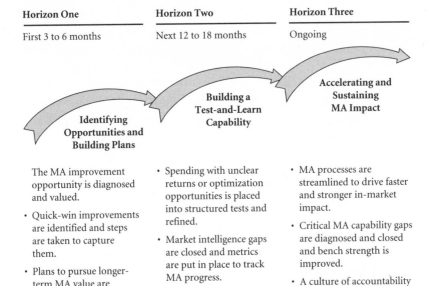

Horizon One	Horizon Two	Horizon Three
First 3 to 6 months	Next 12 to 18 months	Ongoing

Identifying Opportunities and Building Plans

Building a Test-and-Learn Capability

Accelerating and Sustaining MA Impact

The MA improvement opportunity is diagnosed and valued.

- Quick-win improvements are identified and steps are taken to capture them.

- Plans to pursue longer-term MA value are developed and resources are secured to move forward.

- Spending with unclear returns or optimization opportunities is placed into structured tests and refined.

- Market intelligence gaps are closed and metrics are put in place to track MA progress.

- Test-and-learn capabilities become more sophisticated and efficient.

- MA processes are streamlined to drive faster and stronger in-market impact.

- Critical MA capability gaps are diagnosed and closed and bench strength is improved.

- A culture of accountability and performance is engrained and reinforced.

Figure 7.1.   The Three Horizons of Marketing Accountability Improvement

these opportunities. To accomplish this, a marketing accountability diagnostic is conducted. The diagnostic looks for opportunities to improve the effectiveness or efficiency of marketing spending, or both, by considering each of the marketing accountability value levers described in Part Two of this book. Coming out of the diagnostic, you will have (1) identified several "quick win" improvements that can be captured immediately, (2) begun to close critical data gaps, and (3) built plans for conducting deep dives into longer-term opportunities. Designing and conducting the diagnostic properly is critical to the success of your overall MA program, as the diagnostic will reveal the overall size of the prize that is at stake, identify quick wins, reveal structural bottlenecks to improvement, and set the tone for your long-term marketing accountability effort.

Horizon Two focuses on developing a robust test-and-learn capability to improve in-market program performance, close your ROI-knowledge gaps, and better understand how to access all of the improvement opportunities that may be available in and across the six MA value levers. Testing is the most powerful tool available to resolve remaining issues in your understanding of a program's current returns and its future potential. When standard analyses from the diagnostic phase fail to separate the signal from the noise in your marketing spending programs, structured in-market tests can be designed to provide a clean read on marketing cause and effect and real returns on spending. The basic principles of a test-and-learn approach are presented, followed by two complementary styles of test-and-learn—classic field testing and dynamic experimentation. An ongoing test-and-learn agenda will be your key tool for continual optimization of existing spending programs and the means for continually qualifying new programs.

Horizon Three focuses on how to accelerate and sustain the impact of the performance orientation that you have established during Horizon Two. Most important, with a solid baseline of ROI understanding established and validated through a test-and-learn orientation, we focus on honing the processes, capabilities, and systems to use these insights in real time to respond to competitive actions, fast-breaking market opportunities, or other close-in, top-line or bottom-line pressures. Said another way, how does this emerging marketing accountability capability get turned into a business-driving, forward-looking, in-period, competitive advantage? We focus on three key success factors for sustaining long-term impact: (1) building a culture of real accountability, (2) investing in the infrastructure and processes needed to support real-time response, and (3) creating focused, best-in-class capabilities through a build, buy or partnering approach. As we have discussed, marketing accountability is an ongoing journey rather than a destination. Investing in Horizon Three activities should ensure that you do not lose momentum on this journey or plateau at a spot that fails to capitalize on marketing's full potential to add value and contribute to long-term growth.

UNDERSTANDING TYPICAL LANDMINES IN EARLY ROI EFFORTS

Initiating a dialogue on marketing accountability is bound to unearth a lot of bias throughout the organization about how marketing investment does or does not create value. As you begin to have conversations about the need for a marketing accountability initiative, it may be helpful to revisit some of the topics that were covered back in Chapter Two, about recalibrating basic beliefs about marketing spending. Your mission will be better served by simultaneously creating a shared understanding of some of the structural limitations around marketing spending—namely, that it is a tool better suited to tackling certain kinds of problems than others. By using some of that knowledge to educate your audience—for example, "of course we cannot expect to cost-effectively use advertising investment to overcome a material customer service problem"—you should be able to redirect certain kinds of criticisms and not let the broader dialogue get tripped up by some of these distractions and misconceptions.

In a similar vein, when you get into the specific topic of marketing performance measurement, there are often misconceptions, biases, and general confusion about many of the different aspects of a more robust ROI measurement system. Sometimes these are raised as issues by well-intentioned peers who are genuinely struggling with how to think about marketing measurement challenges. Other times they get raised in more of an obstructionist manner, by individuals who would rather see organizational time and energy devoted to tackling other opportunities or who have a vested interest in maintaining the status quo.

Regardless of how and why these issues surface, in our work we often have come upon situations in which these topical landmines become the mythical Gordian knot, appearing so confusing and complicated to untangle that they effectively block any forward progress on marketing accountability as a topic. There are three landmines in particular that you should be prepared for. Tackling each of these in a thoughtful, preemptive way should allow you to avoid errors that could undermine your attempts to build broad-based enthusiasm for a long-term marketing accountability initiative.

Quantitative Marketing Objectives Versus Specific Financial Outcomes

The largest landmine, but also the easiest to avoid, has to do with the different ways in which marketers and CFOs are accustomed to measuring effective performance. As we have argued earlier in the book, a true focus on marketing accountability necessitates a focus on financial outcomes and financial returns. Although this has its own associated complexities (as we will see with the next two landmines), driving toward a well-understood financial return on investment (reflecting net present value of an investment and the cost of capital) would clearly align with what a CFO is typically expecting to understand when reviewing performance measurement data and findings.

By the middle of 2008, to be fair, most marketers had gotten on board with the fact that they need to demonstrate the effectiveness of their investments using quantitative metrics. Almost everyone had gone quantitative. (In the case of some of those marketers who work in direct response businesses, using direct response marketing vehicles with a good understanding of individual customer-level economics, both they and their CFOs start the measurement game fairly aligned.) However, more often than not marketers focus on the quantitative measurement of intermediate or marketing outcomes—like raising unaided awareness from 25 percent to 40 percent or improving a brand's top-two box favorability scores from 45 percent to 65 percent—and they then evaluate the effectiveness of their investments relative to achieving these quantitative marketing objectives.

Thus marketers may be able to quickly tell you that they have good measurement systems in place and understand how well each investment did in terms of delivering a return on its marketing objective (say, every $2.5 million in spend moves unaided awareness by 2 percent). In some sense, these marketers and their agency partners may sincerely believe that they already have a good understanding of the absolute and relative quantitative performance of their marketing programs. But because they often struggle to defensibly link increases in the intermediate or marketing objectives with specific financial outcomes (say, a 2-percent increase in unaided awareness raises annual operating margins by $2 million or increases sales by 4 percent), a CFO typically finds these assertions about performance understanding less than satisfying.

Some companies with more sophisticated customer insight or market research capabilities may have taken the ball even further down field, investing in more scientific attempts to link changes in intermediate marketing objectives with financial outcomes. They may use discrete choice modeling, purchase funnel analytics, or use one of the other analytic techniques covered in the next part of this chapter to more confidently assert that a 1-percent increase in awareness, preference, or consideration will lead to an incremental $5 million in revenues or margin with a specific customer segment. Obviously there is solid consumer behavior or microeconomic theory behind many of these approaches, and the more robust analytic approaches add a rigor and a sense of defensibility to the answers. However, the in-market results and actual performance do not always follow what might have been predicted by these research-driven approaches; this places a cloud of doubt over these kinds of techniques, even when the root causes of the variance are well explained.

Despite the additional substance that these approaches bring, they nonetheless run into nonmarketers' strong skepticism about using research data to *financially* justify marketing investments and validate financial return on investment. There are too many instances of research outcomes not always correlating to business outcomes; for example, when brand familiarity scores go up but actual trial goes down, or when brand equity strengthens around perceptions of innovation and quality but actual deal margins face escalating compression. Others may focus on the accuracy gaps—hypothesized discrepancies between how people respond in a research environment versus what they actually do in real life; in more technical lingo, the gaps between stated beliefs and actual behavior. Regardless of the reason for the objections, you will often reach an impasse in which research-supported techniques to validate financial return will not pass the sniff test, unless they have been validated over time in a closed-loop system that has measured changes in underlying business performance.

As you can see, you can end up with several large groups in a company with diametrically opposed belief systems about how well the company understands its financial return on marketing investments—each right in its own way, but unable to find a bridge to link these belief systems together. This can bring any early momentum you may be building to a screeching halt unless you get out in front of it. Measurement data that focuses on quantitative marketing outcomes is not bad, just incomplete. It can help tell a part—and at times a very compelling part—of the story yet still not prove financial return.

Equipped with this understanding, though, you can get out in front of this issue. If your organization has a strong tracking discipline in relation to marketing objectives and a rich set of research-driven marketing performance analysis, consider that a strength, and help the financial side of the house see how these data sets can play a highly useful role in a broader accountability effort. As we discussed in Chapter Four, this kind of data is very useful in diagnosing why a set of marketing investments may have strong performance, especially in relation to the value levers of strategy and messaging.

However, it is just as important to help the marketers understand why a solid understanding of return on marketing objectives cannot stand as the only performance metric in lieu of a deeper understanding of specific financial outcomes. Although we can remain sympathetic to the struggle many organizations have in providing solid linkages between achieving marketing-specific objectives and financial business outcomes, that does not mean we can abdicate our fiduciary responsibility to push for a more rigorous and defensible quantification of those relationships.

Baseline Versus Incremental Sales: Who Gets Credit for What?

The next ROI-related landmine often surfaces as soon as you get everyone agreeing to focus on measuring the financial outcomes of marketing investments, which, as shown in the previous discussion, is no easy feat. People start to think about the mechanics of how this might happen, and they almost immediately stumble upon the issue of baseline versus incremental performance. Because the optics are the same irrespective of whether we think about top-line or bottom-line performance, for the sake of simplicity, let's keep this discussion focused on the revenue line.

In a nutshell, the issue can be framed like this: if a business had $500 million in revenues last year and spent $50 million on marketing investments, can we irrefutably say that every $1 in marketing investment yielded $10 in revenues? Obviously the business would have invested in many other distribution, product, or operational initiatives to help support its overall revenue targets. Should the marketing investments get full credit for all of the revenue performance? What if we had only invested $25 million in marketing last year? Would our revenues have fallen to $250 million, as indicated by a straight-line relationship between the revenue line and our marketing investments, or would our revenues have been more in the $375 million, $425 million, or perhaps even $500 million range? What if we had invested $60 million in our marketing programs? Would our revenues have gone up to $600 million?

When you first try to look for causal relationships between marketing investments and business outcomes, you clearly run into some tricky decisions as to what proportion of your base business performance you can credit as being driven by your existing marketing investments. If you took all of the marketing investment away, your organization might continue to generate revenues for an extended period based on the strength of your propositions, your products, your distribution, your sales organization, your brand, and all of the other assets that you are deploying on behalf of the business. But at what level and for how long? Similarly, this base volume has been built up over time, to some degree, by the investments that have been made over time in marketing communications and other levers, so you may currently be reaping the benefits of that accretive effect of past investments. Whether you are focused on decay effects or accretive effects beyond the current investment period, it is critical both to understand the relationship of current marketing investment to your "base" business volume in current and future periods and to better predict the impact of changes in marketing investment on that base business over time. At the same time, you want to understand the potential incremental effect of a marginal increase in marketing investment and so triangulate on the optimal level of marketing investment. Baseline impact or the marginal effect, it is not an either-or proposition—we need both!

Newcomers to the world of marketing accountability often get tripped up when thinking these issues through. And it is further complicated by the issue of short-term sales performance versus medium- to long-term sales performance. A business that dramatically cuts back on its marketing investment may lose only marginal volume in the first year, but then the baseline volume performance in years two and three could start to decelerate dramatically based on that year-one investment decision. Said another way, any company's baseline volume needs a certain amount of care and feeding from an investment perspective to prevent its levels and slope from changing over time. Moreover, current-year investment decisions—in marketing as well as across the other operational levers—can impact both the absolute level and the slope of the baseline volume performance in years two and three, regardless of what other investment decisions get made in years two and three.

Even the idea of tying incremental revenues to incremental marketing investments is not always as straightforward as it seems. Occasionally incremental marketing investments may appear to incrementally grow revenues, but what has actually happened is that customers end up forward-buying in this period and then stop shopping during the next period. In other situations, what appears to be incremental volume is actually just the cannibalizing of other SKUs in the offering that were not the target of the incremental marketing programs; this complicates a clean reading of the overall impact.

Now you can see why we call it a landmine! The obvious challenge for you is to not let this admittedly complex issue deter you and the company from tackling the broader marketing accountability opportunity. Although most businesses would never be so reckless as to take their marketing investments down to $0 just to understand the impact of such a move on base volume, most businesses can, through a combination of robust analytic approaches and a focused use of in-market experiments, start to effectively triangulate on these answers. They develop an initial understanding of both how sensitive their base business is to changes in marketing investments as well as how to effectively isolate the incremental lift from incremental marketing vehicles and then fine-tune that understanding over time. Obviously, in data-rich environments like that of U.S. consumer products, with reams of scanner data available for all of the competitors in the category, very robust models have been developed to disentangle these issues. But even in less data-rich environments, progress can be made. We have already presented one example of volume driver modeling, with our retail gasoline example in Figure 2.8, and additional approaches will be covered in more detail in Chapters Eight and Nine.

The main point for you to retain is that you should not be dismayed when people start to raise questions about baseline versus incremental revenue impact and how existing marketing investments might get attributed across the two. As we've said, there are many robust analytical ways to tackle these issues through econometric modeling and in-market experimentation. Your job is to first compliment them on their razor-sharp instincts for immediately getting at one of the trickiest MA issues on the planet and then reassure them that there are many ways to comprehensively tackle this—so stay tuned. We hope you now have enough perspective to see this issue as it starts to emerge, to acknowledge that it is a major issue that needs to get resolved during the course of any significant marketing accountability effort, and to affirm that there are many well-tested techniques for solving this riddle.

The Ever-Elusive ROI Measurement Standards

The final major ROI-related landmine involves the general lack of commonly accepted standards for calculating and quantifying marketing-related ROI, both within and across companies. There is often a high degree of variability in (1) how different kinds of ROI understanding have been arrived at, (2) our confidence that we have specific ROI measures to accurately describe past performance, and (3) the strength of our belief that those ROI measures can be used to predict future performance and guide investment. Usually there is also a wide degree of variation in how much any given analysis has looked at only the individual effects of any given marketing vehicle or program rather than including the incremental interaction or portfolio effects created by the fact that a particular marketing effort was part of an integrated, multivehicle campaign. And because we know that the financial returns that we may have experienced for any given marketing campaign are also a function of a specific marketing and competitive context, we often struggle with how to apply historical performance outcomes to our current situation. So for someone who is expected to integrate all of this knowledge into something coherent for the CEO, it can become almost like a Tower of Babel, impossible to organize, decode, and then reassemble.

Of course, the individual or group who came up with any specific ROI calculation may be convinced of its merit and also highly confident in its applicability across diverse competitive and market contexts. So again we may have a divergent set of beliefs spreading through the organization about how much we actually know about our financial return on marketing investment and thus what our priorities should be for expanding and improving our level of understanding in order to drive in-market performance.

We again encourage you not to be intimidated by this issue and let it undermine your momentum, but rather to take a more optimistic posture by proactively acknowledging that most organizations will have a high degree of variability in their measurement standards and accepting that as reality. If you do this, you can simultaneously educate all of the key stakeholders about the implications of this wide degree of variability—specifically, that it impacts the level of precision with which we can deploy these findings.

In fact, each existing ROI calculation must be assessed for its quality, accuracy, applicability, and usefulness as a future performance indicator. We encourage you to use the Short-term Financial ROI Precision Scale shown in Figure 7.2, or something similar, to put a "usefulness and actionability" rating on all of the existing ROI analyses. There are four levels in this scale, starting with the self-evident

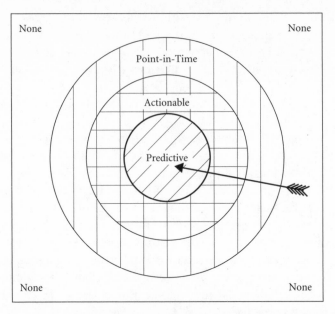

Figure 7.2.   Short-Term Financial ROI Precision Scale

None, moving through Point-in-Time and Actionable, and finally to Predictive, on the bull's-eye. The None designation is used when the existing ROI measures for an activity are not useful or sound, notwithstanding the fact that you may have other performance measurements like return on marketing targets, brand equity, or purchase funnel metrics. You would give an ROI finding a Point-in-Time designation if you have only a few isolated attempts at ROI measurements from one-off historical campaigns. An activity would be given an Actionable designation if you have multiple, robust estimates of historical ROI for that activity across a range of business conditions and feel confident using that range of estimates for business planning purposes. An activity would be given a Predictive designation if you have consistently forecasted and executed your operating plans based on these ROI estimates, the activity is held accountable for delivering that business performance, and its ROI variance over time is well analyzed and well understood.

As all three of these brief ROI landmine discussions have illuminated, you can very quickly end up in some messy and tricky conversations right out of the gate. If marketing ROI as a topic were so straightforward, everyone would have conquered it long ago! Our main goal with this section is to equip you with enough knowledge to stay one step ahead of your colleagues, enabling you to acknowledge the complexity of the topic without letting it become a roadblock to moving forward.

A QUICK PRIMER OF AVAILABLE ANALYTIC TOOLS AND APPROACHES

In the same way that knowledge of ROI-related landmines is helpful when building a commitment to pursuing marketing accountability, so is having some familiarity and fluency in the available analytic tools and approaches for determining spend effectiveness. This quick primer will showcase some of the most prominent approaches and give you a sense of the kinds of insights they provide and when they can be used to best effect. It is not meant to be an exhaustive list of the available approaches or a detailed how-to guide for conducting each of these analyses. We will highlight a list of other good reference materials for specific analytic approaches at the end of this chapter.

The five different analytic approaches that we will discuss are presented in Figure 7.3. The first, competitive benchmarking and best

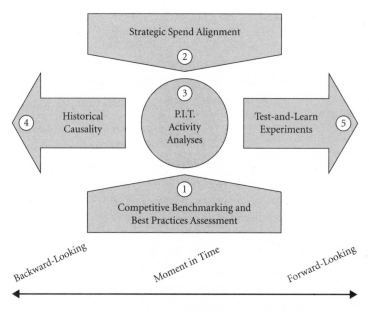

Figure 7.3.   A Primer of Analytic Approaches

practices assessment, is always a good place to start. It can produce high-level insights into the differences in marketing investment models across categories and competitors, and it can usually be done relatively quickly. The second approach, strategic spend alignment, is more inwardly focused and top-down, but can highlight immediate discrepancies between business objectives and marketing investment that can be quickly remedied. The third approach, point-in-time activity analysis, can help to establish baseline performance levels across a range of marketing activities, even if it reflects only a specific moment-in-time measure. The fourth approach, historical causality, attempts to use more robust statistical analyses between past marketing investment and past business outcomes to determine the relative effectiveness of different kinds of strategies and tactics. The more sophisticated versions of this may also address the interaction effects across marketing vehicles as well as isolate both the average and marginal effectiveness of different kinds of marketing investment strategies. The final approach, test-and-learn experiments, will be touched on lightly here, as we will devote all of Chapter Nine to this topic.

Competitive Benchmarking and Best Practices Assessment

Competitive benchmarking analysis inventories current or historical investment levels and activities of relevant companies within your category; best practices assessment attempts to identify analogous situations both in and out of category to extrapolate reasonable investment levels and likely impact. In both situations, analysts are encouraged to use a range of primary and secondary research techniques, leveraging both proprietary and syndicated data sources, to create as complete a snapshot as possible of a company's marketing investment patterns.

For best practice assessments, you have the added complexity of determining which outside companies constitute a best practice—an art in its own right. The starting point should be a collection of leading companies that share some set of like characteristics relative to financial performance, operating models, go-to-market strategies, line-of-business or geographic complexity, marketing investment levels, or other such fundamental factors. But do not overlook the importance of selecting companies that are highly admired inside your organization, especially by key decision makers. Providing a directionally correct best practice assessment about a company whose management practices are highly admired is infinitely more powerful and persuasive than a highly accurate analysis of a company that is seen as more of a peer or, even worse, a sloppy competitor.

In an ideal world, you are striving for as granular a view of marketing investments as possible, capturing data on investment levels, media vehicles, campaign types, any product or geographic market skews, timing, and duration. Obviously you have a speed versus accuracy trade-off here, but many marketers are often surprised by the high quality of the third-party competitive spending sources, notwithstanding the variability across industries and spending categories. The collected data would be compiled in a way to allow for insightful comparisons across competitors and between competitors and your company's own situation.

The graphs depicted in Figure 7.4 are typical of the output from a competitive benchmarking analysis. This illustrative data, from four competitive companies and "us," reflects the total amount of marketing investment that all five companies had deployed in the current and prior year, as well as the percentage of their investment that went into each of eight different types of marketing vehicles. Competitor C is clearly the eight-hundred-pound gorilla in this category from a marketing investment perspective; they have grown their investment in the current year, while we invest at levels comparable to Competitor A, with Competitor D investing at a significantly lower absolute level.

From a marketing mix perspective, you can also see a dramatic difference in strategy. Although both companies invest a proportional amount in direct marketing, Competitor C focuses its other investment on cable TV and radio, whereas we focus our investment in national TV, magazines, and newspaper. Competitor A, on other hand, invests more similarly to Competitor C, but they dial down the direct marketing percentage and invest in internet vehicles instead.

This short example also effectively illuminates the strengths and weaknesses of this type of analytic approach. With a little persistence and elbow grease, this kind of analysis can be pulled from readily available data in fairly short order, especially relative to the alternatives. It also may allow you to frame up some competitive comparisons that have real shock value at both a substantive and a symbolic level. And if your critical first objective is to get senior executives to sit up and pay attention, this may be exactly what the doctor ordered.

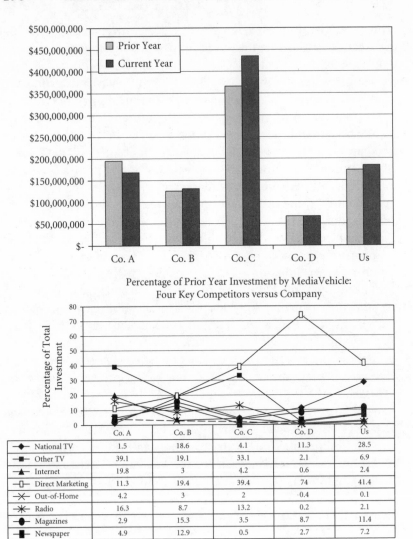

Figure 7.4.   Benchmarking Marketing Mix Patterns

But it tends to fall short of the mark in determining the actionable implications for your company. If your business is twice the size of Competitor C but they spend twice as much on marketing, which company has the better strategy? Are you wasting your money on network TV or are they wasting it on cable, or are both equally effective, given everything else at play? As you know, no two companies are exactly alike in terms of their capabilities, strategic differentiators, or requirements. Simply understanding the gaps between the approaches of two different companies does not help you understand which answer is right. If a competitor had better bottom-line results in a given period, you might be able to infer that their investments were more effective, but you could not irrefutably conclude that their investment levels or mix are the right prescription for *your* business.

So we like to think of competitive benchmarking and best practice assessments as necessary but not sufficient approaches in the overall MA toolkit. If you need to move quickly and you do not have a lot to work with, they are a great place to start. They can help put your company's current situation in a relevant context, which can be especially helpful for senior executives with a nonmarketing background. Typically, however, these types of analyses raise just as many questions as they answer, and you need to supplement them with incremental analytic approaches.

Strategic Spend Alignment

This analytic approach identifies more precise value-creating objectives for your marketing investments, then compares the allocation of your existing marketing investments against those priorities. These more precise "value-creating" objectives are typically sourced either from existing business plans (for specific products, markets, or channels) or from the kinds of strategic marketing analyses (segmentation, purchase funnel blockages, targeting) that were discussed at length in Chapter Four, such as markets targeted for new growth, markets targeted for maintenance, markets targeted for divesting, and so on. You use these materials to help understand a company's most promising growth and volume opportunities or its biggest inhibitors to growth; then the analysis helps ensure that the marketing investments are optimized to address those opportunities and challenges. When a company has had a history of grandfathering a lot of prior-year spending programs into the current year as a matter of course, strategic spend alignment analyses provide an effective and quick way to see how far out of line the existing investment portfolio is, relative to a company's growth priorities.

Figure 7.5 provides a typical example of how this kind of analytic approach might work. On the left-hand side of the figure, seven country markets are plotted on a two-by-two grid comparing forecasted market growth with forecasted operating margin. Some of the

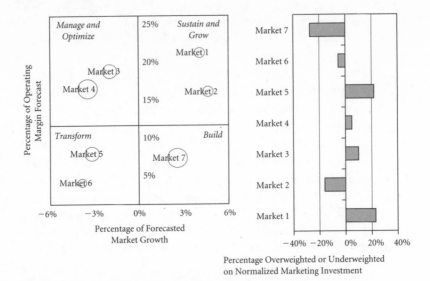

Figure 7.5. Aligning Relative Investment Levels to Forecasted
Growth Prospects

markets are larger and some are smaller, as denoted by the size of the
circle, but they naturally fall into four strategic quadrants: Sustain and
Grow, Manage and Optimize, Build, and Transform. Without additional market-specific context, it is fair to assume that each market
within a given market type would be given a similar marketing investment treatment. But as the graph on the right-hand side of the figure
shows, even when normalized by market size, the current investment
allocation is all over the place. Market 1 is at least 20-percent overweighted from an investment perspective, and Market 2 is 15-percent
underweighted, even though both are Sustain and Grow markets. The
same kinds of discrepancies exist between Markets 5 and 6, both of
which are in the Transform quadrant. Finally Market 7 is seriously
underweighted from an investment perspective, even though it is in
the Build quadrant. Given our competitive position and growth prospects in each of these markets, this kind of analysis raises some very
obvious questions about investment reallocation.

In a similar vein, Figure 7.6 raises comparable kinds of questions
in light of the output of strategic marketing analysis. The graph on
the left-hand side of the page highlights the company's performance
gaps compared with its core competitors at each step of the purchase

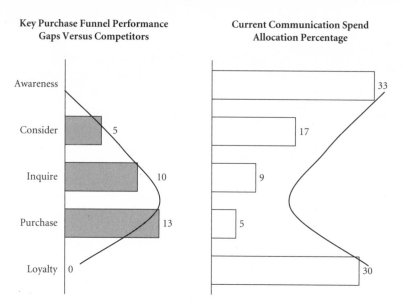

Key Purchase Funnel Performance
Gaps Versus Competitors

Current Communication Spend
Allocation Percentage

Figure 7.6.   Aligning Relative Investment Levels to Purchase Funnel Blockages

funnel. The company is actually at parity with its competitors at the first stage in the funnel, brand awareness, and, at the final stage of the funnel, loyalty. The company has significant deficits, however, in the middle part of the purchase funnel, in terms of converting awareness to consideration, consideration into actual inquiries, and then those inquiries into actual purchases. These gaps range from 5 percent to 13 percent. On the right-hand side of the figure, where current marketing investments have been allocated based on the stage of the purchase funnel that the vehicles target, you can clearly see that the company invests in a way that is inversely proportional to its purchase funnel gaps. The purchase step gets the smallest proportion of the budget (5 percent), whereas the awareness stage and the loyalty stage get the lion's share of the budget (33 percent and 30 percent, respectively). At first glance, it appears that there may be opportunities to divert some of the awareness-focused investment to the consideration and purchase gaps.

These two examples highlight the strengths and shortcomings of this analytic approach. In organizations with highly calcified marketing budgets, this approach provides a fast mechanism for pinpointing spend misalignment and refocusing investment in a way that should be inherently more productive. The data about growth or volume priorities is usually readily available and can often be sliced and diced in a way that quickly reveals major and insightful mismatches between investment and growth. However, this kind of analysis allows you to answer only questions about relative allocation across competing business priorities. It does not help you understand the optimal level of investment or mix of vehicles for pursuing any given opportunity. You will need to use other analytic approaches to get a more precise answer to those kinds of questions.

Point-in-Time Activity Analysis

These kinds of analyses attempt to isolate the cause and effect of a specific marketing activity, like an e-mail campaign or a direct marketing drop or a NASCAR sponsorship. Typically these are customized to deal with the unique characteristics of the specific activity and can vary widely in sophistication, from simple payout calculators to more complex pre- and postadvertising or sponsorship analysis with custom tracking. Sometimes this kind of analysis uses financial outcome data that is directly attributable to the specific marketing activity, but in other cases the financial outcomes may be inferred using a variety of techniques. It is essential to have a clear understanding of how the financial outcome data has been derived, because it is the critical linchpin in any point-in-time analysis. Finally, these kinds of analyses may also track performance against specific marketing outcomes (like perceptual metrics or recall) in addition to financial outcomes.

Table 7.1 provides a typical example of how a set of point-in-time activity analyses might get framed. This is a masked illustrative example from a fast-growing consumer technology company that sells big-ticket devices directly on its website and through its call centers. In a recent quarter, it had ten discrete marketing campaigns in market, across a variety of direct response marketing vehicles like paid search, internet affiliate programs, e-mail, and print catalog marketing. All of its affiliate, banner ad, paid search, and e-mail vehicles are credited for sales that result when a prospective customer directly clicks through to the site and purchases. The print catalogs get assigned sales through some type of source code process for call center orders and through a match-back process that attempts to match orders with people who received a catalog. There was a wide degree of effectiveness

	Number of Impressions or Pieces	Total Cost	Cost per Impression	Total Sales	Cost/ Sale
Google Paid Search	1,693,135	$980,326	$0.58	$5,079,407	19.3%
Yahoo Paid Search	1,262,562	$221,959	$0.18	$757,538	29.3%
Affiliate Program #1	1,486,881	$535,508	$0.36	$1,657,921	32.3%
Affiliate Program #2	4,050,943	$950,621	$0.23	$5,401,257	17.6%
Banner Advertising	6,540,000	$763,453	$0.12	$1,583,926	48.2%
E-mail Drop #1	1,165,000	$38,452	$0.03	$674,592	5.7%
E-mail Drop #2	4,326,500	$114,202	$0.03	$1,202,128	9.5%
E-mail Drop #3	2,540,000	$71,334	$0.03	$2,468,297	2.9%
Catalog Drop #1	2,010,000	$2,480,279	$1.23	$4,788,182	51.8%
Catalog Drop #2	1,105,435	$1,262,413	$1.14	$3,220,441	39.2%
Total Attributable Sales		$7,418,545		$26,833,688	27.6%
Unattributable Sales				$8,563,412	
Total Sales				**$35,397,100**	

Table 7.1.   Q2 Marketing Programs: Point-in-Time Effectiveness Analysis of Marketing Vehicles for High-Tech Consumer Company.

of the various activities—with the most efficient performing at under 3 percent cost of sale and the least efficient performing at more than 50 percent cost of sale. Also, almost 25 percent of the company's total sales for this quarter could not be attributed to any specific marketing activity.

As is immediately evident from this example, the ability to effec-tively isolate the sales impact of any specific point-in-time activity in a rigorous and defensible manner is what separates great point-in-time analyses from their more mediocre brethren. With address-able vehicles like direct mail, Internet, or point-of-purchase, you have better mechanisms for assigning specific sales to a specific activity, so your confidence goes up—but even these do not have foolproof tracking mechanisms. For other kinds of activities, more advanced analytical techniques (simple correlation, regression, test and control, bump/lift) and market research can be used to assign the sales effects and calculate the relative effectiveness of a given point-in-time activ-ity. Over time, the cumulative results of a series of PIT analyses can provide a well-understood range of potential performance outcomes for any given type of marketing activity.

Seeing as these tend to be simpler to do than more robust his-torical modeling and do not require the patience of experiments, PIT activity analyses usually are an important part of the overall analytic toolkit. If you can gain confidence in a way to isolate and allocate the sales effects to individual activities, these analyses begin to provide a solid foundation of ROI ranges for standard marketing activities. However, if you cannot get comfortable with how the sales effects have been allocated, the believability of these analyses begins to break down. Moreover, this kind of analysis also will always miss any of the dynamic interaction effects and synergies across the total mix of marketing investment, as well as the impact of lags, carryovers, and stock effects, which it is not usually designed to capture. Not accounting for these effects may marginally or materially underrep-resent the effectiveness of any given marketing activity. You will need to familiarize yourself with the two final analytic approaches to be able to confidently tackle some of those issues.

Historical Causality

This analytic approach attempts to establish the correlation between historical marketing spending patterns and financial measures of business performance, usually focusing on short-term sales response. At its simplest, you may be running simple linear regressions between marketing spending and sales, looking for statistically significant cor-relations between the variables. The more advanced approaches—which could involve techniques known as mix modeling, dynamic mapping, or other forms of advanced econometric modeling—attempt to perform this analysis all within the context of the total marketing environment, controlling for actions taken across the broader Four P's marketing lever, any relevant competitive actions or response, and potentially other exogenous factors like macroeconomic growth or other market forces that might impact demand and, ultimately, the relative effectiveness of the marketing stimuli. With these approaches, you attempt to study the whole marketing ecosystem and look for significant relationships and interactions across and among all of the potential sales drivers. Some of these more advanced approaches may also try to model the impact of marketing spending on other intermediate or long-term marketing outcome variables, like awareness or consideration or brand equity, as well as on short-term sales.

As you can discern already, these analyses tend to devolve into statistical modeling exercises fairly quickly, and they require a fair amount of historical data to be collected. The specific kind and amount of data required depends on how rich and robust an analysis you would like to conduct. Said another way, working from broader, richer, deeper, and more granular data sets typically leads to more powerful insights and more robust findings about historical causality. Being able to look at granular cuts of the analysis by geographic market or product type or distribution channel will definitely lead to a richer set of insights. But most companies are not naturally set up to store such market-related data in structured formats in readily accessible systems, which can then turn the data extraction, compilation, and quality testing into a monumental task in and of itself, even before the analyzing of historical causality gets started. Sometimes it is even a challenge to just get the short-term sales data cut in a way that easily maps to the marketing vehicles.

But if you are up to the data task and you can access the statistical and analytical support to run the analyses, the insights from historical causality can be compelling. The graph in Figure 7.7 depicts the historical average effectiveness of over twenty different campaigns in generating new orders for two different kinds of products, in both emerging and mature markets. Almost all of the TV campaigns were dramatically more effective in the mature markets than in the emerging markets on a per–gross rating point (GRP) basis. Two specific TV campaigns, TV-c and TV-k, popped for emerging markets, but the rest of the TV investment was dramatically less effective. All of the radio campaigns and the on-line campaign were highly effective for

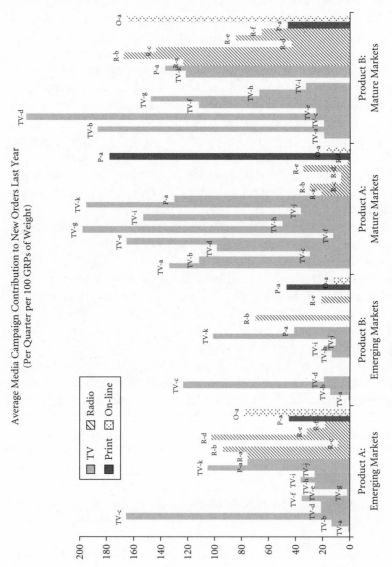

Figure 7.7.   Sample Output from a Historical Causality Analysis

Product B in mature markets; the print campaign was highly effective for Product A in mature markets, but radio less so. For emerging markets across product types, there were some strong performers, but none of the investments had a performance comparable to that in mature markets. When done right, you can quickly assess the relative historical effectiveness and do interesting comparative analyses as well.

The graph in Figure 7.8 depicts a different kind of illustrative output from a more advanced modeling exercise, in which the elasticities of specific marketing levers have been precisely estimated using historical modeling techniques. In addition to the four promotional levers of TV, out-of-home, point-of-purchase, and weekly inserts, the price elasticities for two of the different formats have also been estimated. At the macro level, brand volume is much more sensitive to price changes than to promotional changes. But among the promotional tactics, sales are much more responsive to increases in point-of-purchase and weekly insert activities than to TV advertising or out-of-home advertising. Although there are some variations in performance across distribution channels A and B, you can clearly see how you would be able to use these historical elasticities, combined with investment data, to do detailed ROI calculations on all six levers.

You need to get comfortable with one key aspect of this approach: most of the insights will be inferred through advanced statistical

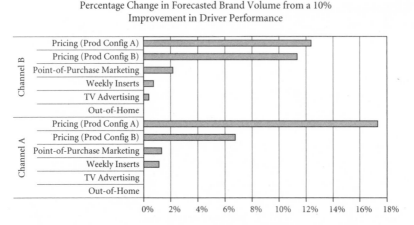

Percentage Change in Forecasted Brand Volume from a 10% Improvement in Driver Performance

Figure 7.8.   Sample Elasticities and Marginal Effectiveness of Various Marketing Levers for Two Different Distribution Channels

analyses. Said another way, the more robust estimates of marketing effectiveness will be mathematically modeled based on natural variations that are detected in the historical data. Although these observed relationships are typically sound, there must be enough material variance in the data for this approach to lead to statistically significant findings. If a company has little historical variance in its marketing investment levels or marketing mix, or too much random noise in the data, then these approaches may not yield any helpful findings, despite the Herculean efforts that may have gone into collecting and scrubbing the historical data. The academic literature is also clear that there are risks inherent in this type of modeling. If not properly managed, these risks—related to not identifying the right variables to model, the statistical independence of some of the variables, model specification, and so on—can undermine the legitimacy of the findings. A capable econometric modeler should be able to help you understand the extent to which these risks could impact your ability to draw readable and reliable conclusions.

The final two precautions that warn against an overreliance on this analytic approach have to do with the "black box" nature of some of the tools and the projectability of the findings. As you can see, you will need to have some pretty strong mathematical chops on staff to perform and then interpret these models. But many of these analyses can appear to spit out the results without a lot of transparency in terms of the underlying scaffolding or modeling assumptions. The model may be right or the model may be wrong, but at a minimum all of the core components that shaped the answer should be well understood and open for debate. If you do not feel confident that someone in your organization has done that, tread cautiously before taking it to the senior leadership team. Finally, the results of historical causality exercises are relevant for future decision making only to the extent that the past patterns still hold true. In stable market situations without a lot of disruption from innovating competitors or substitute offers or new entrants, this may be fine. But if you suddenly find your company in a highly dynamic and rapidly evolving market situation, an overreliance on these kinds of analyses may lead you down a very wrong investment path. Moreover, if you have not had a lot of historical variation in your investments or you are experimenting with a number of new marketing vehicles that your company has never used, the usefulness of this analytic approach drops off dramatically.

Test-and-Learn Experiments

The final analytic approach involves test-and-learn experiments. The idea here is that you use solid experimental design thinking to structure a series of experiments in which you vary marketing stimuli and then analyze the absolute and relative effectiveness of the competing approaches. As we have mentioned, we will be devoting a whole chapter to two distinct variants of this approach—classic field testing and dynamic experimentation—discussing when and how to use these approaches to best effect. We believe that this will become a fundamental component of any long-term marketing accountability agenda, although it is not without its drawbacks in terms of providing immediate answers to outstanding marketing questions.

This closes our primer on the various types of analytic approaches. Although each has its own inherent strengths and weaknesses, notwithstanding that, we feel that all of these approaches can play a role in your overall diagnostic toolkit. As will become patently obvious, it takes a lot of analysis to confidently move an organization through the three horizons of marketing accountability, any particular one of which may have greater requirements for speed versus accuracy versus predictability versus defensibility. Having a flexible set of diverse tools that you can deploy as needed will put you in the most powerful position. And as we step through the details of diagnostic design in Chapter Eight, we will help you figure out how to tailor your early stage analytic techniques for the diagnostic that makes the most sense for your company.

FAMILIARIZING YOURSELF WITH INTERNAL AND EXTERNAL MA ENABLERS

After such a passionate exposition concerning ROI landmines and wide-ranging analytic approaches, you might well arch a skeptical eyebrow if we were to suddenly assert that there is more to marketing accountability than analytics. A strong analytic orientation is obviously at the heart of all accountable marketing cultures. But this analytic orientation gets developed within a broader ecosystem of accountability enablers, without which long-term progress cannot be made. These enablers, which we divide into an internal and an external group, speak to a more holistic set of capabilities, processes, infrastructure, and relationships, all of which must interoperate effectively over time to support a transformation. You may be able to develop one-off, short-term work-arounds for major deficiencies in some of the enablers during the diagnostic phase, but you ignore material gaps at your long-term peril. As with the previous section, the purpose here is to briefly familiarize yourself with these enablers, so that you can anticipate potential enabler-related roadblocks that surface and more proactively take enablers into account as you design your approach to the diagnostic discussed at length in the next chapter.

Internal Enablers

The primary focus of this exercise is to understand how well developed the marketing planning process is, how well it is integrated into the broader business planning process, and how accountable the process owners are for delivering measurable outcomes. There are five core components to the internal ecosystem of MA enablers, as depicted in Figure 7.9. Essentially, by diagnosing a company's existing

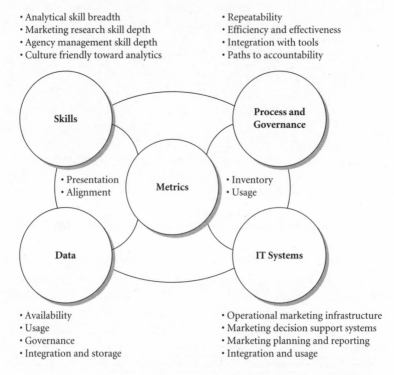

Figure 7.9.   The Internal Ecosystem of Marketing Accountability Enablers

stage of development with regard to metrics, skills, process and governance, data, and supporting IT systems, we attempt to understand how tight an intersection already exists between the business planning process and the marketing planning process, and whether that linkage is supported with a robust, closed-loop system for tracking in-market execution and monitoring performance on the back end. Companies with strong linkages between business planning and marketing planning tend to be better positioned to make faster gains from an accountability perspective. Companies with weak linkages or none at all have a steeper road to climb and usually find themselves in this condition because of some material weaknesses in a few or all of the underlying components. We will quickly step through a discussion of each underlying component, so that you have a better understanding of the role it plays and how to assess your organization's current state of maturity with regard to this component.

METRICS Metrics sit at the center of the internal enablers and are really the linchpin; all of the other enablers play supporting roles. By metrics, we mean the inventory of measurements that the company currently uses to explain business performance and marketing performance. Among a range of other issues, we want to understand whether those metrics are used and presented in consistent ways throughout the organization. For example, how are these metrics calculated? How often are they used, and are they available in a timely way to support planning, forecasting, and course correction activities? Who is the target audience for any resulting output or analysis? Do the marketing metrics align with the other important business metrics? Do the existing metrics answer the toughest and most frequently asked senior executive questions?

Ideally, you would discover a broad inventory of metrics to help manage marketing decisions, with well-understood and well-supported metrics that comprehensively link brand equity, marketing initiatives, and tactical programs to baseline and incremental volume. These metrics should provide a broad and deep understanding of the drivers of volume and should have the political support of all of the key stakeholders in the business. Ideally, these metrics would roll up into a consolidated view of marketing performance and could be used to predict volume. Of course, your company's existing metrics may meet none of these criteria. As disappointing as that conclusion may be, there is a silver lining even in that outcome: it represents a great jumping-off point for hypothesis generation for your MA diagnostic! So at a minimum, take detailed notes and then put them in a safe place.

SKILLS As we discussed in detail in the chapters on the six key value levers, there are a number of different skill sets that are essential to deploying highly accountable marketing investments. Strategic marketing skills, agency management skills, media planning skills, and in-market execution discipline are all at the heart of marketing-driven value creation. At the same time, if an organization wants to make significant headway on marketing measurement, it needs a broad cross-section of analytical skills as well as deep specialist skills in quantitative market research. It's best if the organization has the skills to blend world-class analyses in econometrics, brand measurement, test and control, and market structure with a solid, operationally quantitative decision support capability rooted in solid financial analysis, business planning, data query and manipulation, and the like. Another critical prerequisite is a decision-making culture that is predisposed to analytics as a way to frame problems and present solutions.

PROCESS AND GOVERNANCE Although process and governance are fairly broad themes, when it comes to internal MA enablers we are primarily focusing on the marketing planning process, how it links to the business planning process, and how performance monitoring and course correction happen postplanning. You want to understand whether there are well-understood, repeatable, and effective processes in place for key planning activities like marketing strategy development, key insights generation, business planning, forecasting, budgeting, integrated marketing planning, program development, performance monitoring, and course correction. You want the processes to tightly, directly link strategy to execution decisions, with analytics and insights integrated in a way that is efficient and transparent and with clear ownership of and accountability for process outcomes. The questions of who participates in which steps, how final decisions get reached, and how well the outputs link to inputs for downstream process steps all speak to the tightness and effectiveness of the governance mechanisms. Material process and governance weaknesses are at the center of many failed accountability initiatives.

DATA By data, we mean specifically the marketing data infrastructure and how well it integrates with other operational, transactional data. In the best of all worlds, you would have a holistic approach to marketing data management, with all high-priority data types—including but not limited to sales and volume data, marketing investment data, customer data, marketing vehicle-specific data streams, and transactional data—highly available at the right granularity and frequency, with clear rules about ownership, usage, and enterprise integration. The reality of many organizations, however, is a mishmash of approaches to marketing data, with a hodgepodge of data sources, managed in silos, where the data is usually treated as a perishable asset—a consumable without much shelf life. Data is as much the Achilles heel of so many efforts as it is the enabling currency that supports or undermines the entire MA ecosystem.

IT SYSTEMS This final component addresses the enabling marketing technology systems through which so much of this data and analysis flows. Your objective is to understand how many of the core operational marketing processes and decision-support marketing processes are supported by formal custom or packaged marketing technology systems and the extent to which they interface with customer relationship management and sales force automation software. Because no vendor has come along to provide a SAP equivalent for the marketing value chain, typically what you find here is another hodgepodge of approaches, ranging from paper and Microsoft Excel–enabled processes to those with robust database-driven IT systems and interfaces. And where the operational systems are weak, the analytic systems tend to be even weaker. Conversely though, some organizations have started to tackle this challenge through the building of marketing data warehouses that integrate much of this disparate system data into a single technology with a common interface. Regardless of which end of the spectrum you sit on, inventorying the systems infrastructure closes out the final piece of the internal puzzle.

External Enablers

By *external enablers* we are primarily referring to the kinds of long-term partners or project-based vendors who may be mandatory participants in the first phase of your MA journey and whose support you may want to proactively line up in advance of your diagnostic. Figure 7.10 depicts the five most common types of companies that you might partner with.

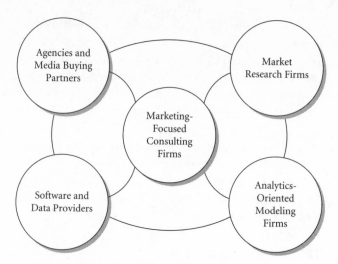

Figure 7.10.   The External Ecosystem of Marketing
Accountability Enablers

AGENCIES AND MEDIA BUYING PARTNERS In many up-or-out marketing organizations with fast rotations through brand management
and field marketing jobs, the advertising, direct marketing, on-line,
or media buying agencies may have the most comprehensive institutional memory for what the company has done and why. Obviously
the kind of agency that will matter most to your company will depend
on your historical marketing mix choices, but you get the point.
These agencies usually have access to much more granular spending
data by market for you and your category competitors. Moreover, an
agency is also the gatekeeper of real media costing information, which
is critical for analyzing new "what if" scenarios needed to optimize
your spending mix. As you can imagine, digging into these issues
of historical advertising performance and media cost may appear
threatening to your agency team and could generate some passive-
aggressive resistance, so you'll need to position the overall effort
through effective top-to-top communications. Most agencies ultimately get on board to support the effort or face the ultimate threat
of being walked off of the account.

MARKETING-ORIENTED MANAGEMENT CONSULTANTS Management consultants can provide quick traction and leverage to firms who either

cannot secure sufficient team resources internally or want the benefit of a highly skilled outside resource to bring speed, efficiency, and objectivity to your overall efforts. The right kind of management consulting partner will have the ability to drive the whole process in a way that jump-starts your efforts, anticipates potential roadblocks, and leverages a wide range of preexisting case history. The best specialist consulting firms may also be able to bring to bear new analytic techniques and the pattern recognition that comes from doing this work over and over again across numerous industries. A consultant should also provide objectivity that is not constrained by entrenched practices or internal politics; this objectivity is sometimes needed to gain consensus among disparate stakeholders. Moreover, a management consulting organization rarely has a vested interest in any specific marketing mix answer, which cannot be said for most agency or agency-network-affiliated entity. This objectivity, coupled with greater analytic rigor, may also be what is needed to meet the CEO's or CFO's high burden of proof for the value of marketing investments. Consulting firms are expensive, though, so the decision to use them should have the right risk-reward payoff. Make sure, too, that you get the benefit of the most experienced practitioners on your project team.

MARKET RESEARCH FIRMS Market research vendors may be called on to recut existing research data in new ways or conduct new gap-fill research. New analysis of existing data could be needed to better match existing research to geographies where particular marketing spending events occurred or to statistically correlate softer metrics such as brand awareness and preference to hard dollar measures of financial performance, such as switching behavior and share of requirements.

ANALYTICS-ORIENTED MODELING FIRMS There are firms that specialize in performing advanced modeling of historical marketing investment data. Typically they combine strong data structuring and manipulation skills with advanced modeling techniques. Many of these firms also have a library of previous analyses that can be used for benchmarking purposes, although most have deep expertise in only a single category, like pharmaceuticals or packaged goods. Sometimes they struggle to connect the analytics insights with the broader strategic context for the company, and obviously the data requirements are intense, but the support of such specialist firms can be a powerful weapon to line up, especially if your company's previous attempts at linking marketing investment to financial reward have underwhelmed the senior executive team.

SOFTWARE AND THIRD-PARTY DATA PROVIDERS A number of newer providers have emerged with software tools and subscription data services that can play a meaningful role in your initiative. Many of these specialists focus on specific aspects of the measurement problem, like data aggregation or industry benchmarking or econometric modeling, and have used packaged approaches with flexible user interfaces to support insights generation and the overall approach to analysis. Other firms focus more on industry-level data capture, with comprehensive views of marketing spending and sales performance. Nielsen, IRI, and IMS are some of the heavyweights for the packaged goods and pharmaceutical industries. All of these areas have been getting a lot of venture capital investment recently, and new providers are pushing innovative solutions with some frequency.

PRACTICAL TIPS FOR GETTING STARTED

Armed with this much deeper understanding of ROI landmines, analytic approaches, and MA enablers—understanding that we will continue to apply when designing your custom diagnostic in the next chapter—you are now more prepared to lay the groundwork and build support for a substantive push for marketing accountability. As we suggested earlier, how far and how fast you go with MA improvement is less a function of where you start and more about the choices you make along the way. No choices are more critical to determining your ultimate success than those you will make in this initial planning phase, in which you begin to set expectations about what problems are going to get tackled, define what success from your efforts will look like, and begin to secure the resources to support the overall effort. Although many of the harder short-term content trade-offs are addressed as part of diagnostic design in the next chapter, there are some practical macro considerations around initiative structure, framing, and resourcing that merit some discussion before we go there.

This kind of an accountability initiative is one of the last great undermanaged investment areas in a company, so the political and cultural tension that may unleashed by merely talking about it can be overwhelming. Thus it will be in your best interest to get out in front of this and to set a proper tone. From a structural perspective, as with any major transformation initiative, this means being thoughtful about questions of executive sponsorship, cross-functional participation, core team dynamics, steering committee roles, and overall initiative governance. Many factors will inform the right solution for your situation, including the internal political landscape, the degree of decentralization or centralization in core marketing processes, who owns what kinds of data, and where the most competent resources lie. Striking the right balance between solutions that are politically or organizationally expedient and solutions that put the best caliber talent in the right kind of roles is one indicator of great leadership. Be prepared to at least invest the time and energy to make thoughtful, conscious decisions with regard to initiative structure. It can save you a lot of backtracking and wasted effort down the line.

The second key issue is how to frame the overriding purpose for this initiative, especially in its earliest days. It is helpful to get your core early stakeholders engaged in a dialogue about where the primary emphasis should be, which then sets the proper tone for the mandate. Typically you want to have thoughtful debates about the relative emphasis of cost-cutting (efficiency) versus volume growth (effectiveness) in the overall scheme of things, as well as about the merits of narrower themes related to ROI quantification (measurement) or marketing analytics skills and infrastructure (capability building).

Efficiency-anchored initiatives, which promise to accomplish the same in-market results while spending less, tend to be the dominant focus these days. The benefit of improved efficiency as a primary objective, particularly when it is accompanied by a very specific target (for example, reduce spending by 15 percent within six months), is that it is a very tangible goal with a high likelihood of being achieved. The drawback to a narrow focus on efficiency or savings is that it is unlikely to coincidentally uncover improvements to strategies and plans that will drive incremental revenue growth. Alternatively, emphasizing spend effectiveness is a more inspirational and motivating goal to marketers than a focus on efficiency, and it is usually more consistent with a CEO and board's search for ever more organic growth. It has the potential to create the more long-term value for the company, if well-executed, but it also may prematurely raise expectations about the power of the initiative before you understand how a steep a hill will need to be climbed. Whether you choose something bold like effectiveness or something tangible like efficiency or something even narrower still, you can see the important implications for the tone and sense of expectations for the whole initiative. So choose wisely.

The final issue involves questions of initiative resourcing. As you will have sensed by now, this is not something that the average Joe can pile on top of his day job. Many companies that have gotten serious about marketing accountability have built out whole departments, working under an SVP of marketing analytics or customer analytics or marketing measurement, who work nonstop with both internal and external resources to continually improve and refine the organization's marketing performance. And as we saw through the discussion of the analytic approaches and MA enablers, the marketing value chain and enabling ecosystem can be complex and the analytic techniques deployed may require some specialist, technical skills. So finding the right resources with the right breadth of experience to support this initiative, even in its first phase, can be a challenge. To the extent these people already live in the business, you may run into a lot of kicking and screaming if you try to pull them from their day jobs.

The most important point is to do some level-setting with your senior sponsors about potential resource requirements before you move too far down any one path. To get started in Horizon One, you are going to need some small core team that is 100-percent dedicated to this effort. It can be as small as one or two people or as large as six to eight. You can then be prepared to supplement those resources with part-time players or extended-team members from across the business, but you are unlikely to make material progress without that dedicated core. Second, given the range of issues to be addressed, the core team will need access to a pool of discretionary funding that allows them to work with some subset of the external enablers identified earlier in the chapter, especially during Horizon One. Finally, it is important to remind everyone that although a long-term commitment to marketing accountability may require substantial investment in measurement capabilities and infrastructure, the findings from a well-constructed diagnostic will give them the information they need to evaluate whether the opportunity justifies the increased investment to assess the relative attractiveness of any self-funding opportunities.

You are now ready to launch into the details of Horizon One, during which we design and execute a custom-built diagnostic that ultimately allows us to identify major improvement opportunities and begin to build a long-term road map for enhanced marketing accountability.

Horizon One: Identifying Your Marketing Accountability Improvement Opportunities

Designing a Fit-for-Purpose Marketing Accountability Diagnostic

T opics covered in Chapter Eight:

- Determining your company's current state of play
- Potential discrete work streams within an MA diagnostic
- Designing the diagnostic that makes sense for you
- Distilling your findings into a compelling three-year road map

Bedside manners are no substitute for the right diagnosis.
—Alfred P. Sloan, GM

If you have stuck with us to this point you are probably pretty serious about embarking on a marketing accountability program of your own. This chapter will help prepare you for that journey by providing you with the frameworks and tools you will need to conduct

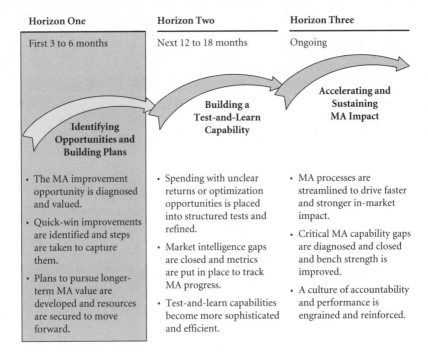

Horizon One	Horizon Two	Horizon Three
First 3 to 6 months	Next 12 to 18 months	Ongoing

Identifying Opportunities and Building Plans

Building a Test-and-Learn Capability

Accelerating and Sustaining MA Impact

- The MA improvement opportunity is diagnosed and valued.
- Quick-win improvements are identified and steps are taken to capture them.
- Plans to pursue longer-term MA value are developed and resources are secured to move forward.

- Spending with unclear returns or optimization opportunities is placed into structured tests and refined.
- Market intelligence gaps are closed and metrics are put in place to track MA progress.
- Test-and-learn capabilities become more sophisticated and efficient.

- MA processes are streamlined to drive faster and stronger in-market impact.
- Critical MA capability gaps are diagnosed and closed and bench strength is improved.
- A culture of accountability and performance is engrained and reinforced.

Figure 8.1. The Three Horizons of Marketing Accountability Improvement

an initial marketing accountability opportunity scan. As we discussed in Chapter Seven, this opportunity scan, or diagnostic, is the first horizon in a long-term marketing accountability program (see Figure 8.1). The diagnostic will help you size up the marketing accountability prize in your company and the challenges you will face in capturing it, so that you can begin to plan a robust and credible long-term MA improvement program.

Depending on the complexity of your issues and the resources you have available to you, this initial diagnostic can take anywhere from twelve weeks to several quarters to complete. An initial diagnostic is necessary before embarking on a long-term MA program, because you just "don't know what you don't know." The diagnostic may reveal that MA is not a significant priority for your organization after all, or it may point you toward improvement opportunities that you had not previously considered. For these reasons and others, a focused up-front diagnostic should be the first step on your path toward greater marketing accountability.

Done properly, the MA opportunity diagnostic will deliver the following:

1. An estimate of the "size of the prize" available from MA improvement

2. Several specific "quick win" improvement opportunities, which will create immediate value through cost savings, improved effectiveness, or both

3. A preliminary plan for capturing longer-term MA improvement opportunities, which includes a testing agenda, capability improvement pilots, and other process, infrastructure, and governance changes needed to support the MA effort

4. A shared understanding of MA concepts and a common language for discussing MA priorities across marketing, sales, finance, operations, and senior management

5. Organizational alignment to pursue MA improvement as a corporate priority, along with the resources needed to make it happen

The first and most important stop on this journey is determining your company's current state of play. We will discuss the five factors that help set the context for the diagnostic and fundamentally shape your approach to it. In the following section, we will highlight the kinds of individual work streams that can and may have a role in the diagnostic process. Then we will bring all these components together with the different types of MA analytic tools that we discussed in Chapter Seven to help you understand how you can design a diagnostic that suits your specific situation, with the pacing, scope, and hypothesis orientation that optimizes your chances for a wildly successful outcome.

Finally, we close with a discussion of how you can distill what we anticipate will be a rich array of findings from the diagnostic into a compelling and focused road map that everyone in the organization understands and supports. This will require a careful blend of art and science, as even vanguard MA innovators know that maintaining a disciplined MA agenda with a solid blend of short-term and long-term payouts remains a huge challenge in the face of ever-changing priorities and short-term performance pressures.

DETERMINING YOUR COMPANY'S CURRENT STATE OF PLAY

Although the overall purpose of the diagnostic is to develop a comprehensive and precise view of your company's state of play in relation to a broader MA agenda, it is critically important for you to take a first pass at assessing the current state of play in order to design the appropriate diagnostic. Having internal hypotheses about the company's current level of MA understanding and capabilities across its business footprint, as well as the perceived priorities for learning and improvement, is incredibly useful in shaping your activities during the diagnostic. For example, does the CEO think the emphasis should be on efficiency (spend less) or effectiveness (get more)? Does the organization believe that data issues are the insurmountable barrier to further improvement, or is it more about analytical and modeling skills? Does the CMO need to be ready to defend a budget request within the next four weeks or are you building a ten-year strategic road map that is not due for a couple of quarters? How you answer these and similar questions will help determine your current state of play.

Figure 8.2 highlights the five critical factors that inform how to determine your company's current state of play. It and the subsequent frameworks should enable you to move through this assessment very quickly. You may need only ninety minutes with a whiteboard in a quiet room or a few three-hour work sessions over a week or two with a motivated cross-functional team to map this out. Even if you cannot get complete alignment around all of these questions, taking the time to craft an internal point of view will save you a lot of wasted effort and missteps further down the road.

The Nature of the High-Priority MA Questions

The first factor highlighted in Figure 8.2 is labeled "Nature of the High-Priority Questions." This is placed at the top of the diagram, for even though in some ways this builds on your assessment of the other factors, it is also an overarching consideration. With this factor, we want to understand the underlying motivations of the powers that be inside your company for pursuing an MA agenda and how those translate into specific sets of questions that must be answered in a prioritized order.

Based on years of advising companies on these kinds of issues, we have seen a huge range in the nature and focus of such questions.

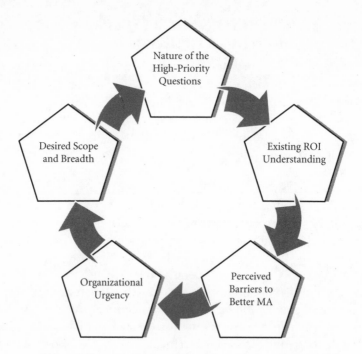

Figure 8.2.   Five Factors That Inform Your State of Play

You would be surprised what can bubble to the top of the list and why. For example, the questions could be primarily strategic. The board may have a gut instinct that the company can be equally effective but spend 15 percent less. The CMO may want to understand how to take an episodic, historically focused ROI approach and transform it into a forward-looking, real-time optimization capability. Or a new CEO may doubt the ROI approach used to date and want a bottom-up justification for how increasing spend could help him achieve the company's organic growth objectives more quickly.

Alternatively, the questions could also be primarily tactical or technical. You could have one major marketing investment under consideration, like a twelve-year Olympic or football sponsorship or a significant shift into a new marketing vehicle type, which needs a sound business case. Perhaps the direct, on-line, and promotional marketing teams understand the ROI of any given campaign in each of their areas, but no one really understands the interplay across the three areas or whether higher effectiveness could be driven through better cross-campaign coordination. Or your organization may feel highly confident in its short-term ROI understanding but want a methodologically sound technique for understanding the longer-term equity impacts of different kinds of investments.

Whether the dominant questions are strategic or tactical in nature, driving for as much transparency as possible around both the nature and the relative prioritization of these questions will help set the table for an effective diagnostic. Do your best to ensure that everyone's agendas are clearly out on the table. It is natural for different stakeholders to have a slightly different take on the high-priority questions—finance's or procurement's priorities may be different from marketing's, which may in turn be different from the board's. Just capture all of the differences for now—do not worry about reconciling them yet. Ultimately you will need to use some strategic judgment to prioritize which questions to tackle to finalize the diagnostic's design, but this should be done only as any timeline, resource, or bandwidth constraints associated with the initial MA diagnostic effort become clearer. Finally, the questions can be oriented toward spend efficiency, spend effectiveness, capability, or some combination of the three. Distinguishing among these themes has important implications for the diagnostic, as you will see.

Existing ROI Understanding

The next critical factor is labeled "Existing ROI Understanding." This is probably the most important factor to address with thoughtful consideration. The core idea here is to quickly assess, but not worry about validating, how much your organization believes it already knows about its marketing investment's ROI. We have a couple of easy frameworks to help you think this through. Because we spent a fair amount of time in Chapter Five outlining the right mix of marketing spending activities, we will not repeat them all here. But the first step is to quickly list what you believe all of the material spending activity is by activity type, across business division or geography as appropriate, and then use the Short-term Financial ROI Precision Scale discussed in Chapter Seven to assess the current state of your existing short-term ROI measures. Recall that the scale has four levels—none, point-in-time, actionable, and predictive—and is used to assess our confidence in the quality, accuracy, and usefulness of our existing ROI analysis. If you find yourself struggling to do the first part of this exercise—let alone the second—this is also good to understand early on!

Once you have determined the existing state of short-term financial ROI precision at the activity level, you can then use the ROI game board, depicted in Figure 8.3, to map out how well different marketing investment pools are understood in relation to different marketing performance measurement approaches and existing insights into marketing portfolio effects.

With marketing performance, in addition to the short-term financial ROI measurements we just discussed, you may also have estimates for nonfinancial returns across a wide array of potentially strategic or tactical marketing objectives (such as returns as measured in increases in brand awareness or stated brand consideration), usually captured through point-in-time or ongoing market research–centered processes. Although many nonmarketers tend to push back on these performance proxies if they are not linked financially to specific business outcomes, these nonetheless represent a material set of measurements that may prove insightful, as you will see when we get further into the diagnostic.

At the other end of the spectrum, your organization may also have processes to estimate the long-term financial impact of marketing investment, often referred to as the brand equity, customer equity, or balance sheet impact. Sometimes these are baked into financially driven brand valuation processes. Alternatively, they may get appended to preexisting processes like price premium or customer lifetime value analyses. Any given pool of marketing investment may be using only one type of performance measurement approach or it may have two or even all three measurement approaches at work.

The other important axis on the game board focuses on marketing portfolio effects. As has been well-debated and documented throughout the marketing literature, target audiences are promiscuous across media, hearing and absorbing messages from TV, magazines, websites, billboards, sponsorships, radio, and usage varies widely across any given day, week, or month. So it is important to assess whether all of your ROI estimates look at marketing activity performance in isolation or take these interactions and cross-effects into account. Thus the axis moves from examining the occasional vehicle to studying multiple marketing activities in isolation to understanding complex multivehicle interactions.

As you can see from Figure 8.3, you are encouraged to plot each of the major pools of marketing investment activity on the game board. In this example, we took a divisional view of a hypothetical

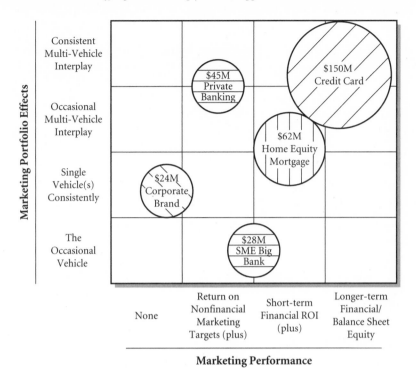

Figure 8.3.   The ROI Game Board

U.S. commercial bank. You can see the wide degree of variance across the divisions and with corporate marketing in terms of the types of performance measurement being used and the extent of portfolio effects being examined.

Finally, Figure 8.4 presents a slightly tongue-in-cheek framework for thinking about your company's potential starting point. On the far left, we start with the "Let's Just Find the Money" crowd, where the primary priority is just to unearth all of the ongoing marketing spending inside the organization, with very little expectation that any ROI figures are attached to that spending. Many readers would be surprised at how many very successful non-CPG companies have to start right here, but it happens more often than not. These organizations are often set up to drive and manage financial or operational performance, or return on invested capital, not marketing-driven financial performance. On the far right, we have "Yin and Yang, in Perfect Balance," in which all material marketing activities have

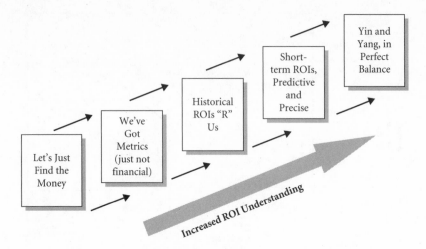

Figure 8.4.   Potential Starting Points for Your Company's Existing
ROI Understanding

predictive financial ROI estimates, complex marketing portfolio effects are taken in account across the business footprint, and the interplay between short-term and long-term financial effects is well understood.

The reality for many U.S. organizations, however, is somewhere between these two extremes. The "We Got Metrics" crowd, often characterized by very tight and mutually beneficial agency relationships, is awash with metrics for marketing outcomes, but very little that links directly into financially based business outcomes. The "Historical ROIs 'R' Us" crowd has built an array of point-in-time and some actionable estimates at the isolated activity level but has not consistently looked at portfolio effects or expected actionable predictability from its ROI estimates. "Short-Term ROIs, Predictive and Precise" tends to be the starting point of many data-rich companies like global CPG or pharmaceutical companies, for whom the main hole in their game is in understanding the interplay between short-term and long-term impacts. All joking aside, the main point is to determine which descriptor best fits the current state of your organization.

Perceived Barriers to Better MA

The underlying components of this factor have been presented during the discussion of MA-readiness segments in Chapter Seven.

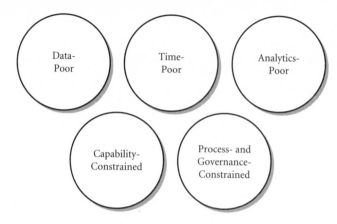

Figure 8.5. Perceived Barriers to Better MA Understanding

Figure 8.5 reinforces the five major themes that emerged—irrespective of industry type, business models, or company size—which can be used to self-assess the most relevant barriers in your company situation. Is your company predominantly (1) data-poor, (2) time-poor, (3) analytics-poor, (4) capability-constrained, (5) process and governance-constrained, or (6) the elusive "none of the above"?

Now, we understand that many companies believe they have some or all of these perceived barriers at play—remember, only 15 percent of companies we surveyed sensed *none* of these barriers inhibiting their MA prowess—but for this state-of-play assessment we are focused on just a quick snapshot of the preexisting belief system inside the company about the perceived barriers and, most important, which barrier serves as the most critical bottleneck.

So as a quick exercise, ask each team member to (1) rate, on a scale of 1 to 10, how relevant each barrier is to better MA understanding in your company, (2) force rank among the five, and (3) provide some detailed qualitative context for your choices. Because each of these perceived barriers has a different diagnosis and a different ultimate fix associated with it, you need to drive toward an aligned view, in which barriers present the biggest challenges, so that you can adequately design the diagnostic. For example, if a company felt that being data-poor was its top barrier, more energy might get directed to auditing a company's underlying customer information architecture and using quick-hit, gap-fill research techniques to create a limited but valuable fact base for basic effectiveness analytics during the diagnostic. Conversely, if a company felt that being analytics-poor was its top barrier, more effort might be devoted to sourcing and then partnering with the right kind of external analytics supplier during the early phase of the diagnostic. We also acknowledge that some participants may see some of these factors as interrelated; for example, we are data-poor because we are capability-constrained. Admittedly, sometimes it will difficult to disentangle which is the root cause and which may be the symptom. During the state-of-play assessment, it is less important to try to resolve this issue—because it may be futile to settle it among yourselves without the perspective of outside seasoned experts—and more important to just note the open or unanswered nature of the question, put it in a parking lot, and move on. A completed diagnostic process should eventually shed more light on these kinds of open issues, with the additional benefit of a richer fact base—not just people's opinions—to inform the discussion.

Organizational Urgency

This factor is fairly self-descriptive. What you are looking for here is an understanding of how quickly the company needs answers to how many of its high-priority questions, and the penalty or downside risk associated with not being able to hit some of the requested time frames. If there are apparent hard stops around some of the questions, are these being internally driven or externally driven? Are there partial or interim responses that can satisfy some of the requirements to get questions answered without forcing unrealistic time frames onto the overall effort?

The objective here is to have a nuanced understanding of the drivers of organizational urgency, the surrounding context for each driver, and a detailed understanding of the implications of hitting or failing to hit the desired time frames. Then as you are designing the diagnostic in light of the other state-of-play factors, you will have a better understanding of how and where you have the flexibility to make what specific kinds of trade-offs.

Desired Scope and Breadth

When we refer to scope and breadth, we are thinking of this factor across multiple dimensions. Geographic scope is the place to start—do we care about specific DMAs (Designated Market Areas) or states or specific countries or regions of the world? Business scope is the next place to go—do we care about specific business divisions, or only specific product lines within those divisions, or perhaps only specific product lines sold through specific distribution channels? Marketing spending type is the next obvious place to go—do we care about only our one or two most important vehicles that get the lion's share of the budget, or should every activity be included? Finally, there is scope across the MA value levers—do we primarily care about investment levels within specific activities or are we interested in exploring all six value levers, from strategy and messaging through in-market execution and fixed cost management?

This final factor serves as the accordion file for most state-of-play analyses. Unless a specific scope or breadth specification is baked into one of the top two or three high-priority questions, this is the one factor that we can expand or collapse based on what we learn while considering the other four factors, as well as what we learn about the resources that the company is willing to put in play to support the diagnostic. The starting point, of course, should be the desired or ideal scope and breadth, all other things being equal. Having seen this story a few too many times, though, we can say that this is consistently the area in which most companies' eyes are bigger than their stomachs—or at least bigger than their wallets. Usually some of the desired scope ultimately has be sacrificed to hit the time lines or resource constraints of the diagnostic.

Concluding the State-of-Play Assessment

Figure 8.6 provides an evaluation tool that allows you to quickly summarize the implications of this state-of-play assessment in relation to a "speed versus rigor" trade-off that is embedded in any significant corporate initiative. Clearly, if this quick and dirty evaluation of the five factors places you on the left-hand side of the diagram for most or many of these elements, your company's current state of play either requires or allows you to put speed at the top of your priority list for this diagnostic. If you ended up checking spots closer to the right-hand side of the diagram for most of the elements, comprehensiveness and rigor will need to be your predominant concern—perhaps to the chagrin of you, the CMO, or the CEO.

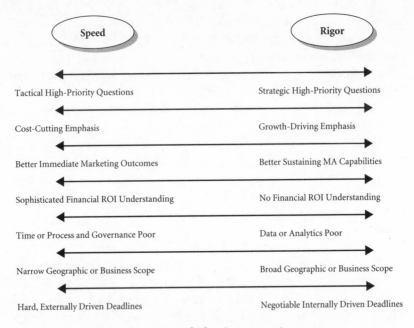

Figure 8.6.   State-of-Play Summary Assessment

Finally, we want to reemphasize that many of these key framing tools for the state-of-play assessment are useful to revisit as you
are stepping through the full-blown diagnostic itself. You should be
cross-checking your initial state-of-play hypotheses about existing
ROI understanding or perceived MA barriers with the actual data as
you have the time and resources to uncover it.

POTENTIAL DISCRETE WORK STREAMS WITHIN AN MA DIAGNOSTIC

Now we will ask you to put your company's state-of-play assessment
aside for a few pages while you familiarize yourself with the types
of discrete work streams that may serve as components within your
overall diagnostic. All ten of the potential discrete work stream
components are depicted in Figure 8.7. As you can see from the diagram, they fall into three basic categories: (1) data collection and
aggregation work streams, (2) analytics-oriented work streams, and (3)
capability and process-oriented work streams. Our main focus
in this section is to help you build a better understanding of each

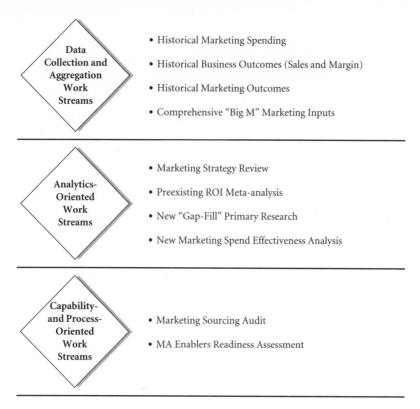

Figure 8.7.   Potential Diagnostic Work Streams

component, what it is used for, and the basic outline of how it gets executed.

Admittedly, however, not every discrete work stream component is relevant in every situation. After you develop a basic understanding of these alternatives, though, we will show you how to combine this with the state-of-play assessment and the available analytic alternatives to design the diagnostic that makes the most sense for your company.

Data Collection and Aggregation Work Streams

The data collection and aggregation work streams are the foundational elements to any MA diagnostic. We have outlined four discrete work streams here—focusing respectively on marketing spending, business outcomes, marketing outcomes, and comprehensive "Big

M" marketing inputs. Typically the source data lives in different IT systems, if it is in a database format at all. Regardless, the guardians and owners of the information for each work stream are usually different; this implies that you ignore the political overtones of any given data request at your own risk and practically ensures a high degree of variability in the ease and speed of data access within and across work streams. As will become obvious, each data set can be captured with varying degrees of granularity or specificity and aggregation (such as weekly sales by channel versus quarterly sales by country). Being purposeful about your choices here will save a lot of heartache and rework on the back end.

Historical Marketing Spending Data Inventory

This work stream is fairly self-explanatory—find out how, where, and when money has been spent, and how much! But as with all of these data collection work streams, the devil is in the details. Ideally you would collect actual marketing spending data by activity extending back at least two to three years, more if it is not too painful. You want the data to be as granular as possible, from a periodicity, geographic, and product-market perspective. Weekly data is better than monthly data, which in turn is better than quarterly data. Similarly, DMA-level data is better than state-level data, which is better than country-level data. Often you will be working closely with your agency partners across your marketing mix to assemble this data, and more often than not it will be available at a campaign level—that's how it was bought. Because each vehicle type has its own intrinsic economics, purchasing dynamics, and in-field idiosyncrasies, harmonizing the data across activity type is often trickier than first envisioned.

Although the goal is to map the spending to specific types of business scope—spend targeted at specific geographies or customer types or channels of distribution or the like—this may not always fall out neatly from the datasets, especially if they are supplied by agency partners. Rather, someone with historical organizational context may need to build these linkages manually, using business judgment as appropriate. Ideally you would able to classify each spending stream in relation to a number of more nuanced conditions—like the specific marketing problem the program was targeting, whether it was part of a broader campaign, its messaging themes, its various creative executions, the fixed or variable nature of its cost, its media or day-part choices, and so on. For the direct response vehicles and con-sumer promotions, if campaign-specific response levels are available, the investment levels and some of these more nuanced conditions should be captured in this work stream as well.

Historical Business Outcomes (Sales/Margin) Data Inventory

This work stream is also fairly self-explanatory, but as with the previous work stream, the devil is really in the details. On the sales side, you will have to decide whether you will collect unit vol-ume data, monetary sales value, or both. On the margin side, you are constrained by whatever cost accounting or profitability regime dominates your business, and whether it is stable and well-supported or in flux and disputed. One of the main challenges with this work stream is to collect the data such that you can flexibly aggregate or disaggregate the sales and margin data to map to the marketing inputs. For certain kinds of analyses, looking at the data by geography or DMA may make sense. For other analyses, being able to recut the sales or margin data by channel or customer type may be more powerful.

Historical Marketing Outcomes Data Inventory

The goal of this work stream is to inventory as much preexisting historical information as possible about nonfinancial marketing or perceptual outcomes. This should include data on customer fun-nel strength (awareness, consideration, trial, and repeat purchase), brand equity and perception data, customer satisfaction data, cus-tomer loyalty and likelihood to recommend data, and so on. This may also include more tactical campaign performance measurement data, like ad recall or sponsorship tracking studies. Typically this data is sourced from a wide range of market research studies; some of this may be collected using a frequent, systematic process; others may come from ad-hoc, one-off research efforts. Often you must aggre-gate the data from a series of hard-copy research reports, many of which have different methodological and data capture approaches that need to be understood and noted. As with the other data collec-tion work streams, the trick here is to try to get the data at a granular enough level (say, by customer segment or by geography) to allow linkages, ideally both qualitative and analytical, with specific marketing inputs or business outcomes.

Comprehensive "Big M" Marketing Inputs Data Inventory

This work stream takes aim at a more ambitious marketing input data set than simply marketing spending activities. The idea is to build a comprehensive view of the strategic marketing intent and the competitive context for any given line of business by capturing incremental data sets for pricing strategy, channel strategy, product strategy, market characteristics, and competitive response. If we thought just about price, for instance, then capturing information on list pricing strategy, realized actual pricing, relative price position, perceived price position, and so on during the same historical time period of your marketing spending across product types would provide you with a rich set of insights on the interplay between marketing investments and pricing. Similar data sets exist for the other "Big M" marketing criteria. Engineering such a comprehensive data view opens up a richer set of analytic possibilities on the back end of the diagnostic. For example, you would be able to discern the effectiveness of certain marketing investments in light of your price position or a certain kind of competitive response or certain market characteristics. Because we know that these effects of these actions are interrelated, this can be a powerful additional lens to have.

All four data collection and aggregation work streams clearly provide the building blocks for much of what comes next. Executing any one of these requires ample planning and thoughtful attention to detail.

In closing this discussion, it is helpful to remember that many diagnostics bog down when the data collection work streams are scoped too ambitiously. It is hard to ignore that very tempting siren song of ever more robust data sets—*Why not? Someone inside the company has to have this data somewhere.* There is also a very real risk that you will not have collected a broad enough information set to do even the most basic MA analyses. But there is some art and some science in understanding how much to bite off initially and knowing when to call it quits. We have seen some companies spend three or four quarters trying to execute these work streams, only to be repeatedly disappointed in both the quality and the completeness of their results.

Analytics-Oriented Work Streams

The analytics-oriented work streams leverage the data foundation built up during the previous steps and turn these into powerful MA-driven insights that help shape our long-term improvement plan. Some of these components, like the preexisting ROI meta-analysis, have a more quantitative skew; others, like the marketing strategy review, have more of an expert-led, qualitative orientation. But whether you do one of these analytic work streams or all four, the overarching goal is to unearth those killer insights that illuminate a range of quick-win action items and a range of longer-term improvement opportunities.

Marketing Strategy Review

Whenever the high-priority questions are strategic in nature, the marketing strategy review work stream needs to be a part of the broader diagnostic. The goal is to thoroughly understand the big-picture, strategic context for the marketing programs that were in place, as well as the underlying rationale for each of the tactical decisions that were made in regard to four of the six MA value levers—strategy, messaging, spending activities, and investment levels. Often this will be distilled by reviewing the following data:

1. Strategic marketing plans

2. Analyses that support the segmentation, target selection, value proposition, and messaging decisions underneath any given program

3. Creative and media briefs that articulate the strategy and desired outcomes for agency partners

4. Any other customer, competitive, or category-level research

5. The in-market media schedules and plans

The availability of these resources depends on the rigor surrounding a company's marketing planning process. Sometimes there is a clean paper trail to all of these items. If not, you may need to compile the strategic intent through more of an oral history approach, using deep-dive interviews to flesh out the analysis. Either way, the point is to be able to clearly assess whether the marketing programs rested on

a logical strategic foundation, supported by reasonable interpretations of the right kind of data, applied with a rigorous internal consistency across the MA value levers.

Preexisting ROI Meta-Analysis

For many large global companies tackling this issue for the first
time, isolated pockets of preexisting ROI analyses may lie scattered
across the organization. Occasionally rumors about the existence
of this or that ROI study get amplified and passed along verbally
inside an organization; these start to feel more like an urban legend
than a solid set of data and analysis that someone can actually forward to you electronically. Nonetheless, the results of these preexisting studies often form the organization's operative belief system
about MA.

The main objective of this work stream is to audit all of these
efforts, integrate and compile the findings in one place, and, as is
methodologically feasible, perform some meta-analysis across the
studies to see whether some set of data-supported existing truths can
be identified. As we pointed out in the earlier discussion on existing ROI understanding, both the level of precision of specific ROI
findings and the extent to which they incorporate interaction effects
and longer-term value drivers can vary widely. All of these components should be clarified as part of the audit, as well as the other
aspects of the strategic context and the methodological approach
associated with each ROI finding. In the best of all possible worlds,
this work stream might allow you to unequivocally state something
as specific as the fact that national TV advertising has a consistent
elasticity of .05 to .08 or that a direct marketing approach has been
perfected inside the company that consistently performs with a $30
to $36 cost to acquire. Even if you cannot get this specific, you should
exit this work stream with an excellent understanding of the quality
and applicability of the existing ROI data points on the company's
go-forward situation.

New "Gap-Fill" Market Research

The focus of this work stream is to design, field, and do preliminary
analysis on a new piece of quantitative, custom market research,
used when companies are worried about the quality and breadth of

the data that may result from their data work streams. Typical data limitations might include

1. The absence of a fact base to support underlying strategic rationale of existing programs
2. Performance tracking that is too infrequent
3. The lack of customer value metrics around frequency, share of wallet, or purchase funnel blockages
4. Aggregate data views that ignore segment-specific differences
5. Lack of messaging or other vehicle-specific recall and effectiveness data

Rather than suspend the MA diagnostic until ongoing tracking and other research are created or fixed, or proceed with insufficient data to create new insight, often you can launch a quick and focused piece of "gap-fill" research in parallel with your diagnostic—an expedient middle course that can yield strong benefits.

If your team has access to someone who is research proficient, it is possible that a single piece of new quantitative customer research can be put in place in as little as six to eight weeks. The nature of the specific questions depends on the nature of your data gaps, but ideally you will have a clearer understanding of the strategic marketing issues at play and some understanding of customer-level sales response and similar findings coming out of the research. Although it will not solve the longer-term challenges of how to keep weaving insights on these kinds of issues into the business, it may allow you to validate emerging findings in a more robust way and take the analysis to a level of detail and insight that will be more compelling to senior management.

New Marketing Spend Effectiveness Analyses

The idea with this work stream, of course, is that some set of new, incremental marketing spend effectiveness analyses will have to be performed during the diagnostic. Think of this work stream as the placeholder for all of those activities. These additional analyses could range in breadth from more qualitative efforts around best practices assessment to highly complex and quantitative statistical modeling of historical performance. These analytic approaches were showcased in the "Quick Primer of Available Analytic Tools and Approaches" in Chapter Seven. Clearly, data and information availability, as well as the analytical skills across the team, will dictate which of these alternatives are available to you. The nature of the high-priority MA questions, however, should be what drives you to prioritize certain incremental analyses over others. And the risk, as always, is in trying to tackle so many new analyses that you overpromise to the executive stakeholders and then materially underdeliver. So plan this work stream with care.

Capability and Process-Oriented Work Streams

Rather than focusing on analyzing the specific business and financial outcomes marketing has driven, the capability and process-oriented work streams uncover strengths and gaps in the underlying system of skills, people, and decision making that lead to those outcomes. Depending on your company's stage of evolution, adding these to your broader diagnostic may be exactly the right thing to help determine how you can accelerate performance to the next level.

Marketing Sourcing Audit

This work stream is focused on benchmarking your company's marketing sourcing and procurement performance against best practice companies. Because marketers tend to have a strong entrepreneurial and creative streak—with highly fragmented buying and execution, and vendor decisions driven more around chemistry, creativity, and other noncost attributes—applying a procurement-led, strategic sourcing approach to the marketing cost center is fraught with challenges. Yet by (1) identifying a consolidated vendor base with preferred specialists with transparent pricing and terms and (2) applying clear value management across the marketing materials and service value chains, best practice companies have demonstrated that they can drive material cost efficiencies, sometimes north of 30 percent. As with any strategic sourcing effort, successful efforts here do not focus just on finding the lowest cost suppliers. Rather, marketers need to incorporate the full value being received from these vendors into the analysis, including all of the tangible and intangible benefits that a company may be receiving by working with, for instance, a premium-priced supplier. But engaging in this type of process forces the marketers to be clearer about how and where any given supplier is delivering value and to evaluate the overall value equation in light of the supplier's cost position.

This work stream is run like a typical audit, during which you will collaborate with finance and procurement to map out the existing supplier ecosystem across all elements of the marketing value chain—from media buying to production to creative services to research and analytics—for each critical marketing vehicle. All material commercial aspects of these relationships are diagnosed and some straightforward financial analysis is done to see whether the organization is currently using relevant price, cost, and demand levers to look for economies of scale and drive efficiencies. This process may be supplemented with an interview-driven information-gathering process, in which internal stakeholders provide a snapshot of the demand drivers for specific suppliers or processes, how and why the status quo functions, and where they might look for performance improvements. Ultimately all of this is synthesized into an assessment of where the largest sourcing-driven opportunities might be and how to realize them.

MA Enablers Readiness Assessment

This work stream is focused on benchmarking the mission-readiness of the MA enablers inside your company relative to those in best practice companies. In the detailed discussion in Chapter Seven, critical elements of a broader MA ecosystem were identified as *MA enablers*. These enablers fall into five different categories: (1) metrics, (2) skills, (3) process and governance, (4) data, and (5) IT systems. Although none of these items individually provides an immediate and direct link to better marketing performance, trying to orchestrate a multiyear MA improvement program when all of the MA enablers are stacked against you is definitely a fool's errand. You may be able to deliver compelling one-off performance improvements, but you will struggle with repeatability if the underlying MA enablers are not addressed.

So this work stream is run like a typical best practices assessment, during which you are triangulating on some assessment of your company's current state by interviewing a cross-section of relevant stakeholders inside the organization, using whatever well-established mechanisms are acceptable inside your organization to assess performance (Harvey balls, five-point rating scales, and the like). Figure 8.8 gives you a good sense of the questions you should explore for each

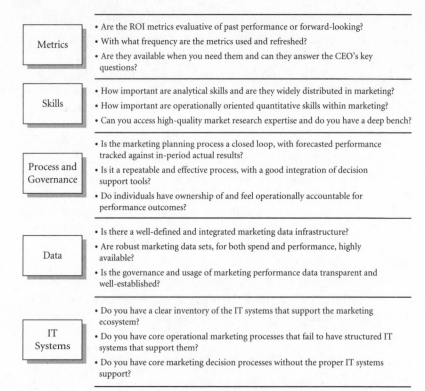

Metrics	• Are the ROI metrics evaluative of past performance or forward-looking? • With what frequency are the metrics used and refreshed? • Are they available when you need them and can they answer the CEO's key questions?
Skills	• How important are analytical skills and are they widely distributed in marketing? • How important are operationally oriented quantitative skills within marketing? • Can you access high-quality market research expertise and do you have a deep bench?
Process and Governance	• Is the marketing planning process a closed loop, with forecasted performance tracked against in-period actual results? • Is it a repeatable and effective process, with a good integration of decision support tools? • Do individuals have ownership of and feel operationally accountable for performance outcomes?
Data	• Is there a well-defined and integrated marketing data infrastructure? • Are robust marketing data sets, for both spend and performance, highly available? • Is the governance and usage of marketing performance data transparent and well-established?
IT Systems	• Do you have a clear inventory of the IT systems that support the marketing ecosystem? • Do you have core operational marketing processes that fail to have structured IT systems that support them? • Do you have core marketing decision processes without the proper IT systems support?

Figure 8.8.   Readiness Assessment Questions for MA Enablers

of the key enablers. This work stream can probably deliver the most value to the diagnostic when a company has a reasonable degree of confidence in its baseline marketing performance but wants to understand how it can consolidate its learning and start to accelerate its improvement cycle.

DESIGNING THE DIAGNOSTIC THAT MAKES SENSE FOR YOU

Now that you have a better understanding of the potential discrete work streams, we can integrate this with the state-of-play assessment discussed earlier in the chapter and the types of MA analyses highlighted in Chapter Seven to design a custom diagnostic for your situation. The state-of-play assessment helped you map out your starting point regarding key elements like existing ROI understanding and perceived barriers to better marketing accountability. It also helped you understand how other factors may impact your need for speed, rigor, or some combination of both from the diagnostic. Finally, your work on the nature of your company's high-priority MA questions becomes the starting point for further refinement of the fundamental hypotheses that will drive the contours of the diagnostic.

When we refer to the diagnostic's being hypothesis-driven, we mean that the diagnostic should be focused on validating informed hypotheses about material MA opportunities, rather than on "boiling the ocean"—conducting all the analyses that are potentially relevant. Not all of the high-priority MA questions uncovered during the state-of-play assessment may meet this materiality criteria—meaning that even if we rigorously uncover the precise answer to a specific question, these insights may not open up material pots of gold on either the marketing efficiency or effectiveness sides of the equation. These high-priority questions are net losers on a number of fronts and should be avoided, unless the political price for ignoring the question is just too high. What we want for the diagnostic, ideally, are hypotheses that reflect high organizational priorities while simultaneously having the potential to offer real marketing-led upside opportunities after sufficient study and analysis.

We follow three basic steps to home in on the right set of hypotheses. The first step involves disaggregating each MA issue into manageable chunks, rather than immediately tackling intergalactic ones. This can be accomplished by creating issue trees for key problems. Our six value levers are essentially a disaggregation of the macro issues of the overall diagnostic and potential sources of marketing accountability value. You should attempt to cut the branches off your detailed MA issue trees with as little analysis as possible, leaving you with the core issues and opportunities to explore. The second step is to frame these core issues as informed hypotheses, such as "Frequent price promotions are training our customers to purchase our product only when it is on deal, which is only driving pantry loading and may be eroding our long-term premium image." The third step is to take each hypothesis and identify simple analyses that answer the question, "What would you have to believe for this to be true?" We might want to tackle the pantry-loading suspicion from the previous hypothesis by assessing purchase rate changes between pre-, during, and postpromotional periods—at both the geographic and individual customer levels if possible. We might address the brand erosion piece by calculating changes in the brand's price elasticity over the previous three to five years. As you can see, the benefit of using hypotheses to focus the diagnostic is that just as much insight can be gained if you prove them wrong as if you validate them.

Once the high-potential hypotheses have been identified, the rest of the diagnostic—its scope, its key activities, its key analyses, and the time line and resources required to support the work—should naturally fall into place. The detailed design should provide specific answers to these questions. For example, how broad or how narrow will the scope be, and will it be focused on marketing outcomes, marketing capabilities, or both? What specific data-driven, analytics-driven, or process-driven work streams are best suited to explore these hypotheses? What mix of analyses is feasible to include, given our speed and rigor parameters? Will this mix provide the necessary burden of proof to clarify our key hypotheses? How long should the diagnostic take, and what resources, internally or externally sourced, would be required to effectively complete the diagnostic?

Three illustrative diagnostic approaches, presented in Figure 8.9, give you a sense of how this might come together. For each of these hypothetical diagnostics, you can see the key hypotheses at the top of the figure, supported by details of scope, activities, analyses, time ranges, and anticipated resources. Each also has a brief description of the kind of company situation for which the diagnostic works best.

The first diagnostic, labeled "Tackle the Basics," is designed for organizations that are just starting to address marketing accountability issues for the first time. In this situation, an organization can often struggle just to identify all of the sources of marketing investment, let alone systematically tie those investments to reliable ROI measures. Often these organizations are data-poor and capability-constrained, and they may have easy opportunities to drive short-term improvements in marketing performance with the MA value levers of strategy, fixed cost management, and spending activities. The diagnostic combines a set of activities and analyses targeted at these improvement hypotheses, in light of the organization's hypothetical starting point. For example, the sourcing and gap-fill research work streams would play a bigger role for them, as would more straightforward analyses of purchase funnels bottlenecks and strategic spend alignment.

The second diagnostic, labeled "Validate with Confidence," is designed for organizations that are data-rich but relatively analytics-poor, with some point-in-time understanding of marketing's return

	Tackle the Basics	Validate with Confidence	Build Distinctive Advantage
Key Hypothesis	Grab low-hanging fruit improvements around strategy, spending activities, and fixed-loss management	Improvements in messaging, spending activities, and investment levels could dramatically spur performance, but it needs hard-edged proof	Solid analytical foundation can be augmented, but capability process and system-related gaps are the critical bottlenecks
Scope	Mainly high-level, with targeted deep dives based on data availability	Broad but granular, across a wide array of spending types	Most holistic focusing on the whole MA system, not just marketing outcomes
Key Activities	• Historical marketing spending inventory • Marketing sourcing audit • New gap-fill research • Lightweight new MA analysis	• Granular approach to marketing spending and business outcomes work stream • Marketing strategy review • Highly targeted gap-fill research • Robust array of new MA analyses	• Augment existing MA databases with comprehensive "Big M" data inputs • Preexisting ROI meta-analysis • MA enablers readiness assessment • Targeted, sophisticated new MA analyses
Key Analysis	• Best practices assessment • Strategic marketing assessment • Strategic spend alignment	• Robust historical modeling • POT Activity analysis • Strategic marketing assessment	• Advanced econometric modeling, including "Big M" data • Capability-driven Best Practice assessment • Test-and-learn effectiveness analysis
Time and Resource	10 to 14 weeks, depending on marketing spend data availability 3.0 to 6.0 FTE	16 to 20 weeks, depending on data complexity 5.0 to 9.0 FTE	12 to 16 weeks, contingent on complexity of invested analytics 3.0 to 6.0 FTE
Works Best for	Data-poor companies with no financial ROI insights, post-M&A, looking for immediate efficiency gains	Data-rich but analytics-poor companies struggling to confirm marketing investment role in driving growth	Companies with reasonable ROI understanding, but lacking broad alignment on how to move to next level

Figure 8.9.   Illustrative Diagnostic Approaches

but nothing that is seen as bullet-proof. The CMO may be struggling to demonstrate marketing's contribution to business growth in a data-driven manner that convinces the CFO or senior management but may have strong hypotheses that improvements across the MA value levers of messaging, spending activities, and investment levels could drive disproportionate business benefit. The key activities highlight granular data collection work streams for both investment and outcome data combined with highly targeted gap-fill research to support a rich set of additional marketing spend effectiveness analyses on the back end. Process and capability issues take a backseat to attempting to validate improvement opportunities in terms of marketing program outcomes.

The third diagnostic, labeled "Build Distinctive Advantage," is designed for a company that has a reasonable baseline understanding of historical ROI but has then struggled to build that understanding into an actionable, real-time competitive advantage because of perceived capability, process, and systems-related bottlenecks. Although many of the easier gains with the MA value levers have been captured, the organization may have hypotheses about significant improvement opportunities to be realized by optimizing across the value levers, particularly by looking at the interplay between strategy, messaging, spending activities, and investment levels. The key activities and analyses have been adjusted to reflect this set of hypotheses, in an attempt to deliver holistic insights across the broader marketing accountability ecosystem.

Obviously there are many variations on these themes, given the wide range of organizational starting points and equally broad range of improvement hypotheses that may be circulating. But with a reasonable understanding of these concepts, you can see how to employ a Chinese menu–driven approach across activities and analyses to custom build a diagnostic well suited to your situation.

After you put the finishing touches on your custom-built diagnostic and your team resources are in place, the real work can begin! Most diagnostics will be executed in four sequential phases, which will be pretty consistent across diagnostics, regardless of the specific components that you have prioritized. As seen in Figure 8.10, the first phase is about data collection and hypothesis refinement, the second focuses on analysis and synthesis, the third builds these into recommendations and implications, and the fourth socializes these via aligning and refining.

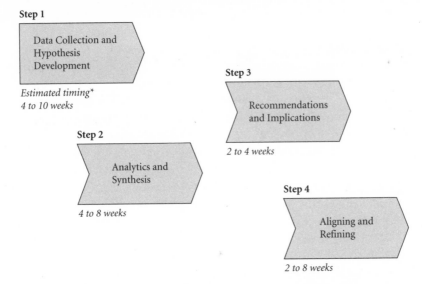

Step 1

Data Collection and
Hypothesis
Development

Estimated timing*
4 to 10 weeks

Step 2

Analytics and
Synthesis

4 to 8 weeks

Step 3

Recommendations
and Implications

2 to 4 weeks

Step 4

Aligning and
Refining

2 to 8 weeks

Figure 8.10. Four Phases of a Typical MA Diagnostic

The first phase has the most amplitude in terms of resource and duration. It is directly related to how ambitious an "ask" you have designed into your data work streams. The core working team is most reliant on the cooperation of a broad array of organizational stakeholders with competing operational priorities, which means this phase can be full of delays, disappointments, and unexpected (usually unpleasant) surprises.

The second phase can be as long as the first, irrespective of whether the analysis is more outcome or process-focused. Expect a fair amount of back and forth as the core team tries to interpret and stress test the soundness of the analytic findings. If your team is new to deploying some of these analytic techniques, make sure you have identified a process for tapping into the necessary expertise on an as-needed basis. Avoid jumping to premature conclusions at this phase, and make sure adequate time has been allowed for synthesis, because you may need to reconcile what appear to be conflicting findings across different sets of analyses. Ideally, at the end of this phase the team will have enough of an understanding of any or all of (1) current program returns, (2) marketing sourcing practices, or (3) MA enabler readiness and what is required to improve these conditions to proceed to the next phase.

In the third phase, the team categorizes the findings identified in the previous phase into either quick wins, for which the burden of proof has been met to make immediate improvements, or longer-term opportunities to test, learn, and refine strategies and plans, build capabilities, and align internal infrastructure. In addition to any near-term marketing plan or budget changes, the key deliverable of this step is a preliminary plan for pursuing longer-term marketing accountability initiatives and a well-quantified estimate of the range of value that these initiatives could create.

The final phase focuses on gaining alignment with near-term spending plan changes and the team's recommended path forward, including resource requirements. Depending on the nature of the recommendations, how contentious they may prove to be, and how decisions get made in your company, this phase can be extremely short, tediously long or somewhere in between. Regardless, the timing of this step should allow for some reworking of the MA recommendations and plans based on the feedback of key stakeholders. We will elaborate on this further in the next and final section of this chapter.

DISTILLING YOUR FINDINGS INTO A COMPELLING THREE-YEAR ROAD MAP

The MA diagnostic will likely generate dozens of ideas on how to improve the efficiency and effectiveness of marketing programs, as well as enhancements to capabilities and infrastructure needed for ongoing impact. These ideas will run the gamut from multimillion-dollar improvements that will require further studying and piloting to simple "no regrets" moves that may save only a few hundred thousand dollars but can be implemented immediately. For many companies, this will seem like an embarrassment of riches—exciting, yes, but also a little overwhelming in terms of figuring out what to tackle first. Depending on your state of play and the hypotheses you had going into the diagnostic, many of your findings may be concentrated in a single value lever, like spending activities or investment levels. That is completely fine—the idea is to find the low-hanging fruit and grab it fast, no matter the source of value.

Many of your findings will also be organizationally and politically controversial—it just goes with the territory. All of that spending has not calcified inside your organization by itself; someone or some group has a vested interest in the specific strategies, programs, marketing service supplier relationships, and so on at the heart of your findings. These stakeholders may sincerely believe in the efficacy or soundness of the status quo, or they may be trying to protect a power base or stack the cards in their favor for incentive compensation or organizational advancement. Either way, this clearly has implications for prioritization as well, because even if something is the right thing to do, with huge potential upside, having to spend eighteen months fighting an internally focused political battle before you can do anything about it will do nothing to advance the broader cause of marketing accountability inside your company.

Taking all of this into account, the challenge for you will, of course, be to weave these findings into a coherent action plan that will deliver gains for the company quickly at appropriate risk and investment levels. Sometimes it is a little tough to jump to a summary view immediately, given the diversity of findings that you will unearth. So usually the most pragmatic first step in planning your path forward is organizing your MA opportunities into either quick wins that can be immediately rolled out or longer-term opportunities that must be carefully planned for. Figure 8.11 provides examples of both quick wins and longer-term opportunities that the diagnostic may unearth, grouped by value lever or process type. In assessing which of your opportunities can be captured immediately, consider the following criteria for quick wins:

- Changes to MA value levers or enablers that can be implemented within the next three to six months and that will begin to create value within the current budget period

- Changes that either do not require consensus to move forward or are so compelling or low risk, or both, that achieving rapid consensus around action is highly likely

Many MA opportunities will not be accessible immediately for myriad reasons. Occasionally longer lead-time capability, process, or systems-driven investments are needed to support specific MA opportunities. Other preliminary findings may require further analysis to determine the true extent of the opportunity. Alternatively, pilot testing may be needed to refine approaches and build organizational consensus on the impact of the changes.

For example, a diagnostic conducted with a beer company suggested that there was a significant opportunity to improve

Value Levers	Quick Wins	Longer-Term Opportunities
Strategy and Objectives	• *Suspend awareness advertising:* Shift next quarter's funds toward critical retention bottleneck	• *Align spending to segments:* Move from mass spend to focus on premium and low-touch segments
Branding and Messaging	• *Call center scripting:* Change Q3 outbound messaging to focus on newly uncovered benefits	• *Copy pretesting process:* Test new copy in development to ensure it meets minimum DWB scores
Spending Activities	• *Reduce scale of catalog prospecting:* Cut bottom 25% of marginal list acquisition	• *Shift from mass to point-of-purchase activities:* Determine the upside available from more $$$$$
In-Market Plans	• *Adopt flighted media:* Adjust Q3 plan based on learning about awareness decay rates	• *Understand interaction effects to amplify SOV effects:* Better cross-vehicle synchronization
Fixed Cost Management	• *Shift immediate production requirements:* Use cost-advantaged suppliers	• *Shorten approval cycles and rework:* Capture 15%+ efficiency gains from creative partners
Investment Levels	• *Apply quick-win saving:* Add $450K to current sub-critical programs and hold $1.2M reserve	• *Optimize media weight:* Create in-market weight tests to identify LT "sweet spot" of investment
Process and Capabilities		
Marketing Sourcing	• *Renegotiate base rates for core marketing materials:* Leverage procurement	• *Intelligently consolidate vendors:* Along with shift to fixed fee structure and transparent pricing
MA Enablers – Process, Skills	• *Roll out ROI payout tool:* Enable team to perform quick analyses to submit with plans	• *Increase analytic capacity:* Add new analyst capacity to support new focus ROI
MA Enablers – Metrics, IT	• *Create C-level MA dashboard:* Incorporate new financial metrics and refresh monthly	• *Operational marketing data-mart:* Design and build IT system to capture continuous marketing data

Figure 8.11.   Examples of Potential Diagnostic Recommendations

trade-spending approaches. Through the diagnostic, the company realized it was spending 3 percent more of its revenue on trade programs than a group of peer companies were, without any greater lift. The company now believed it was overcompensating the trade. Closing this gap would increase the company's earnings by as much as 14 percent, but a wrong move with these powerful customers could spell financial disaster. Clearly this particular MA opportunity needed more study, supported by in-market piloting, before the company was going to make this risky move.

For many legitimate reasons such as these, potentially attractive MA opportunities end up on the medium- to long-term list. But how many of these complex, risky, and financially important initiatives should an organization take on at one time? Companies are of course limited in their capacity to absorb such initiatives successfully before all the spinning plates begin to fall from the air. To consider your company's capacity for supporting multiple longer-term MA initiatives, let's examine the two primary constraints.

The first constraint is problem-solving capacity; that is, the ability to crack the code on the right new approach. In our trade spend example, this involved careful coordination among the heads of marketing and sales and several of their reports. In addition to requiring several half-day problem-solving sessions, this topic dominated all standing meetings between these groups for almost three months before they agreed to a path forward that they could take into piloting. Although the company did not have capacity to take on anything else that involved the interface of these two groups, it did pursue an MA initiative that focused on media optimization because it drew on a different team of leaders.

Another constraint to consider is executional capacity; that is, the ability of staff and markets to absorb changes effectively. Drawing on our trade-spending example, once a "straw man" approach was ready to enter the piloting phase, the team questioned whether it could get enough share of mind among the sales team in the pilot markets to ensure that they delivered new messages and programs to customers while carefully monitoring its impact on their accounts. There were a number of significant product launches happening concurrent with the test, and a new national advertising campaign was also being considered. Ultimately the pilot was delayed by two quarters to accommodate these executional constraints.

Given these limits on your capacity to conduct several MA initiatives in parallel, how do you prioritize which one to three of them should be launched first? Figure 8.12 suggests that a simple "pain or gain" matrix can be helpful in making this prioritization trade-offs. In this case "gain" represents the value at stake and "pain" is a combination of the time, complexity, and risk involved in capturing it. An additional factor that may help resolve any ties that emerge from applying this framework is whether or not the initiatives are at all interdependent or sequential. For example, the beer company example we used previously also identified the opportunity to upgrade its sales calling plan and the sales force resources that would be needed to support it. Although this could create a lot of new value, it was

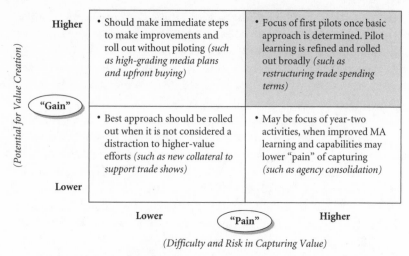

	Lower "Pain"	Higher "Pain"
Higher "Gain"	• Should make immediate steps to make improvements and roll out without piloting *(such as high-grading media plans and upfront buying)*	• Focus of first pilots once basic approach is determined. Pilot learning is refined and rolled out broadly *(such as restructuring trade spending terms)*
Lower "Gain"	• Best approach should be rolled out when it is not considered a distraction to higher-value efforts *(such as new collateral to support trade shows)*	• May be focus of year-two activities, when improved MA learning and capabilities may lower "pain" of capturing *(such as agency consolidation)*

(Potential for Value Creation)

Lower   "Pain"   Higher

(Difficulty and Risk in Capturing Value)

Figure 8.12.   Approach for Prioritizing Longer-Term Marketing Accountability Improvements

logical that the calling plan should build on the trade approaches that were in development, and as such it was deferred until after the trade initiative was completed.

BUILDING A PRELIMINARY PLAN FOR CAPTURING LONGER-TERM MA OPPORTUNITIES

By this point we have determined which of our diagnostic's recommendations are quick wins versus longer-term opportunities, and we have established the relative priority and sequence of these longer-term initiatives. We also have an understanding of what these initiatives will involve and how many of them our organization could act on in parallel. With an understanding of all these factors, you can begin to put together a preliminary plan for what the next twelve to eighteen months of your MA journey will look like as you begin to capture these opportunities.

Ideally, for each major pool of marketing investment identified when using the ROI game board in the state-of-play assessment (refer back to Figure 8.3), you will be able to loosely categorize all of the investment activities into one of five buckets at the end of the diagnostic: (1) proven to be ineffective, (2) proven to be effective, (3) ineffective due to execution, (4) unproven but strategic, and (5) unproven and nonstrategic. We say *loosely* because, as you have seen with the ROI precision scale in Figure 8.3, the level of precision with which something's effectiveness or ineffectiveness is irrefutably proven or unproven can vary considerably! But just because it is hard and somewhat nuanced does not mean that we should not try, and the kind of conceptual framing reflected in Figure 8.13 can help make the findings focused and accessible to senior stakeholders and the broader organization.

As you can see from the figure, rigorously grouping all of your effectiveness findings into these five segments leads to a set of very specific action steps for Horizon Two of the MA journey. Investment pools that have proven to be ineffective open up a pool of funds that can be either dropped down to the bottom line as savings or redeployed into activities that have proven to be effective or to help

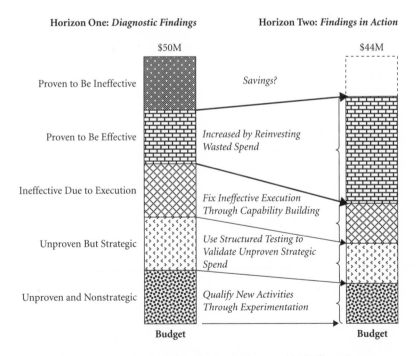

Figure 8.13.   Categorizing the MA Diagnostic Findings into Actionable Buckets

qualify new activities. Investment pools proven to be effective can get a disproportionate share of the budget, driving accelerated business performance. The company can attempt to fix investments that are judged to be underperforming because of execution failures through a focused capability building effort, either with internal resources or through partnering efforts with external resources. Investment pools that are directed at strategic yet unproven activities need to be validated through a structured testing program, which we will explore at much greater length in Chapter Nine. Finally, investments in activities that are unproven yet nonstrategic can also be freed up for redeployment, ideally using some or all of these funds to qualify new investment activities through a structured approach to experimentation. As you can see, if you have the discipline to synthesize your findings into this kind of a framework and you have investment types that fall into each of the segments, you can build a very compelling story around your path forward.

The final consideration in building this plan is what resources you will need for its implementation. In terms of the people needed to pursue these initiatives, you will need to consider whether or not stewarding them will require dedicated staff or can be baked into the current workload of key managers. If there is a need to create a new stewardship role, your core team may provide you with several good candidates to consider. Similarly, if you invested the time to build the right sponsorship and steering committee membership for the diagnostic, chartering the oversight team for the ongoing MA work should be relatively straightforward.

In terms of financial resource needs, the MA initiatives may require new market research, external expertise, or both. In making these choices you should consider the same factors we discussed for the diagnostic. An additional hard cost that may be associated with pursuing these initiatives is that of adding or changing marketing programs related to in-market testing. For example, you may have to add incremental media to several markets to understand the impact of varying investment levels as part of a longer-term media spend optimization program. Ideally, these changes can be more than adequately funded out of any quick-win savings that you have identified.

The considerable time, money, and energy that will go into pursuing longer-term MA improvements must of course make sound economic sense. For this reason, the headline on any set of recommendations arising from an MA diagnostic should include a hard dollar estimate of the size of the prize available from two basic sources of value: (1) revenue enhancement value from improvements that increase in-market impact and (2) cost avoidance value from reducing the cost of delivering programs or eliminating programs with poor returns that cannot be improved. These two sources of value form an estimated total prize, which is critical for senior stakeholders to assess the importance of pursuing longer-term MA improvement opportunities, relative to other corporate goals. To build this alignment, the estimated value at stake must be as specific and robust as possible.

Once the value of a longer-term MA improvement program is weighed against the costs of capturing it, it should be a fairly easy proposition to sell it to a company's leaders. MA diagnostics typically identify 15 to 25 percent of current marketing spending that is either clearly wasted or will yield to rapid improvements. Such quick wins create a self-funding mechanism for pursuing deeper MA initiatives and build strong early management alignment and momentum.

In addition to the human and financial resources needed to pursue long-term MA improvement, there are two additional "asks" to be made of a company's senior leaders. The first is to be a visible champion for marketing accountability improvement. Although this may sound like motherhood and apple pie, it can have several very tangible dimensions. For example, everyone internally and externally pays attention to what the CEO communicates to analysts and investors, and the CEO should feel that MA is a real enough opportunity to be included in that dialogue.

The second ask of senior leaders is for sufficient time to get things right. Leaders who initially bought into long-term plans may make decisions in the following eight to twelve months that seriously jeopardize the success of key initiatives. A common risk is that the CFO will look to the marketing budget to make up a temporary cash shortfall and try to cut programs that are still in test mode. When formulating your ask of senior leaders, you should make these additional requests explicit.

~~∽◦

Anticipating these alignment challenges will allow you to design a sell-in plan for senior business leaders, which ensures that there are no surprises about what can and cannot be accomplished with a long-term MA program. With consensus around the priority of MA improvement and a commitment to the resources and air cover needed to make it happen, your journey toward true marketing accountability has already begun. If you have significant gaps in your understanding of the performance of specific spending activities, which we expect you will, you should expeditiously move to the next chapter on employing a test-and-learn approach to MA. Said a different way, if many of your marketing investment pools still have unproven returns or the returns were proven at a precision level that is not acceptable to you or the broader organization, this chapter will give you access to the necessary thinking and tools to tackle that challenge. If you feel pretty good about your baseline ROI understanding of your existing spend, you may want to move immediately to Chapter Ten and focus on how to turn your MA skills into a sustainable competitive advantage.

Horizon Two: Employing a Test-and-Learn Approach to Drive Continuous Improvement

Systematically Eliminating the Unknown and Improving Returns

T opics covered in Chapter Nine:

- The role of testing in a long-term marketing accountability program
- General principles of a test-and-learn approach
- Designing and executing a classic in-market test
- Embracing the complexity of dynamic optimization
- Committing to an ongoing MA testing agenda

> *We have to develop a mind-set and a capability for continuous experimentation. Most of the experiments don't work, but we have to be out there experimenting and trying. And, of course, what we're trying to do is to create more timely and opportune connections.*
>
> *—A. G. Lafley, P&G*

You have to be fast on your feet and adaptive, or else a
strategy is useless.

—Charles de Gaulle

THE ROLE OF TESTING IN A LONG-TERM MA PROGRAM

Ongoing testing is the secret weapon of sustained marketing accountability improvement. Coming out of a marketing accountability diagnostic, a testing program is the only feasible way to close many of the remaining gaps in our understanding of spending returns, and it is the only practical way to further optimize returns on programs that are already working. As American Express CMO John Hayes recently stated,

> Research is important—we do it. But you cannot learn everything you need to learn with research. So you need to do two other things: First you need a broader set of methods to learn about the consumer besides traditional research, and second, you need to experiment. Experimenting requires a great deal of creativity and a great deal of discipline to ensure that the learning is reapplied in the next set of activities that you might institutionalize.

Market tests can also be used to understand the impact of varying a company's full go-to-market mix, isolating each activity's performance, and quantifying the synergy that their interactions create. Moreover, testing is needed to qualify the new marketing programs that must continually be added to a company's spending mix to adapt to a constantly changing media environment and a brand's ever-evolving priorities. Testing can significantly reduce the probability of making a wrong decision and significantly increase the probability that you will continue to drive steady improvements in marketing performance. Learning derived from MA testing comes the closest to replicating real-world results of any MA analytic approach, because when it is done properly, testing *is* reality—just a smaller slice of it.

A marketing accountability test can focus on understanding or improving any aspect of marketing spending that has a likely correlation to financial performance—including which marketing programs are employed, what they are messaging, where and when they are in field, how much is spent, which incentives or offers are used, and more. Basically, we can design MA tests around any hypothesis that we may have to improve our performance relative to any of the key MA value levers—strategy, messaging, spending activities, in-market execution, fixed cost management, or investment levels. Tests can also be designed to probe the interactions between some subset of these marketing spending variables and other aspects of the marketing mix, like target customer selection, pricing, relative product strength, and distribution channel strength.

Because MA testing can cut both ways, helping you get laser-like precision on extremely tactical choices while concurrently tackling big, long-term accountability questions, it can sometimes appear to be an unwieldy beast. At the tactical level, you can run a series of successive experiments that maximize short-run direct response newspaper advertising by getting smarter about the trade-offs among elements like copy, imagery, incentives or offer components, section placement within the paper, and day-of-week decisions, all across different newspaper vehicles (say, *New York Times* versus *USA Today*). At the subtactical level, you could be trying to learn how to trade off elements around specific words or phrases, different types of 800 numbers, color, graphics or font choices, copy placement in an ad, imagery style, and so on. This is getting way down into the weeds, but if you were spending $50 million or $25 million or even $5 million on these kinds of marketing vehicles, continually optimizing your approach to yield small percentage improvements in sales response could drive significant economic benefits to the business over time.

At the same time, you can be using MA testing to tackle core strategic issues that get at the heart of marketing-driven value creation. These can include testing core hypotheses about customer behavior, purchase funnel blockages, brand positioning, and competitive response. You could also be testing core hypotheses about material marketing program investments; for example, should you be investing $250 million in promotional direct mail offers or $100 million in an integrated marketing program to build brand favorability and preference? Perhaps someone is asking whether a $3.5-million investment to run thirty-second spots during the Super Bowl makes economic sense. You may also be trying to optimize your marketing investments across customer acquisition and customer retention priorities, or to understand the trade-offs between some of your short-term marketing stimuli and long-term customer behaviors like repeat purchase, recommendation, and loyalty. All of these strategic issues can be systematically tackled and addressed through a disciplined and thoughtful approach to MA testing.

From the extremely tactical to the extremely strategic, it's important to remember that the general principles of test-and-learn that we will introduce in the next section apply no matter what level we are operating at. It is a fluid and flexible construct that, when embraced wholeheartedly, should be embedded into the annual operating rhythm and used to bring clarity to the highest-priority MA-related issues, be they tactical or strategic.

GENERAL PRINCIPLES OF A TEST-AND-LEARN APPROACH

At their simplest, all MA tests are just conscious attempts to link marketing cause and effect, by introducing some variation that we can easily read. We say that testing is a *conscious* attempt to link cause and effect, because with our day-to-day market spending decisions, measurability rightly takes a back seat to impact. Said another way, the primary objective of a full-scale marketing program is to work well, whereas the primary objective of a marketing accountability test is to determine *how* well a marketing effort works.

To measure the impact created by changes to these variables or inputs, an MA test divides the world into two different conditions: *test* and *control*. In the test condition, participants are exposed to the change in marketing stimuli; in the control condition, participants are not. Depending on the nature of the MA test, we could be working at the market level, as in geographically defined markets like the country of Italy or the DMA of Boston, or working at the individual customer level, as in cohorts of current or prospective customers, or at a level somewhere in between. In most tests, everything else about the test and control conditions—in terms of economic attractiveness, demographic characteristics, brand strength, competitive intensity, and so on—should be exactly the same. The only variation that we are looking for is the one that is purposefully designed into the experiment. This is why a great deal of care goes into the selection of representative and homogeneous test and control groups.

Figure 9.1 shows the three phases that characterize a typical MA test. The purpose of the pre-test phase is to establish a baseline level of expected company performance in our test and control groups.

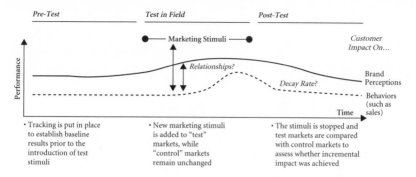

Figure 9.1.   Marketing Accountability Testing Overview

The length of this phase is highly variable, depending on whether comprehensive baseline response or sales metrics already exist or need to be established to support the test. In addition to these baseline business outcome metrics, it is extremely helpful to have baseline data around individual customer perceptions and behavior, to better contextualize the "what" and the "why" of your test results. This may require putting in place customer tracking research that is unique to your test—but not always.

During the test phase, the new marketing stimuli is introduced to the test groups and withheld from the control. The duration of the test phase is determined by the type of variable you are testing, the customer outcome you are targeting, and the extent of variation you are introducing. Finally, the post-test phase reveals what happens to performance once the test activity ends. Specifically, we may be curious about how the lifetime value of the customers that we acquired under the test condition differs from our historic norm, or how long we may continue to benefit from any lift created from the test activity, or the presence of any unintended consequences that lagged our initial results. Because the financial impact of these lagging metrics can sometimes be much greater than our test period results, post-test performance must be included as a critical part of our test's evaluation.

In relation to this basic structure, six core principles emerge to differentiate outstanding MA test-and-learn approaches from all of the rest. These six R's of effective MA testing, presented in Table 9.1, all speak to the key challenge that all MA tests must meet— providing a reliable learning or insight regarding the MA hypothesis or hypotheses being tested. We will introduce two primary experimentation approaches over the course of this chapter. We call the first

1. Right Focus	Focusing the test on the most critical issue, as each additional variable can have a multiplicative effect on the financial and organizational resources required to execute and assess the test
2 and 3. Randomized and Representative	Selecting MA test and control groups that are randomized and representative, so results can be reliably projected across the broader population
4. Reproducible	Avoiding the common trap of creating test conditions supported by marketing activities that cannot be practically reproduced on a broad scale at the same cost or quality levels
5. Risk-Managed	Identifying and potentially mitigating all material test-related risks, from competitive signaling to damaging of customer relationships to hampering of control market performance to the need for redundancy
6. Readable	Maintaining a clean test environment by minimizing test variables and competing marketing programs, tracking changes in customer attitudes and behaviors, monitoring competitive actions, and keeping the test in field for an adequate time frame

Table 9.1.   The Six R's of Effective MA Testing.

the *classic* approach and the second the *dynamic* approach. With the classic approach to MA test-and-learn, we achieve this by *limiting the impact of background noise on our test results by executing clean field tests.* With the dynamic approach to MA, we use more complex multivariate econometric modeling during the post-test phase to achieve the same basic effect.

When done well, MA tests can isolate the impact of the variation we introduce, by simplifying the marketing ecosystem to that single change. A well-structured MA test attempts to remove, control for, or at least understand any other variations that could impact the company's performance with the test group. These factors include changes to the company's other marketing activities, channel partners' and competitors' actions, and environmental factors in the test market such as changes in the local economy or even weather disruptions. The less extraneous noise that we have in our test markets or control groups, the purer the read of our test variable's performance and the higher degree of confidence we can have when we move to extrapolate the insights and findings from the test across a broader field of play.

The classic field test assumes that you can get a read that something is effective by eliminating the background noise in the rollout. However, that is often an unrealistic hope, especially for tests with a relatively long duration. It is usually a challenge to control for everything, even in the most well-planned experiments. A prime example of something that is 100 percent completely out of your control is the weather. So although dynamic optimization involves a more complex analytic process, it is perhaps more real and maybe more realistic, particularly in terms of its implicit understanding that everything cannot be controlled for exogenously when you execute an experiment. Dynamic optimization accepts this basic truth and then finds robust ways for you to still gain valuable learning and insights about accountability while simultaneously driving the in-period business performance as usual. Both approaches have merit in your overall toolkit, though, so let's first take a deeper look at the classic field test.

DESIGNING AND EXECUTING A CLASSIC IN-MARKET TEST

At this point we will begin to translate the basic concepts and principles of MA testing into a systematic business process that you can use to construct your own powerful MA tests. The MA tests that you will be designing and executing will depend on a number of factors, including the kinds of behavioral response you want to be measuring (such as short-term unit sales versus longer-term repeat purchase patterns), the level of aggregation at which you can or would like to measure it (such as the individual customer level versus the DMA level), and the extent to which the marketing stimuli that you want to test are addressable at the individual channel or customer level (such as broadcast TV versus loyalty marketing programs).

At one level, the nature of your overall business model predetermines the most appropriate MA tests. If you are in a business that has a direct sales relationship with your end customer and you track sales data at the individual customer or consumer level (think Dell or Vodafone), you have the most flexibility to pursue a varied and at times very granular testing agenda to understand the impact of marketing programs on short-term and long-term individual customer economics, as well as at higher levels of aggregation. If you are in a business that has an intermediated sales relationship through varied, multi-tier distribution (think P&G or Guinness) or in a direct-to-customer business that does not track sales at an individual customer level (Walmart, Starbucks), you may need to target your testing agenda at the market or store level, and you will be able to track individual customer response only with the help of prefabricated panels (Marketscan, Homescan, Worldpanel, InfoScan) or custom tracking studies.

Most classic in-market tests focus on measuring short-term sales response as the primary outcome variable. This is a reasonable place to start, because the explicit purpose of most marketing activity is to generate in-period demand. Even given that, we still need to decide at what level of aggregation we are going to measure our sales performance: at the DMA or other geographic-market level (store trading area, ZIP code–based, and so on), the store or channel level, or the individual customer level. We can focus on one, two, or all three of these levels, depending on the quality of our sales data and the relevance of that level of aggregation in relation to the marketing actions that we are testing.

The other key determinant of the nature of our in-market tests is the kind of marketing stimuli we are testing. If we are testing mass market stimuli that are harder to address to a known, specific individual customer—like broadcast TV, radio, outdoor, national print, or newspaper—the nature of this nonaddressable media requires us to design a market-level field test; the effects of these stimuli are depicted in Figure 9.2. Said another way, because the marketing stimuli hits the whole DMA or geographic market, the market level is the most appropriate level of analysis. We can attempt to introduce tracking studies to understand the extent to which any given individual customer was exposed to our marketing activities and went on to purchase, but without the help of additional tracking studies it would be impossible to disaggregate the sales response to these nonaddressable marketing activities at a channel or individual customer level.

If we are testing marketing stimuli that are structured around our distribution channel—like in-store merchandising displays, point-of-purchase coupons, or store-specific price promotions—we will want to design a channel-level field test. If we are testing marketing stimuli that are addressable at the individual customer level—e-mail, direct mail letters or postcards, catalogs, direct-response cable

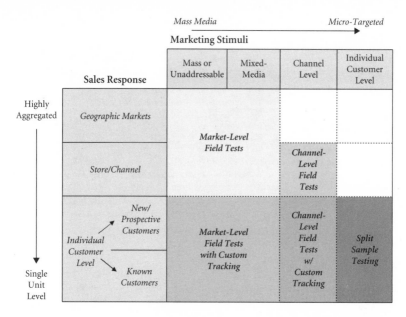

Figure 9.2. Impact of Sales Response Level and Marketing Stimuli on Test Design Alternatives

TV, and so on—the nature of this media allows us to deploy a standard split sample test, again as depicted in Figure 9.2.

Most companies, of course, pursue go-to-market plans that combine all of these media types in an integrated fashion. Even for marketers in direct response businesses—where you might at first assume that all of the marketing programs are focused on addressable media vehicles—national TV, outdoor, or radio-based marketing investments may still play a useful role in the overall mix. Any time you want to test the effectiveness of a mix of activities that includes addressable and nonaddressable marketing vehicles, you will need to design market-level field tests, even if you have the ability to track individual customer-level response. So market-level field tests will be a dominant MA test type across many industries and categories.

Figure 9.3 provides an overview of all the steps involved in the MA testing process. As we address the twelve steps outlined in the process, we will address how each step is relevant for two predominant kinds of in-market tests: market-level field tests and split sample tests at the individual customer level.

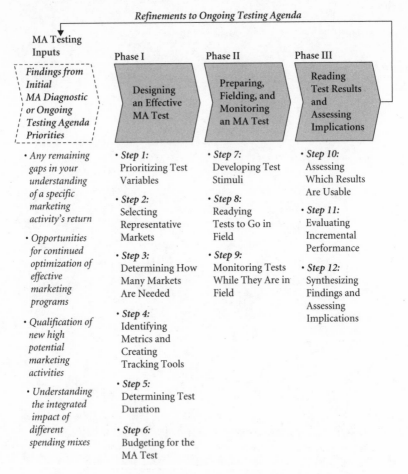

Figure 9.3.   The Marketing Accountability Testing Process

Step 1: Prioritizing Test Variables

As we highlighted in the Six R's of effective MA testing, getting the right focus for your tests means prioritizing your test variables. Each variable that we test requires a minimum of one test cell, group, or market to test it in, assuming the variable has only one value that is interesting to us. If each variable has a couple of values we need to evaluate, this adds a couple of test cells. Each additional value and each additional variable that we introduce has a multiplier effect on the number of test groups or markets required. Depending on the cost and relative scarcity of each test group, there is no getting around the need for focus when prioritizing your test variables.

Let's use a simple example to bring this point home. If we want to hypothetically test the role that broadcast TV advertising versus outdoor media can play to help us introduce a new product, we have one variable (media type), in a couple of different values (TV-only, outdoor-only, some TV-outdoor hybrid), requiring three test cells. If, however, we also have some questions about *how much* TV or outdoor is required, we add a second variable (investment level) to the test. This variable may have three discrete values (low, medium, high). As seen in Figure 9.4, to cover both variables in each of the three combinations, we need nine test cells. If we were to add another variable—say, brand messaging—with three different values, we would need twenty-seven test cells to test all of the relevant combinations.

Now, depending on the nature of the MA test, twenty-seven test conditions may seem more or less manageable. If we are using it to test something with low variable cost to deploy and manage—say, internet banner advertising or search word marketing—this might be

| | Investment Level | | |
	Low	Medium	High
TV-Only	*Market #1*	*Market #4*	*Market #7*
Outdoor-Only	*Market #2*	*Market #5*	*Market #8*
TV+Outdoor	*Market #3*	*Market #6*	*Market #9*

Figure 9.4.   Impact of an Increase in Test Variables and Variable Values on Test Design

fine. However, if we are exploring spending vehicles that will require market-level field tests, all of a sudden the thought of twenty-seven test markets with different test conditions feels expensive, complex, perhaps even overwhelming. As long as we have a continuous-improvement mind-set, we can eventually get to all of the key open questions. But for any given MA test, we encourage everyone to focus, focus, focus.

Fortunately we have the learning provided by the MA diagnostic as an important input to shape our first round of testing. The MA diagnostic will have already classified a company's marketing programs into those with proven returns and those without. Clearly any large programs that still have unclear returns coming out of the diagnostic should be candidates for testing, especially if there is a desire to continue with these investments. These must take precedence over proven programs of similar scale, which may be further optimized through testing.

Step 2. Selecting Representative and Randomized Markets

In the ideal world, your selection of test and control groups would be completely randomized. You could employ some high-tech methods for randomizing your process or some low-tech methods (like heads or tails with a standard coin toss). The idea is to construct test and control groups that have no systemic bias and are indicative of your total market. For example, if key demographics or customer segments, category penetration levels, brand strength levels, or other factors are not representative across your test and control groups, your test results may be skewed and thus less reliable.

With split sample tests in direct-to-customer businesses, this is both fairly easy to do and fairly easy to test, especially with MA tests targeted at existing customers. You can profile the individual customer cohorts in the test and control groups against all the relevant variables that you track—gender, income level, average order size, customer lifetime value, recency of last purchase, frequency of ordering, your attitudinal segmentation, and so on—to ensure that these two groups reflect identical samples with an absence of any systemic differences.

With market-level field tests, ensuring that each market included in a test or control group is representative takes a little more work. In the same way that the different customer cohorts are profiled for split sample tests, you will also want to profile your individual geographies or DMAs against key variables. These variables might include the following:

- *Demographics/firmographics:* Understanding the customer characteristics (income levels, buying behavior, product mix, and so on) of each market
- *Brand and category development:* Understanding the brand's development (for example, local market share similar to national market share), category sales development, or both
- *Brand and category growth:* Ensuring that brand and category growth rates are consistent with national averages
- *Channel:* Understanding which tiers or types of distribution partners are most prominent and their relative market shares
- *Competitive intensity:* Understanding the nature of competitive factors in each market, especially in highly fragmented categories
- *Economic health:* Evaluating relevant local economic factors that are significantly different than national averages (such as unemployment rate or inflation) that could impact the market's response to test stimuli

Ideally you would choose a test market or two with a similar profile against these core profiling variables to your overall market, be that at the regional, national, or international level.

Of course, for many companies it may not be feasible to make each test and control market entirely representative of the total market. A company in the rapid growth phase of its lifecycle may find little meaning in test markets that solely reflect national average company performance, when awareness, distribution, and share may vary widely across their markets. Instead it may be necessary to create peer groups of like markets that are currently trending toward the peak or trough of the development cycle curve. Table 9.2 shows an example of how key market-level profiling variables like those just mentioned were used as inputs into a quantitative cluster analysis to create peer market groups within the United States for a B2B financial services provider.

Finally, it is usually important to work with key peers in your company to do one last gut check on the final list of test markets, especially when conducting a market-level field test. You will want

Profiling Variable	Detailed Description	Peer Group #1	Peer Group #2	Peer Group #3
Firmographics	Number of SMEs requiring product	72,000	19,500	11,750
Brand Development	Company's local market share over national market share	1.2	1.7	.8
Sales Force Strength	Customer satisfaction measures around sales relationships	High	High	Low
Channel Coverage	Percent of Tier 1 brokers carrying product	68%	84%	56%
Competitive Industry	Market share ratios of top four competitors	High	Low	Medium
Matched Markets		Austin, TX Boston, MA Baltimore, MD Phoenix, AZ Seattle, WA	Lexington, KYTallahassee, FL Harrisburg, PA South Bend, IN Medford, OR	Modesto, CA Trenton, NJ Colorado Springs, CO Lansing, MI Burlington, VT

Table 9.2.   Matched Market Selection Using Cluster Analysis: B2B Financial Services Example.

to remove any specific markets or groups that may be subject to anomalous circumstances that will make the results less reliable. So, for example, if there has been M&A activity or unusual competitive activity in a specific geographic market or a certain distribution channel, it's a good idea to steer clear of the affected groups in your test and control selection. Similarly, avoiding markets with one-time local idiosyncrasies, like a recent natural disaster, highly seasonal visitation patterns, or some recent economic disruption, makes the most sense whenever possible.

Step 3: Determining How Many Markets Are Needed

Determining the right size for your test and control groups, in terms of customers for split sample tests or markets for market-level field tests, is about trading off costs, risks, and the projectability of the results. Smaller numbers at either the customer or the market level will result in MA tests that will be cheaper, allowing you to potentially accommodate more variables in your test and limiting your business risk. These smaller tests are also potentially easier to manage. In contrast, tests with larger numbers (more customers or more markets) increase the likelihood that the results will be projectable and are less likely to be completely derailed by one-off externalities. Figure 9.5 contextualizes this with more depth, identifying the driving forces in determining how many test groups or markets you need and the continuum presented by each factor.

Number of test variables used: As we have discussed, the number of test variables you use generally has a direct multiplier effect on the number of test groups or markets you will require, especially with a classic in-market test. In the next section, we will demonstrate how some companies use more of an adaptive experimentation approach,

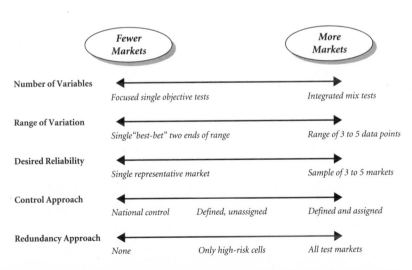

Figure 9.5. Factors Affecting the Number of Markets Needed in a Test

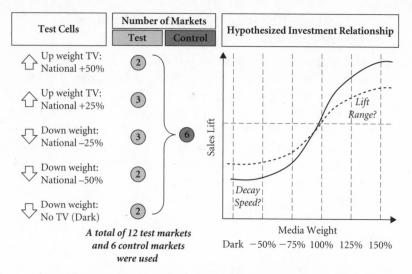

Example: Testing TV Advertising Investment Levels at a Software Company

Figure 9.6.   Determining the Number of Markets Needed for an MA Test

combined with advanced modeling, to circumvent this limitation. But for now, let's take this as a given.

Range of required variation: Most MA test variables will not be a binary, yes or no issue, but rather represent a range of possible values. So determining the right number of variations for each variable is critical. Again, each different value of a test variable requires a discrete test cell, so it's not always feasible to test many variations of any given variable. The difficulties are compounded by the fact that for many marketing investments, many companies do not have a good sense of whether their existing spending levels are within the optimal range to drive sales response.

Figure 9.6 presents a masked example of a software company that was attempting to optimize their investment in television advertising—a program that they believed was working well but were not certain of. The company had only anecdotal data about investment levels gathered from observing their competitors' spending levels and growth. They hypothesized that there was an S-curve relationship between spending and sales, on which a point of diminishing returns was reached at around 140 percent of their current spend. From their observations, they believed there was also a point, at 60 to 70 percent of their current spend, at which it was suboptimal to spend anything on advertising.

Given this hypothesis, ideally they would probably want to test at least three values in advertising spending: their current spend, and then plus and minus 50 percent of that number; these would allow them to have test cells reasonably above and below their hypothesized inflection points on the curve. If there were no limits on their ability to select test markets, they might want to have two other spend levels at the plus and minus 25-percent levels, to give them five plot points on a rudimentary S curve.

Although many academic researchers dispute the existence of an S-curve-like relationship between TV advertising and sales, the software company example also highlights another useful point. The range of variation in values of the variables must be appropriate for the kind of marketing stimuli being tested. For highly targetable vehicles with a high degree of proven efficacy, plus and minus 10 percent of the current investment levels could be more than adequate. For totally new marketing programs, like on-line video or mobile advertising, significantly wider ranges of variation—plus and minus 150 percent or 200 percent—may be appropriate.

Desired reliability of results: Is it enough to have a single group or market representing each test cell or variable? Or, if you have chosen more of a peer group approach, is it enough to have a single group or market representing each peer group? Perhaps it is enough if you assume that you have chosen a market that is precisely representative of the whole and if you further assume that the customers in this market will respond to your stimuli exactly as the rest of the country would. But why take the chance? You don't draw your traditional customer research samples from a single population, so why would you take such a risk with your MA test design?

Although it is wise to not rely on a single group or market for each key test cell, each market you add can come with a hefty price tag, depending on the nature of the MA test. So we offer you these rules of thumb to help determine how much redundancy you should bake into any given MA test design:

- A good starting point is to have two groups or markets representing each unique test cell, more if they are reasonably affordable. This will increase the reliability of your answer and will also build in some redundancy if testing in one market fails.

• For critical research questions, it may be necessary to have three duplicate markets covering this cell—even if it means eliminating other cells in the test.

• Regional customer differences, or the management perception that regional differences exist, may also drive the need for three or more markets for each key cell.

Control market approach: There are essentially three ways to read control or baseline performance results within a MA test: (1) use defined control markets that provide baseline results for the entire test but are not matched to a particular test cells, (2) use control markets that are matched to particular test cells, or (3) use a national or total market control. Each of these approaches will imply a different number of required control markets. Although you won't have the expense of test stimuli in your control markets—which can often be the most frustrating costs to bear, because you are paying more to block media out of a market or do split regional print runs—the number of control markets may still be constrained by tracking costs, market availability, and the opportunity cost associated with constraining incremental marketing activities in these markets during the test period.

The benefit of using defined control markets (matched or not) is that unlike using a national control, you can see what, if any, range of results could be expected in your baseline market performance. Given that these defined controls will be selected with the same principles and filters as used with the active tests, this expected baseline variation can be helpful in explaining why variation exists among like test market cells, and in turn, in understanding what truly incremental growth due to test changes is.

Redundancy approach: There are also potential risks to the test itself that must be considered. In 2005 we designed a large MA test for a national retailer, which had to be suspended just as it was about to go into field because Hurricane Katrina hit and made it impossible to get a clean read across too many of our test markets. Although it is impossible to anticipate a major natural disaster, you can build enough redundancy into your testing plan that if you have to throw out the results from one or two markets, you can still draw meaningful conclusions from your test. Plant closures, unseasonable weather, or intentional disruptions made by your competitors—these are the sorts of circumstances that could force you to throw a market's results out of your test. If you put all your eggs in one basket and try to add markets back into your test after problems emerge, your test results may be valid, but your test's internal credibility could be damaged beyond repair. Of course, ensuring a lot of redundancy across the test design will drive up the number of markets that you need, which will drive up costs.

By balancing your strategic requirements across the five factors shown in Figure 9.5, you will start to zero in on how many test groups or markets are needed. Typically this is an iterative process, during which different, competing test approaches are developed, with the pros and cons of each evaluated and openly debated by the team. As is shown, you can trade off less variation in variable values for more redundancy, or you can trade off higher degrees of reliability relative to constraints imposed by your control approach. Ultimately you have to rely on your business judgment to determine what trade-offs you are willing to live with, relative to the must-have requirements for any given MA test to be seen as credible and effective. With split sample in-market tests, the only real limit to the number of test cells and test groups that you can have is the number of customers or prospective customers you can sample. If you are a wireless carrier with five million active subscribers and five million lapsed subscribers, you should not have too many constraints. With market-level field testing, obviously the number of potential test markets is nowhere near as fungible, and you will face higher cost hurdles for MA tests with a need for too many active test markets.

Step 4: Identifying Metrics and Creating Tracking Tools

The cornerstone of an MA testing approach is robust tracking. At a minimum, the organization needs to have reliable tracking mechanisms for the sales response itself, at whatever level of aggregation—individual customer, channel, or market—is necessitated by the test. For many companies who are new to MA testing, just getting the sales response tracking to deliver accurate, reliable, and timely reads can be a significant challenge, especially when the MA test requires data to get cut in nontraditional ways. If you do nothing else from a tracking standpoint, please get the sales response tracking right!

Tracking sales response is usually only the first step to building a comprehensive measurement approach. More often than not, an effective MA test can create almost as many additional questions as it answers. The sales response performance by test cell typically tells you what happened, but it does not always give you in-depth insights into why it happened. For example, thinking of the straightforward test design in Figure 9.4, we may learn that we get a positive sales response only if we have heavy investment in TV or TV plus outdoor (test cells Market #7 and Market #9), which for some organizations may be enough. However, we will not know the "whys"—why the low or medium investment levels were not effective, why outdoor by itself was not effective, or why our winning test cells won.

Thus we strongly encourage you to supplement the sales response data with additional data sets that provide further insights into customer perceptions and behavior. Some of this data may come from existing sources, whether operational or market research–based, like customer satisfaction surveys, call center reports, or brand health tracking. It can be difficult to get preexisting data sources cut in a way that it can be appended specifically to test groups or markets, but this is usually a good place to start.

Often, however, it will be helpful to augment our existing customer-level data sources with a custom tracking survey specific to the MA test at hand. This can turbocharge your ability to drive deep insights from your MA tests—confidently tackling the "what," as in what happened, the "why," as in why this outcome occurred, and the "how long," as in how long you need a certain kind of investment to get specific shifts in attitudes, perceptions, or beliefs. This can be incredibly valuable as you develop your own set of metrics to help better understand the interplay between specific marketing actions, the sales response, and the impact on brand/customer equity. The downside of customized tracking research is that it can considerably drive up the cost of conducting the MA test, while adding additional time and complexity to the fielding itself. Thus it may not be an appropriate or feasible alternative in every MA test situation.

Customized tracking studies can drive toward measuring different kinds of issues—with questions from as narrow as "Who received the marketing stimuli?" to as broad as "Did it change their individual attitudes, perceptions, or purchase behaviors?" Figure 9.7 suggests the four categories of metrics that your tracking survey could encompass, as well as the cross-tab lenses that may be helpful for interpreting your survey results. Starting with a comprehensive view of customer metrics, you can then narrow these down as appropriate to consider the specific test at hand. You will likely have to reduce the length of

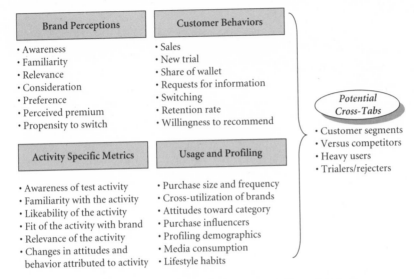

Figure 9.7.   Examples of MA Test Tracking Metrics

your final survey, but this can now be done with an informed view of your data trade-offs.

In an ideal world, you would use three waves of tracking research across your test and control groups—one for each phase of your test. This would give you pre-test, during-test, and post-test measures to compare with each other. If you can afford it, adding additional test waves during the test in-field phase will help you understand the speed of potential changes, whereas additional test waves during the post-period phase make sense if you have a particular interest in decay rates or lag effects. If your baseline performance is highly dynamic, additional preperiod waves might make sense. As you will see from the budgeting discussion that follows, tracking research can be your single biggest test expense, so it is important to think through these research design questions very carefully.

Step 5: Determining Test Duration

There are two sequential steps in determining the appropriate duration for your MA test, the first focusing on the appropriate length of the test-in-field phase and the second focusing on the appropriate proportion of the pre-test and post-test phases, relative to the active

Length of Test-in-Field Phase

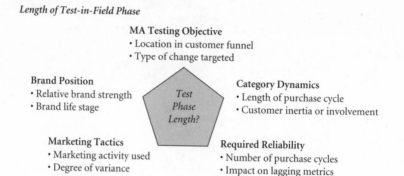

MA Testing Objective
* Location in customer funnel
* Type of change targeted

Brand Position
* Relative brand strength
* Brand life stage

Test Phase Length?

Category Dynamics
* Length of purchase cycle
* Customer inertia or involvement

Marketing Tactics
* Marketing activity used
* Degree of variance

Required Reliability
* Number of purchase cycles
* Impact on lagging metrics

Length of Pre and Post Phases Relative to Test Phase

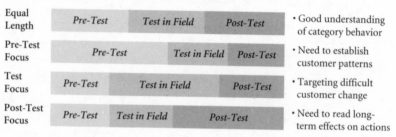

Equal Length	Pre-Test	Test in Field	Post-Test	* Good understanding of category behavior
Pre-Test Focus	Pre-Test	Test in Field	Post-Test	* Need to establish customer patterns
Test Focus	Pre-Test	Test in Field	Post-Test	* Targeting difficult customer change
Post-Test Focus	Pre-Test	Test in Field	Post-Test	* Need to read long-term effects on actions

Figure 9.8.   Factors Affecting MA Test Duration

testing phase. When determining how long your customers will be exposed to your test stimuli, there are five factors to consider, as outlined in Figure 9.8.

For example, we need to understand which objective in the customer decision funnel your test is targeting. We have been asserting that we are looking for changes in sales response, which will take longer to register than changes in top-of-the-funnel metrics like aided or unaided brand awareness. Category dynamics—including issues like the length of the purchase cycle, repeat purchase frequency, and the level of customer involvement within the category—are also important drivers of test length. Categories with longer purchase cycles and less frequency will, on average, require longer test periods than those with a faster, more frequent turn. In the same way, variations in brand position, marketing tactic being tested, and the required reliability of the MA test results will drive either shorter or longer in-field test periods.

With an understanding of the factors that will determine how long your test stimuli remains in field, you can examine the relationship of the test phase to the pre- and post-test phases. Figure 9.8 offers examples of the different situations in which the three phases of your test may not be of equal length. For example, if you are trying to understand decay rates or impact on longer-term customer behavior, your post-test phase may need to be in market for many more purchase cycles than your pre- and test phases.

As you can see, there can be a high degree of variability in the length of each of these phases. On the shorter end, for certain split sample MA tests on quick-turn marketing vehicles like search marketing, you may not have any specific pre-test period per se, just your baseline performance data, and your test period may only last a few days. You may then act on your results immediately at the end of the test period, keeping some post-period tracking in place to periodically validate the initial findings. However, for certain market-level field tests with multiple marketing vehicles in categories with seasonal purchase cycles, your test period may be six or twelve months, with equally long pre- and post-test periods.

Step 6: Budgeting for MA Testing

MA tests can be very expensive, but keep in mind that this is only a fraction of the money that you are currently spending on the tests' full-scale national doppelgänger, which may or not be working, or could be performing much better. So it is always helpful to frame the incremental, out-of-pocket costs required to conduct any given MA test in light of these broader improvement opportunities.

In Figure 9.3 we placed budgeting as the sixth and final step in the design phase. In reality, however, budgeting is an integral part of what tends to be a highly iterative MA test design process, during which cost issues can drive significant choices in terms of variable prioritization, test group selection, and tracking approaches. Each significant design choice has cost implications. People who proactively understand what those are and who can nimbly navigate through different costing scenarios have the upper hand in steering the trade-off conversations that are an inevitable part of MA test design.

There are three main cost components to any MA test—marketing production, media, and monitoring and measurement. The complexity of your overall MA test design—in terms of the number of variables, the number of test cells, the amount of redundancy, the length of the test, and so on—will be directly correlated with your incremental costs for the production and media components. More complexity makes for more expensive production and media costs, and these costs typically cannot be avoided without compromising your test design. Furthermore, many MA test designs do not allow you to purchase different types of media as cost-effectively as possible, because typically you are not getting any scale advantages and may be suboptimizing some of the media deployment to keep your test reads as clean as possible. Given this, you will have some additional cost penalties that should be factored into your budgeting process.

It is with the third cost component, monitoring and measuring, that most companies tend to seek more discretion. If you decide to do custom tracking research in each of your test markets, you have made a decision that increases your costs by a step-function. You can move those costs up and down somewhat based on research design decisions like sample size, number of test cells covered, and the number of research waves, but there is no avoiding the fact that you will probably increase the overall costs of the MA test by anywhere from 15 percent to 40 percent, perhaps more, by including custom tracking. So you need to have a high degree of confidence that the incremental insights are worth the incremental investment, which we believe they usually are. Given this, it is also not surprising that this is usually the first place where companies tend to economize if funding gets tight.

Occasionally other cost components prove to be material. If your test design and analysis capabilities are nascent, you may need external vendor support for that part of the process. Your test design may also have some incremental operational implications—like driving incremental call volume to a call center or driving incremental demand for specific kinds of inventory—that should be factored in.

Step 7: Developing Test Stimuli

We don't need to say much about this step in the testing process because you are probably already closely involved in preparing full-scale marketing programs. We will provide just a couple of cautions. First, ensure that nothing gets lost in translation when scaling down or developing unique stimuli for your test. If you are working with new vendors, make sure that they undergo as rigorous a briefing about your brand, strategies, and goals as you would give to your ongoing national partners. You should also follow any typical approval processes you have in place for getting new creative in field. Second, watch out when you are doing a test that may include marketing vehicles that are not a part of your existing marketing mix, whether they are "new to the world" tactics like location-based mobile marketing or "new to the company" tactics. In these situations, you clearly have more risk at this step, because of your lack of familiarity with the medium, how it works creatively, and its idiosyncrasies when it comes to in-market execution.

Step 8: Readying Tests to Go in Field

In the rush to get MA tests in market, this step is often overlooked. And depending on the complexity of the MA test at hand, this step may need more resources and mental energy than many people initially expect. Typically we organize this step into five key activity streams: (1) organizational readiness, (2) stakeholder communications, (3) capacity management, (4) test monitoring, and (5) test results tracking. For a standard split sample test of direct marketing investment, we may move through the prep work in all of these activities fairly quickly, with small circles of communication. For a complex market-level test, however, this can be a material step that becomes a critical bottleneck to MA test deployment. Figure 9.9 gives an example of a streamlined checklist for just such a test.

Step 9: Monitoring Tests While They Are in Field

There are several factors that could potentially corrupt one or more of your test groups or markets and compel you to throw out their results. These are factors that create variations in your results not explained by proper application of your test stimuli. Although some factors, such as weather or local economic changes, can be read after the test has concluded, others, such as competitive tampering or supply issues, may be lost if you have not created some in-field monitoring mechanism. This could be as simple as designating a sales manager or trusted intermediary as a steward for each test market. These individuals can be given a simple checklist of factors; they will then observe for changes and bring any red flags to the attention of the test owner while the test is in field.

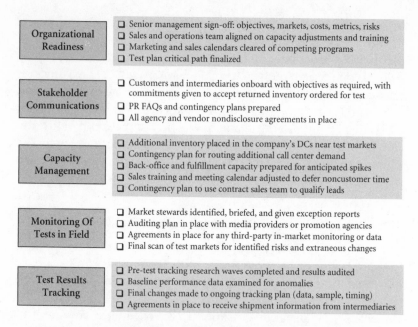

Organizational Readiness	❏ Senior management sign-off: objectives, markets, costs, metrics, risks ❏ Sales and operations team aligned on capacity adjustments and training ❏ Marketing and sales calendars cleared of competing programs ❏ Test plan critical path finalized
Stakeholder Communications	❏ Customers and intermediaries onboard with objectives as required, with commitments given to accept returned inventory ordered for test ❏ PR FAQs and contingency plans prepared ❏ All agency and vendor nondisclosure agreements in place
Capacity Management	❏ Additional inventory placed in the company's DCs near test markets ❏ Contingency plan for routing additional call center demand ❏ Back-office and fulfillment capacity prepared for anticipated spikes ❏ Sales training and meeting calendar adjusted to defer noncustomer time ❏ Contingency plan to use contract sales team to qualify leads
Monitoring Of Tests in Field	❏ Market stewards identified, briefed, and given exception reports ❏ Auditing plan in place with media providers or promotion agencies ❏ Agreements in place for any third-party in-market monitoring or data ❏ Final scan of test markets for identified risks and extraneous changes
Test Results Tracking	❏ Pre-test tracking research waves completed and results audited ❏ Baseline performance data examined for anomalies ❏ Final changes made to ongoing tracking plan (data, sample, timing) ❏ Agreements in place to receive shipment information from intermediaries

Figure 9.9.   Sample Launch Readiness Checklist for an MA Test

The factors that you should consider for real-time monitoring, or retroactive review, fall into three categories: company-introduced noise, testing failure, and environmental changes. Company-introduced noise, like a call center going down or key sales force turnover, is usually the easiest to track but also the most prone to reinterpretation to explain away unwanted test results. Testing failure can occur when test marketing stimuli have been improperly applied; for example, TV advertisements were trafficked at the wrong time or in the wrong DMA, or your custom tracking was not executed properly, or your distribution partners encountered operational problems that artificially muted sales response. Finally, broader environmental disruptions may occur in relation to local economic conditions, the weather, or unusual competitive activity that corrupt the results with one or more of your test groups or markets. By staying vigilant across all of these dimensions in real time, you will save yourself some unnecessary time and effort during the final three steps of the MA testing process.

Step 10: Assessing Which Test Market Results Are Usable

The decision to throw out the results of a given test market because of the interference of exogenous factors should of course not be taken lightly—particularly if there was not adequate market redundancy in your test design, so that excluding the results of a single market could put the entire test in jeopardy. It does, however, sometimes become necessary to exclude some test group results, not only to ensure that overall test findings are accurate but also to protect the credibility of your company's long-term MA testing program. You may even be able to salvage some meaningful insights out of a situation in which you need to exclude the most important market from the test results, by using some more advanced statistical techniques and overlaying that with some business judgment.

When you discover an external anomaly in one of your test groups or markets, the first task is to gauge whether this factor could have had a material impact on your test results and, where possible, to attempt to quantify it. If you can sufficiently quantify or isolate the impact of this factor, you may want to adjust your test market results rather than totally exclude the market. For example, during a test an electronics manufacturer may lose its distribution with a local retail chain that represents 15 percent of the company's sales in a given test market. If chain-level scanner data is available, this impact can be isolated, and the test market's results will not have to be excluded.

If it is determined that the results in a particular market should be excluded from your primary test findings, these results should be fully excluded. We have seen more than one CEO become frustrated with asterisked MA test findings, in which marketers attempted to explain why only certain results should be considered and not the others. This perceived hedging around test results does much more to widen the marketing accountability gap than the test itself does to reduce it.

When a particular test market result is excluded, it is also important to fully document the rationale for this decision. Given expected marketing department turnover, if these factors are not properly documented it is possible for previously excluded results to be reintroduced and reshape the test's findings at some point in the future. Proper documentation of excluded markets will also avoid any perception that marketers were gaming MA tests by excluding market results that did not agree with their desired outcome.

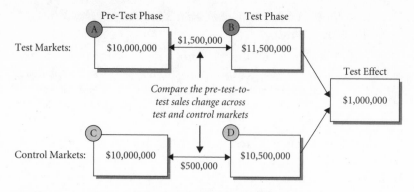

Figure 9.10.   Evaluating Incremental Test Market Performance: Example
Targeting Sales Performance

Step 11: Evaluating Incremental Performance

With a clean data set of test results, you can now consider whether your test activity moved the dial on your targeted perceptions and behaviors and what returns the movements gave you on your investment. Because our test design and subsequent auditing have removed the impact of other factors, only a straightforward calculation (see Figure 9.10) is needed to read incremental performance for each of our test conditions. First we compare the pre-test period and test period results for our key performance variable (such as sales) for each of our groups in the test condition and the control condition. In this simple example, our test markets sales increased by $1,500,000 and our control markets sales increased by $500,000. The difference between these two outcomes, $1,000,000, is the incremental sales growth that we can attribute to our test activity. We refer to this as our *test effect*.

As soon as we have captured the test effect sales impact, we can usually calculate the incremental gross margin or net operating margin associated with those incremental sales gains, using the company's standard cost algorithms. Once the incremental margin is calculated, we then subtract the production and media costs associated with each test condition to determine whether the test itself had a positive or negative ROI. For example, if our business in Figure 9.10 had 25 percent net operating margins and we incurred $100,000 in incremental production and media costs in the test condition, this MA test would have yielded a 150-percent return on investment.

Assuming we have chosen representative test and control markets and do not need to make any further adjustments, we could then also use these figures as a basis for understanding the financial impact of rolling this test condition out across our full market. Obviously more care would be needed in doing this type of extrapolation, making sure that the cost assumptions incorporate the efficiencies of scale purchasing and the test effect assumptions reflect any matched market findings that you may have designed into the MA test. But looking for directionally correct full-market extrapolations is the natural next step in this kind of analysis.

For MA tests with a post-test period, you will need to do additional analyses to help understand the change in sales response between the test period and the post-test period, across the test and control groups. With most MA tests, typically there are no incremental production or media costs associated with the post-test phase, but there could be some lagged incremental sales benefit or sales decline that needs to be monitored. For example, if your MA test stimuli caused some of your customers to forward-buy additional inventory in the test period, and because of that they do not make their usual purchases during the post-test period, then you may have a negative sales effect in the post-period that you'll need to track and model. By continuing to monitor performance, you can determine whether your initial ROI calculations are enhanced or degraded by post-purchase sales effects.

Any time you have the mechanism to evaluate sales response at the individual customer level, either by executing market-level or channel-level field tests with custom tracking or when conducting split sample tests, you also can add additional texture and depth to the sales response modeling. For example, you may learn that the test condition increased sales by inducing trial from new customers, or by stimulating existing customers to purchase larger baskets of higher-priced items more frequently, or by any other realistic variation in individual customer level response.

Table 9.3 presents an example of how this type of an approach can provide richer insights into how and why each test condition delivered the test effect that it did. These are masked results from a catalog retailer who was trying to assess how changes in two test variables—the brand proposition and its creative execution, and

Test Response	Test Condition #1	Test Condition #2	Test Condition #3	Control
Pieces mailed	45,100	45,098	45,099	45,110
Orders	623	615	712	607
Percent of orders per pieces mailed	1.38%	1.36%	1.58%	1.35%
Response difference relative to control	0.04%	0.02%	0.23%	
Average orders per customer during test period	1.20	1.03	1.1	1.03
Number of new customers acquired	519	597	647	589
Total Sales Effects				
Average number of items per order	1.25	1.75	1.47	1.30
Average unit price per item	$131	$75	$89	$95
Total sales effect	$102,016	$80,719	$93,151	$74,965
Sales response versus control	$27,052	$5,754	$18,186	
Percent difference	36 percent	8 percent	24 percent	
Disaggregated Sales Effects				
Response effect versus control	3%	1%	17%	
Number of items effect versus control	–4%	35%	13%	
Average unit retail effect versus control	38%	–21%	–6%	
Disaggregated Customer Effects				
New customer acquisition effect to control	–11.9%	1.3%	9.8%	
Purchase frequency effect	16.5%	0.0%	6.8%	

Table 9.3.   Disaggregated Sales and Customer Effects from a Split Sample Field Test.

the use of a promotional offer (get 50 percent off the second item purchased for specific SKUs)—impacted the effectiveness of one of its traditional new customer acquisition vehicles. There were three test conditions: one group got the new brand/creative alone (Test Condition #1), one got the promotional offer (Test Condition #2), and one got both (Test Condition #3); a control group got neither.

As you can see, all three test conditions yielded a positive total sales response, but when you study the disaggregated sales effects, you see very different paths to value creation. Condition #1, which yielded the strongest test effect, got there by stimulating slightly more total orders than the control, with each order having slightly fewer average items but at significantly higher unit retail prices. Condition #2, which yielded the relatively weakest (but still positive) test effect, got there by stimulating slightly more total orders than the control, with each order having significantly more items at materially lower average unit retail prices. Condition #3, which finished in second place from a test effect standpoint, got there by stimulating significantly more orders than the control group, as well as having higher average items per order, offset by somewhat lower average unit retail prices per item. The disaggregated customer effects also show the relative winners and losers from both a new customer acquisition and a repeat purchase frequency standpoint.

No matter which way this particular company turned, they had relatively better alternatives than the status quo—probably allowing everyone to breathe a sigh of relief! The new brand proposition and creative is a clear winner for this company; the two test cells where it was active were clear relative winners. We can infer from this test that it helps drive appeal among customers with a propensity to purchase its higher-price-point items and materially higher purchase frequency. If this is the only change we roll out nationally, life will be good, at least for a couple of quarters. However, it is a relative loser from a new customer acquisition standpoint. If the company is worried about more aggressive replenishment of its house file with more active buyers, episodically coupling the new brand proposition and creative with the promotional offer will accelerate the growth of its customer roster. If the company has other ways to monetize these relationships, a strong business case could be built for occasionally pulling this lever.

Step 12: Synthesizing Findings and Assessing Implications

The last step in the MA testing process focuses on synthesizing the findings from your test and assessing the implications. From the previous example, you should be able to clearly see how having a deeper understanding of the underlying drivers of sales response can help you make smarter decisions about your marketing investments. To the extent you have the ability to look at sales effects at various levels of aggregation—market, channel, and individual customer—your MA test results will become that much more actionable and relevant.

For each major hypothesis that you are testing with any given MA test, you would expect to have one of three very clear outcomes: (1) "Roll it out (everywhere)!" (2) "Kill it!" or (3) "Scale it gradually." The first two outcomes are fairly self-explanatory. The clear winners should be leveraged on a global scale as soon as feasible. The clear losers should never be rolled out at all or, if they represent components of preexisting spending programs, should get stopped immediately. Typically you land on the "Scale it gradually" outcome only when either the test effect was positive but the idea may still be perceived as too risky to roll out across the full market, or the test results pointed to significant further optimization opportunities.

Of course, for some MA test hypotheses, we occasionally land in the fourth, less comfortable bucket of *inconclusive*. Well-designed MA field tests should not land here often, but it can occasionally happen. For example, for cost reasons we may not have had enough variation in the investment levels for a given program to determine the upper limits of its effectiveness. Or we may have return-on-investment numbers that are right at our hurdle rate, or test effects that are not statistically significant in either positive or negative territory. This may not be enough to warrant killing a preexisting program with a lot of organizational momentum and political support, but the data does not support scaling the program more broadly. Sometimes the existence of attractive alternative investment opportunities is enough to push these programs into the win or loss column. Occasionally you may have to refine your testing approach and go at the question again from a sharper angle.

Depending on the richness of your tracking approach and the robustness of your analytic support, you can augment the basic recommendations with additional insights into the underlying whys and hows that drove each MA test cell recommendation. Many people start by profiling the winning and losing test cells with key brand strength, customer behavior, or activity effectiveness measures pulled from the custom tracking studies. This is a fairly straightforward approach that usually yields meaningful insights, even if they are more directional and descriptive.

More comprehensive econometric modeling can also be done, like that described in the previous chapter, to tease out more subtle and quantitatively rigorous insights. We may want to understand complex interaction effects across some of the decision variables or to better understand the interplay between short-term and long-term outcome variables. In this case, the complexity of the analysis will increase dramatically, but you can end up with a richer storyline around the findings that has fewer detractors as you socialize it with senior executives throughout the organization, especially with your peers in more financially or operationally driven roles.

EMBRACING THE COMPLEXITY OF DYNAMIC OPTIMIZATION

Now that you understand how to execute different approaches to classic in-market field experiments, the compelling benefits of a test-and-learn approach to MA improvement may be patently evident. However, somewhere in the back of your mind you may already be hearing, fearing, or anticipating some of the questioning looks and pushback from people in your organization:

"We need answers faster, faster, faster . . . "

"We cannot put the business 'at risk' and withhold critical marketing investments from key areas while we wait for these tests to play out."

"I will have already moved on to my next assignment/posting/unit by the time the test finishes—I need to get points on the board sooner!"

"The company pays me to use my well-honed instincts and business judgment to guide our investment decisions. And I have a pretty good track record at making the right calls."

"I do not have the luxury to vary only one thing at a time and hold everything else constant. There is too much competitive/market/financial pressure."

If you are already anticipating these responses, do not beat yourself up too much—you clearly are not alone. We have been in conversations with countless executives over the years in which similar objections were raised. Although we firmly believe that the insights to be gained from a continuous test-and-learn approach to marketing accountability clearly outweigh the perceived limitations just described, you also need to be responsive to this kind of push-back and find pragmatic, flexible ways to address these concerns.

You're in luck—we may have some answers for you. We have seen companies pursue another approach to experimentation in addition to the classic approach. We have come to label this other approach the *dynamic* approach or *dynamic optimization*. These two approaches are not mutually exclusive by any means, and they share many of the same core principles and underlying processes. Some organizations may even use both concurrently. However, the dynamic approach has aspects that allow you to offset some of the traditional barriers to adoption of the classic approach. It gives you the ability to continue to drive your strategy and its ongoing execution while concurrently extracting powerful learning and insights. You can then use this learning in a faster way to optimize the execution of the strategy and continue to build the business while you get smarter about what works and what doesn't. You are not forced to put the business on hold while you do your experiments. Despite the additional analytical complexity that it entails, pursuing test-and-learn via dynamic opti-mization may be the most expedient way to get your organization started—as counterintuitive as that may seem!

The classic approach hits the five R's of effective MA testing—right focus, randomized, reproducible, risk-managed, and readable—right out of the ballpark. By exogenously varying the marketing stimuli in direct field testing, you directly observe and assess the sales impact in market between the test and the control groups around a narrow set of hypotheses. So you end up with unbiased, objective reads of performance with regard to those specific hypotheses, which is a more elegant and scientifically pure way to do experimentation. The experiments are cleanly designed and usually simpler to imple-ment. You do not need a Ph.D. in advanced mathematics to have a seat at the table! It is also fairly straightforward to read the financial results of each test, and over time the iterative testing approach can sharpen up all elements of your marketing performance.

The classic approach's detractors typically come at it from a few sides. The most direct criticism has to do with the fact that it is perceived to be time-consuming and expensive, is subject to competitive tampering, may withhold necessary marketing support from key markets for a certain period of time, and appears to turn a deaf ear to the operator's urgent need to *drive this quarter's numbers, now!* Another concern may be that each experiment is testing only a limited number of variables in a very specific market and competitive context. Will the test effect insights still apply in situations in which we are in a different stage of the brand maturity curve or under a different pricing regime or facing a dramatically different competitive response? The shorter the tests, the more narrowly defined the customer cohorts, and the more disciplined you are in tracking post-test performance—a la Capital One—the higher your confidence will be in applying the insights. However, for tests with a longer time frame, with less tightly defined test and control groups, across a more diverse competitive set, spread over a diverse set of geographic markets, using less addressable marketing vehicles—for these, concern about the relevance and applicability of the insights increases significantly.

For companies that share some or all of these concerns, advances in information technology, data management and analytics over the past fifteen to twenty years have made a slightly more complex approach to test-and-learn viable. This approach blends more sophisticated experimental design approaches with advanced econometric analysis, allowing you to pursue several hypotheses simultaneously or sequentially. Its more holistic systems-based approach accommodates the messier, real-world complexity of the typical go-to-market environment more easily, especially when compared to the more single-threaded mind-set discussed in the previous section. The advanced modeling allows for the test to be understood in a more complex system of customer response and competitive reactions. The test effect is understood in conjunction with the other key nonpromotional determinants of sales.

To confidently employ this approach, however, you need to get comfortable with one key fact—most of the insights that you glean from this approach will be inferred through advanced statistical analyses. Said another way, although some aspect of the test effect may be directly observed through the field work, using straightforward calculations, the more robust estimates of business impact will be mathematically modeled based on natural variations detected in the data. Although these observed relationships are typically sound, the academic literature is also clear that there are risks inherent in this type of modeling. These risks are similar to those described in the historical modeling section of Chapter Seven—about not capturing the right variables, about the statistical independence of some of the variables, and so on. A capable econometric modeler should be able to help you understand the extent to which these risks might impact your ability to draw readable and reliable conclusions from a dynamic experimentation approach in general, as well as to help evaluate the specific findings of any given experiment or study.

To the extent that you can get comfortable with this key fact, it opens up a world of richer analytical possibilities. In addition to understanding the test effect associated with your specific marketing stimuli at specific investment levels, you can estimate the elasticity of those marketing stimuli across a continuous range of investment levels. In addition to just focusing on the isolated impact of any specific variable, you can unearth the interdependencies and interactions across the various combinations of your key marketing stimuli. Do some marketing stimuli work better in specific combinations or in a specific market or competitive context? With all of this additional richness, of course, comes the additional task of getting people comfortable with the underlying modeling approaches and the math. If people do not understand the math, they will not sign off on the learning—it is as simple as that.

Figure 9.11 depicts the relative appeal of both approaches to MA testing, very consistent with the preceding discussion. It is not an either/or proposition for any given organization. There is usually a place for the classic approach to MA testing in every organization's toolkit. However, many marketers are faced with the dilemma of having an organization that does not have the patience for a classic approach across all of the critical unresolved MA questions. Dynamic experimentation gives those marketers a pragmatic fallback position, allowing them to advance an MA agenda in a manner more palatable to the organization. The irony here is that fallback positions often reflect simpler alternatives, whereas in this case it actually involves more complexity, across multiple dimensions.

Typically people look for opportunities to dovetail some in-market experimentation on top of the organization's preexisting go-to-market activities for the upcoming quarter or year. Rather than let MA testing get positioned as "We have to wait twelve months while we test," you show up with this position: "I can take what we were going to do next quarter and make it better, while guaranteeing that

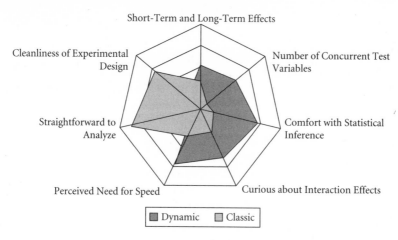

Figure 9.11. Comparing Strengths of the Classic and Dynamic Approaches to Experimentation

we get systematically smarter about our key marketing investments." The goal is to seamlessly weave the two agendas together, remembering that the overarching goal is to drive the business next quarter or next year. Of course, you are simultaneously exploring clever ways to layer in some natural experimentation around any open MA-related questions without being overly rigid about test design issues.

Rather than leaving the business feeling overly constrained by an MA testing agenda, this pragmatic approach allows you to position your efforts as a critical enabler of immediate business performance. Of course, you also know that it is also an important step toward continuous MA improvement. In reality, you may still need to force some uncomfortable trade-offs during the design discussions to get what the company needs from a learning standpoint. But you also have the ability to make more compromises during the design phase, with the option of trying to tease out related important insights through advanced modeling on the back end when you cannot accommodate something as cleanly through your up-front test design decisions.

Key Implementation Differences with Dynamic Experimentation

In terms of detailed execution, dynamic experimentation follows many of the same process steps as the classic approach. There is a design phase, an in-field phase, and an analysis phase, with many of the same subprocesses. For now, we will just focus on the critical differences between the two approaches, which occur primarily in the design and the analysis phases. We will use one specific real-world example as a reference throughout the section to illuminate the discussion.

DESIGN PHASE DIFFERENCES   A key difference between the two approaches relates to the relative prioritization of variables and markets. The dynamic approach can accommodate more complexity in both the types of variables that you test and the possible range in values. Figure 9.12 gives an example of the range of variables in one company's recent dynamic market-level field test. This company identified key variables inside the narrower sphere of "little m" marketing communications spending that is the focus of this book, as well as the broader set of "Big M" marketing activities—related to pricing, product, and channel decisions.

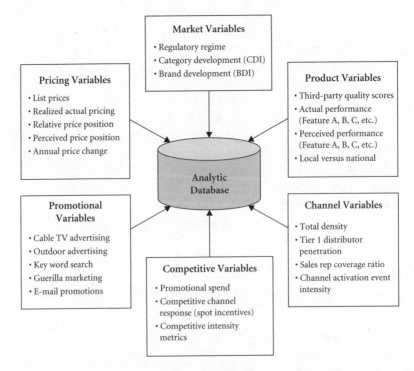

Figure 9.12.   Variable Identification for Dynamic
Optimization Approach

The CMO had a number of unanswered questions about the role that different promotional activity—including cable TV and outdoor advertising, search and e-mail marketing, and guerilla promotional activities—had on driving short-term sales outcomes. But the company needed to tease out these insights in the context of an integrated approach to addressing a broader CEO-level business problem—market share erosion in a critical customer segment in core geographies.

In this case, the CEO had some clear principles guiding his go-to-market approach. The company intended to center its counterpunch on the relaunch of a relatively new product—think of it as more of a line extension than a new-to-the-world breakthrough. This featured product, with revamped merchandising and improved pricing, would be relaunched across all markets. However, the company was also interested in understanding the impact of taking supplementary pricing actions in specific markets relative to this new product and other products, as well as exploring the impact of different combinations of promotional activities and investment levels and different channel activation strategies on overall business outcomes in light of these pricing actions.

Hmmm . . . a daunting challenge, you say? At first glance, it clearly violates one of the critical tenets of the classic approach: to isolate changes to very specific variables while keeping everything else constant. But rather than be stymied by this, the CMO reframed the intended actions into a set of four higher-order themes: (1) baseline changes, (2) incremental pricing actions, (3) incremental promotional activities, and (4) incremental channel activation efforts.

With this reframing, the CMO then convinced the CEO to divide the country into five market groups, as depicted in Figure 9.13. One group received only the baseline changes, two groups received the baseline changes plus one additional change, and the two highest-priority groups from a market share erosion perspective experienced the baseline changes plus two or three of the incremental actions. Although these groupings are clearly not a randomized sample of representative markets, and there is some geographic clustering within the market groups, it reflects a fair compromise that gets at the spirit of the principle. Moreover, the CMO understood that at the DMA level they would be able to do some detailed matched markets analysis (as shown in Table 9.2) across and within each of the five market groups to compensate for the fact that the market selection was not completely randomized and to better understand how that design decision might affect the test results.

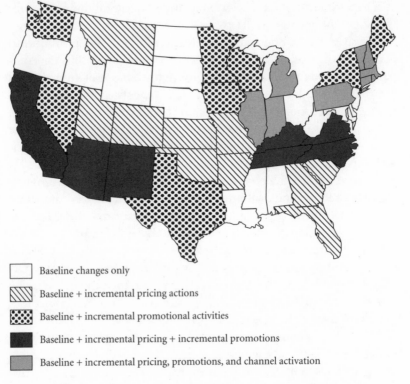

Baseline changes only

Baseline + incremental pricing actions

Baseline + incremental promotional activities

Baseline + incremental pricing + incremental promotions

Baseline + incremental pricing, promotions, and channel activation

Figure 9.13.   Sample Test Design for Dynamic Optimization

The CMO then took the two market groups that were going to get incremental promotional activity, divided them up at the DMA level, and used a fairly classic test design approach to tackle the highest-priority MA questions:

1. Was there still a material role for their two preferred traditional advertising vehicles—cable TV and business print?
2. How quickly should investment be moving into e-mail and search marketing?
3. Could more innovative guerilla marketing activities be used to supplant existing programs?

With over seventy DMAs to work with across the two market groups, the CMO could test various combinations of these vehicles at various investment levels and still have some redundancy in terms of market coverage.

For the most critical questions, the guiding principle was still to maintain discrete relationships between unique test cells and specific variable values. For second-order questions, the CMO allowed for a little more bleed or overlap between the variables and the test cells, with the belief that anything that could not be read directly as a clean pre-post test effect between test and control markets could be statistically inferred through more advanced modeling. In a different situation, the CMO might even have explored the use of fractional factorial analysis, which has been stress-tested in other disciplines, to find the bare minimum required subset of combinations that would need to be tested to answer questions about the effectiveness of any of the variables, in any combination, during the back-end analysis.

As you can see from this overall example, even though you have more complexity with dynamic optimization, the overriding desire is still to drive toward simplifying constructs and themes. Distill the issues down to a few core concepts and weave them into a narrative that everyone throughout the organization can understand. In this example, for instance, that simplifying narrative went something like this: "Do incremental investments in pricing or promotional activities, either by themselves or in some combination, drive enough incremental volume to have a positive ROI?"

As you move through each of the key design steps—selecting variables, representative markets, test duration, and so on—your decision making should reflect intelligent compromises between adhering to the clean design principles described in the classic approach and putting actions in the market that support the overriding business priority. As long as we do not do the same things the same way in all of our markets, we will have enough variation in the activities to tease out meaningful insights about the relative value and impact of each action, in isolation and in combination.

It should also be abundantly clear that for this approach to be effective, you need great data tracking and data management skills. To get accurate monthly reads on all of the variables in Figure 9.12, for twelve months in the pre-test period and an additional twelve months of test phase period, at the DMA level across over two hundred DMAs, is no easy task. During the design phase, key data sources must be identified, processes must be mapped to collect and harmonize the data in a way that will be conducive to modeling, and so on. If additional variables have been identified that do not have preexisting data sources, custom tracking may be necessary to capture the required data.

It would be unwise to underestimate the amount of time and effort that is required to get this part of the equation right. This is the one clear Achilles heel of dynamic experimentation and the place where many first-time MA tests end up falling short, especially when the analysis phase kicks in. It can also become the one place where the relative perceived speed and flexibility advantages of dynamic experimentation start to bog down and turn into distinct disadvantages. Here the devil is in the data.

ANALYSIS PHASE DIFFERENCES Based on everything that we have said so far, it should be self-evident that the analysis phase in dynamic experimentation can be significantly more complicated and time-consuming than in the classic approach. In addition to the straightforward analyses associated with determining test effects across the various test cells in the experiment and synthesizing those findings, whole other sets of analyses need to be prepped, run, QA'd, and interpreted. You need to have access to advanced quantitative modeling skills, either in-house or through outside relationships. You should work with these players to build a detailed analytical plan that accommodates the iterative nature of most modeling endeavors and allows for the necessary time to peel back the various layers of the onion to get to the critical insights.

Although some of this can be addressed during the design phase, most of the meaningful quality assurance work starts once the team gets its hands on the data. You may face a whole range of data issues requiring attention—from decisions on how to handle missing data values to harmonizing mismatched data frequencies to dealing with abnormal data values. You will also have a host of model development issues to address based on your final set of intact variables—from understanding the need for synthetic variables to figuring out how any specific model gets specified to who knows what else. It is beyond the scope of this book to go into all of these technical details, but for those practitioners with the appetite, marketing science textbooks like *Market Response Models* can serve as an excellent reference source. But this is where it will be critical to have some strong players who can bridge the two worlds of marketing practice and marketing science to run this interface.

As you gain some experience with these analytics, you will come to appreciate how flexible and customizable these approaches truly are. You can often cut the data and run the analyses in an infinite number of ways, looking for unexpected insights in every nook and cranny. Depending on the situation, this can be both a blessing and a curse. When you are wrestling with murky unanswered MA issues, having that infinite analytical flexibility can give you the confidence that you are truly wrestling an issue to the ground in a comprehensive and systematic manner, in a way that a simple go/no go decision, based on the test effect read from a single test cell, may not. Ultimately, though, we are using this approach to try to prove or disprove very specific hypotheses about the effectiveness of our marketing actions, and that fact can sometimes get buried somewhere near the bottom of the pile. Striking the right balance is critical. Unfortunately, many first-timers often kill confidence in and enthusiasm for the approach by getting both enamored of and then bogged down in the technical complexity.

At the end of the day, the analytic outputs that one would expect to see might get summarized in a graph like the one shown in Figure 9.14. This is synthesized (but masked) output from our

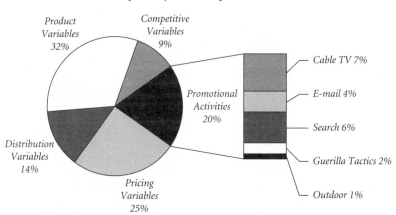

Percentage weightings indicate overall relative importance of variables in explaining incremental sales response

Figure 9.14.   Sample Model Results from Dynamic Optimization Example

earlier example. The company built various models to understand how the impact of changes in marketing actions across product, pricing, channel, and promotional dimensions impacted in-period sales performance. At the highest level, the findings were that specific elements across the product, promotional, and pricing levers accounted for almost 80 percent of the overall variance in sales outcomes, with the product variables being slightly more important (32 percent) than the pricing (25 percent) and promotional (24 percent) variables. This was a somewhat surprising finding for this executive team, whose members were predisposed to believing that pricing was the dominant driver of customer decision making. Of course we tested a wide range of detailed product and pricing variables, and although we are showing this as an aggregate pricing or product effect, there were only one or two very specific variables in each category that were statistically relevant.

Of the 20 percent of the sales impact that was attributed to promotional variables, you can see that the cable TV, search, and e-mail activities accounted for more than 80 percent of that impact. Figure 9.15 builds on these insights about program effectiveness,

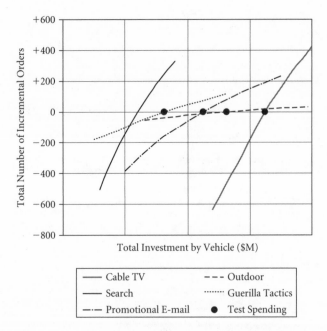

Figure 9.15.   Sample Projected Order Elasticities by Type
of Marketing Vehicle

basically presenting elasticity curve estimates for the five main promotional vehicle types tested during this exercise. Steeper curves mean higher elasticities, which means these variables are more powerful drivers of sales. Said a different way, putting more investment behind a variable with a steep curve will drive more pronounced changes in sales outcomes than for variables with flatter curves. In this particular example, cable TV and search appear to have the most room for profitable expansion, while outdoor, with the flattest slope, would clearly not merit additional investment relative to the other vehicles.

This only begins to scratch the surface around the kind of insights that you can glean. You may want to understand the residual lag effects of certain kinds of promotional investments. Or you may want to understand the key differences between winning and losing markets. Or you may want to understand how favorable changes in two, three, or four of the marketing levers happening concurrently might have an accelerated, not just an additive, effect on your sales outcomes. As you get more comfortable with the approach and the tools, many of these more subtle but important distinctions can be explored in a timely and cost-effective manner.

In conclusion, dynamic optimization opens up an alternative path to drive an MA testing agenda that is well suited to specific business situations. It may allow you to get at many of the comparable MA-related insights of the classic approach without creating the perception that the business has to take a time-out while we go run our tests. But the additional complexity that it entails may not be appropriate for every organization, especially for those that are not so far along in their MA journey.

COMMITTING TO AN ONGOING MA TESTING AGENDA

Whether you moved down the classic or the dynamic path to MA testing, implementing your first few marketing accountability tests will likely be a painful but, we hope, rewarding experience—akin to the experience of implementing an enterprise resource planning (ERP) system, or perhaps of giving birth. Despite the challenges, you should resist the urge to delay getting back into the market with the next wave of MA tests. The goal now is to build on the initial momentum you have created and begin to transition from ad-hoc tests to an ongoing MA testing agenda. The first one or two MA tests conducted in your company should give you a sense of the speed at which your organization can place new tests in field, as well as your organizational capacity to absorb the tests and their learning. This initial read on organizational capability, along with the approach to prioritizing testing goals that we discussed earlier, will allow you to build an MA testing agenda for the next twelve months.

Initially, the amount of money that a company must dedicate to MA testing will be inversely proportional to their understanding of their activity's returns and their business performance relative to their peers. In the first couple of years of an MA testing program, the amount of investment dollars deployed against the testing agenda might represent as much as 25 or 30 percent or more of a company's total marketing spending. This number appears high, but it must be remembered that (1) not all of the money is nonworking, in that more than 50 to 70 percent of test market spending will reach your customers; (2) testing will quickly become self-funding, as savings and performance gains are identified; and (3) initially any money that is not being spent on testing could be languishing in a program that is either not working or not working up to its full potential. Even the most accountable, high-performing companies should always expect to invest at least 5 to 15 percent or more on ongoing testing. Customers, competitors, technologies, and brands do not remain static, so all knowledge is perishable and must be continually renewed.

So you may wonder, when can I stop testing? We assert that organizations committed to a long-term MA program will never stop testing. This must be seen as a continual and evolving process, whose objectives are to learn, modify, and improve in systematic ways that improve business outcomes, enable breakthrough performance, and mitigate risk. Although you can anticipate what your testing priorities might be beyond the next twelve months, it will be difficult to plan for specific tests with great precision. By its very nature, the testing agenda should be flexible and dynamic, because the outcome of tests that are in field today may morph your planned testing priorities for twelve months from now. The nature of your testing portfolio, however, should evolve in a fairly predictable way. At any given time you will have a portfolio of the three basic types of MA tests—validation, optimization, and qualification—that are driving your overall priorities.

Figure 9.16 shows how this portfolio of MA tests is expected to evolve over time. The number and proportion of tests in each category will differ from company to company, but this basic pattern of evolution should hold true for all.

In the first twelve months after you have completed your MA opportunity scan, your company should focus its testing efforts primarily on validating the returns (if any) of any big-ticket programs still in question. Capacity allowing, the biggest opportunities to optimize existing programs should be examined. By year two of your testing agenda, legacy programs are validated or eliminated and the focus shifts to the next wave of programs that can be optimized. Some of your expanded testing capacity in year two will be directed to qualifying high-potential new marketing activities that are not yet in your spending mix. By either year four or five of your testing program, you will have hit the steady state of what your ongoing testing agenda will look like.

As you transition from ad-hoc MA tests to an ongoing testing agenda, your approach will become more standardized and efficient. Ideally, testing will become just another one of your company's routine marketing processes. We have other additional thoughts on a more advanced testing agenda, which should allow you to increase your capacity while reducing costs, which we will share with you in the next chapter as part of your longer-term MA objectives.

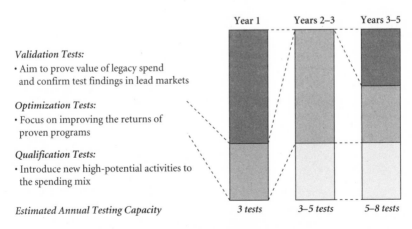

Figure 9.16.   Evolution of the MA Testing Agenda: Illustrative Proportion of Tests by Type

We believe testing is the cornerstone on which a truly accountable marketing organization is built. A testing approach does not intend to change marketers into bean counters or to stifle the art of marketing. Testing is just a means to an end. But when used properly, testing is a tool that can empower creativity, enable breakthrough results, and forge a more productive and enduring alchemy between the art and science of marketing.

CHAPTER TEN

Horizon Three: Sustaining and Accelerating Marketing Accountability Impact

Building Sustainable Competitive Advantage via Deeper Capabilities, Faster Processes, and More Intelligent Brand Equity Development

Topics covered in Chapter Ten:

- "Go on—be a tiger": committing to long-term change
- Selecting where to build deeper capabilities
- Committing to faster, more effective processes
- Driving strategic long-term equity and short-term performance
- Envisioning the end game: the final stages to establishing MA prowess

I skate to where the puck is going to be, not where it has been.
—*Wayne Gretzky*

The first horizon of marketing accountability that we discussed addressed how to begin your journey by diagnosing your company's MA opportunities and gaining top management alignment with immediate improvements and long-term priorities and plans. Horizon Two focused on how to capture these opportunities, through a test-and-learn orientation and capability. Having passed through these two horizons, you already have a strong foundation for accountable marketing. What you build on top of that—the capabilities and infrastructure needed to accelerate and sustain marketing accountability impact—is the focus of Horizon Three.

It may take your company as little as one year and as many as three or four years to reach the third horizon of marketing accountability. Here are some of the signs that your company is entering Horizon Three:

- There are no marketing activities with unclear or inadequate returns remaining in your budget.

- The focus of your testing agenda shifts to continuous performance improvement and qualification of new high-potential marketing activities.

- Marketing accountability begins to feel more like a way of doing business, having seeped into your organization's DNA and lifeblood.

When you have achieved these milestones, you are ready to think about how to accelerate impact and turn this into a source of strategic competitive advantage.

"GO ON—BE A TIGER": COMMITTING TO LONG-TERM CHANGE

The initial improvement prize from pursuing marketing accountability is just the appetizer. The meatier prize—driving continuous financial impact from a self-renewing competitive weapon—will come only from committing to long-term change. The ROI truths that may get unearthed via a diagnostic or confirmed during a market test stay true for only so long before some structural change in the market or some aggressive competitive action changes the underlying customer dynamics and corresponding marketing lever economics. A company must have the capacity to quickly refresh its understanding about what works and then apply this knowledge rapidly through new offers and programs in an ever-evolving market and competitive context. Only a focus on continuous improvement, grounded in the solid empirical understanding of what is known, while pushing hard to uncover new truths about customer behavior and marketing impact, has the staying power to deliver the marketing accountability goods on a consistent basis. Companies that have done this—like Capital One, Procter & Gamble, Tesco, Anheuser-Busch, Google, Progressive, McDonald's, Harrah's Entertainment, and American Express—have delivered faster growth rates and disproportionate financial returns over time, especially when combined with other core capabilities in proposition development, pricing, distribution, supply chain management, and so on.

As we have seen throughout the book, in the discussion of the six MA value levers and the three horizons of MA improvement, four kinds of contributions are needed to guarantee powerful marketing performance—great strategy, great creativity, great execution, and great analytics. When these contributions are reinforced with a great measurement system and a culture of openness, cross-competency understanding, and mutual respect, they lead to consistently great decision making. As depicted in Figure 10.1, these contributions feed off each other to form a virtuous cycle of performance improvement and continuous learning. Sometimes the gains are episodic, with sudden step-function improvements followed by longer periods in which you stay on the same plateau, but you get the picture. Again, it is important to underscore that the competency domains are not an end unto themselves, but rather a means to a deeper understanding; smarter, more powerful decision making; and increasingly effective activation.

Now, we understand that this framing might lead you to believe that each kind of contribution comes from a different functional area in your company. Although in many organizations that may be true, sometimes all contributions can come from a single entrepreneur who instinctively excels in and respects each discipline, as with Apple's Steve Jobs or Nike's Phil Knight. No matter how your company sources these contributions, a complete breakdown in any single area can severely undermine your marketing performance, although minor deficiencies in one or two of the areas may be overcome by distinctive strengths in others for some period of time. Capital One, the

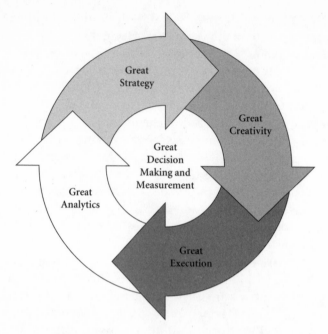

Figure 10.1.   When the Core Drivers of Marketing Performance Form a
Virtuous Cycle of Continuous Improvement

U.S. credit card company, began its journey with an aggressive commitment to analytics and strategy, following quickly with execution,
but creativity lagged. Anheuser-Busch, on the other hand, always led
with creativity and strategy competencies, but committed to analytics
more recently. However, at different points in time both companies
acknowledged that they would not meet their full potential unless
they built incremental competencies in an area in which they had a
material deficit.

So when we borrow so blatantly from Accenture's well-known "Go
on. Be a Tiger" advertising campaign, what we mean is precisely this:
does your leadership have the courage to create the right conditions
for long-term MA impact and change? Unless you are blessed with a
Steve Jobs or a Phil Knight (or a leadership team with the tenacity and
commitment of Tiger Woods himself), it is clearly not easy to deliver
excellence across all of these disciplines or to effectively integrate
and harmonize the diverse perspectives that spring from each. Many

people who excel in analytics or marketing strategy are hard-wired very differently from people who excel in execution or creativity. Not only do leaders need to commit to developing some fluency in each of these disparate areas, but they also need to commit to developing processes and culture in which the value from each kind of contribution is respected and people know how to apply and integrate the insights from across these disciplines into the specific area that they are driving. The blending of art and science is not easy—we acknowledge that—but is critical to achieve if there is desire to aggressively move forward on your MA journey.

Creating the right conditions for long-term MA impact thus requires commitment, focus, and specificity, none of which are easy to come by. By commitment, we mean a number of things: commitment to the idea of investing in strategy, creativity, execution, and analytics; commitment to the idea of fact-based decision making; commitment to measure financial impact no matter how challenging the mechanics; and commitment to act on the insights, results, and findings. By focus, we mean having the discipline to make real choices about where to be great versus where to be just good enough, and then investing judiciously to achieve your targets. By specificity, we mean having the vision to build robust long-term plans, and also peppering them with tangible intermediate goals and specific, measurable milestones.

If you are able to bring commitment, focus, and specificity to this endeavor, answering the "what" part of this question—what you need to do—is a lot more straightforward. Ultimately you will be in a position to sustain and accelerate long-term MA impact by developing deeper capabilities, faster processes, and a mechanism to holistically integrate long-term equity and short-term performance considerations. Figure 10.2 frames each of these as a pillar of sustainability, built on top of the solid marketing accountability foundation that should have been established during the first two MA horizons. Over the course of the rest of this chapter, we will discuss each of these pillars in more depth, weaving in some real-life stories and experiences from some of the leading-edge companies, like Capital One, P&G, Harrah's Entertainment, and American Express. We will then close the chapter and the book with a section that helps you envision the final few stages on your path to distinctive MA prowess (and world domination!).

So go on—be a tiger. Think boldly and dream big, but then follow through with discipline and focus. As you envision the unique mix of

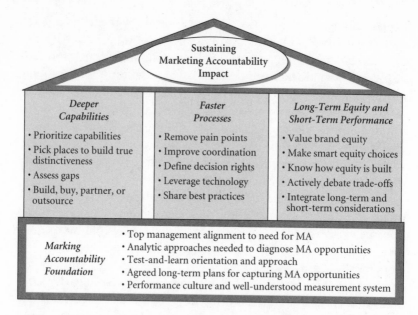

Deeper Capabilities	Faster Processes	Long-Term Equity and Short-Term Performance
• Prioritize capabilities • Pick places to build true distinctiveness • Assess gaps • Build, buy, partner, or outsource	• Remove pain points • Improve coordination • Define decision rights • Leverage technology • Share best practices	• Value brand equity • Make smart equity choices • Know how equity is built • Actively debate trade-offs • Integrate long-term and short-term considerations

Marking Accountability Foundation
• Top management alignment to need for MA
• Analytic approaches needed to diagnose MA opportunities
• Test-and-learn orientation and approach
• Agreed long-term plans for capturing MA opportunities
• Performance culture and well-understood measurement system

Figure 10.2.   The Three Pillars of Ongoing Marketing Accountability Impact

strategic, creative, execution-oriented, and analytical capabilities, processes, and technologies for your situation, visualize and then bring to life a package that is uniquely suited to your company's competitive strategy and that competitors would find hard to duplicate. The next few pages provide some fresh thinking to help you decide where to place those bets and how to do it in a way that allows for flexibility, adaptability, and continual renewal.

SELECTING WHERE TO BUILD DEEPER CAPABILITIES

Looking down from the hundred-thousand-foot perspective, the capability part of the value equation is fairly straightforward—develop deeper competence in the people you have, while at the same time vastly expanding your reservoir of skilled marketing talent. Using sports as a metaphor, the major league team owners want a team with bench strength that is as talented as it is broad. Of course this is easier said than done. It is made even more challenging by the conflicting pressures put on the capability agenda by the ever-evolving marketing landscape: at the same time that every company needs much more skilled and competent marketing generalists—with reasonable fluency across the strategic, creative, execution, and analytic disciplines—the pressure is growing to develop a range of highly targeted specialist capabilities that must be seamlessly stitched into the overall fabric of the marketing organization. Jim Stengel, the former CMO at Procter & Gamble, addresses this need for better generalists and outstanding specialists: "Expect people to have more diversified experience and more extreme experiences . . . The demand for more mastery and specialized skills is much higher than it was twenty-four years ago . . . There will always be a role for generalists; we need to train more generalists. But we will also need more specialists . . . who are absolutely outstanding [in their respective areas]."[1]

Determining the right mix of specialist versus generalist skills and devising how to upgrade the general competency levels of both pools of talent become the critical issues to address on the capabilities side. Some skills may be too strategically important to outsource but too specialized to develop in a broad group of marketers. For example, it may be necessary to have enough internal cross-media planning skill to effectively manage your roster of agencies, but it may be impractical to embed this skill in each of the several brand or product teams that would draw on this skill. A flexible organizational structure that creates a home for these specialist skills, with clearly defined access and integration points for the generalist marketers, may be a better way to go. In this way you gain a great deal of leverage from a small cadre of specialized experts, without overburdening your generalists with unreasonable expectations.

Even when a company embraces this specialist/generalist division, that still leaves the open question of where to build distinctive skills. We have not come across a company that was universally best in class in all of the various skills associated with delivering high-performing marketing investments. Moreover, we are not sure it's possible, or even desirable, to invest the time and energy in being great at everything. Strong-performing, highly accountable companies can succeed by being great at a handful of mission-critical MA activities and just good enough at the rest.

The trick is to identify which MA skills have the greatest role in creating value with your particular business model, brand, and customer mix, then focus on building these. For example, it is commonly accepted that Capital One is great at direct marketing and Pepsi has exceptional creative development. Given Capital One's lack of a physical branch network (unlike its major multiline retail banking competitors like Chase, Bank of America, or Citibank) and Pepsi's distribution disadvantage (compared with the ubiquitous presence of Coca-Cola), these choices made instinctive sense for each of those companies. You have to establish the right hierarchy of priorities for your company, differentiating between the places where having ticket-to-the-game skill levels is good enough and the places where you aspire to be truly distinctive. In the next section, we will offer up some attractive candidates for distinctive capability building; in the section that follows that, we will address different strategies for acquiring those skills.

Attractive Targets for Distinctive Capability Building

Given all of the competing forces at work in the marketing landscape, we firmly believe that there are some attractive places to consider building distinctive capabilities in each of the four competency domains. Although some best-in-class companies have started to move forward along specific dimensions, there is still plenty of room for other forward-looking companies to establish their own distinguishing MA capability competencies. As seen in Figure 10.3, in the strategic quadrant, we think that there are some interesting opportunities in customer insight generation, experimental design, and strategic integrators. In the realm of creativity, we think capabilities associated with the Big Idea, open source creativity, and deep vehicle-specific spikes all show promise. From an execution standpoint, capabilities tied to vendor collaboration, cross-media planning and buying, and rapid piloting and execution have attractive characteristics. Finally, on the analytic side, the areas of data mining, econometric modeling, and customer value modeling have proven particularly fruitful for certain companies. Let's explore each of these ideas in a little more depth.

In terms of strategy-centered capabilities, customer insight generation is an excellent starting point. Procter & Gamble has anchored its whole reinvention of marketing on the idea of "going back to what we do best, and that is putting the consumer at the heart of what we do, having a higher kind of purpose to help improve her life." The

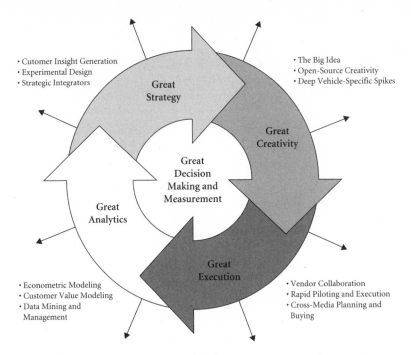

• Cutomer Insight Generation
• Experimental Design
• Strategic Integrators

Great Strategy

• The Big Idea
• Open-Source Creativity
• Deep Vehicle-Specific Spikes

Great Creativity

Great Decision Making and Measurement

Great Analytics

Great Execution

• Econometric Modeling
• Customer Value Modeling
• Data Mining and Management

• Vendor Collaboration
• Rapid Piloting and Execution
• Cross-Media Planning and Buying

Figure 10.3.   Some Potential Attractive Candidates for Distinctive Capability Building

company doubled its investments in consumer insights—obtained through deep immersion, anthropological research, which helps the company develop a deeper understanding of the customer—in a much more complete and holistic way. P&G reinforces this commitment by ensuring that everyone in senior leadership walks the walk by actively engaging in discussions and experiences that are very consumer-centered, ranging from doing field visits to poor consumers in Latin America or China to orchestrating workshops with media-savvy mothers to understand the impact of the Internet on their media habits. The investment is not directed toward research that checks or validates existing beliefs, but rather is focused on unearthing new knowledge about consumer drivers and consumer behavior. For P&G, renewed emphasis on these capabilities has been a clear winner, with paybacks that stretch significantly farther than marketing communications into product innovation, channel management, pricing strategy, and the like.

Consistent with our emphasis on the test-and-learn approach as a core foundational element of long-term marketing accountability, building a strategic and pervasive capability in experimental design is another prime area in which a company can distinguish itself. At its core, this skill is about maintaining a ruthless focus on the big unanswered questions that drive customer behavior and market opportunity, then artfully designing experiments that balance the value of the incremental information to be gained from the test against the hard and soft costs of conducting the test. Capital One is probably the exemplar of the successful development and utilization of this kind of a capability for competitive advantage. Capital One uses controlled experiments to understand what factors correlate with individual risk, to build predictive models for customer response and post-purchase behavior, and then to continually refine its understanding through cohort tracking and ongoing experimentation. Basic statistical design helps ensure that the tests are only large enough to ensure a statistically significant outcome, and more advanced techniques can be used to embed multiple tests into a single test design to lower costs while still allowing reads for all of the primary test effects and cross-variable interaction. All decision makers are trained in this method, and given that their hiring process is geared toward getting the best analytic minds around, people have embraced the approach. Because ideas for experiments can come from anywhere, Capital One also helped democratize the culture, unleashing the inner entrepreneur in everyone. This passionate commitment to experimental design enabled Capital One to keep their products and marketing relevant, such that at any given point in time, anywhere from 60 to 75 percent of their marketing budget might be focused on products and offers that did not exist twelve months earlier.

The final idea at the strategic level involves the concept of strategic integrators. In his recently published book, *Spanning Silos: The New CMO Imperative*, Prophet vice chairman David Aaker talks about the multifaceted yet destructive role that organizational silos can play in impeding progress around a marketing-led, customer-centered agenda. Nobody knows how to effectively weave together the disparate but potentially valuable contributions of the various groups into something coherent and captivating, so an organization might have the parts working hard yet fail to make any material progress. In a similar way, we see a real need for the contributions of strategic marketers who are equally strong in left-brain and right-brain approaches and have the ability to integrate the insights and contributions from the analytic, creative, and strategic realms. These people tend to be highly effective at building bridges to connect what may seem like disparate insights and weave them into a coherent, strategic narrative that is vigorously supported by the data and retains its emotional—and perhaps even inspirational—appeal. Achieving this kind of strategic outcome can be extraordinarily powerful, with logically consistent, financially sound activation road maps naturally flowing as a result. Given that the strategy value lever is the one with which the most costly MA mistakes tend to happen, even pushing to develop a handful of strategic integrators scattered throughout the company can yield disproportionate rewards.

In the creativity quadrant, all three elements for potential distinctiveness feature skills that help make marketing communications more interesting, more engaging, more emotionally persuasive, more compelling, and more fun. The Big Idea speaks to that ability to take solid strategic input and create a simple, unifying, and captivating communications idea on which to build a platform. Big Idea capabilities helped unearth the "Priceless" idea for a trailing MasterCard brand, the "Ecomagination" platform for a GE needing to infuse environmental protection and innovation back into its core identity, and the "easy" button for one-time leader Staples, which had started to lose its luster. Companies like Apple and Nike lean heavily on these kinds of skills to deliver consistently breakthrough, resonant communications. Clearly more art than science, often more resident in outside agency partners than in internal resources, Big Idea thinking tends to marry a deep empathy and understanding of both the target audience and the target media with creativity, intuition, and emotional intelligence to unearth simple, powerful communication ideas. Big Idea capabilities help your company be more right than wrong when it comes to the messaging value lever, which is a critical driver of effective marketing investment.

Open-source creativity approaches this problem from a different angle. The idea is to build a capability that efficiently and effectively harnesses the creative talents of individuals or groups outside of the organization, but in a way that is more democratic than a typical agency relationship, perhaps even promiscuous. In its simplest form, this can involve the development of an external creative network— either formally, as with furniture designer Herman Miller's collaboration with Charles Eames, Isamu Noguchi, and Bill Stumpf, or informally, as in American Express's CMO John Hayes's informal consultations with a select team of influencers like Robert De Niro, Jerry Seinfeld, and Annie Leibowitz. Herman Miller's CEO highlights the balancing act that is required to get the most out of such a model: "We give our creative network an outline of a perceived problem and let them share their insights as to whether we're on the right path and then enable them to bring their own gifts to the search for a solution. We follow them in their journey without judging too quickly."[2]

As the Internet continues to lower collaboration costs, open-source creativity may drive you away from a small group of paid experts to a wider group of passionate users who bring their own creativity to bear on behalf of your brand. Many companies are experimenting with user-generated media and content, some going so far as to ask users to create actual TV advertisements for them. In the United States, Heinz's Top This TV Challenge and Frito-Lay's Doritos brand Super Bowl spots are recent high-profile success stories in user-generated creativity. Some internet sites are taking the ideas in James Surowiecki's best-selling *The Wisdom of Crowds* to the extreme, proactively attempting to harness the insights and creative talents from random strangers on behalf of companies. Regardless of which flavor of open-source creativity you pursue, the hope is that it generates a steady flow of disruptive yet inspiring ideas that keeps your company's creative perspective fresh and disarming. When paired up with a well-thought-out process for harnessing, managing, sifting through, and recognizing the gems as they emerge, perhaps led by the strategic integrators described earlier in this section, a company can truly maximize the effectiveness of this approach.

Although this final idea probably sits at the intersection of creativity and execution, we decided to anchor vehicle-specific spikes with creativity because it starts with great vehicle-appropriate creativity. The general thinking here is to pick one or two marketing vehicles that are critically important to your business model and build distinctive capability in that vehicle. We have already spoken about Nike being best-in-class in creating endorsement and sponsorship marketing opportunities or Capital One being world-class in print direct marketing. In a similar vein, P&G has invested in building world-class capabilities around in-store and point-of-purchase marketing programs. There is clearly something to be said for having a distinctive capability in a vehicle that is so central to a company's overall business model and value creation system. The risk in only going down this route, however, is that in a world of ever-evolving cross-vehicle media consumption, your chosen vehicle gets gradually or dramatically disintermediated and you are left with little else in your toolkit.

As we move squarely into the execution quadrant, one initial place to explore building distinctive capability is the area of vendor collaboration. The reality of the emerging marketing landscape, with its increased need for specialized skills, is mirrored in a company's vendor base. We touched on the financial and quality benefits of some level of vendor consolidation in the discussion of the fixed cost management value lever in Chapter Six; that does not change the fact that most world-class companies will be working with a wide variety of marketing services suppliers for the foreseeable future. In fact, the pressure is growing to work with a diverse portfolio of suppliers, all of which have their own idiosyncrasies and unique management challenges—great interactive agencies, great PR agencies, great direct marketing agencies, great design agencies, great media agencies, and yes, we should not forget to mention great advertising agencies. Developing distinctive competencies on how to collaborate with these suppliers—in terms of briefing, selecting the best supplier for a given problem, getting their best talent excited about working on your specific projects, effectively managing to high quality interim and final deliverables, and aligning performance incentives—can become a source of powerful advantage. The most effective models involve managing and motivating these suppliers like you would any high-performing internal team—showering them with love and encouragement yet keeping on the heat, putting the best available talent together while ensuring they have shared goals and solid communication norms, and giving them access to the tools and resources that they need to succeed.

We will spend a lot of time on the rapid piloting and execution idea in the next section on faster processes, so we will not belabor the point here. Suffice to say that a rapid piloting and execution capability requires mind-sets, skills, processes, and technology geared toward speed and flexibility.

Cross-media communications planning and buying is another interesting place to focus on building distinctive execution capability. Building a reservoir of talent that can integrate a deep understanding of the target audience with a deep understanding of their media habits across media vehicles in a rapidly evolving media landscape is not an easy task. But it is exactly in this intersection of target audiences and media that we find the real opportunities for reach and frequency amplification, at a total cost of delivery that can be significantly lower than a comparable effort in a TV-dominant world. Moreover, if you do not bring a cross-media perspective to certain communication opportunities, in a worst-case scenario you may totally miss certain audiences. And the questions are only getting more challenging. For example, various on-line, direct marketing, and emerging mobile vehicles provide the perfect media to effectively cast a relevant message to a micro-segmented audience, but they cannot always efficiently deliver those segments at sufficient scale. "Conversational" marketing—inviting your audience into a conversation, listening to them, and giving them a voice—is all the rage, but what vehicles are best suited for dialogue or for monologue, and what relative weighting should those conversational vehicles have in the overall media plan? There are still plenty of opportunities to use traditional and emerging mass media vehicles like Captivate's elevator advertising network, but how do you address the risk of having your messages TiVo'd over, tuned out, or turned off? A distinctive cross-media planning capability should be able to incorporate all of this context to help you find ways to drive relevant share of voice at much more effective cost levels than the competition's.

We have spent a fair amount of time addressing the analytics sphere in this last part of the book. So it should come as no surprise that we offer up econometric modeling as one idea for a place to build distinctive capability. Kraft was an early leader here, with ex-Kraft people actually starting a number of the pioneering independent marketing modeling firms in this space. One of the next frontiers for this capability is the integration of econometric modeling techniques with perceptual brand equity data and choice driver analysis, developing integrated mechanisms to trade off short-term and longer-term financial implications of current-period marketing investment choices. Again, you may not need a lot of this capability spread around the company, but having some of it in-house, such that the techniques can be developed and applied in a unique and proprietary way, can become a powerful source of advantage.

A more pervasive capability alternative in which to build excellence is data mining and management. We have seen what a critical role data gathering and data analysis plays in all parts of the marketing value equation. Whether we are talking about product data, customer experience data, customer purchase data, marketing response data, competitive sales data, or what have you, it takes a fair amount of skill to turn all of that data into useful information that becomes the basis for business-driving insights. Many direct-response retailers—like 1-800-FLOWERS, Williams-Sonoma, Amazon.com, and Staples—have invested heavily in this capability to optimize the effectiveness of their marketing investments via better targeting, messaging, and offer development, helping them to spend smarter rather than more to drive solid growth. Whether they are working with a database of ten million or thirty million households, their data miners sift through the data to discover trends, help explain outcomes, and build models to more accurately predict future results. Your company may never reach the pinnacle of one best-in-class company, whose people are able to quickly identify meaningful patterns from reams of data, just by eyeballing the data, but developing a deep capability in the artful slicing and dicing of data to drive meaningful insights can lead to huge long-term rewards.

The final area for consideration in the analytic sphere is an off-shoot of data mining and analysis, something that we have labeled *customer value modeling*. The idea is to leverage deep, diverse data sets about customer preferences and customer behavior to build highly actionable understanding of the drivers of customer value for every prospective customer. This understanding must help you identify the potential worth of any given type of customer as well as predict the hypothetical worth of targeted but not-yet-acquired prospects. It must also help you understand what kinds of offers are required to keep existing customers at those value levels, as well as what triggers can help grow a customer's total worth potential. Harrah's Entertainment has a category-trouncing customer value modeling capability, which it has used to drive dramatic increases in customer share of wallet and commensurately high returns on invested capital. Harrah's started building this capability in 1998 and over time has developed a highly accurate estimate of each customer's potential worth through its Total Rewards loyalty program. Moreover, it uses differences between a customer's theoretical or predicted value and his or her actual observed value to identify high-impact marketing opportunities and aggressively push high-yielding offers in that direction. Building a distinctive capability here sharpens your ability to have smart hypotheses for experimental design and unearth fast-breaking, profitable growth opportunities.

So now that you understand all of the discreet ideas depicted in Figure 10.3, how should you decide where to anchor your distinctive capability bets? As we discussed earlier, many of these choices should be driven by your company's operating model, competitive environment, and underlying category dynamics. For example, companies in low-involvement consumable categories may want to start by investing in the creative and execution quadrants, because much of their marketing may be driven by mass advertising and channel-specific vehicles. Alternatively, companies in direct response retail or service businesses may want to prioritize capabilities in the strategic or analytic quadrants, because a primary way to build sustainable competitive advantage for those businesses lies in individual-customer-level analytics and the strategic choices made to optimize around it. It is hard to generalize what the right answer for your company might be without getting into the specifics, but this should help you understand how to frame the relative attractiveness of the various choices.

It is also important to note that you have some interesting alternatives for sourcing any of these distinctive capabilities. One route may be to outsource, by entering into some relatively exclusive long-term relationships with an external individual or company who can give you relevant and timely access to the capability. Another route is to hire a few dedicated experts who can serve as deep subject matter experts, perhaps forming a center of excellence, and then deploy them as needed. A third route is attempting to embed the distinctive skill into the overall capabilities of the broader marketing organization, evolving into a baseline requirement for most generalist marketers.

The plus side of the outsourcing route is that you do not have to undertake the challenge of organically growing and embedding an unusual capability that might have cultural or talent requirements that even a larger company may struggle to meet. The downside is that you will not own the capability directly, and the intellectual property may leak out into the market at large, or to specific competitors. The center-of-excellence route is attractive, for it both focuses the investment and limits the risk, but you will need to figure out how to integrate and link the specialists into the overall decision-making process. You would probably take the last route only if the skill was going to be seen as absolutely vital to your competitive strategy.

Building Strong Generalists

Irrespective of where you decide to build distinctive capabilities, every marketing organization will continue to need strong generalists.

A strong generalist is someone who knows how to process information and drive activities across the strategic, creative, execution-oriented, and analytic realms, without necessarily being able to do a specialist's job in any given area. So this person may not know how to generate the Big Idea, but he or she will know how to brief the creative team to stay on strategy and objectively evaluate the merits of any output that they create. In the same way, a strong generalist may not know how to run the SAS programs and perform the econometric modeling but will know how to ask the right questions to stress test the integrity of the findings and how the potential findings should be applied in decision making.

Some generalists may have a deep spike in one of the competency realms and then adequate fluency in the other areas. Others may be fairly strong in most or all of the competency realms. What is most important is that strong generalists drive informed decision making that benefits from the diverse contributions and thinking of all of the areas and are completely comfortable working in cross-functional situations however the different functional areas are defined. They are also able to troubleshoot and problem-solve marketing investment challenges driven by the under-performance of any one of the six MA value levers. And in many organizations, strong marketing generalists have roles that span more broadly than just marketing communications, potentially including new product innovation, customer experience, channel management, revenue management, and so on.

So now that you understand what a strong generalist looks like, how do you develop and grow a talented crop of your own? Typically, a good starting point is having well-thought-out career paths in the marketing function. If you live in a classic consumer products organization with a brand management structure, the formula, although evolving, is fairly well understood. If you live in a company in most of the rest of economy, it usually is not as clear. Giving your emerging stars the opportunity to contribute or lead activities in a narrower part of the marketing value chain—for instance, in marketing strategy or across the advertising and sponsorship vehicles—may provide good foundational exposure to specific elements. Involving them in specific initiatives or projects that require cross-functional collaboration in marketing or between marketing and other groups provides excellent development opportunities. Some of your best generalists are also individuals that have spent some time in adjacent operating areas, like in the field organization, a P&L-focused geographic unit, high-priority shared service areas like customer service, or post-sales installation and support. Finally, many companies are pushing for more seasoning in their generalists by having them do fewer quick-turn job rotations, but rather having them go deeper and longer in a smaller set of roles.

Build, Buy, or Partner?

After you have picked a few areas for distinctive capability building and understand your overall need for strong marketing generalists, you then must decide whether you should build it, try to acquire it, or partner with a third-party organization to access the capability in a consistent and predictable manner. Typically you might start by benchmarking your current state in relation to any of the core skill areas, then diagnosing gaps and prioritizing improvement programs in all of the key areas. We have used the framework in Figure 10.4 to help sort priorities and related action steps by capability area, based on the overall importance of a given skill area to the company's

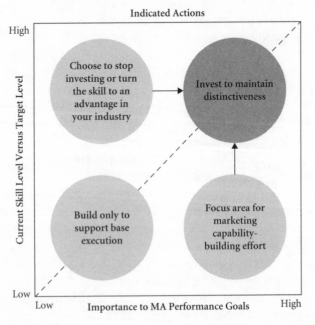

Figure 10.4.   Prioritizing MA Capability Improvement Areas

overall MA improvement goals and the perceived existing gap between the company's current state and desired state regarding that capability. The important thing is to ensure that your investment levels are appropriate to the strategic necessity and the perceived shortfalls in each capability area.

For some skill gaps, it may not be feasible or economically viable to try and close the gap on your own. If you need a lot of the capability and it is mission-critical, using M&A to leapfrog ahead may be your best bet. Alternatively, strategic partnering or outsourcing may be a viable option for highly specialized capabilities that you will not need in high volume or frequently. Outsourcing, of course, is a concept not foreign to marketing. The vast majority of companies are already essentially outsourcing several activities, including advertising development, media planning and buying, and market research design and fieldwork. Although it is not wise to outsource MA skills that are critical to strategy, managing others through specialized external firms will likely have a positive impact on their ROI and will allow the firm to focus its attention on the MA skills that matter most to their brand and business model. Whole marketing programs, which may be part of your spending mix but not its most critical elements, may be candidates for outsourcing. These programs could include management of event marketing programs, database marketing, and even your CRM activities.

COMMITTING TO FASTER, MORE EFFECTIVE PROCESSES

In addition to building deeper capabilities, another way to accelerate your MA performance is to commit to faster, more effective processes. Given the often complex ecosystem of decision makers involved, as well as the number of internal and external teams whose activities need to be managed, marketing probably stands second only to IT in terms of how long it apparently takes to get things done. By systematically applying a Six Sigma–like discipline to your existing processes across the strategic, creative, execution, and analytic areas, you can drive better linkages between the capabilities that you are building, the underlying infrastructure that supports them, and the resulting in-market actions they produce. What you want is better-informed decision making that allows you to get new programs in market before you have missed the window of opportunity. When this kind of an orientation is applied to marketing processes that drive your most material, highest-ROI investments, the results can be astounding, as demonstrated in the next Capital One example.

Capital One probably stands out as the leading practitioner of this pillar of long-term MA sustainability. Just as much as its statistical wizardry, the company's commitment to faster, more effective processes stands out as a critical element in executing against its information-based competitive strategy. Over the 1990s, Capital One developed an unduplicated ability to rapidly form cross-functional teams between operations, technology, marketing, and analysis; get stuff done; disband the teams; and then reform a new team for a different opportunity—and then another and another and another. Analysts rode herd over the in-market experimentation process, coordinating the tasks required for a test to proceed from idea to rollout, soliciting input from these cross-functional team members, and then handing it off to a product manager to get the tests into production via operations scheduling, call center training, and so on. The organization became proficient at using IT code jockeys to trick the call center software to support a test, dropping the lead time for IT systems changes from two years to one week. It presented an interesting paradox, for at the same time the infrastructure needed to work flawlessly to support a rapidly growing base business, it also had to be flexible enough to allow for hundreds of system exceptions to test new concepts—effectively a series of smart, quick work-arounds that could be backfilled with more scalable solutions if any given test was successful. With this approach Capital One was able to exponentially increase its rate of in-market experimentation, as depicted in Figure 10.5, and it emerged as one of the fastest-growing, most profitable consumer credit companies.

The Capital One example highlights some of the basic requirements for faster, more effective processes. First, many marketing-driven processes are slower than they need to be due to basic process failures like a lack of standardized process inputs and outputs, poor synchronization of upstream outputs and downstream process steps, and unclear decision rights. This is often made more complicated by the cross-functional and multiorganizational nature of the team structures. Second, a flexible yet scalable operations and technology infrastructure provides the backbone for all such process improvement. Third, you will need to manage the tension between a desire for speed and the need for scalability in an artful and creative manner.

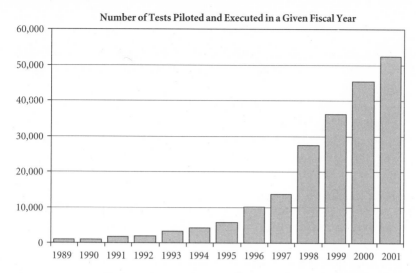

Figure 10.5.   Capital One's Dramatic Acceleration of Testing Throughput in the 1990s

We will discuss each of these ideas in greater depth in the rest of this section.

Removing MA Process Pain Points

MA process pain points are recurring points of friction that cause rework, delays, and frustration in bringing your spending programs to market. Think about it. How long did it take to get your last outbound campaign, sales promotion, or advertisement ready for market? Equally important, how much variance do you experience in the time it takes to develop similar marketing spending programs? Streamlining core MA processes and improving their coordination is a critical impact accelerator, getting programs in front of customers more quickly and effectively multiplying the size and capacity of your marketing department. If a regularly repeated MA process ties up the equivalent of five full-time marketers for twenty-five weeks at a time, reducing this process cycle time to sixteen weeks is like adding two new permanent members to your team—at no extra cost.

We think your initial efforts should focus on practical process simplification and the removal of repeated pain points. Think of it as a poor man's attempt at Six Sigma. By enrolling key stakeholders in some brainstorming meetings and using some basic process mapping techniques, you can begin to identify pain points and diagnose their root causes. This allows you to quickly get to what's broken. Then the idea is to leverage the process owners to come up with alternative solutions and propose some pilot fixes that can be refined over time. This is not about clean-sheet process redesign or creating an official process binder that will gather dust on someone's credenza, but rather practical solutions for tough problems. Figure 10.6 provides an example of this approach in action, whereby a large services firm was able to effectively reduce elapsed time for print and TV ad development from twenty-five weeks to sixteen weeks by tightening up the creative development cycle, doing structured preproduction test and refinement, and clarifying decision rights with all stakeholders.

A consistent theme that will emerge from your examination of pain points is that MA process cycle time is dependent on how well everyone works and plays together. To build better marketing spending programs and get them to market faster, you must facilitate smoother coordination at four levels: within the marketing group, across cross-functional business teams, with and among external

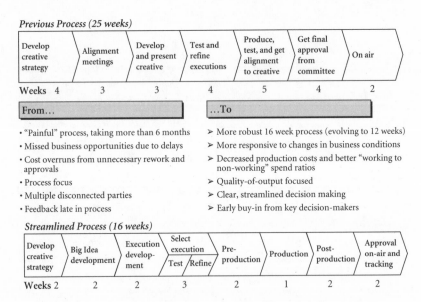

Figure 10.6.   Streamlining Critical MA Processes: Print and TV
Ad Development for a Services Firm

agencies, and finally across the top management team. Common ways to achieve better organizational coordination are clarifying the process steps, developing shared expectations and standards for common process inputs and outputs, requiring downstream process elements to effectively and transparently incorporate upstream output, and improving overall written and verbal communication. Process steps that transition between competency areas—from strategic to creative, from creative to execution, from execution to analytic, and from analytic back to strategic—tend to be hardest to get right, even when you have a cross-functional team structure. Layer this on top of an external vendor structure that may involve many unrelated entities, and you can quickly see why these aspects of the process warrant the most care and feeding. Finally, as you focus on systematically removing pain points from your highest impact processes, a commitment to informal or formal best practice sharing and knowledge management within and across your company's broader marketing community can lead to a more rapid adoption of improved approaches throughout the organization.

Another critical success factor for all of this is a system of clear decision rights for major marketing program decisions. A lack of clear decision rights across the marketing value chain is a critical impediment to faster cycle times and overall efficiency, and it is often the root cause of excessive rework that drives up production costs. These decision rights establish who is involved and when and how they are drawn upon. These rules clear up the confusion about who is being informed on an FYI basis, who is providing input to a decision, who is providing a preliminary approval, and who has the final sign-off. Figure 10.7 shows an example of what one company's decision rights look like for the development of a new television advertisement. This more streamlined and, we believe, appropriate allocation of decision rights allows you to minimize approval rights to the least number of critical points, while helping to avoid the risks that the process gets stretched out endlessly or involves a series of people who have a vote but no accountability for the outcome.

A Flexible, Scalable, Comprehensive Marketing Technology Infrastructure

As some observers wryly note, even though global enterprises invest more than $1 trillion annually in marketing activities, it is still one

	Creative Strategy	Story Board	Claims Support	Testing Animatic	Copy Testing	Pre-Pro Choices	Rough Cut	Final Edit
Top Executives								
CEO								▓
CMO	■	▓						■
Other Execs								▓
Marketing Team								
Director	▓	■	▓	▓				■
Project Owner	▓	▓	▓	▓	▓		■	
Shared Services								
Legal			▓					
Insights				▓				
Corporate Comm.								
Business Team		▓						▓

				Preliminary Sign-off	Final Sign-off
	No Role	Inform	Input		
Key		▓	■	▓	■

Figure 10.7.   Establishing Decision Rights for Program Development: Advertising with Low Assessed Risk

area of the enterprise where many of the critical processes are supported by technology that is stuck in the late 1980s—spreadsheets, word processing documents, e-mail, voicemail, and the occasional fax! Marketing has stubbornly resisted any attempt to get onto the enterprise technology backbone, and given how tone-deaf many of the large ERP providers like SAP and Oracle are around marketing's functional requirements, the status quo has been easy to maintain. Yet in the first decade of the twenty-first century, many trends have been at work to change these underlying dynamics, with incumbents and new entrants attempting to capitalize on this untapped opportunity.

And this is happening just in the nick of time, because as the Capital One example made abundantly clear, having a comprehensive technology architecture that flexibly and quickly integrates customer data, marketing investment data, and marketing response data with information from other customer-facing systems—like POS, CRM, e-commerce, and call center—is a critical enabler of faster cycle times and better accountability for marketing. As one player from Capital One noted, "The systems piece was one-hundred-percent critical. If it is tedious or cumbersome to pull insights, it just will not happen. Our systems were set up in a way that allowed us to get at the meaningful analysis quickly, which made the marketers and the analysts that much more effective at their jobs."

The technology that enables marketing accountability, though rapidly changing, has three enduring main components: (1) customer data infrastructure, (2) other customer-facing operational technology, and (3) marketing-specific operational and decision-support technology components, as shown in Figure 10.8. The customer data infrastructure sits at the hub of this ecosystem, and it tends to be supported by large enterprise-ready software players like Teradata, Oracle, and SAP. The customer data infrastructure aggregates behavioral data about each individual customer's myriad interactions with a company—what they buy, how frequently they buy, what channels they buy through, how profitable they are, how many service interactions they have had, what marketing offers they responded to or ignore, and so on. The customer data infrastructure includes databases and data management tools, and probably also has a business intelligence layer that is used to do baseline analysis and reporting around the data. The other customer-facing operational technology

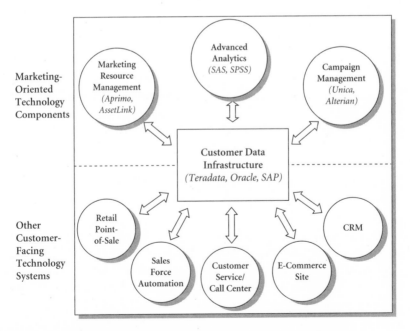

Figure 10.8. The MA-Related Technology Landscape

systems, like point-of-sale or sales force automation or e-commerce engines, in addition to supporting the core operational process, also feed data into the customer data infrastructure and help keep the data views of any given customer as up to date as possible.

The third and final element of this ecosystem is the marketing-specific technology components. Here we have three alternatives, all with very disparate heritages grounded in addressing distinct aspects of the marketing process, starting to converge through aggressive M&A into more comprehensive solutions. From the one direction, we have technologies that were rooted in automating the strategy, analytics, and execution of direct marketing campaigns. This started in the off-line world, incorporated on-line vehicles like e-mail over time, and now includes comprehensive multichannel perspectives, typically handling things like segment and offer management, campaign management, content optimization, and some level of customer analytics. Unica and Alterian are the leading vendors with this pedigree. From the other direction, we have technologies that were focused exclusively on the analytical sphere, like SAS or SPSS. These technologies are much more technical but throw an extreme amount of horsepower at challenging analytical and modeling problems. Finally, we have some newer technologies that focus more on a comprehensive, process-led view of marketing resource management, providing integrated views into planning and budgeting, calendaring and workflow management, automating creative operational processes via on-line approvals, and digital asset management capabilities, as well as potentially handling some production management issues. Aprimo and Assetlink are emerging leaders that attack from this angle.

As you can see, all of these technologies help to improve the process of delivering accountable marketing, even if some are more anchored in the analytic sphere than the creative sphere, or more in the execution sphere than the strategic sphere. But as we mentioned, the value propositions of many of these technologies are starting to converge as each provider expands its offerings through home-grown product development and M&A. Each of these technologies has its benefits, but depending on your company's marketing model and competitive strategy, you may be better off initially investing in an analytics-led solution or a workflow- or process-led solution. Moreover, if you have significant gaps in your customer data infrastructure, you may be better off investing in closing those gaps in parallel with investing in more advanced marketing technology solutions. Part of what an MA enabler assessment would deliver during the diagnostic phase (discussed in Chapter Eight) is a clearer understanding of what this road map should look like for your company. It is most important that you start to get the interfaces among the three components—customer data infrastructure, other customer-facing technology, and marketing-specific technology—right, and that each of the new investments builds off and takes advantage of the information assets generated by the earlier investments.

But wait, you may be thinking—that $1 trillion seems to move around the global economy quite nicely on its own right now, with the help of spreadsheets and faxes, so if it ain't broke, why fix it? Although that may be technically true, companies that have taken the time to develop a comprehensive technology vision for the marketing arena and have invested in that vision are reaping huge rewards. Kraft, which pioneered the use of mix modeling to drive ROI understanding, has been able to move to just-in-time planning by automating the company's analytics. By moving away from labor-intensive program evaluations to technology-driven platforms, Kraft has cut the time it takes to analyze program ROI from several weeks to only a few days. Best Buy, a U.S. retailer, had a tenfold increase in campaign-level ROI after introducing a comprehensive campaign management solution, increasing customer profitability and loyalty while decreasing the time to market for a new campaign from weeks to hours. Topdanmark, a Danish insurer, found that the process optimization enabled by one of these technologies allowed them to run more campaigns, with better results, with fewer resources, actually doubling the number of campaigns its internal resources could support during the course of a year and halving the time to market per campaign.

Managing the Tension Between Speed and Scalability

The final aspect to delivering faster, more effective processes is in managing the constant tension that you will feel between the desire for speed—fast, faster, fastest—and the need for the processes to be not only efficient, but also effective and scalable. As you start to get the technology and data infrastructure in place per the preceding discussion, some of the tools and resulting process optimization should enable you to achieve both. But without some of these enabling technology investments, you will often be forced into seemingly suboptimal trade-offs between these two competing priorities. Use your common sense and general management instincts to help guide your decisions here. Obviously, for high-volume, high-repeat processes, faster approaches that are not cost-effectively scalable are far less attractive than low-turn processes. It is most important that you do not compromise the effectiveness of your decision making in the quest for speed and efficiency. That would definitely be putting the cart before the horse.

DRIVING STRATEGIC LONG-TERM EQUITY AND SHORT-TERM PERFORMANCE

In addition to deeper capabilities and faster processes, the final key component of long-term MA sustainability in Horizon Three is developing a disciplined approach to building brand equity in conjunction with delivering short-term financial performance. Brand equity is an intangible asset that, when it is built correctly, should have a shelf life much longer than that of any specific marketing campaign. If the equity is of the right kind for your target customers (high performance or cutting-edge design, irreverent humor or empathetic listening)—what we call *strategic equity*—that perceptual equity should continue to pay back dividends to the brand over a longer time horizon, which is why we often refer to this as the balance sheet effect, as opposed to the income statement effect, of marketing investments.

Now, we will be the first to acknowledge that marketing communication investments play only a partial—and at times an extraordinarily narrow—role in building strategic equity. Clearly these activities do not and should not bear the full burden of strategic equity building. As one of this book's coauthors wrote in *Building the Brand-Driven Business* and as Prophet vice chairman David Aaker has written in multiple books, we firmly believe that brand equity is built by the complete experience that a customer has with a brand and a company, through every customer interaction with the company's products, services, distributors, and employees.

Nonetheless, finding a way to put out marketing programs that build strategic equity and drive short-term financial performance is the Holy Grail of marketing accountability. It can be hard, but it is not impossible. As American Express CMO John Hayes notes, "Some marketing programs have long fuses, while others demonstrate a shorter-term impact. You need to prioritize opportunities to align with the best interests of your customers and your business goals." Given the de facto requirement that most campaigns be delivered in an integrated, multichannel fashion, there is usually enough flexibility and coverage across the vehicles to potentially support both objectives, if it is on strategy to do so. When you take the conversation back up to the hundred-thousand-foot level, this same idea must apply across the full portfolio of marketing investments that you are making to support a brand. Ask yourself: are you managing a portfolio of activities and investments over the course of a year that are doing an excellent job reinforcing and extending a brand's strategic equity while driving exceptional sales response and short-term financial performance?

It is important to remember that not every campaign or marketing program necessarily reflects a trade-off between the two requirements of strategic equity and sales response. The wildly successful repositioning of McDonald's in the early part of this decade, with the "I'm loving it" campaign, is an excellent example of a messaging platform and creative execution that allowed for multichannel communication investments to be made that delivered both strategic equity and sales response. BMW's efforts around "The ultimate driving machine," UBS's global investments in its "You & Us" campaign, and Staples' push around "That was easy" and the "easy" button are all comparable examples for which the strategic and creative levers work so effectively that most vehicle-specific investments, when working inside this broader ecosystem, are able to build strategic equity while delivering short-term sales response.

That said, some marketing investment decisions are better positioned than others to deliver strategic equity building or sales response, just by the very nature of the medium; how targeted and relevant its delivery mechanism is in relation to purchase occasions and purchase decision making; the extent of engagement it provides to the target audience; and how easy it is for the audience to skip, bypass, or ignore your marketing efforts. Some of these characteristics have been addressed in the Chapter Five discussion of the vehicles value lever. Figure 10.9 provides a hypothetical framework for thinking about the natural "equity-building versus sales response" trade-offs driven mainly by the intrinsic characteristics of these different marketing vehicles. Investments in sports sponsorships, mass TV, and PR are more effective at building strategic equity but less effective at

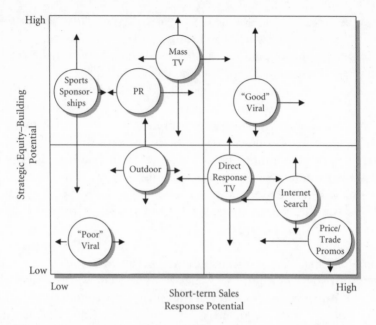

Figure 10.9.   Hypothetical Strategic Equity versus Sales Response
Trade-offs of Different Marketing Vehicles

driving short-term sales response. Internet search, trade promotions, and direct response TV, on the other hand, are more effective at driving sales response but may have more questionable strategic equity effects. As the arrows around each circle in the figure indicate, some of these vehicles have significantly more amplitude than others on the sales response and strategic equity levers, and all of this assumes that smart decisions were made against the strategic, creative, in-market execution, and investment level value levers.

Kraft, an early leader in marketing accountability, provides a sobering example of a firm that lost its leadership position over a five- to seven-year period (and has since been fighting hard to gain it back), specifically because it took its eye off of this particular aspect of the ball. Kraft, which had pioneered some of the earliest use of econometric modeling and mix modeling to study marketing investment performance, ended up with a decision-making process that overweighted the short-term sales response metrics while ignoring the strategic equity piece. To be fair, Kraft's approach allowed it to perform very effectively for a few years, because the sales response effect of its chosen vehicles—primarily trade promotions and point-of-purchase marketing—was so dramatically better than some of its other choices that sales increased robustly. But these choices were also slowly eroding the consumer dynamics in the category, because the consumers became trained to purchase the brands only when on sale, load up their pantries on trade-promoted items, and then strictly avoid paying for the brands at full price. A commensurate focus on strategic equity should have given Kraft an early warning system about these corrosive effects so it could potentially shift the mix of marketing investments to a combination of activities to rebuild any strategic equity that might be getting undermined via its high sales response tactics. Instead, although Kraft believed that it was optimizing its marketing investments to drive in-market performance and shareholder value, the company actually ended up increasing the price sensitivity for its brands, eroding the price premium it had traditionally been able to command and undermining its fundamental economics.

To be effective in this area and avoid an outcome like Kraft's, you need to have a well-aligned structure for managing and monitoring strategic equity development. But clearly there are challenges with this, some of which we covered in the discussion of marketing outcomes versus financial outcomes in Chapter Seven, related to the skepticism that many nonmarketers have for the research techniques that are typically used to measure strategic equity. There are no real-time cost-effective mechanisms to track what is happening with perceptions and equity across all of the relevant customer groups or geographic markets. So the monitoring is episodic and directional at best and is usually a backward-looking, lagging indicator. Brand tracking studies, a technique commonly used to measure equity, are often not granular enough to provide actionable insights from a purchase occasion or customer segment perspective. Although some new providers have deployed disruptive technology-enabled solutions to address some of these gaps in the monitoring tools, this still remains a challenge.

The other challenging aspect of this is that intangible assets are by their very nature extremely tricky to monitor and control. Sometimes they are highly stable and have a phenomenally long tail, the existence of which can confound even that hardest of skeptics. In other market situations, the asset value of strategic equity can suddenly become very volatile—a lot of asset value can deflate very quickly in a crisis (think of the UK's 2007 banking crisis with Northern Rock) or with the emergence of a highly disruptive and innovative competitor (think of Sony Walkman in the face of Apple's iPod). Moreover, everyone has to be crystal clear that strategic equity does not live in the ether or in the stars; rather, it resides inside the hearts and minds of very specific individual customers. So a company needs to understand which segments it has equity with, how those segments are evolving over time as they age and move into different life phases, and how the appearance of newer, younger customer cohorts impacts the existing strategic equity that has been built.

As you can see, strategic equity presents quite a paradox, for although it can be very fluid and evaporate quickly in the face of dynamic change, when properly built it can also live on for decades longer than most people expect. And given the lack of robustness and timeliness in the measurement mechanisms, it is hard to understand reliably whether any given activity is actually making a positive, neutral, or negative contribution to strategic equity. Finally, because these market research–led measurement techniques are often owned and controlled by marketing, there is some well-placed fear among non-marketing executives that low-ROI activities will get papered over as strategic equity builders, without any independent third-party process to audit the measurement results!

Even though strategic equity has all of these complications and is not a straightforward asset to work with, at the same time, you ignore it at your peril. If you only drive the business toward short-term sales response, you may be fatally wounding the business's ability to effectively compete over the long run. As we highlighted already, the consumer products industry is littered with players that went down this route only to have their lunches eaten by private label brands and other, less short-sighted rivals. Figuring out who should monitor this phenomenon is also rarely straightforward. Given the relatively short tenure of many brand, product, and marketing managers in their existing roles and the overweighting of their incentives toward short-term performance, it may be asking too much to expect them to step outside of that box and ladder up to this broader perspective. Perhaps it is something that only a global CMO, a CEO, or even a board needs to help monitor, because they have an easier time balancing a short-term and longer-term view. Although there is no single mechanistic formula for figuring out how to incorporate this into your company's suite of capabilities, these thoughts from P&G's Jim Stengel provide excellent food for thought and perhaps a solid starting point:

> ... the CEO and I regularly do get involved with our top brands—we look at how they're doing on the big questions. We ask about their choices on equity. Are they building the right things? We're trying to build the consumers' image and perception of our product. So we need to know what we're aspiring to. ... We look at the equity attributes that drive share and the value attributes that drive share and we report those to the senior leadership team. In the areas related to brand equity, brand value and ROI, I'm on point for it, making sure we're looking for the right things at the right levels.[3]

ENVISIONING THE END GAME: THE FINAL STAGES TO MA PROWESS

We would like to close the chapter and the book by describing a best-case development path that details the final stages that your organization should move through in the acquisition of marketing accountability prowess. As we emphasized repeatedly throughout the book, the nature of highly competitive markets, the constant threat from disruptive innovators, and the ever-evolving media landscape mean that a commitment to accountable marketing needs constant attention, investment, and vigilance. It is not something that can get checked off with a concentrated two-year focus, like a Sarbanes-Oxley implementation or Y2K software compliance, and then recede into the background. We have discussed how to think about capability, process, and technology improvements, as well as the control mechanism for balancing long-term equity considerations with short-term performance, that form the pillars of continuous improvement in the preceding sections. Now we would like to specifically focus on how the measurement system and the decisions that it drives will and must evolve when supported by adequate investments across the three pillars.

We showcased some of this thinking in Chapter Eight, in the diagnostic section that addressed defining your state of play. In particular we discussed two factors—the level of existing knowledge about ROI and the perceived barriers to better MA performance—that are very relevant for this current discussion (see Figures 8.2, 8.4, and 8.5). The framework that we are about to discuss specifically addresses how to migrate the emphasis of your focus and, in particular, the kinds of business decisions you are expected to support, as your existing knowledge of ROI performance increases and the perceived and actual structural barriers to better MA performance begin to fall by the wayside.

As highlighted in Figure 10.10, we believe that there are three discrete stages that your organization will move through. The first stage, which we have labeled "Baseline ROI Established," is the stage at which you should have entered Horizon Three. In this stage, the organization should have a reasonable degree of confidence in the historical ROI of the majority of marketing investments and be bullish on the more holistic approach to marketing measurement that is being implemented. A company transitions to the second stage, which we have labeled "Competent Decision Support," when its understanding of drivers and marketing vehicle interplay has significantly

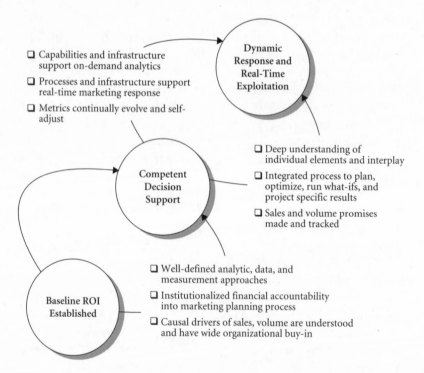

Figure 10.10.   Best-Case Development Path for Your Company's Marketing Accountability Prowess

deepened, and it is using this information to do planning, most likely on an episodic basis. A company transitions to the final stage, which we have labeled "Dynamic Response and Real-Time Exploitation," when the infrastructure, processes, and decision-making pace support real-time marketing responses to new insights that are continually culled via on-demand analytics. In the rest of this section, we will go into slightly more detail about each of the stages and show-case specific examples of companies operating at each of the levels.

Baseline ROI Established

We expect that most companies enter Horizon Three at the Baseline ROI Established stage. During this stage, marketing has increased visibility into and understanding of the causal drivers of sales, volume, or both, as well as the role that specific marketing investments play in supporting those outcomes. The test-and-learn agenda that you moved forward with in Horizon Two should have eliminated the largest ROI unknowns from your material marketing investment programs, even if your baseline ROI understanding reflects only a more static, point-in-time test effect outcome or the results from some limited historical econometric modeling. So the material measurement gaps should be closed or at least well on their way to being closed. Ideally, you have preliminary answers to the big C-suite questions about whether the company is spending the directionally right amount on the right activities.

In addition, the marketing team should also have achieved organizational alignment on an ROI measurement approach that it has started to effectively implement. This should include a well-understood and standard process for diagnosing marketing performance, including the analytic, data, and measurement techniques that will be used, as well as the socialization of a common metrics framework. This is supported by a better-defined marketing planning process, which is both cross-functional and infused with a renewed sense of financial accountability. Marketing-driven financial performance metrics should start to show up in business and operating plans. In addition, some of the distinctive skill-building investments have started to show material returns.

Ideally, the series of experiments conducted in Horizon Two, in combination with measured progress against some of the MA enabler gaps identified in the diagnostic, has provided cumulative empirical evidence that the overall approach works, and the organization is intrigued by the potential of what might come next. CMO Becky Saeger's recent journey, building organizational momentum to step up investment in the "Talk to Chuck" campaign at U.S. discount brokerage firm Charles Schwab, is an excellent example of a company moving from Horizon Two to confidently operating in the Baseline ROI Established stage. After a massive cost-cutting and restructuring exercise at the company, executive leadership showed a renewed interest in how marketing could be used to drive growth. Using a customer-insight-driven approach with strong strategic and messaging foundations, the team developed a $15 million investment plan across integrated media to be tested in three markets, with a solid mix of business metrics (new accounts, net new assets from new and existing households, attrition rates) and perceptual metrics. Control markets were selected, what proved to be groundbreaking results were reviewed, and the senior team gained confidence to dramatically step up its investment in Q4 2005 and into 2006 and 2007. This example illustrates that by building a string of successes, carefully collecting the data on the results, and then incorporating the insights into decision making, marketers can whet the appetite of the C-suite, and soon everyone will be wanting more!

So what is not yet happening at this stage of development? Typically it can still take a lot of custom effort to collect the data and perform the analysis, because the technology infrastructure does not yet seamlessly integrate with the measurement system. In addition, although a basic level of ROI understanding has been achieved, some of the more complicated econometric or hierarchy-of-effects analyses have probably not been done or done consistently, so you are less confident in how much you know about the marketing portfolio effects and interactions. From a tools perspective, score-carding reports may have been established, but scenario-modeling and optimization tools are probably still in short supply. Finally, there are still a fair number of data gaps to be closed to support more complex analytics and accurate forecasting processes. Until you make progress on some of these shortcomings, your company will probably hover at this stage of development.

Competent Decision Support

A company begins the transition to the "Competent Decision Support" stage of development as it significantly deepens its understanding of ROI performance through a steady improvement in its data, measurement systems, and analytic processes and starts to use this deepened understanding to plan for and forecast future performance, rather than just describe past performance. By the time a company has reached this stage, it will have accumulated a material body of work that analyzes the ROI performance of its individual marketing elements using a variety of analytic techniques, so it has a high degree of confidence in the range of performance outcomes it can reasonably expect at different investment levels. This same body of work should have generated material insights into the portfolio and interaction effects across marketing vehicles, as well as how different mix combinations perform at different investment levels, in the context of hypothesized external market conditions and hypothesized competitive response.

This degree of confidence in underlying ROI understanding encourages the organization to run a much more integrated and holistic marketing planning process. This integrated process is typically used to plan and optimize marketing investments and to run sophisticated what-if scenarios that model the performance of different vehicle mix and investment level choices—in light of varying macro-environmental factors, anticipated competitive response, and, most important, project-specific results. It is the cumulative body of ROI findings that is typically used to populate the parameters in the simulation tools, and these iterative analyses give the organization a greater degree of confidence in the sales and volume commitments that are made as a result of integrated planning. Just as important, this process closes the loop on the back end, such that performance results are tracked, variances are diligently analyzed, and people are held accountable for specific business outcomes as well as for incorporating any new learning into planning. Consistently executing in this manner will link strategy to execution in a very tight and direct way, with ample management visibility into success criteria, potential risks, and expected outcomes. It will also guarantee that analytics and insights are integrated transparently and that the analytic tools link directly with other insight generation processes. So you can see why this stage has been labeled Competent Decision Support!

Many of the leading companies that we have highlighted throughout the course of this chapter, like Procter & Gamble, Kraft, and American Express, are operating at this stage of MA prowess. The discipline is embedded, the accumulated body of knowledge is impressive, and the combined effect is to shape and drive business decision making on a regular if periodic basis. Even so, these companies have to push hard just to maintain their momentum at the Competent Decision Support stage. Jim Stengel talks about how P&G has "become tremendously creative at how we're using modeling, looking backward and also projecting forward. . . . But there still is a research opportunity. We understand the elements pretty well. And we're not bad at figuring how they interplay. But we're not quite where we need to be in terms of projecting specific results . . . it's important to stay disciplined—to hit the accountability issue very hard and also to be creative."[4] So as you can see, even Olympic-caliber athletes can never afford to let their guard down.

Yet if it is as hard as Stengel implies to maintain effective performance at the Competent Decision Support stage, why not just stop at this level? How and why would any company try to push past this? The main reason is the still somewhat lagging nature of the insights that a company is working with during this phase. Depending on the timing of the planning cycle, the timing of the insight generation and analytics phase, and where you currently are in the operational cycle, you may be working with information that is six, twelve, or even eighteen to twenty-four months behind the business. Although the decisions you are making are still probably orders of magnitude more appropriate than those of a company without any of this capability, in light of the ever-growing number of systems providing real-time information on customer behavior and customer response (websites, POS, call centers, Google analytics, and so on), many organizations sense a missed opportunity and try to find ways to capitalize on that by transitioning to the final stage of MA prowess.

Dynamic Response and Real-Time Exploitation

In this stage, which we have labeled "Dynamic Response and Real-Time Exploitation," a company is still getting all of the core scenario planning and accountability benefits of the Competent Decision Support stage, but those benefits no longer accrue in relation to episodic processes tied to the annual planning cycle. Rather, these benefits are deployed as a market-facing, real-time operational capability that can be used to intelligently shift tactics in-period to respond to any fast-breaking market opportunities or competitive threats or to course-correct against initial investment plans because of poor response or suboptimal business performance. The organization has developed the deeper capabilities, faster processes, and flexible technology infrastructure discussed earlier in the chapter, allowing our MA principles to be applied on a much faster cycle time. The real-time monitoring aspect of this is key, as is having an ability to take real-time actions in response to the rapidly emerging set of insights and information.

Harrah's Entertainment, for example, combines real-time customer analytics about a gamer's current experience in the casino with a variety of real-time marketing mechanisms to proactively and positively influence the gamer's experience and the company's own economics. So for example, if a player runs into a quick run of losses on the slots, losing enough money in a short enough amount of time to dramatically increase the probability that this kind of player will get up and leave the casino for a change of luck, Harrah's real-time system can monitor this and send out an electronic or in-person intervention with an offer for a $40 voucher for a meal at one of the nicer restaurants or two highly discounted tickets to a live concert starting in the next hour or two. The electronic offer, which comes directly via the loyalty card into the player's slot machine, is highly automated and infinitely scalable.

This example may seem extreme or uniquely suited to Harrah's operating environment, but it provides a good sense of how a company operates at this final stage of MA competence. First of all, it has mechanisms that allow it to constantly monitor its performance at a customer level or market level in real time. Clearly the key MA enablers—metrics, data, IT systems, skills, and processes—must be highly developed for this to occur. Second, the example calls for smart algorithms that model anticipated customer behavior based on what is happening, and, ideally, knowledge (or an accurate prediction) of any given individual customer's score or value in terms of these key behavioral predictors. Then based on those values and any additional data collected from the real-time experience, the company needs to have prepared some well-defined and specific cost-effective actions that the company can take to try to elicit the desired response. This is how we get to both the on-demand analytics and real-time response components at the heart of this stage of MA prowess.

Countless other examples abound. Capital One has been operating at this level for years. The data-rich, real-time operating environment of internet retailers is ideal for this approach, and players like Amazon, eBay, and Netflix are confidently operating under this model. Google's whole operating model is built around this idea, and it is proving highly effective and highly disruptive. With the rapid emergence of a whole new set of real-time, relative marketing mechanisms, from mobile marketing to on-line contextual advertising to search advertising to other low-cost, automated mechanisms like e-mail and POS-driven couponing, smart marketers will have an even richer array of choices to incorporate and integrate, notwithstanding any twists and turns caused by concerns about privacy, unwanted interruptions, and any new defense mechanisms consumers erect around themselves. Even if your company is not that enthusiastic about any of these newer marketing techniques, outbound call centers and customer service centers are a much more traditional place to incorporate real-time response, by changing call scripts in a way that reflects the emerging insights from the on-demand analytics.

Even more so at this stage, the work is never done. Although the purpose of the algorithms is to help the company optimize with a core set of data, real-time monitoring drives total transparency to the effectiveness of the algorithms and the real-time response tactics. Diagnosing performance gaps—and there will most definitely be gaps—forces the organization to continue to look for new approaches and new analytic hypotheses to pour back into the top of the funnel. As a result, high-priority metrics continually get tweaked in relation to the emerging on-demand insights and become somewhat self-adjusting. Similarly, marketing investment plans have more flexibility baked into them, and in-period investment can be shifted to emerging high-response activities in a much more fluid manner.

Culture of Real Accountability

Irrespective of which final stage of MA you are operating at, continuing progress through Horizon Three requires an absolute commitment to a culture of real accountability. As American Express's John Hayes notes, "What is most important, though, is having clear measurements for all initiatives, and ensuring that the organization sees the CMO holding him- or herself accountable for all marketplace results." This idea of accountability must shape the beliefs, language, and mind-sets of all marketers in the organization, underscored by a commitment to fact-based decision making, the translation of analytical insights into action, and clear measurement parameters. Accountable behaviors must be recognized and rewarded by the CMO and by everyone on the senior leadership team.

An unexpected insight from the Capital One story is how a commitment to accountability can have a positively radical impact on the culture. Because everyone inside the organization, especially the senior leadership, was so deeply ingrained with a "prove it" orientation and a huge respect for empirical evidence, it quickly became clear that the data talks, and a good data story trumps organizational hierarchy any day of the week. Because the company's commitment to faster, more effective processes allowed it to run highly cost-effective experiments, everyone soon realized that anyone in the company could come up with a good idea on how to improve business performance, get it into the system on a small scale, prove that it works, and then scale it. This democratization of influence ended up creating a culture in which everyone is an entrepreneur, with that deep sense of conviction, commitment, and passion to build, improve, and win.

We hope that you have enjoyed this journey through the twenty-first-century world of marketing accountability and that you feel much more prepared to ascertain how to deploy an accountable approach to marketing investment that will help drive your business forward. As you can see, the gains may be hard fought, but the upside for making progress on this kind of agenda is practically limitless. This approach to marketing accountability, when executed well, applied judiciously, and continually renewed, can become a critical source of sustainable competitive advantage.

Just remember, no matter what the starting point is, building prowess in MA is a multiyear journey—and no matter how much progress your company may be making, you cannot afford to take your eye off the ball. You will need to continually build institutional memory and knowledge as well as information assets to be successful over the long term. But remember, too, that wins come with each step along the journey, and the ultimate rewards are well worth the effort.

⎯∿⎯ Notes

Chapter Four

1. Jamie LeReau, "GM Mulls Spot with Conquest Customers,"*Automotive News*, February 4, 2007, 30.
2. Suzanne Vranica, "Super Bowl Advertisers Play It for Laughs,"*The Wall Street Journal*, February 5, 2007, 1B.
3. Bruce Horovitz, "Suicide Prevention Group Criticizes GM Ad,"*USA Today*, February 8, 2007, 1B.
4. "UBS Profits Soar 71%, Setting Record,"*American Banker*, November 2, 2005, 170 (211): 28.
5. *Advertising Age*, April 7, 2008.

Chapter Five

1. *ANA*, "Technology Briefs: Digital Video Recorders," February 2007.
2. *Advertising Age*, "Study Finds Mixed DVR Effects," March 24, 2008, 8.
3. "Why DVR Viewers Recall Some TV Spots,"*The Wall Street Journal*, February 26, 2008.
4. Jon Vomhof, Jr., "Best Buy to Sponsor NASCAR Race,"*Minneapolis/ St. Paul Business Journal*, April 23, 2008; http://twincities.bizjournals.com/ twincities/stories/2008/04/21/daily17.html
5. Mary Connelly and Laura Clark Geist, "Marketing Maelstrom: Why an Exodus?"*Automotive News*, October 1, 2007, 3.
6. Tim O'Reilly, "O'Reilly—What Is Web 2.0?" September 30, 2005, at http:// www.oreillynet.com/pub/a/oreilly/tim/news/2005/09/30/what-is-web-20.html.
7. Ibid.
8. Anjali Cordeiro, *The Wall Street Journal*, April 22, 2008, B7.
9. Janet Adamy, "Starbucks Moves Aim to Revive Brand, Shares,"*Wall Street Journal*, March 20, 2008, B5.

10. Emily Steel, "Marketers Explore New Virtual Worlds; Some Create Own as Second Life Site Loses Some Luster,"*The Wall Street Journal*, October 23, 2007, B9.
11. Rich Karpinski, "Measuring New Media Not Easy," *B to B*, March 24, 2008, www.btobonline.com/.
12. Hairong Li, Michigan State University, "Advertising Media: Planning & Strategy," http://hairongli.com/admedia/.

Chapter Six

1. "Revlon Vital Radiance,"*The Wall Street Journal*, March 31, 2008.
2. "Yankee Group Forecasts That Internet Advertising Will More Than Double,"*Media Post*, January 21, 2008.
3. Frank Cooper, Vice President Marketing, Pepsi NA, *Media Post*, March 13, 2008.
4. "Designing DaVinci: Dell's New Mouthpiece,"*Austin Sentinel*, February 29, 2008.
5. "Can Dell Make a Success of These Ambitious Changes?"*PR Week*, March 2008.

Chapter Ten

1. Excerpted from an extended interview, *CMO Thought Leaders: Rise of the Strategic Marketer*, published as a *strategy+business Reader* by Booz Allen Hamilton, 2007.
2. "Herman Miller's Creative Network,"*Business Week*, February 15, 2008.
3. Ed Landry, Leslie Moeller, and Will Waugh, *James R. Stengel: Ultimate Marketers*, published as a *strategy+business Reader* by Booz Allen Hamilton, 2007, 270–289.
4. Ibid.

―ᴧᴧᴧ― Bibliography

Chapter 1

Abraham, Magid M., and Leonard M. Lodish. "Marketing Spending Effectiveness: How to Win in a Complex Environment." *Harvard Business Review*, 1990. In: Court, David, and Kathleen McLaughlin. 2000. "Getting the Most out of Advertising and Promotion." *McKinsey Marketing Practice*.

"Brand Investment Traps." OWJ Issue 19, LNA, Schonfeld & Associates, Lippincott Mercer analysis; *Mercer Management Journal*.

Briggs, Rex, and Stuart, Greg. 2006. *What Sticks: Why Most Advertising Fails and How to Guarantee Yours Succeeds*. Chicago: Kaplan Business.

Burner, Rick E., and Marissa Gluck. 2006. "Best Practices of Optimizing Web Advertising Effectiveness." *DoubleClick*.

Cassidy, Fran, et al. 2005. "A Credibility Gap for Marketers." *The McKinsey Quarterly*.

Court, David, et al. 2005. "Boosting returns on marketing investment." *McKinsey Quarterly*.

Court, David, and KathleenMcLaughlin. 2000. "Marketing Spending Effectiveness. How to Win in a Complex Environment." *McKinsey Marketing Practice*.

Fisher, Marc, Hyun Shin, and Dominique Hanssens. 2006. "Marketing spending and the volatility of revenues and cash flows." Working paper. Christian-Albrechts University at Kiel and UCLA.

Loechner, Jack. 2007. "Americans Spend Half Their Spare Time Online." *MediaPost Publication*, May 23, 2007.

Marketing Leadership Council. 2005. "2005 Marketing Investment Benchmarks." *Corporate Executive Board*.

Marketing Science Institute. 2003. "Measuring and allocating marcom budgets: Seven expert points of view." A joint report of the Marketing Science Institute and the University of Michigan Yaffe Center for Persuasive Communications.

Moeller, Leslie, Sharat Mathur, and Randall Rothenberg. 2003. "The better half: The artful science of ROI marketing." *strategy+business*, 30:24–38.

Neff, Jack. 2004. "TV Advertising doesn't work for mature package goods." *Advertising Age*.

Prophet State of the Marketing Study. 2007. "The Effectiveness Imperative." "Renovate to Innovate: Building Performance-Driven Marketing Organizations"; "New Realities and Performance Requirement Mandates Faced by Today's Marketers." CMO Council, November 2005.

Sanders, Holly. 2007. "Chopper Clan's Ubiquity Highlights Ad Trend." *New York Post*.

Wasserman, Todd. 2007. "New Media: Google, Yahoo! Educate Marketers About Testing." *Brandweek*, January 15, 2007.

Chapter 2

Aaker, David A.1991. *Managing Brand Equity: Capitalizing on the Value of a Brand Name*. New York: The Free Press.

Gupta, Sunil, et al. 2006. "Modeling customer lifetime value." *Journal of Service Research*, 9(2):139–155.

Lodish, Leonard M., et al. 1995. "A summary of fifty-five in-market experimental estimates of the long-term effect of TV advertising." *Marketing Science*, 14:133–140.

Lodish, Leonard M., and Carl Mela. 2007. "If brands are built over years, why are they managed over quarters?" *Harvard Business Review*, July-August, p. 104–112.

Oster, Christopher. 2007. "The customer service hall of shame." MSN.Com, April 26.

Rust, Roland. 2007. "Seeking higher ROI? Base strategy on customer equity." *Advertising Age*, September 10.

Stelter, Brian. 2008. "Griping online? Comcast hears and talks back." *New York Times*, July 25.

Uchitelle, Louis. 2003. "U.S. overcapacity stalls new jobs." *New York Times*, October 19.

UPI. 2007. Business News Report: Kraft Meeting Disappoints Analysts, February 21.

Chapter 3

Dunn, Michael, and Scott Davis. 2002. *Building the Brand-Driven Business: Operationalize Your Brand to Drive Profitable Growth*. San Francisco: Jossey-Bass.

Chapter 4

Aaker, David A. 2008. *Strategic Market Management.* New York: Wiley.

Holt, Douglas B. 2001. "Mountain Dew: Selecting new creative – HBS case." Boston: President and Fellows of Harvard College.

Lal, Rajiv, Carin-Isabel Knoop, and Irina Tarsis. 2006. "Best Buy Co., Inc.: Customer-centricity – HBS case." Boston: President and Fellows of Harvard College.

Mark, Ken, and Robert Fisher. 2006. *Capital One: Launching a Mass Media Campaign.* Ontario: Ivey Publishing, Ivey Management Services, The University of Western Ontario.

Chapter 5

Elliott, Stuart. 2008. "For a new brand, Pepsi starts the buzz online." *New York Times,* March 14.

Garfield, Bob. 2007. "The post advertising age." *Advertising Age,* March 26.

Jack Morton Worldwide. 2006. "2006 experiential marketing study: A survey of global response." http://www.jackmorton.com/us/ philosophy/whitePaper.asp.

Johnson, George P. 2007. "The experience marketing imperative." White paper.

Li, Harong. 2007. "Advertising media: Planning and strategy." Michigan State University. http://hairongli.com/admedia.html.

Moon, Youngme. 2006. "Google advertising – HBS case." Boston: President and Fellows of Harvard College.

Nunes, Paul, and Jeffrey Merrihue. 2007. "The continuing power of mass advertising." *MIT Sloan Management Review,* 48:63–71.

O'Reilly, Tim. 2007. "What is Web 2.0? Design patterns and business models for the next generation of software." *Communications & Strategies.*

Stone, Bob, and Ron Jacobs. 2001. *Successful Direct Marketing Methods,* 7th ed. New York: McGraw-Hill.

Thompson, Clive. 2008. "Is the tipping point toast?" *Fast Company,* January 28.

Villaneuva, Julian, Shijin Yoo, and Dominique Hanssens. 2007. "The impact of marketing-induced vs. word-of-mouth customer acquisition on customer equity." Working paper, ISES Business School and UCLA, forthcoming in *Journal of Market Research.*

Watts, Duncan J., and Jonah Peretti. 2007. "Viral marketing for the real world." *Harvard Business Review.*

Chapter 6

"Advertising: A passion for variety."1996. *The Economist*, November 30.

Assetlink. "Top seven best practices in marketing operations." Assetlink Marketing Operations Management. http://www.assetlink.com/ Whitepapers.html.

Economist Intelligence Unit. 2006. "Driving growth through the finance function."*The Economist – Executive Briefing*, July 3.

Greenberg, Karl. 2007. "ANA Confab seeks to define, illuminate integration."*MediaPost Publications*, June 15.

"IBM puts squeeze on ad budget." 2004. *Advertising Age*, March 29.

Institute of Management and Administration. 2000. "Reducing supplier base still top strategy for purchasing pros."*Supplier Selection and Management Report*, September 1.

Mullman, Jeremy. 2007. "Media agency of the year: Retooled starcom makes its own rules."*Advertising Age*, February 26.

"P&G: New and improved: How Jim Stengel is remaking the world's biggest advertiser." 2003. *Adweek*, November 17.

"P&G reads the riot act over client conflict."2005. *Marketing Week*, August 4.

Samsung, The TOP Brand in the World. http://www.123helpme.com/view .asp?id=47241.

Sark, Adrian, and DanReynolds. 2004. "Best practice in agency search and selection." The Institute of Advertising and Communications, http:// www.agencysearch.ca/search/BestPractices.ASP.

Smith, Rob. 2007. "Bright ideas."*Brandweek*, May 16.

Vokurka, Robert J.1998. "Supplier partnerships: A case study." *Production and Inventory Management Journal*, 39:30–35.

Chapter 7

Hansens, Dominique M., Leonard J. Parsons, and Randall L. Schultz. 2001. *Market Response Models: Econometric and Time Series Analysis*, 2nd ed. Boston: Kluwer Academic Publishers.

Chapter 9

DeKimpe, Marnik. "Time series models in marketing: Past, present, and future."*International Journal of Research in Marketing*, 17:183–193.

Lodish, Leonard M., Howard L. Morgan, and Shellye Archambeau. 2007. *Marketing That Works: How Entrepreneurial Marketing Can Add Sustainable Value to Any Sized Company*. Upper Saddle River, NJ: Wharton School Publishing.

Rierson, Michael, and James Lattin. 2003. "Capital One: Leveraging information-based marketing – Stanford GSB case." Palo Alto: Board of Trustees of Stanford University.

Wind, Yoram (Jerry). 2007. "Marketing by experiment."*Marketing Research*, Spring, 10–17.

Chapter 10

Anderson, Elana. 2004. "The marketing technology backbone."*Forrester Research*, September 30.

Anderson, Eric, and Duncan Simester 2004. "The long-run effects of promotion depth on new versus established customers: Three field studies."*Marketing Science*, 23(1):4–20.

Collins, Kimberly. 2008. "Magic quadrant for marketing resource management, 1Q08."*Gartner*, March 3.

DeKimpe, Marnik, and Dominique Hansses. Nov. 1999. "Sustained spending and persistence response: A new look at long-term marketing profitability."*Journal of Marketing Research*, 36(6):397–412.

"Herman Miller's Creative Network." 2008. *Business Week*, February 15.

Landry, Ed, Leslie Moeller, and Will Waugh. 2007. "James R. Stengel: Ultimate marketers."*A strategy+business Reader*, 270–289.

McMahon, Seamus, and Barbara Mirque. 2007. "John Hayes: A culture of reinvention." *A strategy+business Reader*, 174–188.

Noonan, Jack. 2008. SPSS: "A leader in predictive analytics."Presentation given to annual Investor's Conference, New York, March 6–8.

Paige, Christopher H. 2000. "Capital One Financial Corporation – HBS Case." Boston: President and Fellows of Harvard College.

Pauwels, Koen, Dominique Hanssens, and S. Siddarth. 2002. "The long-term effects of price promotions on category incidence, brand choice and purchase quantity."*Journal of Market Research*, 39(4):421–439.

Quelch, John A., and Laura Wing. 2008. "Charles Schwab & Co., Inc.: The 'talk to Chuck' advertising campaign – HBS case." Boston: President and Fellows of Harvard College.

Tedeschi, Bob. 2008. "Putting innovation in the hands of a crowd." *New York Times*, March 3.

Unica. 2004. "Enterprise marketing management (EMM) – Enabling world-class marketing." White paper. Waltham, MA: WP-EMM-0605-PDF, September.

Yoo, Shijin, and Dominique Hanssens. 2005. "Modeling the sales and customer equity effects of the marketing mix." Working paper, Singapore Management University and UCLA.

⟿ The Authors

Michael Dunn is chairman and CEO of the global consultancy firm Prophet and has helped orchestrate the firm's tremendous growth over the past several years. He oversees the development of the firm's people, practices, and thought leadership and also serves as a strategic adviser on client engagements. Most recently, he has provided key insights for clients including Zurich Financial, United HealthCare, Emaar, Harrah's Entertainment, Visa, and T. Rowe Price. Dunn coauthored *Building the Brand-Driven Business* with his colleague Scott Davis in 2002, and he has written numerous white papers and articles. He also frequently serves as a source for professional and mainstream media for insights on companies facing business and brand challenges. He was named one of *Consulting* magazine's Top 25 Consultants of 2008. Dunn received an M.B.A./M.A. in Asian studies from the University of California at Berkeley.

Chris Halsall was a partner in Prophet's New York office. He has deep experience across a variety of sectors, including packaged goods, financial services, retail, and high tech. Halsall has worked with leading companies in over twenty countries on topics ranging from brand portfolio strategy to marketing spending effectiveness, product launch, and mergers and acquisitions. Prior to joining Prophet, he was the senior branding expert with McKinsey & Company. At McKinsey, Halsall led the Marketing Effectiveness Centre, helping give clients the capability to do more with less marketing spending. Before entering consulting in 1999, he was in sales with Bell Canada and in brand management with Procter & Gamble. Halsall has written several articles on marketing effectiveness and building powerful brands and has been a keynote speaker for various marketing organizations, including the American Advertising Association and the Canadian Marketing Association. He received a B.B.A. from the University of New Brunswick and an M.B.A. with a concentration in marketing from the Ivey School of Business at the University of Western Ontario.

──ᴠᴠ── Index